Sibling Relations and the Transformations of European Kinship, 1300–1900

*We would like
to dedicate this book
to the memory of
Bernard Derouet*

Sibling Relations and the Transformations of European Kinship, 1300–1900

Edited by

Christopher H. Johnson
and
David Warren Sabean

berghahn
NEW YORK · OXFORD
www.berghahnbooks.com

First published in 2011 by
Berghahn Books

www.berghahnbooks.com

©2011, 2013 Christopher H. Johnson and David Warren Sabean
First paperback edition published in 2013

Library of Congress Cataloging-in-Publication Data

Sibling relations and the transformations of European kinship, 1300–1900
/ edited by Christopher H. Johnson and David Warren Sabean.
    p. cm.
  Includes bibliographical references and index.
  ISBN 978-1-84545-769-3 (hardback) -- ISBN 978-0-85745-046-3
(institutional ebook) -- ISBN 978-1-78238-087-0 (paperback) --
ISBN 978-1-78238-088-7 (retail ebook)
  1. Brothers and sisters—Europe—History. 2. Kinship—Europe—History.
I. Johnson, Christopher H. II. Sabean, David Warren.
  HQ759.96.S54 2011
  306.875094—dc22

2010029805

British Library Cataloguing in Publication Data

A catalogue record for this book is available from the British Library

Printed in the United States on acid-free paper.

ISBN: 978-1-78238-087-0 paperback
ISBN: 978-1-78238-088-7 retail ebook

Contents

Figures and Illustrations

Figures

Illustrations

Preface

In 2007, Berghahn Books published *Kinship in Europe: Approaches to Long-Term Development (1300–1900)*, edited by David Warren Sabean, Simon Teuscher, and Jon Mathieu. The chapters in that volume were gathered together from three conferences. In Oslo at the International Historical Association Conference in the round table session "Family, Marriage, and Property Rights," we rather tentatively broached the issue of systematic structures of kinship in Europe and the problem of historic change from the Middle Ages through the long processes of modernization. Teuscher and Mathieu, together with Sabean, provided a number of panels at the European Social Science History Conference (ESSHC) in the Hague and went on to bring together seventy scholars and students at Ascona-Monte Verità, Switzerland.

The chapters in *Kinship in Europe* distilled the argument that emerged in the broad comparison of different, mostly Western European, regions and states. They outlined two major transitions in long-term transformations of kinship: one leading from the late Middle Ages into the early modern period, and the other beginning in the mid eighteenth century, working out its course during the first decades of the nineteenth century. Taking into account issues of political modernization, novel economic institutions, and class differentiation, the book documented shifts in kinship but by no means a decline in its importance.

The early comparative work faced many difficulties, not the least of which were the radical differences in the way different countries treat the history of kinship and the family. Some of the most systematic work on kinship emerged earlier in France than anywhere else, and two French historians have been central to our discussions: Gérard Delille, whose detailed and magnificent work on kinship systems in Italy has provided a challenge to continually rethink the issue of structure, and Bernard Derouet, whose work on inheritance systems in France has revolutionized the field.

The first results of discussions from the three conferences provided both a historical grid and a series of theoretical issues. The next years brought new constellations of scholars together to test and broaden our hypotheses and to provide new departures for consideration. Since we were also reflecting on more than a century of social anthropological research on kinship, mostly in non-European areas, we were anxious to consolidate first our understanding of Europe before slowly expanding our geographical coverage. For some of the problems we took up, we gingerly began to step into the twentieth and twenty-first centuries and push back our examination to the ancient world. At the ESSHC in Berlin, we looked at sibling relationships. Here we were most interested in testing and revising the view of kinship over the long run. Many of the essays in this volume were first presented in Berlin, and the editors have rounded out the discussion with a number of solicited manuscripts. At that conference, Simon Teuscher and Jon Mathieu played a major role in setting a high intellectual and critical tone.

At the ESSHC in Amsterdam, we brought together six panels to discuss "international families," once again beginning in the Middle Ages but this time going on into the twentieth century. Here we were concerned less with expanding on a narrative of long-term structural changes than with thinking through the use of certain conceptual tools. On the basis of many decades of work on the family and kinship in Europe, the task was to consider issues of systemic family relations, power and coordination of interests, and material mediations—what kinds of services, properties, activities, and cultural goods help give shape to how family members and kin relate to one another. The German Historical Institute in Washington provided a venue for a follow-up conference, and the revised essays are collected in a volume in preparation, edited by Johnson, Teuscher, Sabean, and Francesca Trivellato.

A final issue to emerge from discussions about Europe has led us to confront directly much of the new kinship understanding in the present-day discipline of anthropology. In the late 1960s David Schneider threw a bomb into kinship studies, and the resulting disarray took many decades to overcome. One of his many objections to the work of his colleagues was based on his contention that Europeans had taken their folk model of blood connection off with them to the field and found, despite masses of evidence to the contrary, that everyone thought like Europeans. Our latest foray into kinship studies in Europe thus has been to examine his assumptions and to ask whether and when kinship was modeled on blood in the European past in the first place. That was the subject of our panels at the Lisbon ESSHC and a follow-up workshop in Frankfurt. The essays for that volume are being edited by Johnson, Bernhard Jussen, Teuscher, and Sabean.

All along throughout the kinship project, we have been supported by Els Hiemstra, who has ably organized each of the European Social Science History Conferences. Antoinette Fauve-Chamoux headed up the network on demography and family and helped us in all kinds of ways to get organized and put together as many panels as we needed to discuss an issue thoroughly. Simon Teuscher and Jon Mathieu encouraged us to edit the essays in the current volume and provided a very useful critical take on each of the chapters. Johnson wishes to thank the members of the Wayne State history department, who participated in a colloquium devoted to an earlier version of the introduction, for their insightful comments. We want to thank Astrid Reinecke for her elegant artwork in preparing the genealogies that appear in this book and Daphne Rozenblatt for her professional and skilled compilation of the bibliography. Many thanks as well to Marion Berghahn and Ann Przyzycki of Berghahn Books for their editorial expertise in guiding this volume to publication and to the anonymous readers who helped give greater focus to several arguments, especially in the introduction.

Christopher H. Johnson, Detroit, and
David Warren Sabean, Los Angeles
3 November 2009

From Siblingship to Siblinghood

Kinship and the Shaping of European Society (1300–1900)

Christopher H. Johnson
and David Warren Sabean

This book is the second in a series arising from the collaboration of a group of historians from a dozen countries interested in mapping the history of kinship in Europe from the Middle Ages to the present. The first, *Kinship in Europe: Approaches to Long-Term Development (1300–1900)*, traced the general dimensions of the project in fifteen chapters by specialists across this broad time span with the goal of convincing the scholarly world that kinship was at every turn a critical force in shaping the general history of Europe.[1] Perhaps the most surprising point was the demonstration that far from receding as a factor of historical significance in face of the grand forces of modernization unfurling in the eighteenth and nineteenth centuries—the common assumption among historians of this era—kinship played a large and increasingly powerful role in European life and indeed energized those very forces, including industrial capitalism, class formation, civil society, nation-building, representative government, rational administration, educational access, and scientific research and its institutions, as well as the revolution in sentiment, romanticism, nationalism, and the changing discourses of sex and gender. According to the leading voices of enlightened thought at the time and to subsequent historical wisdom, the human motor driving these dynamics of the modern world was the self-motivated individual. An enormous amount of work has been poured into the examination of this self, a cultural construction of the era.[2] But everywhere one looks in late eighteenth- and nineteenth-century life, that individuated self was in fact embedded in the web of family and kinship, a whole set of relationships without which its achievements would have been paltry indeed.

We have been able to track two major transitions in the history of European kinship, the first concentrated in the fifteenth and sixteenth centuries, the second in the century between 1750 and 1850.[3] The first involved the decline of the quite flexible forms of medieval kinship and, by and large, their replacement by agnatic lineages where a single male (often the eldest) inherited the intact patrimony while other siblings were excluded, though not without compensation. Succession to title, office, capital, and client connections was often as important as landed property. The dowry became the central mechanism for forming alliances and extending the reach of the lineage. Thus, while women for the most part lost roles as heirs and progenitors of lines, the "sister-wife" became pivotal as an agent for her birth-family's power and potentially for her husband's, as Michaela Hohkamp (Chapter 3) shows in detail for the princely dynasties of the Holy Roman Empire around 1500, though her examples also show that women might be cast away if their connections did not bear fruit. David Sabean and Bernard Derouet, among others, have charted the phenomenon for German and French peasants, so this is not simply a description of kinship practices among the titled and the wealthy.[4]

This lineage model closely resembled the developing structure of authority and practices of expansion of the early modern state. What we see, in fact, is the operation of patrilineal kinship as the binding force of society as a whole, with all units connected hierarchically by patronage, each element with certain "privileges" passed on from father to son. Of course, the operation of patrilineal principles would look considerably different from region to region, but they could be at work even in those places that practiced fundamental equality among all the heirs, undifferentiated by sex. For such situations, Derouet has insisted on the important distinction between "succession" and "inheritance," and both he and Sabean have shown that offices, homesteads, and certain privileges might be reserved for the eldest son with farmland, gardens, buildings, and agricultural equipment distributed with obsessive equality.[5] Furthermore, until well into the eighteenth century, it was quite possible for marriage to unite partners of significantly different fortunes, with a sibling group as a whole combining with other families in different ways. Thus a family of brothers and sisters inheriting portions of similar size and composition could have radically divergent destinies through marriage alliance.

Thus in regions both of partible and of single-son inheritance, the foundations for long-term patron-client relationships, often lasting for many generations, were laid. Patrilines, patrimonial entities, or "houses" in areas of closed inheritance could organize multigenerational reciprocities, utilizing cadets and cadettes to build clientages or to act as demographic reservoirs. Whether equal or unequal, marriages were always exogamous, with partners that one could consider as "strangers," often uniting status with talent.[6] The reigning ideology was patriarchy, conceived as the generous and wise authority of the father, from the highest of the king to the "little monarch" of the meanest family. Jean Bodin theorized this vision of state and society in his great work, *Les six livres de la République* (1586).

The previous passage provides a very general thumbnail sketch of what can be described as the early modern European kinship system. If it is a largely accurate portrayal, this long moment in Western history seems at odds with Jack Goody's vision of bilateral transmission, "diverging devolution," as the essential characteristic of kinship in European societies, which he contrasts with the African pattern of unifiliation and transmission exclusively in a male or female line. In the Eurasian model, siblings as heirs are at the heart of the picture, and it is the dowry that becomes the mode of inheritance for females. Each partner in a marriage thus contributes to the "conjugal fund," which is then redistributed in the next generation.

This apparent contradiction is examined in great depth by Bernard Derouet in Chapter 1 of this volume. Demonstrating his immense knowledge of the wide variety of forms of transmission and succession and their related kinship structures, Derouet builds a highly nuanced picture of these processes by examining how the dowry functioned in various settings, principally in France. He largely verifies the sketch above, focusing on the actual practices that can be observed (mainly via notarial records) as opposed to notions derived from *de jure* protocols. Central was the exclusionary dowry, whose recipient (not always a female) foreswore all claims to inheritance (generally in regions where Roman law predominated, though not at all derived from it) to create the possibility of "unilaterality," in most regions arranged on behalf of a single son. The purpose, most fundamentally, was to preserve the patrimony and to maintain the integrity and continuity of the *maison*. But much of the north in fact practiced equal inheritance, with the "dowry," if the term was used at all, being similar to the marriage portion of a husband. These portions were provided from the pool of resources of their families of origin and would be deducted from the final reckoning upon the death of the parents, the point at which all the siblings would be "made equal." This entire system differed significantly from the south's in that the newly married couple usually set up on their own (neolocality) as opposed to the wife entering the family of the husband (patrilocality). Still, most families devised strategies to maintain the patrimony, especially through advances on inheritance throughout the life cycle and the repurchasing by the designated successor of patrimonial properties, stemming the centrifugal force of *de jure* rights.

Derouet thus introduces the central purpose of this book: to capture the realities of siblings' roles in the making of kinship systems and the societies in which they were embedded. One might think, in a system oriented toward the establishment and maintenance of lineages usually dominated by the eldest brother, that sisters and younger brothers would be marginalized and indeed be viewed as nuisances. While these "others" might at times be cast out or troublesome, all chapters dealing with the pre-modern period document the inaccuracy of this assumption. They had their place and figured fundamentally in the structuring of power and its cultures within early modern societies. It should be understood, however, as Hohkamp argues so eloquently in Chapter 3, that the sex-neutral term "sibling" did not exist in European languages until the modern era and that "brothers" and "sisters" were differently defined, sisters always in relation to their condition (especially as a wife—or not), brothers simply as sons of the same parent(s).[7] Analysis of this gender difference remains a key theme throughout this volume.

The historicity and cultural relativity of the concept we take for granted today when using the term "sibling" (exactly like the other terms central to our discipline, such as "family" or "kinship") cannot be doubted. This is why putting contemporary theories concerning siblings or other familial relationships in the service of our historical analyses must be approached with great caution.[8]

In Chapter 2, Karl-Heinz Spieß explores the earliest manifestations of the process of lineage formation in the high aristocracy and raises the primordial point: would it not have been simpler just to have fewer children and not worry about what to do with the "extra" ones beyond one male heir to the patrimony and a daughter with whom to ally one's house with another? But immediately the problem of child mortality arises and is compounded by questions of competence, vigor, and (for women) attractiveness. Moreover, marriage strategies often required offering up a daughter at a very young age. Hence, lots of children were desired. Large families (and step-families) meant significant age differentials among the children, with older ones often emerging as surrogate parents for the younger in case of parents' deaths. Both Spieß and Sophie Ruppel, dealing with the seventeenth century (Chapter 4), address this issue, but there seems a marked difference in expected roles and treatment, with late medieval relations more formalized and lacking in warmth. Both sons and daughters were fixed in a hierarchy based mainly on age, with the older ones destined for secular roles (successors and wives) and the younger bound for celibacy and the Church, with—mainly for the males—potential political significance. Age hierarchies among siblings figure in several chapters of this volume but, as one might expect, allow for considerably more flexibility in modern times. If, for example, eldest brother Werner von Siemens, the industrialist, functioned throughout his lifetime as the effective head of the family, in the case of the Gladstones, recounted by Leonore Davidoff in Chapter 12, William, the fourth son, emerged as "eldest brother." In the Gladstone case, the sisters Anne and Helen seem to have played out roles more determined by birth order, but there were many other large bourgeois nineteenth-century families, like the German-Italian Brentanos, where this was not the case.[9]

For the most part, late medieval brothers and sisters in the high aristocracy were not close but divided from one another at an early age and often put in situations of rivalry, which had quite concrete bases not requiring psychological explanation. Although Spieß found occasional expressions of tenderness, emotional indifference was particularly noteworthy from brother to sister, especially if she were a nun. Sisters who became wives cementing *alliances* (a term universally used by both great and small) were obviously enormously useful and achieved recognized status as the "Schwesterfraw" or "rechte Schwester." It is this relationship that Michaela Hohkamp (Chapter 3) explores in depth, using fifteenth- and sixteenth-century examples. She argues that the sister chosen to create a link with another house, one who potentially brought with her person material assets and enhanced prestige for her husband, possessed clear significance and could be a key agent in building powerful lineages on both sides of the marriage equation. If, however, the expected return on the investment did not work out, the sister-wife could be cast to the wolves in a separation initiated by her husband and followed by ignominious banishment to nowhere by her successor brother(s). In short, no longer a Schwesterfraw, she was useless, therefore no longer kin.

It has been argued, however, that the instrumentalism in intrafamilial relations in the early days of the emergent lineage system—which was matched, but with less drama, in the world of the peasantry—was less in evidence as one moves to the urban context.[10] Steven Ozment, working with family correspondence mainly from sixteenth-century Nuremberg, claims that the solid *Bürgertum* led family lives in a web of emotional attachment—though with clear paternal authority—that prized child development in an atmosphere of positive reinforcement, thus trying to push Philippe Ariès's "discovery of childhood" back two centuries. In Ozment's view, considerable agency was enjoyed by the emergent generation—at least for the young men.[11] When observed from a structural perspective, however, urban patricians produced lineages not at all dissimilar to aristocrats', favoring elder sons and so forth.[12] Younger sons and daughters did what they were told (however they might have been conditioned to do so), the sons often going off mostly on their own, though usually with convenient assistance from relatives at their destination, either establishing themselves away or waiting in the wings, should the successor son die or resign his duties. Resentment and conflict were always possible, and the positions of daughters mirrored those of aristocratic women.

Was it the same among the ordinary people of towns—the artisans and small merchants, the laborers and servants? Although much more research needs to be done, it would appear that their kin relations were more flexible, rigidifying in proportion to a family's status and wealth.[13] Male household authority remained a constant, but widowhood might bring a degree of autonomy if there was sufficient income.[14] In general, then, in contexts where real property and ample liquid assets did not provide the foundation of existence, different, more fluid patterns of kinship subsisted, and the nexus of siblingship might lose the structural/instrumental dimensions so clearly delineated by Derouet and Spieß for the propertied classes in the peasant world and the aristocracy.

As we move forward to the seventeenth century, we arrive at the moment when lineage kinship had reached its zenith and many of its rough edges had softened. The expectations of the various levels of siblings in the age hierarchy had been routinized, and the functions of younger brothers and sisters were more highly valued. Meanwhile, siblingship had become more politicized. Although siblings were often of great value to the interests of a house, at the highest levels of statecraft sibling differences, not only among themselves but with their fathers, might lead to conflict that could only be settled by the intercession of superior authority or indeed by war or the threat of it. Sophie Ruppel (Chapter 4) and Benjamin Marschke (Chapter 5) illustrate each of these points in detail.

Ruppel's study of the dynasties of prominent imperial princes in the later seventeenth century shows the extent to which the lineage system had evolved since 1500 and the central contributions of siblings to its full flowering at this time. While large families remained normal in the high aristocracy and age hierarchy (now integrated with an elaborate system of social precedence and honor) still defined roles and relationships, it is clear that younger siblings were more esteemed and that the emotional bonds between all siblings were much stronger. Their attachment to their house and its state (for the term is now becoming relevant), though still expressed through veneration of the head of the dynasty, was deep, and their work on its behalf, whether as a sister-wife married into another house, a younger brother, or even an unmarried sister, was considered crucial to the advancement of its interests.

In contrast to the picture presented by Karl-Heinz Spieß for the same milieu two centuries earlier, Ruppel's brothers and sisters, though placed like his in other courts as "apprentices," were usually educated and trained by uncles and aunts at those courts and remained in intimate contact with their own inner family, writing letters almost daily in an art now prized perhaps above all others.[15] Once they were sent out into the world, their privileges were ensured in contract and culture by the head of their line, and in return their obligations were many, above all to provide information ("spying" would not be too strong a word) about their new court and its dealings, often in coded messages, and even to act as envoys and negotiators in an age when formal diplomatic structures were in their infancy, especially for smaller political entities. Younger siblings were honored, indeed, as "the living potential of a dynasty." In the most obvious difference from the early days of dynasty building, the mortar of siblingship and its benefits was sincere emotional attachment, which Ruppel documents thoroughly. Although hierarchy was respected, seen especially in terms of address, letters reveal deep love, especially between brothers and sisters, reminding one, she notes, "of a much later period." The interface between interest and emotion is clear and indeed, though here in the service of the vertical aristocratic lineage and the dynastic order, presages the transition to the new kinship system of the later eighteenth and nineteenth centuries, where the horizontal ties among siblings move fully to center stage within all propertied classes.

The sibling dynamics of the seventeenth- and earlier eighteenth-century dynastic order were not, however, all peace and concord. Ruppel concludes with an examination of the quarrels within the house of the Palatinate (charged by the mercurial personality of the famous warrior who had served the Stuarts in the Civil War, "Rupert of the Rhine"), which love certainly could not heal, nor could the agents of the emperor; the enmities ended with the collapse of the dynasty. But it is the revisionist analysis of the house of Brandenburg-Prussia by Benjamin Marschke that takes us into a world where power and its pursuit trumped filial loyalty (the true heart of dynastic continuity, after all) and siblings became pawns in the game. His work also carries the story forward into the age when father-dominant patriarchy was being destabilized by a generation of sons, a process that culminated in the wholesale transformation of kinship structures and, hardly incidentally, the collapse of the French monarchy in 1789 at a point when the king as father of his nation lost all credibility.[16]

Marschke's project is nothing less than the explosion of the myth that the rise of Prussia owed its success, at least in part, to the continuity of succession by primogeniture, an ideal mandated for electors but rarely accomplished by this elite of imperial dynasties. Beginning with Frederick William, the Great Elector (1640–1688), and ending with Frederick the Great (1740–1786), Marschke shows that far from being untroubled, each of the four successions to the crown was marked by "reversionary politics," defined as "the opposition to the ruling monarch posed by (or coalescing around) his own heir apparent." The reasons for the formation of such "crown prince's parties" were varied. They often involved foreign influence seeking policy redirection or differences with regard to marriage alliances, but they also had much to do with the ways the crown prince's siblings might be deployed, including the possibility of a brother replacing him.

Only reading the detail of each succession crisis can do justice to the ways Marschke's argument alters our perception of the history of Prussia's emergence as a great power, but the critical point for our purposes is that this chapter provides a fascinating exploration of how dynasticism could be undermined from within. Its weakest links were all too human, for they involved people destined to lead and rule merely on the basis of their birth, which could not guarantee intelligence, vitality, leadership qualities, or even the ability to reproduce—an issue across the European aristocracy as lines increasingly died out in the eighteenth century. As it turned out, the Prussian monarchy luckily withstood its succession storms and was possibly even strengthened by them. But one thing was certain: its most powerful occupant, Frederick II, found that bureaucracy at home, competent diplomats abroad, and a professional military were infinitely more effective in forging an eighteenth-century state than relying on siblings (whom he mostly isolated) or the kinds of alliances that they might build to allay the power of lesser rivals or spy on greater ones. Frederick and his father, Frederick William I, were only two of the most significant rulers to make this shift.[17] The old lineage model was fading fast.

Kings and other large territorial rulers found that while brothers and sisters might still remain important in cementing alliances (though sometimes disastrously so for the recipient, as in the case of Marie Antoinette), they progressively lost much of their earlier usefulness, so carefully documented by Ruppel. More fundamental, however, was the fact that the continuing intermediate power of aristocratic lineages within their realms weakened monarchs' claims to sovereignty.[18] Thus, in a process familiar to all, rulers built bureaucracies and militaries often bypassing powerful lineages or thoroughly integrating them into positions of state authority, but in either case subordinating officers of the state to the crown.[19] Focusing on the Kingdom of Naples in a brilliant study of this process, which he has now expanded to include all of Europe, Gérard Delille demonstrated through remarkable genealogical research that in the eighteenth century, noble lineages, having lost their political significance and beset demographically by the demands of primogeniture, tended to break down into their collateral branches (*lignées*), which in turn began to intermarry with each other, forming a new kind of consanguineal solidarity.[20] He examines the complexities of this process with various examples in Chapter 6. It serves as a marvelous overview of the general process of the transformation of lineage-based kinship structures and the aristocratic society associated with them. This transformation was hardly limited to the highest levels of society, for Sabean exhaustively demonstrated the same eighteenth-century process in his village of Neckarhausen among property-owning peasants, as have dozens of other scholars across Europe.[21]

In a relatively brief period of time, virtually everywhere in Western and Central Europe, the old system retreats. A new kinship regime where affection was a prerequisite emerges, one based on close marriage of social equals, many of them violating the "incest" prohibitions of the church. For the most part, siblings came to inherit equally (as became law in the Napoleonic Code), though "arrangements" were still made to preserve the patrimony.[22] A wholesale transformation in the structure and practices of kinship in which vertical patrilineages gave way to horizontally organized consanguineal kindreds occurred during the century surrounding the age of the French Revolution.

Let us flesh out the nature of this new kinship regime in a bit more detail. If the heart of the old system was the father-succeeding-son dyad and the object of marriage the expansion of the options of the lineage, the heart of the new was what can be termed the "sibling archipelago," which at first generated second cousins and then, increasingly, first cousins as preferred marriage partners.[23] Besides consanguineal marriage, sibling exchange, doubly uniting two families, was an important option, as were repeated marriages with in-laws' families. Close marriage also included brothers' best friends from school or those of the same milieu in a given locality. But just as central to the system as all these forms of close marriage and repeated alliance were exogamous marriages. Research on the elite families of nineteenth-century Vannes (Morbihan) shows that these families practiced close marriage and radical exogamy *simultaneously*, marrying most of their progeny locally and often consanguineally, but reserving one or more children for marriages with totally unrelated people of their own social status whose families had either recently moved to Vannes or who themselves resided elsewhere. Such complementary practices served to consolidate power locally while extending connections with the wider world.[24] But distant marriages were rarely "arranged" with "strangers"; rather, they were nurtured via social gatherings in national and regional capitals and often confirmed in stays at the families' country homes. Ideally, all matches bloomed in an atmosphere of love, where sibling love becomes cousin love, and so on, out to the borders of one's "society," that is, one's class. Whatever the match, the families of marriage partners, the "in-laws," were embraced as one's own. Affinity became a bond far deeper than the "alliance" that characterized the old kinship regime.

Jane Austen depicted all this best, of course, but literature across the West captures the same reality, often exploring, as in Chateaubriand, Goethe, Melville, and a host of others, tensions of incestuous love—crucially, in this era, almost always between brother and sister.[25] Research into the correspondence of the age—every bit as dense as that of the aristocrats studied by Ruppel—goes well beyond, while also corroborating, the evidence provided by literature. The chapters below dealing with this period are a mixture of the two and complement one another. Two interesting points gleaned from the close study of (at least) French family letters over time can serve to measure the emergence of deeper intragenerational intimacy. One is the emergence, among *haut-bourgeois* families, of the familiar, second-person singular *tu*, previously reserved only for children and pets, as the mode of communication, first between adult siblings and married couples, and then (by the early nineteenth century) also between children and their parents (but not grandparents). The other is the *immediacy* of letters and journals, specifically, their lack of reference to the past or to kin of the past. There is really no sense of lineage, proud or otherwise, to be found in the period of transition through the middle of the nineteenth century. However, the constant reference to the living members of their own generation and that of their parents, and then, as they age, that of their children, is overwhelming. Retrospective memoirs spend little time on ancestors but heap praise on parents and aunts (especially) and uncles, none of whom are forgotten. A habitus of present-bound familiarity was being established, which in turn during the second half of the nineteenth century issued into a new consciousness of agnatic lineages and forms of associations that tried to gather together the larger family—based on surname recognition—into the "old" intimacy slowly being lost with the turnover of generations and the proliferation of offspring.[26]

We are talking here about families of a certain level of wealth and status, but studies of small-business and peasant milieus suggest similar patterns. All are linked by one fact: small or great, these were people of property. In the working-class world of urban laborers and landless industrial out-workers, tenants, and agricultural workers, consanguineal and other forms of close marriage appear to be rare, though more research needs to be done. Many studies touching on the issue suggest that non-propertied classes maintained their own flexible systems of kinship reciprocities for support in the midst of the increasingly brutal swings of the emerging market economy and, as Michael Anderson and Leslie Moch among others have shown, as conduits between job-seeking migrants and factory towns.[27] But kinship practice among wage-earners seems more a response to new economic imperatives than an active element in shaping them.

Let us turn now to the ways that sibling-based kinship among the propertied, whose wealth, thought, and talent sparked the multiple transformations of modernity, articulated with these powerful forces. We will focus briefly on the first phase of the market/industrial revolution, bourgeois class formation, civil society, political power in the liberal state, and nation-building.[28]

What happened as marriage became more endogamous and inheritance more equal was the consolidation of family interest around not a single line but a constellation of loving relatives made as extensive as possible. In the simplest sense, when the children of brothers (parallel cousins) married, the assets bequeathed by the grandparents stayed fully in the family. This, however, amounted to a holding operation, assuring only the continuity of social standing and the patrimony. More crucial—and more common—were cross-cousin marriages, others with more distant kin, and those within one's milieu but with a non-relative whose family reciprocated with a second marriage in a sibling exchange. This was often followed by the linking of these two families with a third, and yet another sibling exchange binding together their allied families. Such affinal complexes were often reinforced in the next generation by further marriages among more distant kin of each of the families, along with a cousin marriage or two. What came into being, then, were large constellations (kindreds) including multiple families of two active gen-

erations. This created a very large marriage pool for the next generation, who could link up further in the various manners already noted. In
short, a small army of relatives was produced. Who were their officers?
Why, those who kept up with all these folk—the sisters, who became
mothers and, especially, aunts.[29]

Before going any farther, it must be stressed that the later eighteenth
and first half of the nineteenth century was an age, especially among the
bourgeoisie (like aristocrats coming to power in an earlier time), when
large families predominated, often the consequence of repeated marriages in this age of high female death rates due to childbed fever. Small
property owners in France, however, tended to limit births to limit the
number of heirs. (French peasants became notorious for this and were
ultimately blamed for depopulation and waning French power in the
nineteenth century.) This difference is pertinent because it underlines
the distinctiveness of bourgeois class formation: it was cemented everywhere by connections of kinship, and the more relatives the merrier—
not least in that they represented all the more people who could be
trusted in the pursuit of profit, leadership, and power.

Although it was an age of new horizons and thrilling possibilities, the
instability of virtually every aspect of life in the mad century of unprecedented transformation bridging the year 1800 cannot be doubted. The
new kinship regime served, especially for those most directly involved in
the whirlwind, as ballast as well as navigator amid the variable currents
of these new waters. Is it any wonder, then, that the *family partnership*
was far and away the dominant form of business organization, from the
highest levels of international finance to the production of chocolate,
throughout this era? Even great undertakings like canal and rail building involved the mobilization of capital by congeries of family firms
in England to finance its private companies. The boards of directors of
state-regulated limited liability companies on the continent comprised
alliances of members connected by family ties that often overlapped
with elite school ties. The École Polytechnique, France's leading *grande
école*, gave preferential admission to sons and nephews of graduates
while forming new bonds that would be replicated in the next generation through marriage. Dozens of business histories stress the importance of mobilizing family capital, tapping family members for new
positions (especially for branch establishments at home and abroad),
and the continuation of the firm down the generations.

But no longer did the eldest son have the inside track on succession;
rather, the most talented or most compatible with the firm's culture
would get the nod. In the third generation of the massively expanding
Siemens company, for example, a second cousin once removed (who had

often disagreed with the patriarch) was tapped to head up the considerable family holdings in England.[30] Exogamous marriages would incorporate sons-in-law who might in fact take the family name and see one or more children marry back into the family. Correspondence between family partners (mainly brothers, cousins, and brothers-in-law) far and near spoke of new deals and problems of production, but always spoke of love as well. All firms that have been studied in detail, many of them among the most famous names in nineteenth-century business—Rothschild, Pereire, Courtauld, Wedgwood, Cadbury, Montgolfier, Motte, Oberkampf, Siemens, Bleichroder, to cite a few—made their fortunes within the grid of kinship.[31] The name, of course, became a guarantee of quality, and companies built images of iconic founding fathers (and a few founding mothers such as Veuve Cliquot) of what they might call dynasties or lineages, but it was the bilateral cousinage that defined the actual operations of the business.[32] Only very late in the century did the corporation begin to outflank the family firm, and even then the same rationale of kinship and trust caused some to resist the trend (witness Siemens, Ford, or Firestone).

The same argument can be made for the professions, government service—including the military—and intellectual and artistic circles. Adam Kuper, a British anthropologist, offers a fascinating study of the intertwining of the Wedgwood and Darwin families. They initially brought together artistic and manufacturing genius with medical practice and research and distinction in literature and learning, but then expanded into banking, supplementing the material side, and a range of scientific achievement of which Charles Darwin's was only the most monumental. Over four generations, some dozen cousin marriages (including Charles's) reconnected the families, satisfying the powerful sentiments that sibling love generated. Kuper argues that they were matched by scores of such kinship constellations constituting the "intellectual aristocracy" of later Victorian Britain, a notion advanced at the time in statistician Francis Galton's book, *Hereditary Genius*.[33] Such variety of occupations and interests seems characteristic of many evolving kindreds in the nineteenth century. The Wedgwoods and Darwins were freethinkers, but in many constellations in Protestant countries men of the cloth figured prominently; their sectarian allegiance often defined their cohesion and coincided with political persuasion. Leonore Davidoff and Catherine Hall's pathbreaking book *Family Fortunes* shows in detail this interpenetration of religion, politics, and the congeries of kin in the making of the English middle class.[34]

Laced through all these connections were the bonds of siblings, that primordial love cementing first families as well as those of second-family siblings-in-law who in the minds of many were virtual brothers and sisters. Such bonds were then infinitely ramified as the children of siblings became cousins who, as Johnson argues in Chapter 8, were themselves often "like brothers and sisters" but eminently marriageable despite their consanguinity—ironically unlike one's sister-in-law, seen, at least in the eyes of many Christians and the law of England, as embodying "one flesh" with her brother-in-law. Mary Jean Corbett sorts out this delicious conundrum elegantly in Chapter 11. In contrast with the early modern kinship system—where, as we have emphasized, siblings nevertheless played crucial functional roles—they were at the very heart of the kinship grid intertwining with the emergent forces of modernity. In this book we adopt the word "siblingship" to denote the more functional connections among brothers and sisters in the early modern context, and "siblinghood" to characterize a state of being in the modern era.

Crucially, an understanding of sibling-based nineteenth-century kinship provides a new way of looking at the embattled problematic of bourgeois class formation. If we begin by picturing the people involved not as individuals but as members of families and kin groups, and realize that these groups are linked by exogamous marriage (which can readily become endogamous in the next generation) to many other such groups locally, regionally, nationally, and, for some, internationally, in a pool created by friendship, mutual interests and concerns, compatible worldviews, and accepted manners of behavior—what Bourdieu named the habitus—then we have a vast human chain bound by affection and understanding that is fairly clearly distinguished from other elements of society by virtue of their biological relationships.[35]

Obviously not all groups within a nation were linked to all others, religious minorities being the clearest examples, but even here shared values and interests and common school ties led to occasional strategic interfaith marriages among the more secular families within them. Regina Schulte provides detailed insight into the latter phenomenon from the interior workings of the Mendelssohn family and its circle in Chapter 11. By the end of the century, entire national elites of the economy, politics, and intellectual life had many kin across them—what royalist critic Beau de Loménie in France called *les dynasties bourgeoises*.[36] Assistance was only a cousin away, went the saying. Locally and regionally, the bourgeois elites seemed in fact to be remarkably intertwined and always had kinship links to the centers of power.[37] Everywhere, within these linked kin groups we find enormous diversity of occupations and economic undertakings, civic and political activities, religious stewardship, and intellectual and artistic pursuits, which tended to be the province of men, while the work of maintaining and advancing this bourgeois culture through its web of kinship fell principally to women. It was a thoroughly joint enterprise.

Men were certainly involved in guiding the education, the orientation of interests and careers, and the marital choices of families' children, but the day-to-day advice on these matters, the correspondence necessary to facilitate their positive fruition, and all the arrangements required to present their offspring in proper "society" were dominated by sisters, mothers, and aunts. In this world where the public and private spheres were thoroughly intermingled, women obviously played a central role in the provision of inherited wealth and dowries for investment in family firms, money for schooling and marriage settlements, and endowments for churches and charitable foundations (in this area, especially as the nineteenth century rolled on, they became major players directly). Women also brought social status and political connection, which could be of great significance to the men of the families they married into. And they became directly involved in political debate, usually with the strong support of their families and utilizing their wider kin connections in every way possible to promote not only major causes of specific interest to women, such as suffrage, birth control, or temperance, but also on behalf of political programs and parties—and not just behind the scenes. But their activities "in society" could also be crucial in framing political action and shaping political discourses, as Steven Kale, Whitney Walton, and Anne Martin-Fugier have shown for France.[38]

Jointly then, men and women of the bourgeoisie, embedded in a world of interconnected kin, promoted a way of life centered around ideals of happiness and peaceful progress in all realms of activity, where economic growth was but one aspect.[39] That it was also insular and inattentive to the concerns and demands of those beneath it goes without saying, but it was assumed that bourgeois culture would one day become synonymous with culture in general, an assumption explored trenchantly by Roland Barthes when he designated the bourgeoisie as the "class which ex-nominates itself" that is, universalizes its being.[40] A focus on kinship allows us to understand in a much more nuanced way what nineteenth-century bourgeois society and bourgeois consciousness were about. Both were literally inbred.

The new kinship system also contributed centrally to the consolidation of the nation-state. The nineteenth century was an era of unprecedented movement of people, and above all, *within* nations, which for the first time became truly integrated. Obvious for new nations like Italy and Germany, this was true even for Great Britain and France, which had long been pink or green on the map but in reality were a hodgepodge of provinces and subordinated peoples where different dialects and languages prevailed.[41] But in the nineteenth century, at all levels of society, temporary migration from every corner of the nation gave way to permanent relocation. With whom, near whom, would they relocate? Even if the relocation was not with kin initially, the next generation provided a kin-grid of attraction. Among the bourgeois, this was an age when provincials made their way in the nation as never before. They never abandoned the culture of their origin because there were always family members building their businesses and their status back home, even though they might marry away or to people from away. Even if marrying locally, kin served in branch offices of the family firm, took positions in other firms (often of their wives' families), became employees and officers of the state, and increasingly carried the nation's banner in the wider world as soldiers, bureaucrats, businessmen, and professionals in the vast enterprise of colonialism.[42]

Everywhere, siblinghood was in play. The Rothschilds and the Siemenses were only the most prominent families to dot as many European capitals as possible with brothers, each integrating rapidly into their adopted nation's elites and contributing mightily themselves and in following generations to their countries' development, drawing upon their kin-based experience to spawn new networks among their in-laws and cousins.[43] And the intellectual and artistic elites of London, Paris, Berlin, and Vienna, whose contributions to their nations' prestige cannot be underestimated, were similarly entwined, with brothers or sisters often nurturing the careers of the most talented among them.[44] Finally, we must not forget that the binding ideology of the nation owed much of its rhetoric (and why was it so convincing?) to kinship terminology—though it was almost exclusively male, cleansed in the French Revolution of its original feminine component as daughters and sisters of liberty went to the guillotine while the *symbol* of Liberty marched on, bare breasts and all.[45]

The chapters in this book dealing with eighteenth- and nineteenth-century sibling relations all explore what might be called the emotional underpinnings, both fruitful and limiting, of the new kinship system, whose interaction with key dynamics of emergent modernity we have sketched above. We are not arguing for the epistemological priority of this affective universe nor indeed of its associated kinship regime in relationship with social, economic, and political forces of change that marked the age, but rather the interpenetration of all with all.

The emergence of a sibling-based kinship order required a fundamental change in the nature of sibling relationships, in which emotional ties and instrumentality were reconfigured and outfitted with a new language of sentimentality (where love and its expectations could easily give way to murderous hate) and a new dynamics of functionality, replacing the formal logics of lineages with the flexible practices of kindreds. Almost dialectically, however, the full flowering of the lineage system as it peaked in the later seventeenth century was accompanied by a growing emotional intensity among siblings participating in it that then flowed into eighteenth-century cultural life—sometimes described as a "culture of sensibility"—among aristocracy, gentry, and wide swathes of property-owning society, most notably the upper bourgeoisie. As Johnson emphasizes in the opening of Chapter 8, this phenomenon was just an aspect of what Michel Foucault called the "deployment of sexuality," which arose in face of the inadequacies of the instrumental marriage system of "alliance" characteristic of the lineage kinship system, now under duress in the rapidly changing social, economic, and political climate of the eighteenth century. The nuclear family thus, in Johnson's words, became "the crucible of sexuality," a training ground for new affective modalities that was inherently incestuous. In a culture where parental authority was fading, one that prized instead the young "couple" with its claims to autonomy, brother and sister—less separated than before in the new warmth of homes that themselves were becoming less public, even in their design—were thrown into each other's arms and hearts in radically new ways.[46] And indeed, as Sabean argues in Chapter 9, it was here that the "self," that notional child of the Enlightenment, refined by Romanticism, was formed.[47]

As already noted, much of the literature of the later eighteenth and early nineteenth century reflects this flowering of sibling love, both celebrating it and wringing its hands at its excesses. It is here that we encounter the great and flagrant contradiction that the sex-neutral term "Gechwister" (sibling) tried to cover up: the islands of the sibling archipelago were not of equal size, with the high promontories of the brothers looming over the lush, lagoon-dotted gems of the sisters. A new gender order had arrived with the new affective and kinship regimes, but it was far from equal, despite the multiple, more significant roles that sisters and aunts played within them. Carole Pateman's "sexual contract" traced the constitution of authority from "father-right" to "husband-right," but brother and husband were now blurred indiscriminately on several levels. The new power relations, however, were disputed at every turn during the revolutionary age, a phenomenon analyzed with consummate authority by Susanne Desan.[48]

All six chapters of Part Two grapple with this problematic and explore different dimensions of it. All deal with the (sometimes explosive) emotional relationships of siblings and touch on incest from various perspectives. Ruth Perry's approach in Chapter 7 is transitional. Her starting point chronologically is a popular ballad of the seventeenth century in which a brother and sister indeed commit incest and run away together. She dies in childbirth, but he, deeply saddened, lovingly preserves the child and then dies by his own sword. It is a classic story of "star-crossed lovers" rather than a cautionary tale about incest. A much more renowned ballad of the late eighteenth century follows a similar scenario, but the sister bids the brother to slay her after the birth of the child, who also conveniently dies. He has truly loved her and is filled with remorse—but not with guilt. Both tales use the metaphor of a lost "sheath and knife" that can never again be matched, an obvious allusion to the perfect sexual union with their sisters.

Perry argues that these tales symbolize a transition in which incest between brother and sister loses its framework of mutual volition. The brother now runs the show, survives handily, gets away with murder, and does not have to worry about the fruit of the union, but we are supposed to feel sorry for him as he wanders sadly around his father's castle. She sees therefore a marked decline in sisterly agency (mirroring women's in general) from the seventeenth century on, an argument she makes at length in her book, *Novel Relations*, even though the structure of kinship in England has morphed substantially in the direction outlined in this introduction. The new age heralded a new form of victimization for women, though now, she argues, in the more suffocating confines of the nuclear family. This interpretation thus establishes her work on the darker side of the new kinship's consequences, with gender oppression as the dominant theme.[49]

Christopher Johnson (Chapter 8) is more positive and optimistic, though clearly appreciating the power relations operating between brother and sister. Relying on extensive correspondence within increasingly prominent bourgeois families in Vannes over the century spanning the year 1800, he maps the various roles of sisters and brothers, aunts and uncles, within the daily lives of these people. He focuses first on key moments in the making of the new kinship system: a courtship and marriage between cousins, virtual siblings, orchestrated by the young man's sisters, one of whom sees the bride as a surrogate for herself; and the overwhelmingly important place of siblings and aunts and uncles in times of trial and joy, such as the birth of a niece or nephew, or of tragedy, such as death. Johnson then shows how ordinary family life revolved around and was coordinated by siblings, often of the older generation, and how most aspects of these families' interface with bourgeois society and its politics—private soirées, gatherings at country houses, public banquets and balls, the activities of voluntary organizations, and so on—seemed always to also be family affairs where kin or kin of kin made the connections.

But most important of all, perhaps, were the ways in which the paths to success of the younger generation—for males in careers, for females in good and happy marriages (though these counted for the men as well)—were facilitated especially by aunts and uncles, who were also very often their namesakes and godparents. Johnson's study underlines, in particular, the pervasive influence of an aunt, Marie Jollivet Le Ridant, who had special links with the royal court under the Restoration and was a member of Parisian high society, in the lives of her nieces and nephews and those of their children. But this form of empowerment must be taken for what it was: an ability to use influence on behalf of "her men," her brother and her husband first, then her nephews, and finally her grand-nephews.

In Chapter 9, David Sabean offers a close analysis of two less well-known but classic novels of late eighteenth-century Germany, a novel and epic by Clemens Brentano, supplemented by his correspondence, especially with his sister Bettine (von Arnim), and ruminations on Hegel's views on the family. Sabean argues that a, perhaps the, central discourse on the formation of the self in this era involved the intense emotional interaction between brother and sister in their formative (postpubescent) years. It was summed up in Brentano's simple phrase in writing to a female friend: "Bettine is my double." Although erotic attraction is at play and critical in creating the bond, it is the discovery of a higher and purer love that defines the relationship where the philosophical (Kantian) moral ideal of virtue is enshrined. The critical point, however, is that this ideal comes to be transferred to the vision of the perfect wife and, in courtship, sister and lover "fade into each other." This, of course, was one reason why cousin marriage was so attractive, because, as Johnson shows, the cousins were virtually sisters in any case but were not off-limits as partners, and such a match was ideal since it united people who had lived "like brother and sister all their lives."

In concluding with Hegel, Sabean moves to a different level in this discourse. For Hegel, the brother-sister bond is indeed the foundation of ethical life, but it is devoid of sexual content. Of course, it is possible to read his passage in different ways—as a brother commenting about how he thinks a sister ought to develop as a personality or as a theoretical statement about the position of the (bourgeois) sister/wife. Here it makes little difference for a woman whom she marries or who her children turn out to be, since the foundations of her personhood are rooted in the dynamics of sibling affection. Was his contention that the loss of a brother could bring no consolation but a myth to which young men might attach themselves? Was it the reverse image, in which her selfhood really was irrelevant, her function being essentially to worship him and guide him toward a good choice in marriage? Was it not he who had to face the world with fierce independence bred of ethical certainty, fitted for the market and a revolutionary age, obscuring the fact that men were reliant for training in love on their sisters, for the pursuit of knowledge on aunts' largesse, for opportunities in the professions on uncles' connections, and for success in business on a place in the family firm.

Regina Schulte in Chapter 10 presents a charming picture of what may well have been the very heart of cultural life of earlier nineteenth-century Berlin: the Mendelssohn-Bartholdy family, its welcoming home, and its multitude of artistic and intellectual connections, which spanned the religious range of the Prussian capital by virtue of Abraham Mendelssohn's conversion. The entrance of the brilliant Pietist minister's son from Pomerania, Gustav Droysen, as tutor for the talented Felix and Fanny set off a dynamic of three-way (ultimately four-way upon the appearance of Fanny's suitor, the painter Wilhelm Hensel) emotional fire that deeply affected all their lives. Most importantly, this study is unique in this collection in highlighting the homoerotic potential arising from the "crucible of sexuality" from which sibling love was molded, for Gustav and Felix entered a friendship—encouraged by Fanny at every step, though undoubtedly tinged with jealousy in light of her love for each of them—that seemed something more than friendship.[50] These experiences, visible through correspondence, lived with them always. All were cooled and redirected by noteworthy marriages, Fanny at a quite young age to Hensel, much later Felix veering farther away from his Jewish roots into a Frankfurt Huguenot family, and Droysen into the famed Friedländer family of Berlin, Jewish converts to Protestantism. While the young men further integrated the cultural elite of the capital and went on to fabulous careers, Fanny, forbidden by her husband to write any more songs from Droysen's poetry upon their marriage, drifted into wifely duties though continuing to compose in a desultory fashion—the fate of many female artists of this age and beyond.

Mary Jean Corbett (Chapter 11) takes us into a different terrain on the subject of incest: the fascinating history of the British prohibition of a man's marriage to his deceased wife's sister—a notion that today hardly strikes us as compelling. The various reasons for doing so were both practical (maintaining an alliance) and emotional (familiarity, children's interests, etc.), given the intensity in this period of the aura of sister and aunt. But for opponents, largely from the practicing Christian community across denominations (whose interests got the 1835 law passed in the first place as the prohibitions of the church faded in authority), this intensity of sisterhood was precisely the source of one of their main arguments: that as sister-in-law she became a virtual sister to the husband and their union would thus be incestuous. While the conflict drew on traditional doctrine that husband and wife became "one flesh" through carnal intercourse (Gen. 2:24) and sisters shared a single substance through generation, the nineteenth-century discourse added sociological analyses about the nature of domestic arrangements, moral arguments about the attachment of siblings, and lurid scenarios of seduction and murder.[51]

Corbett shows that the issue had a surprisingly large place in the fiction of the age, complementing the raging pamphlet literature. She underlines that this was overwhelmingly a male combat, above all because of the supposed man's "prerogative of unfettered selection." Once again, the gendered structure of sibling relationships comes to the fore. Corbett concludes with a critique of Ruth Perry's claim that the nineteenth century saw the ever-increasing dominance of the place of the "conjugal family" over the "consanguineal family" in ego's (female or male) reckoning and lived experience, arguing instead that the two were more likely to be "blurred," as they obviously were in the "one flesh" notion. The study of continental family experiences among the propertied classes (represented in this volume and citing a wide literature) would sustain this perspective, as would cousin-marriage studies such as Kuper's and detailed research in family papers such as Davidoff and Hall's *Family Fortunes* for Britain itself.

In Chapter 12 Leonore Davidoff concludes the volume with a tragedy in two acts (or perhaps not quite, if we add a third), and we return with a vengeance to the centrality of gender oppression in the history of siblings. Her investigation of brother-sister relations within the Gladstone family features two types of sister: Anne, the saintly eldest sister who, classically, replaced the ailing mother as the nurturing and sustaining female force in the lives of her brothers, especially for the third-born, young William; and Helen, the youngest sibling, whose headstrong character and questionable life-choices provoked William to effectively replace their father (who unlike the mother lived to a ripe old age) as her guide and disciplinarian. A massive collection of family papers and correspondence allows Davidoff to plumb the depths of these interactions, though in much more detail for Helen than for Anne, who herself died young without marrying. Yet Anne lives on in the correspondence as the symbol of everything a sister should be—self-sacrificing, homebound, responsible, and attentive to every need of the men in her life. Had she lived, this is what she would have been for her husband, no doubt selected for his moral resemblance to her brothers, for this is the formula—outlined sternly and in great depth—that William proposed to the teenaged Helen when she appeared to be veering in the wrong direction.

The rest of the story unfolds as William enters into his political career and simultaneously attempts to corral Helen, whose mental and physical health seems always on the edge of collapse and whose ability to manage her familial sinecure seems always in doubt. Surrounded by doctors, visiting various spas, and apparently drugged half the time, Helen seems confined under the dome of her brother's (solicitous) authority. Escape disappears as a marriage proposal collapses before William can even prohibit it. Intellectually and spiritually adventurous, Helen finally converts to Catholicism, throwing her evangelical family into a fit, but rebuffs their every effort to discourage her decision. She ends her life as a secular sister in a French nunnery doing good works, fading from William's correspondence. Davidoff cannot say how typical this tale is, but it says volumes about the ways the lives of brothers and sisters played out in the nineteenth century and the expectations brothers had of their sisters. Davidoff's unrelenting presentation of Helen as a victim of her brother's gender assumptions nevertheless opens a small window for a third act. Did she not achieve a degree of autonomy in her final vocation?

This book does not seek to provide a unitary thesis, and on occasion its authors disagree with one another. Its intention is to create a multifaceted conversation about siblings, a neglected subject but one that we believe opens doors to a deeper understanding of European kinship and its ramifications for the general history and culture of the West. The most persistent, and vexed, theme throughout the book is gender, the analysis of which, given its enmeshment in the tapestry of history, changes everything.[52] The issue here, above all, is the sisters. Whatever the context, and however important and influential a sister or an aunt may have been, each of these chapters demonstrates again and again that their work was *on behalf* of a male, a brother, or a nephew, that the vessel of love was the sister, its idealizer the brother, and that the consequences of their love, whether consummated or not, fell upon her, not him. Although the extreme sacrifice was death, as with the "sheath" of Scottish ballads' lore, Chateaubriand's Atala, or Hegel's sister, some, like Johnson's Aimée Galles or Schulte's Fanny Mendelssohn or even Davidoff's Helen Gladstone learned to live with their disappointment, achieving some degree of fulfillment if not autonomy, though less than what might have been.

In much of the literature examined here, the discourse is established by males, totally so in Corbett's case, and the focus of the females' attention is upon them. In this reading, then, autonomous selfhood is in fact denied to women, whose role and place, however important they might be, are in reaction to men. But one of the lessons we learn from kinship analysis is how much the ideology of autonomy was just that—ideology.

Men relied on the dense network of kin at every phase of their lives to make their way in the world. And, of course, there are other examples of women to weave into the story, such as Bettine von Arnim or Fanny Lewald, who deserve further study before we take the male representation at face value. Despite all of Clemens Brentano's sultry rhetoric about himself and his sister being fashioned together in an almost incestuous intimacy, Bettine simply brushed all that aside and turned herself into a major—can we say autonomous?—social critic and central intellectual figure of the *Vormärz*.

In approaching gender in the nineteenth century, the close study of the kinship system organized around siblings allows one to come to an assessment that transcends the victimization/empowerment dialogue, just as it does the debate over the gendered character of the private and public spheres. We are only at the beginning of understanding the dynamics of familial interaction. One of the problems is that treating the nineteenth-century family implicitly as "mom, dad, and the kids" distorts the reality of webs of relationships organized around complex interactions of families who recognize the social, moral, sentimental, economic, and political ties that bind them. Families cannot be reduced to simple power relationships, and gender relations as an analytical problem cannot be cast in a triumphal (or tragic) story devoid of context and without close attention to the details of action within the constraints of given possibilities.

Notes

1. David Warren Sabean, Simon Teuscher, and Jon Mathieu, eds., *Kinship in Europe: Approaches to Long-Term Development (1300–1900)* (Oxford and New York, 2007). A third book is in preparation: Christopher H. Johnson, David Warren Sabean, Simon Teuscher, and Francesca Trivellato, eds., *Trans-regional and Transnational Families in Europe and Beyond: Experiences Since the Middle Ages.*
2. The modern historiographic agenda was set by a famous essay by Marcel Mauss, "A Category of the Human Mind: The Notion of Person; The Notion of Self," *Journal of the Royal Anthropological Institute* 68 (1938), reprinted and discussed in *The Category of the Person: Anthropology, Philosophy, History*, ed. Michael Carrithers, Steven Collins, and Steven Lukes (Cambridge, 1985), 1–25. Following upon that, Charles Taylor surveyed the field in *Sources of the Self: The Making of Modern Identity* (Cambridge, MA, 1989). The most recent attempt to dig up the roots of the self is Jerrold Seigel, *The Idea of the Self: Thought and Experience in Western Europe since the Seventeenth Century* (Cambridge, 2005). An important attempt to look at the issues in the context of nineteenth-century France and the educational system is Jan Goldstein, *The Post-Revolutionary Self: Politics and Psyche in France, 1750–1850* (Cambridge MA, 2005).

3. For a general overview, see David Warren Sabean and Simon Teuscher, "Kinship in Europe: A New Approach to Long Term Development," in Sabean, Teuscher, and Mathieu, eds., *Kinship in Europe*, 1–32.

4. See the series of articles by Bernard Derouet, "Parenté et marché foncier à l'époque moderne: une réinterprétation," *Annales HSS* 56, no. 2 (2001): 337–368; "La transmission égalitaire du patrimoine dans la France rurale (xvie–xixe siècles): Nouvelles perspectives de recherche," in *Historia de la Familia*, 3 vols., vol. 3: *Familia, Casa Y Trabajo*, ed. F. Chacón Jiménez (Murcia, 1997), 73–92; "Pratiques de l'alliance en milieu de communautés familiales (Bourbonnais, 1600–1750)," in *Le choix du conjoint*, ed. G. Brunet, A. Fauve-Chamoux, and M. Oris (Lyon, 1998), 227–251; with Joseph Goy, "Transmettre la terre: Les inflexions d'une problématique de la différence," *Mélanges de l'école française de Rome, Italie et Méditerranée (MEFRIM)* 110 (1998): 117–151; "Le partage des frères: Héritage masculin et reproduction sociale en Franche-Comté aux xviiie et xixe siècles," *Annales ESC* 48, no. 2 (1993): 453–474; "Pratiques successorales et rapport à la terre: Les sociétés paysannes d'ancien régime," in *Annales ESC* 44, no. 1 (1989): 173–206; "Territoire et parenté: Pour une mise en perspective de la communauté rurale et des formes de reproduction familiale," *Annales HSS* 50, no. 3 (1995): 645–686; "Cycle de vie, marché du travail et transferts fonciers: Chayanov et la paysannerie française d'Ancien Régime," in D. Barjot and O. Faron, *Migrations, cycle de vie familial et marché du travail (Cahier des Annales de démographie historique*, Nr. 3) (Paris, 2002), 305–317; "Les pratiques familiales, le droit et la construction des différences (15e–19e siècles)," *Annales HSS* 52, no. 2 (1997): 369–391; "La terre, la personne et le contrat: exploitation et associations familiales en Bourbonnais (xviie–xviiie siècles)," *Revue d'histoire moderne et contemporaine* 50, no. 2 (2003): 27–51. See also the discussions throughout David Warren Sabean, *Kinship in Neckarhausen, 1700–1870* (Cambridge, 1998).

5. Bernard Derouet develops the distinction between "succession" and "inheritance" in "Political Power, Inheritance, and Kinship Relations: The Unique Features of Southern France (Sixteenth–Eighteenth Centuries)," in Sabean, Teuscher, and Mathieu, eds., *Kinship in Europe*, 105–124, here esp. 105–108. See also the discussions throughout David Warren Sabean, *Property, Production and Family in Neckarhausen, 1700–1870* (Cambridge, 1990), where the substance of the issue is discussed without the precise conceptualization.

6. See Gérard Delille, *Famille et proprieté dans le royaume de Naples (XVe–XIXe siècle)* (Rome and Paris, 1985); Elisabeth Claverie and Pierre Lamaison, *L'impossible mariage: Violence et parenté en Gévaudan XVIIe, XVIIIe, et XIXe siècles* (Paris, 1982). Both of these books are summarized and discussed in detail in Sabean, *Property*, 399–416.

7. "Sib" or "sibbe" has a deep history in English, in written form dating at least to *Beowulf*, meaning at first "kinship, membership," as well as "peace, amity, concord," and becoming more specific (toward "blood kin") over time. Anthropologists adopted and refined such usage in the nineteenth century. It was not until the early twentieth century that "sibling," defined as "each of two or more children of a common parent or parents," entered the English language, again first employed by anthropologists. *The Compact Oxford English Dictionary*, 2 edition (Oxford, 1991), 1759–60.

8. For a recent discussion, see Juliet Mitchell, *Siblings: Sex and Violence* (Cambridge, 2003).

9. On this issue, see Martine Segalen, "'Avoir sa part': Sibling Relations in Partible Inheritance Brittany," in *Interest and Emotion: Essays on the Study of Family and Kinship*, ed. Hans Medick and David Warren Sabean (Cambridge, 1984), 129–144. For

the Siemenses, see the forthcoming article by David Warren Sabean, "German International Families in the Nineteenth Century: The Siemens Family as a Thought Experiment," in Johnson et al., *Trans-regional and Transnational Families*.

10. With regard to the structure and expectations of gender roles, while Derouet does not address the issue explicitly, the patterns he describes left little to choice among participants. It does seem, however, that daughters and wives exhibited more agency among peasants in this age than did aristocratic women. Barbara Hanawalt has argued this point for English peasants in the late Middle Ages in *The Ties that Bound: Peasant Families in Medieval England* (Oxford, 1986).

11. Steven Ozment, *When Fathers Ruled: Family Life in Reformation Europe* (Cambridge, MA, 1985).

12. Simon Teuscher, *Bekannte, Klienten, Verwandte: Soziabilität und Politik in der Stadt Bern um 1500* (Vienna and Cologne, 1998). See also Teuscher, "Property Regimes and Migration of Patrician Families in Western Europe around 1500," in Johnson et al., *Trans-regional and Transnational Families*.

13. In a large literature, see James R. Farr, *Hands of Honor: Artisans and their World in Dijon, 1550–1650* (Ithaca and London, 1988); Daniel Roche, *The People of Paris: An Essay in Popular Culture in the Eighteenth Century*, trans. Marie Evans in association with Gwynne Lewis (Berkeley, 1987); Roche, "Work, Fellowship, and some Economic Realities of Eighteenth-Century France," in *Work in France: Representations, Meaning, Organization, and Practice*, ed. Steven Laurence Kaplan and Cynthia J. Koepp (Ithaca and London, 1986), 54–73 [on Jacques Ménétra, glazier]; Maurice Garden, *Lyon et les Lyonnais au XVIIIe siècle* (Paris, 1970), 173–354; Jean-Pierre Bardet, *Rouen aux XVIIe et XVIIIe siècle: Les mutations d'un espace social*, vol. 1 (Paris, 1981), 230–265; Gay Gullickson, *The Spinners and Weavers of Auffay: Rural Industry and the Sexual Division of Labor in a French Village, 1750–1850* (Cambridge, 1986); Mary Jo Maynes, "Women and Kinship in the Propertyless Classes in Western Europe in the Nineteenth Century," in *Gender, Kinship, Power: A Comparative and Interdisciplinary History*, ed. Mary Jo Maynes, Ann Waltner, Brigette Soland, and Ulrike Strasser (New York, 1996), 261–274.

14. See especially Janine Lanza, *From Wives to Widows in Early Modern Paris: Gender, Economy and Law* (Aldershot and Burlington, VT, 2008).

15. On the emergence of epistolary culture in Europe, see Roger Chartier, Alain Boureau, and Cécile Dauphin, eds,, *Correspondence: Models of Letter-Writing from the Middle Ages to the Nineteenth Century*, trans. Christopher Woodhall (Princeton, 1997); Jane Couchman and Ann Crabb, eds., *Women's Letters Across Europe, 1400–1700: Form and Persuasion* (Aldershot and Burlington, VT, 2005); Thomas O. Beebee, *Epistolary Fiction in Europe, 1500–1850* (Cambridge, 1999); Anita Pacheco, ed., *A Companion to Early Modern Women's Writing* (Oxford, 2002); Elizabeth C Goldsmith, *Exclusive Conversations: The Art of Interaction in Seventeenth-Century France* (Philadelphia, 1988); Janet Gurkin Altman, "The Letter Book as a Literary Institution, 1539–1789: Toward a Cultural History of Published Correspondences in France," *Yale French Studies* 71 (1986): 17–62; Elizabeth Heckendorn Cook, *Epistolary Bodies: Gender and Genre in the Eighteenth-Century Republic of Letters* (Stanford, 1996).

16. On this issue, see above all Roger Chartier, *The Cultural Origins of the French Revolution* (Durham, NC, 1989).

17. See Sabean and Teuscher, "Kinship." For an interesting treatment of princely families and their role in state development, see Jonathan Spangler, "Those in Between: Princely Families on the Margins of the Great Powers," in Johnson et al., *Transregional and Transnational Families*.

18. This, of course, was lauded by Montesquieu and later Tocqueville as a means of preventing "tyranny."

19. See the brilliant study by William Beik on the strategies of Louis XIV, *Absolutism and Society in Seventeenth-Century France: State and Provincial Aristocracy in Languedoc* (Cambridge, 1985), as well as the recent work of Jay Smith on the adaptation of the French nobility to the changing circumstances of the power and leverage, *Nobility Re-imagined: The Patriotic Nation in Eighteenth-Century France* (Ithaca and London, 2005).

20. Gérard Delille, *Famille*; idem, *Le maire et le prieur : Pouvoir central et pouvoir local en Méditerranée occidentale (XVe–XVIIIe siècle)* (Paris, 2003)

21. See Gérard Delille, "Kinship, Marriage, and Politics," in Sabean, Teuscher, and Mathieu, *Kinship*, 163–183; Sabean, *Kinship in Neckarhausen*, passim and the bibliography.

22. See Ulrike Vedder, "Continuity and Death: Literature and the Law of Succession in the Nineteenth Century," and David Warren Sabean, "From Clan to Kindred: Kinship and the Circulation of Property in Pre-modern and Modern Europe," both in *Heredity Produced: At the Crossroads of Biology, Politics, and Culture, 1500–1870*, ed. Staffan Müller-Wille and Hans-Jörg Rheinberger (Cambridge, MA, 2007), 85–102 and 37–60 respectively.

23. Christopher H. Johnson, "Die Geschwister Archipel: Bruder-Schwester-Liebe und Klassenformation in Frankreich des 19. Jahrhunderts," in *Die Liebe des Geschwister*, ed. Karin Hausen and Regina Schulte, in *L'Homme: Zeitschrift für Feministische Geschichtswissenschaft* 13, no. 1 (2003): 50–67. Reprinted as Johnson, "The Sibling Archipelago: Brother-Sister Love and Class Formation in Nineteenth-Century France," in Mary Garrett, Heidi Gottlieb, and Sandra Van Burkleo, eds., *Remapping the Humanities* (Detroit, 2007), 94–111.

24. Christopher H. Johnson, "Into the World: Kinship and Nation-Building in France, 1750–1885," in Johnson et al., *Trans-regional and Transnational Families.*

25. See the excellent summary by Michael Titzmann, "Literarische Strukturen und kulturelles Wissen: Das Beispiel inzestuöser Situationen in der Erzählliteratur der Goethezeit und ihre Funktionen im Denksystem der Epoche," in *Erzählte Kriminalität*, ed. Jörg Schönert, Konstantin Imm, and Joachim Linder (Tübingen, 1991), 229–281.

26. These points are taken up in greater detail in Christopher Johnson's Chapter 8 below and are reflected in a great deal of the collected correspondence of the age.

27. James Lehning, *The Peasants of Marlhes: Economic Development and Family Organization in Nineteenth-Century France* (Chapel Hill, 1980); Christopher H. Johnson, *The Life and Death of Industrial Languedoc, 1700–1920: The Politics of De-industrialization* (Oxford, 1995); Elinor Accampo, *Industrialization, Family Life, and Class Relations: Saint-Chamond, 1815–1924* (Berkeley, 1989); Michael Hanagan, *The Logic of Solidarity: Artisans and Industrial Workers in Three French Towns* (Champaign, IL, 1980); Gullickson, *Spinners and Weavers of Auffay*; Tessie Liu, *The Weaver's Knot: The Contradictions of Class Struggle in Western France, 1750–1914* (Ithaca and London, 1994); Martine Segalen, *Fifteen Generations of Bretons: Kinship and Society in Lower Brittany, 1720–1920*, trans. J. A. Underwood (Cambridge and Paris, 1991); Michael Anderson, *Family Structure in Nineteenth-Century Lancashire* (Cambridge, 1971); Leslie Page Moch, "Bretons in Paris: Regional Ties and Urban Networks in an Age of Urbanization," *Quaderni storici* 86, no. 106 (2001): 177–199; Abel Châtelain, *Les migrations temporaires en France de 1800 à 1914*, 2 vols. (Lille, 1977).

28. Although all these issues are not dealt with in detail in the chapters of this book, the reader is reminded that it is part of a series, two others of which have appeared or will soon appear: Sabean, Teuscher, and Mathieu, *Kinship in Europe* and Johnson

et al., *Trans-regional and Transnational Families*. Please refer to them as well as the specific references below for further evidence of the arguments presented in this introduction.

29. Sabean, *Kinship in Neckarhausen*, 490–510.
30. Sabean, "German International Families."
31. Bertrand Gille, *Histoire de la maison Rothschild*, 2 vols. (Geneva, 1965, 1967); Rondo Cameron, *France and the Economic Development of Europe, 1800–1914* (Princeton, 1961); Leonore Davidoff and Catherine Hall, *Family Fortunes: Men and Women of the English Middle Class, 1780–1850* (Chicago, 1987); D.C. Coleman, *Courtaulds: An Economic and Social History*, vol. 1: *The Nineteenth Century* (Oxford, 1969); Leonard Rosenband, *Papermaking in Eighteenth-Century France: Management, Labor, and the Revolution at the Montgolfier Mill, 1761–1805* (Baltimore, 2000); Louis Bergeron, *Banquiers, négociants et manufacturiers à Paris pendant le Directoire et l'Empire* (The Hague, 1978); Peter Stearns, *Paths to Authority: The Middle Class and the Industrial Labor Force in France, 1820–1848* (Urbana, 1972); Jean Lambert-Dansette, *Quelques familles du patronat textile de Lille-Armentières (1789–1914)* (Lille, 1954); Bonnie G. Smith, *Ladies of the Leisure Class: The Bourgeoises of Northern France in the Nineteenth Century* (Princeton, 1984); Serge Chassagne, *Le coton et ses patrons: France, 1760–1840* (Paris, 1991); Jürgen Kocka, "Familie, Unternehnmer und Kapitalismus. An Beispielen aus der frühen deutschen Industrialisierung," *Zeitschrift für Unternehmergeschichte* 24 (1979): 99–135; David Sabean, "Kinship and Class Formation," chap. 22 of Sabean, *Kinship in Neckarhausen*; Friedrich Zunkel, *Der Rheinisch-Westfälische Unternehmer, 1834–1879* (Cologne, 1962); Marion A. Kaplan, *The Making of the Jewish Middle Class: Women, Family, and Identity in Imperial Germany* (New York, 1991); Philipp Sarasin, *La ville des bourgeois: Élites et société urbaine à Bâle dans la deuxième moitié du XIXe siècle* (Paris, 1998).
32. Sabean, "German International Families."
33. Adam Kuper, "Darwin's Marriage, Theories of Heredity, and the Origins of Eugenics." Paper presented at the European Social Science History Conference, Lisbon, March 2008.
34. Davidoff and Hall, *Family Fortunes*, especially Part One.
35. Bourdieu, *Outline of a Theory of Practice* (Cambridge, 1977); Sabean, *Kinship in Neckarhausen*, 449–489.
36. Emmanuel Beau de Loménie, *Les responsabilités des dynasties bourgeoises*, 5 vols. (Paris, 1977).
37. Johnson, "Into the World"; Sabean, "Kinship and Class Dynamics."
38. Stephen Kale, *French Salons: High Society and Political Sociability from the Old Regime to the Revolution of 1848* (Baltimore, 2004); Whitney Walton, *Eve's Proud Descendants: Four Women Writers and Republican Politics in Nineteenth-Century France* (Stanford, 2000); Anne Martin-Fugier, *La vie élégante ou la formation du Tout-Paris, 1815–1848* (Paris, 1990).
39. Sabean emphasizes the role of annual great-family reunions as one of the crucial elements promoting unity and class feeling. *Kinship in Neckarhausen*, 472–474.
40. Roland Barthes, *Mythologies*, trans. Annette Lavers (New York, 1972), 137–142.
41. The classic study is by Eugen Weber, *Peasants into Frenchmen* (Stanford, 1977), Part I, "The Way Things Were."
42. For a detailed analysis of the building of local civil society and political power on one hand and national connection across kinship grids on the other, see Christopher H. Johnson, "Kinship, Civil Society, and Power in Nineteenth-Century Vannes," in Sabean, Teuscher, and Mathieu, *Kinship in Europe* and Johnson, "Into the World,"

in Johnson et al., *Trans-regional and Transnational Families*. Also, Stéphane Gerson, *Pride of Place: Local Memories and Political Culture in Nineteenth-Century France* (Ithaca, 2003).

43. Niall Ferguson, *The World's Banker: The History of the House of Rothschild* (London, 1998); for genealogical details, see Joseph Valynseele and Henri-Claude Mars, *Le sang des Rothschilds: familles alliées* (Paris, 2004); Sabean, "German International Families."

44. Outside of the work of Adam Kuper, this is a phenomenon that has not received much focused attention, but can be gleaned from biography after biography following Kuper's methodology. Anecdotal evidence arises in Kaplan, *The Making of the Jewish Middle Class*, Carl Schorske, *Fin de Siècle Vienna: Politics and Culture* (New York, 1980), Robert Herbert, *Impressionism: Arts, Leisure, and Parisian Society* (New Haven, 1988).

45. On the reaction to women in Revolutionary politics, see, among others, Lynn Hunt, *The Family Romance of the French Revolution* (Berkeley, 1992), 53–123; Dominique Godineau, *The Women of Paris and Their French Revolution*, trans. Katherine Streip (Berkeley and Los Angeles, 1988); Joan Wallach Scott, *Only Paradoxes To Offer: French Feminists And The Rights Of Man* (Cambridge, MA, 1996), 19–56; and especially Darlene Gray Levy, Harriet Branson Applewhite, and Mary Durham Johnson, eds., *Women in Revolutionary Paris, 1789–1795: Selected Documents* (Urbana and Chicago, 1980), 143–308.

46. On the decline of paternal authority and the rise of the couple, see Maurice Daumas, *Le syndrome des Grieux: La relation père-fils au XVIIIe* (Paris, 1990) and *La tendresse amoureuse, XVIe–XIXe siècles* (Paris, 1997); on the bonds of friendship, Anne Vincent-Buffault, *L'exercice de l'amitié: Pour une histoire des pratiques amicales aux XVIIIe et XIXe siècles* (Paris, 1995); and on the changing material context of family life, Annik Pardailhé-Galabrun, *The Birth of Intimacy: Privacy and Domestic Life in Early Modern Paris*, trans. Jocelyn Phelps (Cambridge, 1991); for an up-to-date survey of the changing modalities of sexuality, see Katherine Crawford, *European Sexualities: 1400–1800* (Cambridge, 2007).

47. See especially the soliloquy by Klinger's character, Haroun, lamenting that he could not marry his sister.

48. Pateman, *The Sexual Contract* (Stanford, 1988); Juliet Flower MacCannell, *The Regime of the Brother: After the Patriarchy* (London, 1991); Susanne Desan, *The Family on Trial in Revolutionary France* (Berkeley, 2004).

49. Perry, *Novel Relations: The Transformation of Kinship in English Literature and Culture, 1748–1818* (Cambridge, 2004). The tale of the dying sister (along with dying female lovers in general) is a recurrent theme in turn-of-the-century literature, most notably in Chateaubriand. See especially Madelyn Gutwirth, "The Engulfed Beloved: Representations of Dead and Dying Women in the Art and Literature of the Revolutionary Era," in Sara E. Melzer and Leslie W. Rabine, eds., *Rebel Daughters: Women and the French Revolution* (Oxford, 1992), 198–227.

50. On the characteristics of male friendship in this era, see Anne-Vincent-Buffault, *L'exercise de l'amitié*, 185ff.

51. On the convoluted history of this prohibition and its further justification by premodern science, in which blood and semen were seen as effectively the same substance, see David Warren Sabean, "Kinship and Prohibited Marriages in Baroque Germany: Divergent Strategies among Jewish and Christian Populations," *Leo Baeck Institute Yearbook* 47 (2002): 91–103.

52. Joan Wallach Scott, *Gender and the Politics of History* (New York, 1988).

PART ONE

PROPERTY, POLITICS, AND SIBLING STRATEGIES (LATE MEDIEVAL AND EARLY MODERN)

Chapter 1

Dowry: Sharing Inheritance or Exclusion?

Timing, Destination, and Contents of Transmission in Late Medieval and Early Modern France

Bernard Derouet

In Europe from the fifteenth to the eighteenth centuries, the relationships among siblings were strongly influenced by the position assigned to each child from the perspective of the family patrimony. In this regard, what was in play concerned a potential inequality among siblings not only in the attribution of wealth and material goods, but also in the way in which those among them were considered—or not—to be the true continuators of the family, bearers of its identity who were charged with its perpetuation. This distribution of roles among different children took place or became manifest at two essential moments: the death of their parents and their own marriage. The focus here is on the respective importance of these two moments and in particular on the significance of the matrimonial *prestation* called the "dowry." By virtue of its diversity of forms, its actual content, and its variable implications in connection with inheritance, the dowry is especially revealing of the character of various family systems and the differential treatment of siblings.

Origins and Implicit Logics of the Exclusionary Dowry (*Dot-exclusion*)

It is well known that under the Ancien Régime, France was a country of great diversity. In matters concerning the family and rules of inheritance, we have become abundantly aware of this diversity especially through the works in the history of the law by Jean Yver—taken up thereafter by Emmanuel LeRoy Ladurie—on the geography of *"coutumes"* (that is, the regional codes applying to private law drafted in the fifteenth and sixteenth centuries).[1] To be sure, the uses that many historians and anthropologists have made of this work have not always been relevant: the classification devised by Jean Yver, valid on the strictly juridical plane, often does not make much sense from the point of view of actual social practices of transmission.[2] The geographical divisions that he proposed can also be questioned. But this author had the merit of shining a bright light on the most important question concerning the devolution of the patrimony: the exclusion (or not) of children receiving dowries (*enfants dotés*) from participation in the inheritance at the time of their parents' death.

Indeed, the dowry as a modality of exclusion from the patrimony constituted the formula most generally employed in France, on the regional or the individual level, in the division of the patrimony among different children. Other methods were occasionally used, wherever the regional customary laws permitted, such as the *préciput* or the possibilities offered by the will (institution of a universal heir), but they often served only as a title of confirmation for an exclusion first put into play at the level of marriage and the dowry.[3]

A difficulty arises from the fact that the word "dowry" was sometimes also used in regions with equal inheritance for sons and daughters, as in several regions in northern France. But there should be no confusion: in this case the "dowry" simply comprised the goods that the woman brought into her new household upon marriage. This did not mean that this matrimonial prestation would constitute the entirety of what she would receive from her family of origin. Upon the death of her father and mother she would be able, by restoring what she had received at the time of her marriage (or its value), to participate in the succession equally with all her brothers and sisters. Moreover, neither did the use of the word "dowry" in such a case signify that in the new couple's relationship, the goods coming from the wife would have a specific juridical status (as in the dowry system born of Roman law).

Let us return to the exclusionary dowry. How to interpret it, from a historical point of view as well as from the perspective of the conceptions of the family to which it bears witness? It had not always existed. Even among the nobility, before the transformations of the eleventh and twelfth centuries (which saw the beginnings of the exclusion of daughters and, partially, of the practice of favoring the eldest son), women generally participated in successions, including rights to landed property. We have little information about the peasant milieu, but in the later Middle Ages (the fourteenth and fifteenth centuries), when peasant practices appear clearly, especially in notarial acts, the practice of dowry exclusion becomes widely evident, particularly in the southern half of France (and sometimes elsewhere as well).

Some writers have connected this with the fact that the French Midi retained traces of Roman culture, or better—which is more credible—with the fact that it was in these regions that Roman law had been rediscovered, coming from Italy (Bologna) in the course of the twelfth and thirteenth centuries, until then having disappeared completely and been forgotten in these regions. It is true, indeed, that in the later Middle Ages the formulation of contracts here was invested with a very "Roman" formal appearance, employing all the juridical concepts connected with this law. Does the exclusionary dowry originate from this influence? This appears to be highly debatable, insofar as Roman law, which carried with it the very idea of the dowry and the principles applicable to it (notably its protection), *never* envisaged that to grant a dowry to a daughter excluded her from her "family" and took away, in matters of inheritance, the rights associated with her filiation. Jurists of the late Middle Ages were so aware of this that in order to justify exclusion of the dowered daughter from succession, they had to rely on thirteenth-century *canonical* decisions justifying by means of "the theory of the oath" the fact that those who renounced their claim to inheritance at the time of their marriage could not be released from their promise. Moreover, except in some regions like Provence, where exclusion of the dowered daughter was "statutory" (that is automatic, deriving from the regional law itself), nowhere did marriage contracts fail to include an explicit and personal renunciation by the married and dowered daughter of any future inheritance, in order to render this decision unassailable.

In fact, the misunderstanding in this regard on the part of numerous historians can be easily explained. It was in the southern half of France that a majority of the non-egalitarian practices concerning the transmission were encountered. This generalization needs to be refined, for it was especially the mountainous areas that adopted these practices, and they did so the earliest.[4] On the other hand, it was also the southern half of France where the Roman law was established as the legislation of reference in matters of private and familial law, even if there already existed specific local *coutumes*. Many specialists have thus made the connection between unequal practices of transmission and the Roman law. Indeed, the latter provided, by the liberty accorded to the *père de famille* thanks to the will, a wide range of possibilities to organize his succession as he wished (though he could also desire that it be egalitarian). But it was forgotten that the exclusionary dowry, the main instrument of and justification for inequality among siblings, in fact had nothing to do with Roman law, which did not recognize it.

Why did the practice of dowry exclusion prevail in certain social milieus and especially in certain regions? This is a question too complex to be grappled with completely here. Let us be content to point out that equal transmission and unequal transmission were, each of them, linked to a very specific conception of the right to benefit concretely from the inheritance: in the case of equality this right was conceived of as something deriving from *filiation*, from the link of kinship, independently of any other consideration. In the other case, this right was conceived as deriving from membership in an entity that was at base "sociological" in nature—from the fact of remaining in it, of keeping interests in it, of working for it, and of maintaining with it a certain way of life. This might involve cohabitation under the same roof (co-residence) or, in a more supple manner, the fact of maintaining spatial proximity and common interests with the family of origin. Under these conditions, the departure from the family upon the occasion of marriage, if it was accompanied by integration into another entity, meant, ipso facto, the loss of any right in the heart of the universe from which one came. In France, the practice of dowry exclusion can thus be found as much in regions of primogeniture and single succession (Pyrenees, Massif Central) as in regions of wide familial communities of the *zadruga* type (Nivernais or Bourbonnais, for example), or in regions of simple "agnatic" practices, with equality only among the male children, and of *frérèches* and temporary joint possession (as in Franche-Comté and numerous regions of the Alps).

I will not pursue here the question of how much the exclusionary dowry owed to cultural traditions and how much to reasons of an economic order or other causes. Let me simply point out that if, as has been shown, these practices were not a *consequence* of Roman law, it is well understood that Roman law—with its organization of the dowry system—was able to constitute for these practices an admirable instrument for establishing juridical "formality" (leaving aside the partial distortion of its spirit): the Roman juridical regime of the dowry secured both a protection of the dowry and a separation of the patrimonies of the couple between husband and wife, which could be adapted quite well to the situation of daughters who were dowry-excluded from their family.[5]

Likewise, the spirit of the Roman law, with its concept of *patria potestas* (the linking up with this *potestas* being more important for inheritance rights than the prerogatives given by filiation), could also be easily "manipulated" to justify a conception of succession rights founded on the principle of "residence."

The Dowry: Unifiliation, Bilaterality, or "Unilaterality"?

Earlier considerations on the separation of assets between husband and wife in the case of the exclusionary dowry led to an examination of the notion of the "conjugal fund" put forward by Jack Goody as a characteristic of all European societies. It is well known that Goody—who draws a fundamental distinction between lineage societies of the African type and Eurasian societies—was much interested in the question of the dowry, whether "direct" (dowry) or "indirect" (dower).[6] To be sure, he attaches great importance to the issue of the chronology of transmission. But in his perspective, the dowry is solely the manner in which daughters participated in inheritance, in Europe as in Asia. This does not mean that daughters were not true heirs; compared with male children, the only difference consisted precisely in that their portion of the patrimony was entrusted to them at a different time, on the occasion of their marriage, while the sons were most often awarded a postmortem transmission. According to Goody, this difference should not detract from the perception of the fundamentally *bilateral* nature of all European systems of transmission, which he characterizes as "diverging devolution." These systems are distinguished in toto from those of African societies, which are based on the lineage, *unifiliation*, and in which transmission takes place without the patrimony passing from one kinship line to another (transmission in the same sex line). In this context, the chronology of the transmission, which in Europe was the main aspect by which a differential treatment of sons and daughters existed, would in the end be only a marginal phenomenon that should not mask the profound truth of practices.

On the other hand, the comparative study of European societies has led historians and anthropologists to put the accent on certain fundamental cleavages that separate different models of transmission practices *within* societies where unifiliation does not prevail. The notion of diverging devolution proves to be inadequate to characterize European societies as a whole, precisely insofar as it is the presence or absence of a veritable bilaterality that constitutes one of the major aspects of their differences. To understand the meaning of this perspective we must abandon the criteria on which Goody relied in assessing the "bilateral-ity" of a system, breaking away from seeing it as a question of filiation, of transmission in a single line or in two lines of kinship. To put it an-other way, the originality of European societies is that they reveal a co-existence between systems of transmission authentically bilateral (with inheritance equally divided among all children, neolocal residence, the centrality of the couple and the new cell founded upon marriage, and communal fusion of goods brought to the marriage), and others, by con-trast, that one can qualify as unilateral but that are not, for all that, based on a principle of unifiliation.

These "unilateral" practices appear in full light upon examination of "*systèmes à maison.*" This concept of "the house" proves to be opera-tive as much in the analysis of certain forms of familial reproduction characteristic of the elites of the medieval and early modern era (nota-bly in noble milieus), as in the peasant world. In the latter, it is known that the practices of transmission to a unique or principal successor—of which the primogeniture (*l'ainesse*) of the Pyrenees is one of the classic examples—can be described as "house systems." It should not be forgot-ten, however, that other practices of transmission, which could involve a plurality of successors, also fit perfectly in this analytical framework, as in the case of certain types of *communautés familiales.*[7]

In these non-bilateral practices where transmission went to "one side only," the notion of "side" does not refer to a criterion of sex (masculine/feminine) and thus to a line of kinship, but refers to an entity definable in terms of "residence" and/or of patrimony (it being understood that here the notion of immaterial or symbolic patrimony is taken into con-sideration as much as that of material patrimony). Although the inheri-tance could be transmitted to daughters as to sons—or rather, "to pass" to certain ones among them—such practices were worlds apart from the logic of diverging devolution and the idea of a centrifugal effect on the patrimony that this term requires. The key notion here is not bilat-erality and equilibrium, but *dissymmetry*, meaning both the division of the patrimony unequally between those children who stayed and those who departed, and the nature of the married couple's relationship, in which one of the spouses "move[d] to the house of the other" and inte-grated into the entity for which the latter took on the responsibility of its continuation.

Not at all subject to a process of splintering and of dissemination, the patrimony was mortared in a politics of continuity, of the perpetuation of an entity that was not a kinship group like a lineage, one whose identity may be described as being more institutional ("*réelle,*" res) than private ("*personnelle*"). This is why such practices can be characterized neither by the notion of bilaterality nor by that of unifiliation, but rather by that of unilaterality (which is very different). A symmetry can certainly exist in "kinship recognition" (which is thus of the cognatic, undifferentiated, bilateral type) without a similar symmetry presiding over the transmission of the patrimony and the forms of identity that are linked with it. The fact that dissymmetry concerns only one specific aspect of the transmission (that of goods and social status, and not that of filiation) does not, for all that, reduce the significance of this phenomenon, for the originality of such practices lies precisely in the fact that the patrimony (in the largest sense) in this case plays, as the foundation of identities and as the principle of social classification and organization, exactly the role played by filiation in unilinear systems (lineage societies).

As we have noted, in France the word "dowry" was also sometimes employed in regions where equal transmission of the patrimony prevailed (for example the north, especially the Parisian Basin, and regions of the west) to designate the goods brought by the wife at the moment of marriage. But in this case, it was a question of anything but what we have just been describing. First of all, in this system the wife, more often than elsewhere, pieces together, on her own, a part or all of her dowry: these goods come from savings realized from wages she has earned, thanks to domestic service, in a rural society where children marry rather late but leave their family of origin early on to be "placed" with others and earn their livelihood personally. To be sure, it was also the case that the young bride received goods given to her by her family at the time of her marriage. But in these regions, marriage and the dowry are not the key moments in the transition between generations and in the devolution of the patrimony. A daughter, just like a male child, could in addition receive goods from her parents progressively, at different times in her life cycle.

The essential moment came at the death of the last parent. The operative principle was that the rights to the patrimony were solidified definitively only at this point. Everything that had been distributed previously was now put into question. It is critically important to make an essential distinction: even though small portions of the patrimony may have been distributed to the children on the occasion of their marriage, these were only *avances d'hoirie* (advances on the inheritance), provisional dispositions liable to new settlement at the time of the distribution of the estate, which gave to each child his or her due, this time irreversibly. Thus the death of the parents made the "liquidation" of a sociological entity and a community of rights the order of the day, and it was from the compost of this decomposition that the creation of new entities could be organized—centered on the couples who constituted them, not on their reattachment to a pre-existing entity. Thus is carried forward an indefinitely repeated alternance of decomposition/re-composition of family units, which is characteristic of truly bilateral systems and rooted in an authentic diverging devolution. A true restructuring occurs with every generation, and the transition is, in a sense, a rupture.

Naturally, the situation existing among siblings within their family of origin inevitably has consequences and ongoing implications for the male/female relationship of the married couple. We must be careful not confuse different planes: that of authority and that of the patrimonial claims within the couple. Even in societies with equal inheritance, the authority of the *chef de famille* and the management of common goods remained masculine prerogatives. But at the least, wherever there existed bilateral practices by which all children were placed on the same level with regard to the transmission of the patrimony, the consequences were not negligible: this situation alone permitted the formation of a couple where the two spouses arrived with marriage portions that were equivalent or at least equilibrated—that is to say, a situation propitious to the creation of a veritable "communauté conjugale" (a precise juridical term, but one that links up with the idea of the conjugal fund) in a logic centered on the couple itself, and not on an entity that it develops and perpetuates.[8]

Is the Dowry a Female Patrimony?

To understand clearly the dowry and its peculiar logic, three types of questions need to be unraveled. The first concerns the content of what has been given the label "matrimonial prestation." The second examines the precise identity of the persons to whom it is granted. The third concerns the *"usages"* (customs or practices) of the dowry, its juridical nature, and the uses that can be made of it (whether by the receiving family or by the dowried individual).

Let us begin with the content of the dowry. It was of course quite different depending on whether it was an exclusionary dowry or another type of matrimonial prestation. In the first case, the dowry differed significantly from the portions of the inheritance received by the true successors of the family: this can be seen as much with regard to the *value* of the goods granted as to their *nature*. This point holds for all social classes, as much for the nobility as for the peasantry, for example. In most cases, the child given a dowry received goods of an appreciably inferior, or very inferior, value compared to those put at the disposition of her siblings who remained integrated in their family of origin. This is not always easily discernible, for while the notarial acts carefully detail the composition of the dowry, they rarely mention the value of what the real successors will receive: indeed, such precision is not legally necessary, since the latter are content to receive "the rest" (once the dowries are subtracted) later on. But this "rest" is indeed the essential portion of the patrimony: in all cases where comparison is possible, documents reveal that the dowry represents very little in relation to the true portion of the inheritance.

Most often the dowry was made up of the trousseau (personal clothing, household linens, several pieces of furniture such as a bed and a chest) and other moveable goods: often two or three small animals (among peasants) and especially a sum of money. In the peasant milieu, this dowry almost never included land or houses, which were the heart of the family patrimony. Some historians have wondered whether the presence of money in dowries did not signify an abundance of available liquid assets (hence a monetized economy). In reality, except for certain rural societies practicing periodic migration outside the region, this explanation is not valid: if one gave the recipient of the dowry only money, it was in order to preserve the means of production of the house for its veritable successors. Moreover, the actual payment of the dowry money took place in stages spread out over a long period—five to thirty or forty years in some peasant societies. Only a very small part of this money was given on the wedding day itself. Finally, these periodic payments, spread out as they were, likened the dowry to a kind of *"rente"* (annuity), which included interest, and whose sums were given in proportion to availability in the family as it was able to generate new liquid assets by its work.[9]

Nevertheless, it is true that we know of several examples in European rural societies where the female dowry was on the contrary often composed of real estate (often a bit of land, and in any case the house where the new couple would live): this seems to have been the case in part of southern Italy, in the Greek islands of the Aegean, and in coastal Galicia in Spain—a situation where it would be erroneous to view it as a "matrilineal" transmission, but rather more pertinently as a form of "matrifocality."[10] In France, however, such situations rarely occurred.

In discussing the composition of the dowry, a problem remains with regard to the nobility (and a very small segment of the peasantry). Among nobles, the female dowry also was often composed simply of sums of money, *rentes*, and other paper assets. Still, in this social milieu, the inclusion of some properties and seigneuries in the dowry was unexceptional. Should we then conclude that the practices of transmission here were somewhat more bilateral? Despite appearances, that would be an interpretive error. In reality, even when real estate and indeed seigneuries figured in the noble dowry, careful examination demonstrates that these lands were "marginal," geographically isolated, and in any case peripheral to the ancestral lands of the family, the basis of its identity and its status—in short, the "heart" and central core of the patrimony. In general, landed properties included in dowries often comprised more or less recent acquisitions; better still, it was a question of property that came into the patrimony via the dowry of another woman, usually the mother of the dowried daughter. The mother had herself received it from her own family of origin, where it was also peripheral to the heart of their patrimony.

In this fashion, passing from dowry to dowry, these properties continually "circulated" from one family to another and were, in the end, treated in the same way as the movable goods ordinarily composing the dowry, from which they in fact differed very little. We can also see here the mark of a specific transmission for certain goods from mother to daughter and thus forward from generation to generation: that is to say, a system that can be styled bilineal, with some goods specifically masculine and others specifically feminine, transmitted separately in each line (father/son, mother/daughter). This practice is not at all incompatible with the dowry system, in that it corresponds to the latter with regard to the distinction maintained between the goods of the husband and those of the wife—a situation where there is no mixture or fusion of the marriage portions of the spouses, the opposite of what prevails in a true conjugal fund. The qualification "bilineal" assuredly applies better to such systems than the term "bilateral." In France of the Ancien Régime, it was especially in the nobility where we can observe such practices, much more rarely in peasant societies. But elsewhere in Europe such systems were often seen beyond the world of the elites.[11]

In France, it is in the rural regions with equal inheritance that one sees the most cases where a woman, at the time of her marriage, received a small amount of land from her parents and/or other means of production (animals, agricultural implements, etc.). This could be the case as much for the advance granted to the man as for that agreed to for the woman by their respective families. This point should be stressed: the practice here was truly bilateral, for each of the two spouses received such a matrimonial prestation from his/her side. In short, this transfer of goods on the occasion of marriage did not constitute a "compensation" that one domestic entity paid to another in order to place one of its children in the latter, but is rather support brought to the children themselves, so that each could, with his/her spouse, participate in the construction of a new cell of existence. In a word, this is the entire rationale of practices centered on *neolocal* marriage, where one does not move in "*chez*" the one or "*chez*" the other, but the newly created family is centered on the couple itself. Here, we are in the presence of a completely different conception of the transition between generations.

Beyond these regions, was the dowry specifically feminine and reserved for a new wife? Generally, yes, but with important nuances. In regions with "agnatic" systems of transmission (inheritance reserved for male children only), daughters were in effect the only persons likely to receive a dowry, which excluded them from the rest of the patrimony. But in systems with a unique or principal heir, things were much more complex. The essential issue here was the preservation of the "house" and its integrity. Generally it was a male child who was designated as successor, but not always: some familial practices in the Pyrenees recognized "*l'ainesse absolue*" where the single successor was the eldest child, whatever the sex (the Basque country, for example); elsewhere, the absence of a male child could lead to the designation of a daughter as the unique successor, and her spouse would be integrated "into the house" in a subordinate position. This explains why certain daughters could not receive a dowry, while on the other hand certain boys could be given a dowry (notably younger sons marrying the female heir of another "house"). In reality, in designating a child as an excluded dowry recipient or a veritable heir, the sex of the person concerned counted less than the fact of being destined to leave or stay, to be integrated into another family unit or to assure the continuity of the "house" of origin. From this perspective, the phenomenon of the dowry in this practice of succession and marriage was asexual.

In another connection, even admitting that the dowry was generally reserved for women, could it be called a true patrimony for them? Here too, the answer calls for important nuances. Officially, for example in marriage contracts, the dowry of a woman was presented most often as serving "to support expenses of the household"—thus it was a contribution from her family of origin to successfully integrate her into another family and profit from the enjoyment of its wealth. However, it is clear that the dowry system, in any case such as it was organized under Roman law, was partially a protection and a guarantee for the *person* of the woman: this regime assured her that her dowry would be protected and not squandered, and that in case of her widowhood it would permit her to remarry with the same dowry or to lead a decent and relatively autonomous existence if she chose to remain a widow. The woman also preserved the possibility of choosing the ways her dowry would be conferred upon her death.[12]

Under these conditions, can the dowry be considered a veritable personal "patrimony" of the woman? In some ways, this point is open to discussion. Above all, the dowry was conceived as a cogwheel in the alliance of different family units. Less than an equivalent of inheritance, the dowry was in this context the means and the instrument of matrimonial exchange between houses. The dowry a house received in the house upon the arrival of a spouse would serve to free up funds for a dowry in its turn for an *"exclu"* from the house, whether this occurred in this generation or the next. Taking account of this recycling of dowries, it is difficult to consider them as true portions of inheritance. Besides, they remained distinct from the assets of the house, available to be put into circulation again. In sum, they were destined to "come and go" without ever really fusing concretely with the patrimonies of the houses with which they intertwined only for a moment before leaving again. We are therefore far, in this case, from the notion of the conjugal fund characteristic of truly bilateral systems.

Marriage and Death: The Paradoxes of the Chronology of Transmission

We have seen that the chronology and the content of transmission are two aspects difficult to dissociate from each other. Depending on the type of succession system, the marriage of the children and the death of the parents did not have the same importance as decisive moments in the process of succession. However, despite the results that we have arrived at so far, it can be asked if, in other regards, it might not be necessary to invert the perspective as to the role of these two key moments. The concept of "transmission" is a complex notion that takes in several elements of transference at once: of rights, of authority, of effective power over property. But the distinctions among these different aspects suggest another, parallel, perspective on the temporal articulations of the transition between generations.

Up to this point, we have considered the respective roles of marriage and death in different types of practices essentially from the point of view of the determination of *rights*. But if we abandon for now this de jure perspective to envisage the transmission de facto, we find ourselves paradoxically in the presence of an inverse situation concerning the respective role of these two key moments, for the moment when the content of the transmission is decided was not necessarily the same as the moment when it took effect.

As we have seen, in a "house" system the successor was designated—or confirmed in his or her position—at the time of his or her marriage. Yet despite the precocity of this designation, on a sociological plane the reality of the system went in an entirely different direction. Most often, the *chef de famille* "passed the hand" to his or her successor only much later. If (s)he could, the successor held on to the real power in the house (family and property) until his or her death. To be sure, circumstances might have led to the relinquishment of this role, planned in advance but ensuring that (s)he would be looked after, cared for, and given a pension. The future successor might also have been involved in some decision-making and in a part of the management of the house. But these occasional mitigations should not mask the profound reality of the actual transmission for persons and property: it came about only with the death of the titular *chef de famille*. The successor, even if long designated as such (at least since marriage), had to wait for this crucial moment, on the spot, in a subordinate position. Moreover, we know that it was this contrast between the theoretically enviable position of the successor—and future *chef de famille*—and the sociological reality of a situation of prolonged minority under the authority of parents that often engendered acute intergenerational tensions that could spill over into violence.[13]

This contrast between the attribution of rights planned since children's marriage and an effectuation that, for those selected as successors, was in fact put off until the death of the parents also existed in those unequal practices organized around the parity of male children while excluding the daughters, as in old Franche-Comté.[14] While the daughters received a *dot divise*—a dowry that excluded them from future inheritance and was tied to their marriage "out" to the household of her spouse and his father—the sons were established, from the time of their marriage, as heirs to the largest part of the patrimony and especially all the real estate (land and houses), but this privilege came to them only at the price of their lack of autonomy and juridical emancipation, and their maintenance—even after marriage—in the home of their parents until the latter's death. Although in this case the patrimonies ended up being divided, such practices did not amount to a real diverging devolution or the bilaterality proper to systems of transmission where all of the children (daughters as well as sons) are placed on the same footing. These latter systems alone permit the formation of a couple where the two spouses enter the marriage with equal or at least equilibrated portions, that is, a situation favorable to the formation of a true conjugal community in a logic centered on the couple itself and not on an entity that it prolongs and perpetuates.

But do not these egalitarian systems also invite an inversion of perspective with regard to the chronology of transmission? Although the death of the parents appeared de jure to be the crucial moment, de facto it often played a much less central role than one might expect. A careful examination of successions in such regions under the Ancien Régime belies the idea that everything came into play at this precise instant, in the sudden splintering of a patrimony and the brusque disintegration of a family unit whose members began only then to disperse. In reality, the autonomy of the children (or some of them) was often achieved well before the death of the parents. The departure of the children while they were still young was often made possible by the labor market, which allowed them to make a living and to save toward a neolocal marriage that would be brought to fulfillment later on. We must also stress the capital role played in most egalitarian systems by the phenomenon of *l'avance d'hoirie* (advance on inheritance), which was essential in order to achieve one's establishment and marriage and to assure the first foundations of a farm—even if it meant that the advance, often small in its first installment, had to be combined with wage work.

Thus in those systems where the transition between generations involved a restructuring, a rearrangement of roles, of locations, and of family units, the moment of the parents' death was in the end only one phase among others and did not necessarily hold the central place that one might presume. The heirs did not have to wait for it, nor were they entirely dependent on it. The idea that needs to be underlined is the *progressive* nature of the process of transition, which by no means always occurred in a brutal rupture upon the parents' death. After the initial *avance d'hoirie*, other transfers could eventually follow. Close observation shows that the parents, well before their death, in the course of time often increasingly gave up the better part of their possessions and especially their means of production in the rhythm of the marriage of their various children and their own aging. A last step often came with the cession of their property *inter vivos* ("between living people"—the *"démission de biens"* of the Ancien Régime): by this act they rescinded their authority over the patrimony in exchange for a life annuity or even for an assumption of full responsibility for their material well-being. Thus it frequently happened that at the time of the parent's death, the inheritance to be shared consisted of only a few crumbs that the parents had kept to assure themselves the bare necessities of their old age, the rest of the patrimony having already been amputated on various occasions. Far from the notion of "rupture," the image arising in this case is one of supple and progressive transition, despite the profound restructuring often involved in the passage from one generation to another.

The chronology of transmission can thus be approached from two different perspectives, each of which has its sphere of pertinence, though they lead to opposite conclusions. To sum up, the object here has been to draw attention to the fact that the "sociological truth" of a system does not necessarily accord with its "juridical truth." It is necessary to bring to bear the distinction between the transmission of property and that of authority or power, and above all not to confuse the moment of the attribution of rights (de jure) with that of their effective transfer. Even so, we remain in the presence of two modes of familial reproduction that at the key moments of marriage and death bring completely opposite roles into play.

Translated by Christopher H. Johnson

Notes

1. Jean Yver, *Essai de géographie coutumière : Egalité entre héritiers et exclusion des enfants dotés* (Paris, 1966); Emmanuel Le Roy Ladurie, "Système de la coutume: Structures familiales et coutumes d'héritage en France au XVIe siècle," *Annales ESC* 27 (1972): 825–846.
2. Allow me to refer to a study that I published on this question, "Les pratiques familiales, le droit et la construction des différences (15e–19e siècles)," in *Annales HSS* 52, no. 2 (1996): 369–391.
3. The practice was to give one of the heirs an advantage *"hors part,"* that is, he would keep the excess benefit while at the same time sharing what remained of the inheritance equally with the other heirs.
4. Several regions of the Midi of France remained rather egalitarian in inheritance, including with regard to daughters.
5. In Rome, the regulations of the dowry system were specified and organized, if in a belated manner, to respond to the necessities of marriage *sine manu*, which permitted the possibilities of divorce and repudiation. Differing from the former marriage *cum manu* (where the wife was *loco filiae* with regard to the husband, and where her matrimonial contribution was integrated into the patrimony of the latter), it was manifestly necessary in the new form of union to organize a separation of patrimonies between the marriage partners to guard against the possible vicissitudes of their future life.
6. Notably in *Production and Reproduction: A Comparative Study of the Domestic Domain* (Cambridge, 1976). He returned to this question in several later books.
7. See Bernard Derouet, "Territoire et parenté: Pour une mise en perspective de la communauté rurale et des formes de la reproduction familiale," *Annales HSS* 50, no. 3 (1995): 645–686, here 662–670.
8. In certain cases it was a question of a *"communauté universelle,"* but these were rather rare because of the notion of *"biens propres"* and of *"biens linagers"* in the old French customary law. Regions of equal inheritance, in France, were those where the matrimonial regime of community between spouses—community of moveable goods and of acquired goods (moveable and real property)—were most broadly developed. The only exception was Normandy, for reasons that would take too long to develop here.

9. In this sense, there is less distance than one might think between "unequal" and "equal" inheritance practices. In the latter, where the death of the parents threatened to dismember their patrimony (especially their property in lands and houses), in real practice one often finds one or two children *"prendre leur suite"* (taking over): they rented the portions of the land belonging to their co-heirs (*rente foncière*), and progressively, when they had the means, they recovered these portions by purchasing them outright from their brother, sister, nephew, or niece. This whole process was not, in the end, so different from what one observes in regard to the dowry, which in some respects was like a *"rente"* due to its distribution over time.

10. See Gérard Delille, *Famille et propriété dans le royaume de Naples, XVe.–XIXe. siècles* (Rome and Paris, 1985); Eythimuos Papataxiarchis and Socrates D. Petmezas, "The Devolution of Property and Kinship Practices in Late- and Post-Ottoman Ethnic Greek Societies: Some Demo-Economic Factors of Nineteenth and Twentieth Century Transformations," *Mélanges de l'Ecole française de Rome* (1998): 217–241; Carmelo Lison Tolosana, *Antropologia cultural de Galicia* (Madrid, 1971).

11. For instance in Greece, on Karpathos, where simultaneous transmission from father to eldest son and mother to eldest daughter was practiced; see Bernard Vernier, *La genèse sociale des sentiments: Aînés et cadets dans l'île grecque de Karpathos* (Paris, 1991).

12. Let us note in passing that what is said here about the "dowry" can not be applied to the *dower* (*douaire*), despite the fact that it could be labeled an "indirect dowry." The dower was a widow's *droit de jouissance* on the property of her dead husband's family and allowed her to end her life in a decent manner and in conformity with her social status. But the dower consisted only of a right to personal use on such property: it included neither the possibility of selling it nor arbitrarily dividing it among descendants. This is therefore not a question of a real property and thus of a true patrimony. In France, the only exception to these remarks concerns certain practices of the nobility before the twelfth century: at the time of his marriage, a man could give his wife certain goods and even certain lands with the right to do what she wanted with them and to dispose of them as she pleased (several examples of this can be found, notably, in the works of Georges Duby). But this type of application of the dower disappeared thereafter.

13. Elisabeth Claverie and Pierre Lamaison, *L'impossible mariage: Violence et parenté en Gévaudan, XVIIe, XVIIIe et XIXe siècles* (Paris, 1982).

14. Bernard Derouet, "Nuptuality and Family Reproduction in Male-Inheritance Systems: Reflections on the Example of Franche-Comté," *The History of the Family: An International Quarterly* 1, no. 2 (1996): 139–158 and "Le partage des frères: Heritage masculin et reproduction sociale en Franche-Comté au XVIIIe et XIXe siècles," *Annales ESC* 48, no. 2 (1993): 453–474.

Chapter 2

Maintenance Regulations and Sibling Relations in the High Nobility of Late Medieval Germany

Karl-Heinz Spieß

This article focuses on the fourteenth and fifteenth centuries, since the lack of source material makes it very difficult to formulate general remarks about sibling relations in the Early and High Middle Ages. Even though many individual cases are known from the early period, such as the problematic relationship between the sons of the emperor Louis the Pious, only the wider scope of sources found for the Late Middle Ages (including letters, testaments, or pictures) allows for more general statements.[1]

The "family order" of the late-medieval high nobility in Germany had two principal aims. To begin with, a central concern was dynastic continuity: the family of a ruler tried to produce a great number of children to compensate for high infant mortality. However (and equally important), dynastic continuity could only take place with the preservation of a dynasty's territorial substance.[2] Both of these aims were easily achieved if a father had only one or two sons. With just two sons, a territory could easily be divided and still maintain dynastic strength. One or two sisters, in turn, could also be allowed to marry. But if many children of a couple survived, resources had to be distributed unequally. Fathers achieved this by imposing different roles on their children through either oral or written contracts. In this context, the father (or, with his death, the reigning successor) played a key role in the formation of sibling relations, which he shaped according to his will.[3] Essentially, there were four different family roles that divided the siblings into four different groups.[4]

The sons succeeding to their father's office constituted the first group; they were expected to take over the rule and to take care of the continuity of the dynasty after their father's death. It was not necessarily the firstborn son who was chosen as successor, for primogeniture was not yet generally accepted among the German nobility. The lords wanted to retain the freedom of choosing the successor according to the latter's abilities to rule.[5] Nevertheless, the order of birth played a certain role, as Figure 2.1 illustrates.[6] Quite often, two or even three or four brothers shared the role of successor if their father had decided to divide the territory among them. Therefore, the first group of siblings consisted of ruling brothers, who were usually married.[7] An exception to this was provided by a "substitute successor" who was allowed to marry only if the first successor should fail to produce sons.[8]

The second group of siblings was formed by brothers who had to enter clerical life and consequently were not allowed to marry. They tried to maintain a lifestyle in accordance with their status by collecting a sufficient number of prebends, but until they did so they were in need of additional maintenance from their secular brothers.[9]

Female siblings were also divided into a secular and an ecclesiastical group. On the one hand, those chosen for a secular life left their parents' household at an average age of seventeen and married into another family.[10] On the other hand, those chosen for an ecclesiastical life were put into nunneries at around ten.[11] The fate of female siblings was also influenced by the order of birth, though this factor was less important than in the case of brothers (Figure 2.2).[12] Obviously, health and beauty played a more decisive part than the order of birth. For example, Margrave Albrecht Achilles of the famous Zollern dynasty had arranged in his testament of 1473 that his daughters should either marry or become nuns. And indeed, two of them were sent into nunneries and seven married. Margaret had to go into the nunnery St. Clara in Hof at the age of thirteen "because of the sickness of her body" ("angesehen blodikeit ires leibs"). She must have been hopeful of recovery because she was allowed to postpone her vow and to wear her secular clothes for one year. She then revolted against the wish of her father but had to give way in the end. Ironically, her sister Ursula tried, at the same time, to become a nun at St. Clara because she did not want to marry the husband her

Sons who died early and 76 families with only one grown-up son are not counted.

Out of 191 first born sons

151 (= 79.1 %) were allowed to marry

26 (= 13.6 %) became clerics

14 (= 7.3 %) became substitute rulers

Out of 191 second born sons

93 (= 48.7 %) were allowed to marry

77 (= 40.3 %) became clerics

21 (= 11.0 %) became substitute rulers

Out of 106 third born sons

34 (= 32.1 %) were allowed to marry

51 (= 48.1 %) became clerics

21 (= 19.8 %) became substitute rulers

Out of 56 fourth born sons

15 (= 26.8 %) were allowed to marry

35 (= 62.5 %) became clerics

6 (= 10.7 %) became substitute rulers

Out of 28 fifth born sons

5 (= 17.9 %) were allowed to marry

21 (= 75.0 %) became clerics

2 (= 7.1 %) became substitute rulers

Out of 16 sixth born sons

2 (= 12.5 %) were allowed to marry

12 (= 75.0 %) became clerics

2 (= 12.5 %) became substitute rulers

Out of 6 seventh born sons

6 (= 100 %) became clerics

Figure 2.1. Order of Birth and Family Roles (1200–1500) of Fifteen German Dynasties (Counts and Barons)

1. Out of 55 families with 2 daughters,

        1 daughter married   in 5 cases

        2 daughters married   in 42 cases

        no daughter married   in 8 cases

2. Out of 18 families with 3 daughters,

        1 daughter married   in 9 cases

        2 daughters married   in 4 cases

        3 daughters married   in 5 cases

3. Out of 26 families with 4 daughters,

        1 daughter married   in 5 cases

        2 daughters married   in 7 cases

        3 daughters married   in 6 cases

        4 daughters married   in 5 cases

        no daughter married   in 3 cases

4. Out of 8 families with 5 daughters,

        1 daughter married   in 0 cases

        2 daughters married   in 3 cases

        3 daughters married   in 4 cases

        4 daughters married   in 1 case

        5 daughters married   in 0 cases

        no daughter married   in 0 cases

5. Out of 9 families with 6 daughters,

        1 daughter married   in 0 cases

        2 daughters married   in 6 cases

        3 daughters married   in 2 cases

        4 daughters married   in 0 cases

        5 daughters married   in 1 case

        6 daughters married   in 0 cases

        no daughters married   in 0 cases

6. Out of 4 families with 7 daughters,	
1 daughter married	in 1 case
2 daughters married	in 0 cases
3 daughters married	in 1 case
4 daughters married	in 1 case
5 daughters married	in 0 cases
6 daughters married	in 0 cases
7 daughters married	in 1 case
no daughter married	in 0 cases

7. A family with 8 daughters could not be found.

8. Out of 1 family with 9 daughters,	
1 daughter married	in 0 cases
2 daughters married	in 1 case.

Figure 2.2. Number of Daughters per Family and Their Family Roles

father had chosen for her. She, too, had no chance of defying her father's will. According to the instructions of their father, both sisters had to be brought to the castle Plassenburg—if necessary tied to the carriage—to be interned until they consented to his wishes. A third daughter was supposed to enter a nunnery at the age of eight because she was ugly.[13]

The distribution of family roles is documented by both written texts and paintings. A good example of pictorial representation is a painting by Hans Baldung Grien (Illustration 2.1).[14] This picture, which is more than two meters wide, shows Margrave Christoph I of Baden in the year 1509 or 1510 with his wife Ottilie and his fifteen children, some of whom were already dead at that time. All of them, whether dead or alive, are clearly separated into the four groups that have just been characterized. Those among the ecclesiastical brothers and sisters who had already reached a high position with ruling rights and sufficient income are marked in a special way. All sisters, whether secular or ecclesiastical, are presented in a standardized manner with regard to their physiognomy and dress. The male siblings are presented in a more individual way: two of them obviously resemble their mother; the others look like their father. Only one of the brothers wears armor, which singles him

Illustration 2.1. The Family of Margrave Christoph I of Baden ca. 1510

out as the future successor. In this case, he was not the firstborn, but the fifth-born son.[15]

A second portrait shows that the pattern of grouping children by present or future status was not unusual. Illustration 2.2 is a painting showing the sixteen children of count Adolf I of Nassau and his wife Margaret of Nuremberg. Once again the four groups of siblings are clearly separated, with the future successor wearing armor to single him out among his secular brothers.[16]

Before proceeding to an investigation of the relations between siblings, I would like to present a central thesis of this essay. I suggest that due to the imposition of different roles and maintenance regulations, the relations between noble siblings were primarily formed and regulated by structures and not by individual attitudes. These structural differences did not exist among young children. Before the age of about seven, brothers and sisters grew up together in the children's quarter of the castle, although, of course, not all of the children lived together at the same time.[17] A great number of births also meant great differences in age. For instance, the firstborn child of the Margrave Christoph of Baden was already an adult of twenty-two when the youngest child was

born.[18] Among stepbrothers and stepsisters, the differences in age may have been even greater.[19] As a structural phenomenon, the difference of age had an impact on the relations between siblings of noble families with many children. Younger siblings quite often lost their father at a relatively early age and, as long as they were underage, found their older brothers as ruling successors fulfilling the father's role.[20] The Gonzaga family of Mantua, for instance, formally expressed this situation by addressing the head of the family as "frater et pater."[21]

At the age of seven, siblings began to follow different paths according to their roles. In some instances, brothers went to school together, but usually they were separated. The secular sons were educated by a private tutor and later sent to a foreign court.[22] On the other hand, those destined to become clerics went to a cathedral school and later to university.[23] The female siblings also left their parents' households in order to join a nunnery or to marry. The physical separation of siblings in their youth may therefore be considered as a further structural moment. Usually, they lived a considerable distance from each other until the end of their lives, with only very sporadic personal contacts.[24] Even at moments of personal crisis they could not expect to be surrounded by their

Illustration 2.2. The Family of Count Adolf I of Nassau (15th century, copied in the 17th century)

siblings. This fact is impressively illustrated in a letter from Duchess Beatrix to her brother, Duke Albrecht of Bavaria, in which she tells him that she is seriously ill and asks him to send one or two counselors who would be able to report to him how she had died.[25] No children, except for future rulers, were expected to return to the parents' household. If any of them did—for instance if the marriage of a daughter proved to be a failure—quarrels concerning maintenance could hardly be avoided.[26]

This brings us to the question of maintenance regulations. Even though the pattern of family roles divided the siblings into four groups of different social status, parents tried to treat at least those within each group equally. The testament of Margrave Jacob of Baden, composed in 1453, typically represents this effort. The three secular sons were given equal parts of the territory. Two sons were expected to become clerics with annuities of 500 fl until their incomes from prebends amounted to 1,000 fl. Secular daughters received dowries of 10,000 fl each, while those who entered nunneries were provided with annual annuities of 100 fl as long as they lived.[27]

Although it was comparatively easy to distribute annuities in equal portions, partitioning a territory into equal parts proved to be more difficult and presented practical and political problems. Each unequal distribution could result in conflicts, as male siblings pursuing secular careers considered themselves as born with equal rights to rule. For this reason, most solutions that favored one of the secular brothers in terms of higher rank sooner or later failed. Having brothers share both rule and income could only work for a short period of time, not in the long run. The proverbial "enemy brothers" is evidence for the competition that necessarily emerged in connection with a small territorial base.[28]

Even though relations between ruling brothers tended to be tense, secular and ecclesiastical brothers were united by mutual dependence, which encouraged them to follow a common strategy of collecting prebends. Thanks to mutual support, an ecclesiastical brother might manage to gain higher income and to even attain a bishopric. A secular brother could profit both from active political support by his ecclesiastical brother and from being relieved from maintaining him. Furthermore, ecclesiastical brothers usually were very supportive of each other when it came to gaining prebends.[29] Only when a clerical brother was not willing to accept his role but claimed a portion of the dynastic territory was the harmony between ecclesiastical and secular brothers disturbed.[30] Fierce quarrels could follow, which in the case of Johann and Heinrich of Nassau even led to the threat of a duel. But such a duel was prohibited by imperial law; brothers from the same womb were only allowed to enter into a judicial fight. In the end, Heinrich succeeded in claiming a part of the territory despite the fact that his brother had ruled alone for fifteen years.[31]

The territory of Baden offers a good example of the issues that influenced the strategies of different siblings. In 1501, Margrave Christoph stipulated, just as his grandfather Jacob had done before him, that each secular son should receive an equal portion of the territory. Two years later, however, for political reasons he chose his son Philipp as single heir. In the following years, his son Ernst, who had been chosen for an ecclesiastical career, insisted on his right to share the rule and to marry. He finally succeeded in 1510 after fierce quarrels. Precisely at this point in time, in 1509 or 1510, the picture (see Illustration 2.1) was painted in order to present Philipp as the single successor and to hide the fact that a fight had occurred between the two brothers.[32] Despite this example and several others, in most cases higher nobles seem to have accepted ecclesiastical careers, which offered a life of good income without heavy burdens. Moreover, if a prince or count managed to become a bishop or even archbishop, which happened quite often, he got the opportunity to govern his own territory anyway.[33] Furthermore, given the wide acceptance of concubinage many ecclesiastics were able to found their own families, whose members, however, had neither a right to succession nor a right to inherit.[34]

Female siblings chosen for marriage were successfully kept from claiming a part of the heritage by having to sign a letter of renunciation after their dowry had been paid. Such letters of renunciation became standard in the fifteenth century. Before their introduction, a daughter could claim a part of the inheritance if her dowry was restituted to the family property.[35] Thereby, maintenance problems were solved once and for all, and friendly relations among secular siblings were not disturbed by competition. A letter from the Electoral Prince Friedrich of Brandenburg to his sister Dorothea, who was married to the duke of Mecklenburg, is a good example of such friendly relations. He began the letter by telling her that it was difficult to send her a special hunting dog because he had none of its kind at his court, but he promised to look for one in adjacent territories. Then he expressed his joy that she was going to visit him in Berlin and informed her that St. Michael's day would be suitable for a meeting.[36] Exchanges of letters and presents between married brothers and sisters were quite common. Another example is the letter from Margaret of Cleves to her brother, Duke William of Berg, in which she tells him how much she longs to see him again and that she is sending him cloth as a present.[37]

In some cases, it appears to have been rather difficult to arrange a meeting between brother and sister. Margarethe of Nassau-Saarbrücken, married to Gerhard of Rodemachern, for example, wrote to her brother, Count Johann II., shortly after Easter 1464 that she had hoped in vain to meet him in Trier during Holy Week. In this letter, she told her brother what she would have preferred to communicate personally, namely that her husband had frequently refused, without good reasons, to grant her wish to travel to her brother. Since she ardently desired to see her brother, she begged him to write to her husband on the lines that he was in need of her support. Only under such circumstances would Gerhard allow her to undertake the travel. Whether or not she was successful is, unfortunately, not documented. It appears, however, that the two brothers-in-law had fairly good relations, since Gerhard asked Johann to support Margarethe during his absence at the French court in 1452, a favor that was immediately granted because of Johann's "affection and friendship."[38]

In fact, married sisters figured as important persons of contact for their ruling brothers, since relatives-in-law were crucial to the social and political activities of the nobility. Sons-in-law were even simply called sons and sisters-in-law called sisters, thus appearing as siblings—a clear indication of the importance of affinity.[39] The application of the term sister rather than sister-in-law is easily understandable, considering the fact that they lived within the household of their parents-in-law. The same, however, did not hold true for sons-in-law, which makes this use of terminology rather remarkable in this instance. In fact, formal adoptions of sons-in-law are attested for the sixteenth century; in one case, a mother-in-law even explicitly assures her son-in-law of her "motherly" affections.[40] The relations between siblings were endangered, however, if payment of the dowry was delayed.[41] The payment of a dowry was often delayed to such an extent that the ruling sons had to carry this financial burden after the death of their father. Albrecht of Hohenlohe, for example, had married Kunigunde of Henneberg in 1240, but her dowry was not paid completely before her father's death in 1245. It was then the responsibility of her brothers to provide for the remaining balance, which appears not to have happened by 1248. It must be presumed that this debt seriously strained the relation between the siblings. In 1266, conflict between Albrecht and Kunigunde's brothers could not be avoided, since the dowry was still not wholly paid.[42] Once again, the maintenance regulations proved to be decisive.

Sisters who had been sent to monasteries often lived far away from their families and were dependent on visits from their siblings for contact. Their suffering from personal neglect is documented by many letters written by nuns who asked their parents or siblings to send a letter or even to come in person.[43] Margaret of Brandenburg, abbess of the Franciscan nunnery of Hof, where she had lived for nineteen years, urgently implored her father in a letter to visit her because she was so much longing for him. Were there a chance, although she was very well aware of the fact that there was none, she herself would make the trip to her father. If she could not walk to him, she would even crawl. Nuns' situations were sometimes improved by sending several sisters to the same monastery.[44] A good example is provided by the daughters of Woldemar I, count of Anhalt. His four surviving daughters all entered the Dominican nunnery of Coswig in the second half of the fourteenth century.[45] Even if a daughter lived in a certain monastery for educational purposes only and was supposed to get married at a later stage of her life, she could still live there together with one of her sisters, as illustrated by the case of Elisabeth of Braunschweig-Lüneburg, daughter of Heinrich. In 1518, she left the Cistercian nunnery Wienhausen in order to get married to Karl, duke of Geldern.[46]

Those nuns who were elected abbesses managed to get more attention from their siblings because their position was politically useful for the dynasty.[47] This was especially true if one of the daughters became abbess of one of the old convents called "*Reichsstifte*," like Quedlinburg, Gandersheim, or Gernrode. Due to the far-reaching authority of these abbesses, the families of Braunschweig and Anhalt had a vital interest in promoting their daughters into one of these positions. In the middle of the fifteenth century, Duke Erich of Braunschweig-Grubenhagen and his daughter Sophia tried legal as well as violent means to get her established in Gandersheim.[48] That even abbesses of nunneries were dependent on their family connections is illustrated by a letter from Margret of Brandenburg, abbess of the Franciscan nunnery of Hof, to her stepbrother Friedrich. First she thanked him for the beautiful bag he had sent her. It softened her heart that he thought of her, but the wine she had received from him had been too sour to enjoy. Next time he should rather send money so that she can buy the wine herself. Then she begged for precious cloth and reminded her brother that the annuity he was paying for her was due only during her lifetime.[49]

According to cultural norms of the period, siblings were supposed to show each other the love, faith, and friendship arising from natural bonds. This obligation, often actually written down in legal documents and contracts, was widely accepted as a standard.[50] Nevertheless, good relations among noble siblings often ran into obstacles. Several of these were structural: the great number of siblings who had to share the family property, considerable differences in age, physical separation from an early age, the exigencies of different roles, and levels of maintenance imposed by a father or reigning brother against the expectations of younger siblings. In most instances, we do not know the reasons for disturbed relations. Zimburga of Nassau wrote a letter of accusation to her brother, Margrave Christoph of Baden, asking him for the reasons why he never contacted her or at least sent a letter through a messenger after she got married in the Netherlands. After the death of her father, he had not kept his promise to be like a father to her. Her clerical uncle, the archbishop of Trier, acted far more like a father to her than he. She asked him not to be insulted by her reproach and to send her a letter. Unfortunately, we do not know the reasons for her brother Christoph's reluctance to contact her.[51]

Harmony among siblings could develop when the secular brothers received sufficiently equal portions, if income from prebends for the clerical brothers was adequate, and after a dowry had been paid. This balanced system of maintenance upheld by dynasties and the Church, and by the reciprocal demands among the siblings themselves, was threatened by the Reformation. Many princes and counts who had adopted Protestantism could no longer send their sons into cathedral chapters and their daughters into nunneries.[52] They obviously did not regard reducing the number of children by changing their reproductive behavior as a solution: the frequent extinction of lines encouraged them to secure the survival of their dynasties by producing as great a number of children as possible.[53] On the other hand, the few rulers who stuck to Catholic belief did not have enough sons to fill all the vacant Episcopal sees, which led to accumulation of bishoprics in the hands of individual clerical brothers.[54]

Protestant rulers were forced either to divide their territories into even more parts in order to supply each son with an income of his own, or to find new careers for them, for example in military service.[55] To marry all of the daughters burdened a family with considerable dowry payments. In any case, the maintenance situation in Protestant dynasties became ever more subject to greater tension, which of course must quite naturally have affected sibling relations within the higher nobility. The essays of Michaela Hohkamp and Sophie Ruppel in this volume explore many of the dimensions of this new situation.

Notes

1. Brigitte Kasten, *Königssöhne und Königsherrschaft. Untersuchungen zur Teilhabe am Reich in der Merowinger- und Karolingerzeit* (Hanover, 1997), 182ff.
2. Karl-Heinz Spieß, *Familie und Verwandtschaft im deutschen Hochadel des Spätmittelalters, 13. bis Anfang des 16. Jahrhunderts* (Stuttgart, 1993), 10–11; Cordula Nolte, *Familie, Hof und Herrschaft: Das verwandtschaftliche Beziehungs- und Kommunika-*

tionsnetz der Reichsfürsten am Beispiel der Markgrafen von Brandenburg-Ansbach (1440–1530) (Ostfildern, 2005), 55ff.

3. Spieß, *Familie und Verwandtschaft*, 454ff.; Nolte, *Familie, Hof und Herrschaft*, 171ff.; Jörg Rogge, *Herrschaftsweitergabe, Konfliktregelung und Familienorganisation im fürstlichen Hochadel: Das Beispiel der Wettiner von der Mitte des 13. bis zum Beginn des 16. Jahrhunderts* (Stuttgart, 2002), 141ff.; Roger Sablonier, "Die Aragonesische Königsfamilie um 1300," in *Emotionen und materielle Interessen: Sozialanthropologische und historische Beiträge zur Familienforschung*, ed. Hans Medick and David Sabean (Göttingen, 1984), 282–317, here 314.

4. Actually, there were fifth and sixth groups that are not discussed in this article. They consisted of illegitimate stepbrothers and stepsisters. See Spieß, *Familie und Verwandtschaft*, 381ff.; Paul-Joachim Heinig, "'Omnia vincit Amor'—Das fürstliche Konkubinat im 15./16. Jahrhundert," in *Principes: Dynastien und Höfe im späten Mittelalter*, ed. Cordula Nolte, Karl-Heinz Spieß, and Ralf-Gunnar Werlich (Stuttgart, 2002), 277–314, here 297ff.; Ellen Widder, "Konkubinen und Bastarde: Günstlinge oder Außenseiter an Höfen des Spätmittelalters," in *Der Fall des Günstlings: Hofparteien in Europa vom 13. bis zum 17. Jahrhundert*, ed. Jan Hirschbiegel and Werner Paravicini (Ostfildern, 2004), 417–480, here 426ff. Also Mikhaël Harsgor, "L'essor des bâtards nobles au XVe siècle," *Revue Historique* 253 (1975): 319–354 and Chris Given-Wilson and Alice Curteis, *The Royal Bastards of Medieval England* (London et al., 1984).

5. Karl-Heinz Spieß, "Lordship, Kinship, and Inheritance among the German High Nobility in the Middle Ages and Early Modern Period," in *Kinship in Europe: Approaches to Long-Term Development (1300–1900)*, ed. David Sabean, Simon Teuscher, and Jon Mathieu (Oxford and New York, 2007), 57–75.

6. The figure is taken from Spieß, *Familie und Verwandtschaft*, 457–458.

7. Ibid., 462ff.

8. Ibid., 288–289.

9. Ibid., 301ff.; Nolte, *Familie, Hof und Herrschaft*, 114ff.; Christine Reinle: "'Id tempus solum': Der Lebensentwurf Herzog Johanns von Mosbach-Neumarkt (†1486) im Spannungsfeld von dynastischem Denken, kirchlicher Karriere und gelehrten Interessen," in *Der Pfälzer Löwe in Bayern: Zur Geschichte der Oberpfalz in der kurpfälzischen Epoche*, ed. Hans-Jürgen Becker (Regensburg, 1997), 157–199, here 165–166, 169; Ellen Widder, "Karriere im Windschatten: Zur Biographie Erzbischof Ruprechts von Köln (1427–1478)," in *Vestigia Monasteriensia: Westfalen—Rheinland—Niederlande*, ed. Peter Johanek, Mark Mersiowsky, and Ellen Widder (Bielefeld, 1995), 29–72, here 52ff.

10. Spieß, *Familie und Verwandtschaft*, 414ff.

11. Spieß, *Familie und Verwandtschaft*, 372–373; Eva Schlotheuber, *Klostereintritt und Bildung: Die Lebenswelt der Nonnen im späten Mittelalter* (Tübingen, 2004), 175ff.; Eva Schlotheuber, "Familienpolitik und geistliche Aufgaben," in *Familie und Gesellschaft im Mittelalter*, ed. Karl-Heinz Spieß (Ostfildern, 2007).

12. The figure is taken from Spieß, *Familie und Verwandtschaft*, 369.

13. Nolte, *Familie, Hof und Herrschaft*, 116ff. See also Christine Kleinjung, "Geistliche Töchter—abgeschoben oder unterstützt? Überlegungen zum Verhältnis hochadeliger Nonnen zu ihren Familien im 13. und 14. Jahrhundert," in *Fürstin und Fürst: Familienbeziehungen und Handlungsmöglichkeiten von hochadeligen Frauen im Mittelalter*, ed. Jörg Rogge (Ostfildern, 2004), 21–44.

14. Dietmar Lüdke et al., eds., *Spätmittelalter am Oberrhein: Große Landesausstellung Baden-Württemberg 29. September 2001–3. Februar 2002, vol. 1: Maler und Werkstätten 1450–1525* (Stuttgart, 2001), 448–449.

15. Konrad Krimm, "Markgraf Christoph I. und die badische Teilung: Zur Deutung der Karlsruher Votivtafel von Hans Baldung Grien," *Zeitschrift für die Geschichte des Oberrheins* 138 (1990): 199–215 with details of the picture.

16. Henrich Dorsen, ed., *Genealogia oder Stammregister der durchläuchtigen hoch- und wohlgeborenen Fürsten, Grafen und Herren des uhralten hochlöblichen Hauses Nassau samt etlichen konterfeitlichen Epitaphien* (Saarbrücken, 1983), 5.

17. Nolte, *Familie, Hof und Herrschaft*, 213ff.

18. Detlev Schwennicke, *Europäische Stammtafeln, Neue Folge*, vol. I.2: *Přemysliden, Askanier, Herzoge von Lothringen, die Häuser Hessen, Württemberg und Zähringen* (Frankfurt am Main, 1999), figure 268.

19. The already mentioned Margrave Albrecht Achilles of Brandenburg married twice. The first daughter was born in 1450, the last in 1478. See Detlev Schwennicke, *Europäische Stammtafeln, Neue Folge*, vol. I.1: *Die fränkischen Könige und die Könige und Kaiser, Stammesherzoge, Kurfürsten, Markgrafen und Herzoge des Heiligen Römischen Reiches Deutscher Nation* (Frankfurt am Main, 1998), figure 129.

20. Rogge, *Herrschaftsweitergabe*, 59ff., 141ff.; Nolte, *Familie, Hof und Herrschaft*, 276ff.; Spieß: *Familie und Verwandtschaft*, 283ff.

21. Ebba Severidt, *Familie, Verwandtschaft und Karriere bei den Gonzaga: Struktur und Funktion von Familie und Verwandtschaft bei den Gonzaga und ihren deutschen Verwandten (1444–1519)* (Leinfelden-Echterdingen, 2002), 125–126; Sablonier, "Königsfamilie," 313 notes the same practice within the Aragonese royal family.

22. Laetitia Boehm, "Konservativismus und Modernität in der Regentenerziehung an deutschen Höfen im 15. und 16. Jahrhundert," in *Humanismus im Bildungswesen des 15. und 16. Jahrhunderts*, ed. Wolfgang Reinhard (Weinheim, 1984), 61–93, here 83–84; Notker Hammerstein, "'Großer fürtrefflicher Leute Kinder': Fürstenerziehung zwischen Humanismus und Reformation," in *Renaissance—Reformation: Gegensätze und Gemeinsamkeiten*, ed. August Buck (Wiesbaden, 1984), 265–285; Spieß, *Familie und Verwandtschaft*, 462ff.; Nolte, *Familie, Hof und Herrschaft*, 215ff.; Karl-Heinz Spieß, "Reisen deutscher Fürsten und Grafen im Spätmittelalter," in *Grand Tour: Adeliges Reisen und europäische Kultur vom 14. bis zum 18. Jahrhundert*, ed. Rainer Babel and Werner Paravicini (Ostfildern, 2005), 33–51, here 38ff.

23. Gerhard Fouquet, *Das Speyerer Domkapitel im späten Mittelalter (ca. 1350–1540): Adlige Freundschaft, fürstliche Patronage und päpstliche Klientel*, vol. 1 (Mainz, 1987), 167ff.

24. Two sisters of Emperor Frederick III were married to other princes of the empire: Margaret became the wife of the elector Frederick II of Saxony in 1431, and Katharina married Margrave Karl I of Baden in 1447. See Schwennicke, *Europäische Stammtafeln, Neue Folge*, vol. I.1, figure 42. Likewise, each of the sisters of Margrave Albrecht Achilles of Brandenburg was married and therefore left the parental court. For instance, Dorothea married Heinrich IV of Mecklenburg-Schwerin in 1432, while Margaret became the wife of Ludwig VIII of Bavaria in 1441. See Schwennicke, *Europäische Stammtafeln, Neue Folge*, vol. I.1, figure 129.

25. Georg Steinhausen, ed., *Deutsche Privatbriefe des Mittelalters*, vol. 1: *Fürsten und Magnaten, Edle und Ritter* (Berlin, 1899), Nr. 63, 17f. (1447-03-11). Beatrix had been a widow since 1443, living in Neumarkt, which lay within her husband's territory, about 100 kilometers north of her brother's residence in Munich. She wrote her letter in vain since she died the following day. Note that a widow generally retired to one of her husband's castles, which often rendered contact and travel to her blood relatives quite difficult. Karl-Heinz Spieß, "Witwenversorgung im Hochadel: Rechtlicher Rahmen und praktische Gestaltung im Spätmittelalter und zu Beginn

der Frühen Neuzeit," in *Witwenschaft in der Frühen Neuzeit: Fürstliche und adlige Witwen zwischen Fremd- und Selbstbestimmung*, ed. Martina Schattkowsky (Leipzig, 2003), 93ff.

26. Nolte, *Familie, Hof und Herrschaft*, 187–188.

27. Hermann Schulze, ed., *Die Hausgesetze der regierenden deutschen Fürstenhäuser*, vol. 1 (Jena, 1862), no. 3, 174–194, here 177ff. Another instance is the "Dispositio Achillea" from 1473. Hermann von Caemmerer, ed., *Die Testamente der Kurfürsten von Brandenburg und der beiden ersten Könige von Preußen* (Munich, 1915), no. 5, 35–36. See also Spieß, *Familie und Verwandtschaft*, 306–307 and Reinle, "'Id tempus solum,'" 165.

28. Many examples of this phenomenon can be found in Spieß, *Familie und Verwandtschaft*, 204ff.; Rogge, *Herrschaftsweitergabe*, 59ff.; Stefan Weinfurter, "Die Einheit Bayerns: Zur Primogeniturordnung des Herzogs Albrecht IV. von 1506," in *Festgabe Heinz Hürten zum 60. Geburtstag*, ed. Harald Dickerhof (Frankfurt am Main, 1998), 225–242.

29. Aloys Schulte, *Der Adel und die deutsche Kirche im Mittelalter: Studien zur Sozial-, Rechts- und Kirchengeschichte* (Stuttgart, 1910), 274ff.; Gerhard Fouquet, "Kaiser, Kurpfalz, Stift: Die Speyerer Bischofswahl von 1513 und die Affäre Ziegler," *Mitteilungen des historischen Vereins der Pfalz* 83 (1985): 193–271, here 195ff.; Franz Machilek, "Markgraf Friedrich von Brandenburg-Ansbach, Dompropst zu Würzburg (1497–1536)," *Fränkische Lebensbilder* 11 (1984): 101–139; Widder, "Karriere im Windschatten," 41ff.; Spieß, *Familie und Verwandtschaft*, 301ff.; Nolte, *Familie, Hof und Herrschaft*, 125ff.

30. Spieß, *Familie und Verwandtschaft*, 208ff., 270; Rogge, *Herrschaftsweitergabe*, 141ff.; Klaus Graf, "Graf Heinrich von Württemberg († 1519): Aspekte eines ungewöhnlichen Fürstenlebens," in *Württemberg und Mömpelgard: 600 Jahre Begegnung*, ed. Sönke Lorenz and Peter Rückert (Leinfelden-Echterdingen, 1999), 107–120, here 109ff.

31. Spieß, *Familie und Verwandtschaft*, 258.

32. Krimm, "Markgraf Christoph I.," 210.

33. Rudolf Holbach, *Stiftsgeistlichkeit im Spannungsfeld von Kirche und Welt: Studien zur Geschichte des Trierer Domkapitels und Domklerus im Spätmittelalter*, vol. 1 (Trier, 1982), 256ff.; Fouquet, *Das Speyerer Domkapitel*, vol. 1, 68ff.; Michael Hollmann, *Das Mainzer Domkapitel im späten Mittelalter (1306–1476)* (Mainz, 1990), 188ff.

34. Heinig, "'Omnia vincit Amor,'" 281ff.; idem, "Fürstenkonkubinat um 1500 zwischen Usus und Devianz," in *"...wir wollen der Liebe Raum geben": Konkubinate geistlicher und weltlicher Fürsten um 1500*, ed. Andreas Tacke (Göttingen, 2006), 11–37.

35. Spieß, *Familie und Verwandtschaft*, 331ff.

36. Steinhausen, *Deutsche Privatbriefe*, Nr. 78, 59 (1458-05-03).

37. Ibid., Nr. 21, 19f. (ca. 1400).

38. Spieß, *Familie und Verwandtschaft*, 484.

39. Ibid., 499; Nolte, *Familie, Hof und Herrschaft*, 65.

40. Ingeborg Mengel, "Politisch-dynastische Beziehungen zwischen Albrecht von Preussen und Elisabeth von Braunschweig-Lüneburg in den Jahren 1546–1555," *Jahrbuch der Albertus-Universität zu Königsberg/Preussen* 5 (1954): 225–241, reprinted in Ingeborg Klettke-Mengel, *Fürsten und Fürstenbriefe* (Cologne, 1986), 11–23, here 18f.

41. Spieß, *Familie und Verwandtschaft*, 168–169.

42. Karl Weller, *Geschichte des Hauses Hohenlohe*, vol. 2 (Stuttgart, 1908), 14ff.

43. Spieß, *Familie und Verwandtschaft*, 376–377, 470–471. Margaret of Brandenburg did not see her father for years; he would not even visit her when passing her nun-

nery. Her brother Friedrich, however, kept close contacts with his half-sister Margaret and his sister Dorothea, who lived in a different nunnery. See Nolte, *Familie, Hof und Herrschaft*, 121ff.

44. Spieß, *Familie und Verwandtschaft*, 485. In some instances, an aunt already lived in the nunnery. Nuns were the only group of siblings that had no chance to have a family. The rulers tried to make life in the nunnery easier for them by helping them to get privileges that allowed them to eat different food, to wear furs, or to receive visits by their mother or their sisters. Nolte, *Familie, Hof und Herrschaft*, 121.

45. Schwennicke, *Europäische Stammtafeln, Neue Folge*, vol. I.2, figure 187.

46. Ida-Christine Riggert, *Die Lüneburger Frauenklöster* (Hanover, 1996), 220.

47. Nolte, *Familie, Hof und Herrschaft*, 121ff.

48. Kurt Kronenberg, *Die Äbtissinnen des Reichsstiftes Gandersheim* (Bad Gandersheim, 1981), 88–91.

49. Steinhausen, *Deutsche Privatbriefe*, Nr. 408, 280–281.

50. Spieß, *Familie und Verwandtschaft*, 483–484.

51. Steinhausen, *Deutsche Privatbriefe*, Nr. 225, 157f. (ca. 1476).

52. Georg Schmidt, *Der Wetterauer Grafenverein: Organisation und Politik einer Reichkorporation zwischen Reformation und Westfälischem Frieden* (Marburg, 1989), 490ff.

53. Paula Sutter Fichtner, *Protestantism and Primogeniture in Early Modern Germany* (London 1989), 38–39.

54. Spieß, "Lordship," 68f.

55. Fichtner, *Protestantism*, 17.

Chapter 3

Do Sisters Have Brothers? The Search for the "rechte Schwester"

Brothers and Sisters in Aristocratic Society at the Turn of the Sixteenth Century

Michaela Hohkamp

As the traditional bourgeois family, a product of early modern Europe, lost its function as a political, social, and cultural motif in the second half of the twentieth century and alternative forms of cohabitation were emerging in Western industrialized societies, European research began to view and study the family as a historical and culturally shifting segment of society. Over time, the classical techniques for studying family networks, such as historical demography, have profited from socio-anthropological theories and methods as well as from gender-specific approaches. The primary outcome of these studies has been twofold: the insight that family and kinship formations have very different historical and cultural representations, and the awareness that—contrary to traditional assumptions—they have lost none of their central value in Western societies.[1] But even though research on families and kin has changed greatly and become highly diversified over the years, it is still not far removed from traditional approaches to the nuclear family. The study of family in the context of wider kinship networks is a relatively recent development.[2] As historiography has turned its attention to cultural studies, this substantive shift has brought about a reorientation within family and kinship research. The main lines of inquiry of this research field—including the techniques and practices of transfer of ownership, the role of family-based economies in the emergence of industrialized production, the reproduction of cultural, social, economic, and political elites, and the study of the relationship between emotions and violence in kinship and family contexts—are now being combined with questions on the significance and quality of special family and kinship relations.[3] Partly on the basis of earlier research into sibling relations (primarily the study of inheritance practices in agrarian societies),[4] relations between siblings are the focus of attention again—but this time as an independent phenomenon.[5]

As earlier socio-anthropological studies have revealed, the relevance of sibling relations in the early modern period is inseparable from the respective rights and practices of inheritance. Insofar as previous research on aristocratic societies has stressed that sons, as future agents of power, were accorded a prominent role in the transfer of rule and ownership, sibling relations—apart from various reports of disputes between brothers—have been pushed to the sidelines in this context. Relations between brothers and sisters have mainly been studied in light of their emotional qualities, or they have been of historical interest due to possible disputes between brothers-in-law or between fathers and their sons-in-law over the dowries of the respective sisters or daughters.

Gender-oriented studies now indicate, however, that daughters or sisters played a role in the transfer of power and ownership not only in agrarian societies but also, under special circumstances and in certain ways, in the European noble society. There is even evidence that daughters, upon marrying, had to renounce all claims to inheritance—the inheritance of their fathers, mothers, and that of their brothers—as of the beginning of the fourteenth century.[6] Among the late medieval and early modern nobility, which increasingly advocated the transfer of power according to linear succession of a male heir, this renunciation (so-called *Fräuleinverzicht*) was most likely practiced because daughters were entitled to allodial inheritance and—if the properties were *Weiberlehen* (female fiefs)—could actually be holders of fiefs.[7] But daughters not only enjoyed such possessions, also called *Kunkellehen* (fief following the female line): in the absence of sons, daughters also became subsidiary heiresses who could gain control over the so-called *Mannlehen* (male fief), with the king's approval.[8] This legal possibility was nothing if not contentious, however.[9] One method that was used to circumvent a daughter's right to ascend to power was the use of contracts, which might secure the succession for a ruler's brother's son (his nephew) instead of his own daughter. The importance of this measure for the constitution of princely houses during the course of early modern history has been investigated in the literature and will not be discussed further here.

With respect to our line of inquiry into brother and sister relationships in late medieval and early modern noble society, it may be pointed out that daughters without brothers had the right (albeit it was difficult to exercise) to their parents' property, whereas daughters with brothers, at least as of the Late Middle Ages, were generally dependent on the dowries granted to them upon marriage.[10] But even daughters with brothers who were royally compensated with dowries were not always willing to renounce their rights. In the period under consideration here, namely, the turn of the sixteenth century, it is possible to find examples of princes' daughters (with brothers) who did not renounce their rights as heiresses. Among the prominent cases is that of Kunigunde, the daughter of Emperor Frederick III and sister of Emperor Maximilian I, who initially did not renounce her inheritance rights upon marrying Duke Albert IV of the Bavarian House of Wittelsbach,[11] or that of Elisabeth of Hesse at the end of the fifteenth century, the daughter of Landgrave Henry of Hesse from his liaison with Anna of Katzenelnbogen, who also refused to renounce her inheritance and thereby provoked an attempted murder.[12]

Certainly, the few cases mentioned here do not stand in contradiction to the real tendency, observable since the Late Middle Ages and the beginning of the early modern period, of power being transferred in whole and by linear succession solely to a male descendant. One plausible argument against revisiting these kinds of cases, which we do below, is that they represent lesser phenomena in view of the greater historical trends. Yet if kinship studies of early modern aristocratic society are not exclusively focused on male succession but strive to keep a broader kinship network in view, then the analysis of inheritance cases that were disputed within a mixed-gendered net of wider kinship relations makes sense precisely because of their special or isolated status.[13] Studying such cases can shed light on the cultural logic behind the transfer of power in the late medieval and early modern period and better depict the transmission of ownership and power in a wider kinship network.

From the point of view that political history is simultaneously a history of culture and gender, it is worthwhile to take a new look at the relations between brothers and sisters, also in the context of transfer of power and ownership. This chapter will do just that. While the first part will discuss problems of definition, the second part of this essay will investigate the relations between sisters and brothers based on the empirical example of European noble families during the transition from the late medieval to the early modern period, viewing them in the light of kinship and inheritance practices. This will allow a reexamination of the significance of brotherhood and sisterhood for the respective historical actors in terms of transfer of power and ownership within noble society in early modern Europe.

Sisters and Brothers: A Problematic Definition

"Geschwister," as the Adelung Dictionary of 1811 tells us, are "Personen, welche einerley Ältern, oder doch Einen Vater oder Eine Mutter haben, [and can be seen] ohne Unterschied des Geschlechts, als ein Collectivum" (Persons who have the same parents or one father or one mother and can be seen as a collective without differentiation of sex).[14] Had this popular reference work been consulted in the previous century for a separate entry for "Geschwister" (sibling), the search would have been in vain. The entry for "Fratrueles" only contains a reference to the word "Geschwister-Kinder" (children of siblings, cousins) in the section about "Nachfolge oder Erbfolge derer Seiten-Freunde" (succession or inheritance of collaterals).[15] The word "sibling" is thus discussed only in relation to inheritance claims, especially those of the uncles and aunts of a deceased person, or their nieces and nephews: in other words, in those cases where a person leaves behind neither father nor mother, brother nor sister, son nor daughter. While the word "Geschwister" existed as its own lemma and was used gender-neutrally at the beginning of the nineteenth century, before 1800 the word "Geschwister" was not a keyword in the popular encyclopedias of the time, but rather was mentioned only in the context of inheritance law. And in this legal arena, as we saw above, the issue of gender and the question of whether one was a brother or a sister were anything but insignificant.[16] In early modern law, inheritance was decided not only by the degree of relation of a person to the deceased or their emotional closeness or distance, but also by their gender.[17]

Zedler's *Universal-Lexicon* from the mid eighteenth century defines a sister in gender-specific terms as a "Weibsperson, welche nebst anderen von einem Vater oder von einer Mutter gezeuget worden" [Female person who along with others has been begotten by one father or one mother].[18] By subjecting the relevant entries to a closer reading, it becomes clear that defining a sister as a "Weibsperson" goes beyond applying a mere "sexed" label. According to Zedler's *Universal-Lexicon*, being a brother or a sister is associated with different cultural concepts. The "Schwester" entry in the encyclopedia goes on to distinguish between different types of sister: there are "vollbürtige[n] leibliche[n], halb- und Stiefschwestern." Whereas the "vollbürtigen, leiblichen, rechten" (full-born, corporal, full) sisters, namely the "sorores germanae," are sisters with the same father and mother, paternal half-sisters—that is, sisters who have the same father but different mothers—are called "sorores consanguineae."[19] Sisters who have different fathers but the same mother are termed "sorores uterinae." Those sisters with neither the same mother nor the same father are referred to as "sorores comprivignae."[20] The entry for "Bruder," by contrast, offers the following concise definition: "Dein Bruder, [seie] Deiner Mutter Sohn" (Your brother is your mother's son), while the superordinate header "Frater" is less ambiguous and contains the sub-categories "frater adoptius," "frater consanguineus," "frater uterinus," and "fratri germani"—i.e., full brothers. The "Frater" entry is completed with the word "fratriae," which denotes "zweyer Brüder-Weiber" (two brothers' wives).[21]

A comparison of the definitions found in the entries for "Bruder" (brother) and "Schwester" (sister) reveals, firstly, that there is no term analogous to "sorores comprivignae" for brothers and, secondly, that the status of adoption is overlooked with respect to sisters. Brothers and sisters differ at this conceptual level, but in another way as well. While the entries under the heading "Frater" do not comment further on the origin of this word, the author of Zedlers's encyclopedia apparently thought the Latin root "soror" called for an explanation. It is said, namely, that a person is called "soror" "weil sie nicht allein ganz besonders … gebohren, sondern auch bey ihrer Verehelichung von dem hause, darinnen sie gebohren, abgesondert, und in eine andere Familie versezet wird" (because she not only is born completely separately but also is separated at her marriage from the house where she was born and is relocated in another family).[22] So a sister is called "sister" not only because she has brothers and is the offspring of a set of parents, but also because she is a wife and thus belongs to a house with a different origin to that of her father and mother. This mid eighteenth-century explanation of the use of the Latin word "soror" is remarkable in that there is no corresponding definition with respect to brothers. Here we see a difference at the level of definition that indicates actual dissimilarities in the lives of brothers and sisters. We can sum up the findings as follows: the brother was a brother because he was a son, while the sister was only a sister because she was by definition also a wife. This insight must have been common knowledge back then. After all, in early modern writings, we encounter the married sister in the figure of the so-called "Schwesterfraw" (sister-wife).[23]

A Definition and Its Significance in Concrete Practice

What then does it mean for a study of the brother-sister constellation in late medieval and early modern society when "sister" is viewed as the married daughter of a set of parents with several offspring, and a brother is a brother simply by virtue of his being the son of a couple with numerous offspring? To answer this question, it is necessary to first review the figure of the sister—the married sister, the "Schwesterfraw." Current research generally sees the married sister as someone who is taken away from her original family and taken into the family of her husband.[24] This view is corroborated by legal textbooks from the mid eighteenth century, for example, when they deliver arguments of why—from the perspective of a male ego—one type of sister-in-law, namely the sister of the deceased wife, may be taken in marriage, while another type of sister-in-law, namely the wife of one's brother, is off limits.

The somewhat rambling line of argumentation in this legal work can be summed up in the following key sentence: the sister of the deceased wife may be taken in marriage "weil die Frau dem Mann, nicht aber der Mann der Frau folget, und er nicht von ihren juribus familiae, dignitatis, sanguinis, eique inherentis reverentiae, sondern sie von seinen partizipieret, … [weshalb] in unserer Schwestern und Muhmen gewesenen Ehe-Männern die ganze ratio und causa impedimenti [cessieret], wodurch wir unseres Bruders und Oncles gewesene Ehe-Frauen propter communicationem reverentiae sanguinis zu heyrathen verhindert werden" (because the wife follows the husband and not the husband the wife, and he does not participate through her rights of family in dignity, blood, and inherent reverence but she does so through his, … that is why in the widowers of our sisters and aunts the whole reason and grounds for the prohibition is laid to rest, but we are forbidden to marry the widows of our brothers and uncles on account of participating in the respect for blood). In other words: the married sister (a possible wife) enters into the "communionem reverentiae sanguinis" with her husband and his family and thus has a legal relationship to them. The married man, by contrast, does not enter into any "communio reverentiae sanguinis" with the family of his spouse, meaning that he is not in the "juribus familiae"[25] of his wife, so he is not prevented from marrying his wife's sister.

This line of argument is essentially based on the notion that the quality of the kinship relationship between two married sisters is different from that of two married brothers. But what about a married sister and a married brother? By this legal definition, brothers and sisters from the same set of parents are clearly related by blood and may not marry each other. But how are kinship relations affected when the sister of a male ego enters into "communio sanguinis" with a husband and thus becomes part of his "jura familiae," while her brother marries but, according to the prevailing law, does not assume the same status as his sister? Does a married sister of a husband have the same kinship relationship to her brother as a married sister of a wife has to her sister? The early modern legal literature seems to be inconsistent in this point. Starting from this issue, it makes sense to study the married sister of a husband not simply as a sister, but through the lens of the early modern formulation "Schwesterfraw." What follows is a micro-study of a married sister with a brother—here the case of Anna of Württemberg—to conceptualize a married sister as a kinship figure in the transfer of power and ownership in the early modern noble society of the Holy Roman Empire.

The "Schwesterfraw" Anna of Württemberg (1408–1471) as a Wife

The story of Anna of Württemberg takes us back into aristocratic society at the threshold of the early modern period and at the interface of four powerful houses in the southwestern corner of the empire: the counts of Katzenelnbogen, the landgraves of Hesse, the margraves of Baden, and the counts of Württemberg before they were elevated to dukes. Connected as they were through a close network of kinship relations, the legacies of these houses and the kinship information they provide are rife with disputes over inheritance, power, and ownership. The inheritance battles waged between the Katzenelnbogen counts and their relatives from Hesse and Baden have been recorded in detail in state and political histories and will not be alluded to further here. These disputes have also already been subjected elsewhere to an extensive revision from the perspective of cultural and gender studies and from the critical viewpoint of the history of historiography.[26] Owing to far-reaching kinship relations, events in the house of Katzenelnbogen were relevant not only to the Baden and Hesse relations, but also to the Württemberg counts with marital ties to the Katzenelnbogens. The first wife of Philipp the Elder (1402–1478 or 1479), Count of Katzenelnbogen, was namely Anna (1408–1471), the daughter of Eberhard IV (1388–1419), Count of Württemberg, and Countess Henriette of Montbéliard (born between 1384 and 1391 and deceased 1444).[27] Anna's brothers were the Württemberg counts Ludwig I (1412–1450) and Ulrich V (1430–1480), later known as "der Vielgeliebte" (the Much Loved).

There is little out of the ordinary to report on the first twenty years of marriage between Anna of Württemberg and Philipp the Elder, Count of Katzenelnbogen. The peace of these years apparently came to an end in the 1440s, however. Reports surface at this time that the countess tried to reignite the extinguished passion of her spouse through love charms. Court hearings were held in 1446 to deal with this delicate situation.[28] In that same year, there is clear evidence of a geographic separation of the married couple. It can be proven that Anna was residing at her dower house, "Schloss Lichtenberg," in 1446.[29] But this arrangement was apparently not tolerable. Count Philipp the Elder successfully petitioned the Pope in 1456 for separation of bed and board. Although it had been impossible during the court hearings to prove that the countess had really engaged in magic spells, and the accused herself insisted until the end that she had only asked a servant for magic recipes, her actions were seen as injurious. As one of the cardinal obligations between married couples was protecting life and limb of the other spouse, the allegations against the countess provided legal grounds for separation. From 1456 on, we find Anna in Waiblingen, Württemberg, at an abode provided to her by her brother, Count Ulrich V of Württemberg.[30] Anna died there in 1471. Two years later, her widower married a second time.

The "Schwesterfraw" Anna of Württemberg as a Daughter

Anna was not simply a wife and sister, she was also the daughter of Henriette of Montbéliard, who was a countess of Montfaucon before her marriage with the Württemberg count Eberhard IV. According to Burgundian custom, she was the legal heir to the fiefdoms of her grandfather, Count Stefan of Montfaucon, after her own father died without leaving behind a male heir. Thus Henriette—as mentioned above—was entitled according to both Burgundian practices and imperial law to assume her grandfather's seat of power: Henriette was a classical "Erbtochter" (daughter as heir).

And Henriette went on to assert her rights. Upon conclusion of her marriage contract in 1397, the territories promised to her became the domains of her father-in-law, Count Eberhard III of Württemberg. But when her husband Eberhard IV died in 1419, Henriette together with the Württemberg counsels took custody of her children, assumed the regency over Württemberg, and also governed Montbéliard. The male kin of her deceased spouse lodged a complaint with the emperor but lost. Henriette retained custody and tended to the affairs of the regency.

Under her rule, the contract of marriage between her daughter Anna and Count Philipp the Elder of Katzenelnbogen was signed on 6 February 1420, and several years later, on 7 December 1427, was amended to grant Philipp the Elder the city and castle of Marbach as a lien instead of the originally promised sum of money (called "Zugeld").[31] After she had ceded territory to her twelve-year-old and thus marriageable daughter for the marriage that was consecrated in 1422, Henriette stepped down from her regency in Württemberg but continued to rule Montbéliard until her death. As an aside, it is interesting to note that Henriette's years as regent have led to opposing verdicts of this princess from French and German political historians. While on the western side of the Rhine the countess has gone down in history as the "bonne comtesse," historians on the eastern side of the Rhine have, since the eighteenth century at the latest, accused Henriette—and her daughter Anna—of being addicted to power.[32] And up to the end of the twentieth century, it may be read that Henriette was "versponnen, gewalttätig und sprunghaft" (crazy, violent, and erratic).[33]

This critical and even disparaging assessment of Henriette of Montbéliard in the German historiography is closely related to her decision, two years before her death in 1444, to remember her daughter Anna generously in her testament and to bequeath to her, in addition, her holdings in Swabia and parts of her own inheritance (namely, the castle of Purrentruy) and to name her co-heiress in case her sons should die without heirs.[34] Such active governance on the part of princesses appears to have been a thorn in the side of early modern historians—and their modern counterparts.[35] By the late eighteenth century, this form of female rule was deemed a failure primarily due to the verdict of the professional historians. From their writings it was often a short hop to the historiographical studies of the late twentieth century.[36]

The "Schwesterfraw" Anna of Württemberg as a Sister

If Henriette's actions are scrutinized from the perspective of gender studies, and if the focus is shifted from the individual to the family and kinship setting, then Henriette's alteration of her testament in favor of her daughter in 1442 can be interpreted not simply as a sign of fickleness, but as a commentary on the marriage of her second oldest son Ulrich, who wed Margarethe, a daughter of Count Adolf II of Cleves and his spouse, a born duchess of Burgundy, on 29 January 1441. What the sources do not disclose is whether Henriette's decision was influenced by an intervention on the part of her son-in-law of Katzenelnbogen, or whether her change of mind was the result of some calculations of her own. It is also not possible to conjecture about territorial speculations or possible expectations that might be behind this new constellation of power involving Henriette and her daughter, for the sources remain silent here as well. What is documented, however, is that both of Anna's brothers, especially brother Ulrich, hotly contested this change to their mother's will and ultimately got it reversed. To achieve this, they kept their mother under house arrest in her Nürtingen residence until she finally rescinded the provision benefiting her daughter and bequeathed her possessions to her sons. When Henriette died in 1444, there were initially some problems in transferring the Montbéliard holdings lying to the west of the Rhine to the two brothers, but in the end the brothers succeeded in incorporating their mother's territories into their own dominion. Montbéliard, situated at the Burgundian Gate, remained part of Württemberg until 1793.

So much for the historical facts. Now, what is their significance for our line of inquiry into the relations between brothers and married sisters in aristocratic society of the late medieval and early modern period? Before addressing this question, it is first necessary to point out that the separation of Philipp and Anna of Katzenelnbogen, as well as the court hearings leading up to the final annulment of their marriage, happened *after* the testament was changed and *after* the disputes between Henriette and her sons regarding the inheritance for the daughter and married sister. Given the instrumental nature of royal and noble marriages in late medieval and early modern Europe—a premise that is strongly supported in the literature—this coincidence of timing leads to the conclusion that the Katzenelnbogen count came to view his marriage with the daughter of Henriette of Montbéliard as politically useless after the extensive loss of Anna's inheritance claims and so took measures to rid himself of this superfluous instrument. Whether the accusations of magic-making against Anna of Württemberg were a simple strategic move by a greedy husband or rather an imaginative form of coercion prevalent at that time that manifested itself during power struggles and marital conflicts among the early modern nobility, cannot be discussed further here.[37]

With a view to a future analysis of such coercive actions, which were not untypical in the context of separations and annulments of royal and noble marriages, it may be said that Anna of Württemberg was not unique in her experiences. Indeed, at the end of her life, she could look back on experiences similar to those of, for example, Sidonie of Wettin (1518–1575) and, before her, Sidonie's aunt Katharina (1468–1524). The two princesses—Sidonie, who was married to Duke Eric II of

Braunschweig-Calenberg, and Katharina, who was wed to the Tyrolean archduke—were likewise accused of posing a threat to the life and limb of their husbands.[38] But unlike Sidonie, who was flanked by her Saxon relatives, especially her brother August (1526–1586), and Katharine, who received support from her father, Saxon Duke Albert the Courageous (1443–1500), Anna was fatherless (Eberhard IV died in 1419) and was moreover at loggerheads with her brothers over their mother's inheritance. It appears to have been this lack of kinpower that ultimately doomed Anna's existence as a princess to failure. Unlike the aunt-niece pair of Katharina and Sidonie, who despite accusations and—at least in Sidonie's case—subsequent witchcraft trials prevailed unscathed (i.e., they were not required to relinquish their princely positions entirely), Anna of Württemberg was banished in the second half of her life by her brothers to a remote Württemberg domain and hence isolated from the political machinery. Having been provided with a meager annual allowance of 1,000 fl. and shunted off to her place of birth in Waiblingen, to a residence provided by her brother, she henceforth led a socially and politically invisible existence until she died in 1471, "verlassen und vergessen" (abandoned and forgotten), at the age of 63.[39]

What we have seen up to now is the close relationship between the quality of the marital relations between Anna of Württemberg and her husband Count Philipp of Katzenelnbogen on the one hand, and her status as "Erbtochter" or as a legal heiress and sister to two living brothers on the other. Anna's brothers refused to accept their married sister's stake in their mother's inheritance; instead, they saw themselves—in keeping with the conventions of the time—as the only legitimate heirs of their father and mother. It was unacceptable to them that Anna should be granted rights that she might have transferred to her own husband before the death of her brothers or before the death of their male offspring. As it was not likely that Anna's brothers would die without male offspring—in the year of her separation and the court proceedings (1446), Anna's brother Ludwig already had two sons, and in the year of her official separation of bed and board (1456), her second brother Ulrich could already look upon two living male offspring—there was little hope for Philipp of Katzenelnbogen that Anna's claims to her mother's territories would ever be realized.

Taking Stock

In the story of Anna and her brothers we find a brother-sister relationship that was strongly defined by the fact that the sister, equipped with a dowry, did not simply turn her back on her original family after her marriage and enter into a "communio reverentiae sanguinis" with the family of her husband. Having been provided in her mother's testament with territorial holdings and even further-reaching rights to the future inheritance of her brothers, Anna was and remained part of the "jura familiae" of her own family, even after marriage. Whether or not Anna of Württemberg had consented to or was even satisfied with the dissolution of her marriage and her new residence in Waiblingen cannot be known, and it is not of central interest here. Two things are important for our line of inquiry; firstly, the fact that Anna, at her final domicile, was unable to play an active role in noble society and therefore no longer had recourse to any instruments of power—whatever these might have been for a princess in late medieval and early modern society; and secondly, and of key importance in understanding the relationship between married sisters and their brothers, the fact that after her separation Anna of Württemberg did not go to live with or near her daughter, who was married to Landgrave Henry III (1440–1483) of Hesse, but rather returned—whether voluntarily or not is not the issue here—to Württemberg under the care of her brother; in other words, she moved back to her original family.

It might be tempting to read into these events some kind of emotional or otherwise special quality in the relationships between brothers and married sisters. But there is something far more interesting in play here. After all, the coincidence of timing mentioned earlier between the transfer of money and property to the count of Katzenelnbogen and the births of Anna's children indicates that Philipp the Elder was clearly willing to uphold the marriage with Anna of Württemberg as long as money and property were forthcoming. One can therefore lay part of the blame for the married couple's separation at the doorstep of the two brothers and their insistence that Anna should be written out of their mother's testament—especially considering that the instrumental nature of, or rather the congruence of emotions and material interests in, royal and lesser marriages is not beyond debate in the literature. But this is beside the point. Of relevance here is that the figure of Anna of Württemberg represents a classical "Schwesterfraw" whose existence as wife and princess was contingent on the conduct of her brothers in legal issues relating to power and possession, and hence also on her status as a sister. The last will and testament of Henriette of Montbéliard certainly had a paradoxical effect if it was explicitly intended to grant her daughter a stake in the transfer of power. On the one hand, she put her daughter in some respects on equal footing with her sons by allowing through her testament her Katzenelnbogen son-in-law to participate in the "jura familiae" of Württemberg. But in doing so, Henriette created a strife-ridden sister-brother constellation in which, in the long run, the "Schwesterfraw" was transformed back into an unmarried woman and, being no longer a wife nor, in the strict sense of the word, a sister, found herself a political, social, and economic outcast.

In answer to our question of how to understand brother and married sister relations in late medieval and early modern aristocratic society, the events surrounding Anna of Württemberg and her brothers reveal the following. A sister was a sister if she was married; she was successfully married as long as her husband participated in the "jura familiae" of her family of origin. As we have seen, however, this participation had the potential to limit or appropriate the rights, power, and possessions of the brothers of married sisters; for their part, the brothers of married sisters had a vested interest in trying to minimize the claims of their sisters. As a result, and as was clearly demonstrated in the case of the count of Katzenelnbogen, brothers were capable of jeopardizing the marriages of their sisters, weakening their position as "Schwesterfraw," and limiting their role as agents in the transfer of power. It is a process that the brothers, as husbands of wives who were sisters in turn, could hardly wish upon themselves. What we see here is an inextricable paradox that not only fueled numerous conflicts between royal and noble brothers-in-law, but also may explain the marital discord in so many royal and noble marriages. Recognizing this brother-married sister paradox enables a departure from the model that has been favored by historians up to now explaining the innumerable marital crises among the noble classes—namely, absence of love, an explanation that can be found in historiographical writings since the seventeenth century—and helps us locate the cause of the strife-ridden relationships of noble and royal couples in the paradoxical structure of the legal and political culture of the time.

The "Schwesterfraw" as Agent between Brother and Husband

The figure of the brother-in-law has been mentioned above. The example of Count Philipp the Elder of Katzenelnbogen has set forth a plausible argument of what the expectations of a husband of a "Schwesterfraw" might be vis-à-vis her original family, specifically her brothers, that is, his brothers-in-law. Yet in the case of Anna of Württemberg and Philipp of Katzenelnbogen, there is a dearth of written evidence with respect to the hopes that could move a prince to marry a "sister." To fill this gap, the conclusion of this paper shall examine the story of Anna of Habsburg.

Anna (1432–1462), a daughter of King Albert II of Habsburg, became engaged to marry the youngest of the three brothers of the House of Wettin, William III, known as the Brave, in April 1439.[40] This marriage between the Habsburg princess and the Wettin prince served political objectives from the very beginning, as it was contrived to give the groom a claim to the Bohemian throne. But after the death of Anna's brother, King Ladislaus Posthumus of Bohemia (born 1440) in 1457, the political situation took an unexpected turn for William III, and another was crowned in his place. William was not about to accept this political setback without a fight and turned to the Pope for support, denouncing the Bohemian coronation as unlawful. William argued that an election only came into question if "von den Königlichen Samen oder geschlechte, Man oder Fraw, Niemand im Leben wehre" (from royal seed or lineage, man or woman, no one was still alive). The thwarted prince went on to say that, since his spouse Anna was still alive, it was the right of "der durchlauchtigsten Frawen Annen, Königin, des vorgenanten Herrn Ladislai etwan Königs, rechten Schwester, von Vater und Mutter meiner lieben Gemaheln" (of the highness Anna, queen, of the previously mentioned Ladislaus ertstwhile king, his full sister from father and mother, my dear spouse) to inherit this Bohemian kingdom "nicht allein von freiheitt und gerechtigkeitt, sondern auch von alten löblichen Herkommen vndt gewohnheitt wegen, von rechtenn Erbs gefelle" (not only from freedom and justice but also from old praiseworthy custom and usage, from rightful inheritance succession).[41] In case the Pope was not disposed to recognize this right of the sister, the "Schwesterfraw," William took the precaution to refer in the same correspondence to the existing inheritance contract between Saxony and Bohemia, which should deliver the Bohemian crown to him, a Wettin of Saxony, by contractual means.[42]

William III failed in his bids to claim the Bohemian throne. The result was that Anna, following the death of her brother, no longer played a role in the transfer of power. William then separated from Anna of Habsburg and compelled her to take up residence in a remote castle.[43] William's separation from his wife subsequent to his political misfortune was very much in keeping with the instrumental character of noble and royal marriages of the age. But the fact that William was able to accomplish the separation without causing any major scandals in aristocratic society may be explained in part by the absence of a royal brother. Unlike the cases of Anna of Württemberg and Sidonie of Saxony, no judicial proceedings investigating witchcraft or magic-making had to take place in this royal separation. William III simply isolated his wife, thus tacitly confirming what had actually transpired: the election of George of Poděbrady as king of Bohemia had made it abundantly clear that Anna's position as an agent of power, which was based on her status as the full sister of King Ladislaus, no longer applied.

Following the death of her brother, Anna no longer existed politically for William as a wife, i.e., an agent of power, because the desired transfer of power did not take place. In other words, after the death of her brother and following the failed bid by her husband to become his successor in Bohemia, Anna was no longer a "rechte Schwester," nor was she a wife or princess any more. Before the death of her brother, Anna still carried the promise of being an agent of power. Through the death of King Ladislaus, wife Anna became, as desired, a rightful heiress to the throne, or as William formulated it in his letter to the Pope: she became a "rechte Schwester." But because her rights as a sister were not enforceable, and Anna the royal "Schwesterfraw" ceased to exist to a certain extent, Anna the wife disappeared as well: William forced her to spend the rest of her life locked, invisible, inside the walls of an isolated castle.

Conclusion

The objective of this essay has been to examine the special quality of relations between brothers and their married sisters among the late medieval and early modern nobility, specifically in terms of their significance in the transfer of power and possessions. A discussion of early definitions of the words "brother" and "sister," and their meanings, particularly in the legal arena, shows that "brotherhood" and "sisterhood" represented two culturally disparate concepts in the transmission process of power within the late medieval and early modern aristocracy. This difference was first of all tied to sex and, secondly, depended on the legal status of being married. Whereas full daughters of a set of parents were only sisters when they were married, sons became brothers simply because their parents had several blood offspring. On the basis of this peculiarity of definition, and using concrete examples of the relations between brothers and their married sisters at the dawn of the early modern period, it has been possible to flesh out the figure of the "Schwesterfraw," who, contrary to early modern juridical-theological discourse, and also contrary to the assumptions in the literature, was not characterized by her change of house and family upon marriage. Instead, this late medieval and early modern "Schwesterfraw" can be viewed as an agent or broker of power in the context of farther-reaching kinship formations.

The figure of the "Schwesterfraw" or, as she was called by her contemporaries, "rechte Schwester" or "leibliche Schwester," was the agent and transmitter of power and possessions and as such helped turn potential power into transferred power, i.e., successful power. Her princely existence was based in large part on the fact that these wives, these princesses, were or could become not only daughters, but also, or perhaps primarily, "rechte Schwestern." This transformation could take place if their brothers had died and they were thus "Erbtöchter"; or if they had not renounced their inheritance as was the custom; or if despite this or subsequently their fathers and mothers had made explicit provision for them in their last will and testament; or if they had ascended to power with the support of the king or emperor. The examples discussed here attest to the fact that contemporaries knew how to exploit this political principle to best effect. As demonstrated here, married daughters and/or sisters of agents of power played a vital role in the transmission and exercise of power in that they transferred power to competing royal families. The events in the lives of Anna of Württemberg or Anna of Habsburg are only two prominent examples.

As we have seen, the position of daughters and sisters in the transmission process of power was conversely dependent on whether or not they had brothers, whether or not these brothers were living or deceased, and whether or not they had blood offspring, that is, their own sons or daughters. Transfers of power and property were thus affairs that affected entire kinship networks, centering on the nodes of "daughters and sons" and "brothers and sisters." This chapter has demonstrated that being a "Leiblehenserbe," that is, being an heir or heiress to the property of parents, was, for daughters at least, not a status derived solely from kinship by blood. To be a "rechte Schwester"—in other words, to be an agent of power and thus a classical "Schwesterfraw"—was, as we have seen, not merely a question of origin or blood kin, but primarily a question of kinship networks. The significance of "rechte Schwester" and "Schwesterfraw" in the context of transfer of power rested namely in at least two things: being married and being a sister. Contemporaries called this phenomenon "Schwesterfraw."

Notes

1. David Warren Sabean and Simon Teuscher, "Kinship in Europe: A New Approach to Long-Term Development," in *Kinship in Europe: Approaches to Long-Term Development (1300–1900)*, ed. David Warren Sabean, Simon Teuscher, and Jon Mathieu (New York, 2007), 1–31. Cf. Carola Lipp, "Verwandtschaft – ein negiertes Element in der politischen Kultur des 19. Jahrhunderts," *HZ* 283 (2006): 31–77.
2. Cf. Ebba Severidt, *Familie, Verwandtschaft und Karriere bei den Gonzaga: Struktur und Funktion von Familie und Verwandtschaft bei den Gonzaga und ihren deutschen*

Verwandten (1444–1519) (Leinfelden-Echterdingen, 2002), 9; Sylvia Schraut, *Das Haus Schönborn: eine Familienbiographie (1640–1840)* (Paderborn, 2005); Christophe Duhamelle, *L'héritage collectif: La noblesse d'Eglise rhénane, 17. et 18. siècles* (Paris, 1998).

3. See David Landes, *Dynasties: Fortunes and Misfortunes of the World's Great Family Businesses* (New York, 2006); David Sabean, *Kinship in Neckarhausen, 1700–1800* (Cambridge, 1998); Jon Mathieu, "Verwandtschaft als historischer Faktor: Schweizer Fallstudien und Trends, 1500–1900," *Historische Anthropologie* 10, no. 2 (2002): 225–244.

4. Concerning siblings, see for instance Martine Segalen, "'Sein Teil haben': Geschwisterbeziehungen in einem egalitären Vererbungssystem," in *Emotionen und materielle Interessen: Sozialanthropologische und historische Beiträge zur Familienforschung*, ed. Hans Medick and David Sabean (Göttingen, 1984), 181–198; concerning relations between siblings in the context of heritage in the German lands, cf. Jürgen Schlumbohm, *Lebensläufe, Familien, Höfe: Die Bauern und Heuerleute des Osnabrückischen Kirchspiels Belm in proto-industrieller Zeit, 1650–1860* (Göttingen, 1994) and Michaela Hohkamp, *Herrschaft in der Herrschaft: Die vorderösterreichische Obervogtei Triberg von 1737 bis 1780* (Göttingen, 1998), 157–215. Concerning relations between brothers in urban economies during the early modern period, see Mark Häberlein, *Brüder, Freunde und Betrüger: Soziale Beziehungen, Normen und Konflikte in der Augsburger Kaufmannschaft um die Mitte des 16. Jahrhundert* (Berlin, 1998), 338–392.

5. Concerning relations between siblings within the high aristocracy of the Holy Roman Empire (hereafter HRE) see Sophie Ruppel, *Verbündtete Rivalen: Geschwisterbeziehungen im Hochadel des 17. Jahrhunderts* (Cologne, 2006).

6. Margareth Lanzinger, "Mitgift," *Enzyklopädie der Neuzeit*, vol. 8 (Stuttgart, 2008), 606ff; concerning rights of daughters in the context of heritage in Westphalia during the early modern period see Heinz Reif, *Westfälischer Adel 1770–1860* (Göttingen, 1979), 81.

7. Concerning women as owners of fiefs see Hedwig Röckelein, "De feudo femineo: Über das Weiberlehen," in *Herrschaftspraxis und soziale Ordnungen im Mittelalter und in der frühen Neuzeit: Ernst Schubert zum Gedenken*, ed. Peter Aufgebauer and Christine van den Heuvel (Hanover, 2006), 267–284.

8. Elisabeth Koch, "Die Frau im Recht der Frühen Neuzeit: Juristische Lehren und Begründungen," in *Frauen in der Geschichte des Rechts: Von der Frühen Neuzeit bis zur Gegenwart*, ed. Ute Gerhard (Munich, 1997), 73–93, here 90–91.

9. Concerning the rights and claims of daughters within the high aristocracy of the Holy Roman Empire, see Karl-Heinz Spieß, *Familie und Verwandtschaft im deutschen Hochadel des Spätmittelalters: 13. bis Anfang des 16. Jahrhunderts* (Stuttgart, 1993), 331ff.

10. Spieß, *Familie*, 13, 135; cf. Reif, *Adel*, 83; Batrix Bastl, *Tugend, Liebe, Ehre: Die adelige Frau in der Frühen Neuzeit* (Vienna, 2000), 64.

11. Concerning Kunigunde see Wilhelm Baum, *Die Habsburger in den Vorlanden 1386–1486: Krise und Höhepunkt der habsburgischen Machtstellung in Schwaben am Ausgang des Mittelalters* (Vienna, 1993), 738.

12. Concerning the counts of Katzenelnbogen see Karl E. Demandt, "Die Grafschaft Katzenelnbogen und ihre Bedeutung für die Landgrafschaft Hessen," *Rheinische Vierteljahresblätter* 29 (1964): 73–105 and Karl E. Demandt, "Die letzten Katzenelnbogener Grafen und der Kampf um ihr Erbe," *Nassauische Annalen* 66 (1955): 93–132; also Michaela Hohkamp, "Eine Tante für alle Fälle: Tanten-Nichten-Beziehungen und

ihre politische Bedeutung für die reichsfürstliche Gesellschaft der Frühen Neuzeit (16. bis 18. Jahrhundert)," in *Politiken der Verwandtschaft*, ed. Margareth Lanzinger and Edith Saurer (Vienna, 2007), 149–171.

13. Concerning case studies, see Carlo Ginzburg, "Ein Plädoyer für den Kasus," in *Fallstudien: Theorie – Geschichte – Methode*, ed. Johannes Süßmann, Susanne Scholz, and Gisela Engel (Berlin, 2007), 29–48.

14. Article: "Geschwister," in Johann Christoph Adelung, *Grammatisch-kritisches Wörterbuch der Hochdeutschen Mundart, mit beständiger Vergleichung der übrigen Mundarten, besonders der Oberdeutschen*, vol. 3 (Leipzig, 1793–1818).

15. Article: "Nachfolge oder Erbfolge deren Seiten-Freunde," in Johann Heinrich Zedler, *Zedlers Universal-Lexicon*, vol. 23 [Leipzig, 1740] (Nachdruck Graz, 1961), col. 171–179, here 171.

16. Concerning the importance of sisters and aunts in the process of transformation of power and property within the high nobilty of the HRE, see Michaela Hohkamp, "Sisters, Aunts and Cousins: Familial Architectures and the Politcal Field in Early Modern Europe," in Sabean, Teuscher, and Mathieu, *Kinship in Europe*, 128–145.

17. Cf. Spieß, *Familie*.

18. Article: "Schwester," in Zedler, *Zedler's Universal-Lexicon*, vol. 36 [Leipzig, 1743], col. 480–483, here 480.

19. Cf. Gianna Pomata, "Blood Ties and Semen Ties: Consanguinity and Agnation in Roman Law," in *Gender, Kinship, Power: A Comparative and Interdisciplinary History*, ed. Mary Jo Maynes, Anne Waltner, Brigitte Soland, and Ulrike Strasser (New York, 1996), 43–64.

20. Article: "Schwester." Concerning the interdiction of marriage, see Samuelis de Cocceji, *Jus controversum civile...* (Frankfurt and Leipzig, 1713–1718), 154.

21. Article: "Frater," in Zedler, *Zedlers Universal-Lexicon*, vol. 9 [Leipzig, 1735], col. 1765.

22. Article: "Schwester."

23. Geheimes Staatsarchiv Berlin (hereafter GStAB) OBA 22068 Bl. 2, letter, August 1518.

24. Concerning the position of women as members of two families see Severidt, *Familie*, 69 and Spieß, "Familie," 128.

25. Article: "Schwester"; Samuelis de Cocceji, *Jus*, 150ff.

26. Hohkamp, "Eine Tante für alle Fälle."

27. Concerning the marriage of Anna of Württemberg and Count Philipp the Elder see Spieß, *Familie*, 108. See also Karl E. Demandt, *Regesten der Grafen von Katzenelnbogen 1060–1486* (Wiesbaden, 1954), vol. 2: *(1418–1482)*, Nr. 3066 (7 December 1421), 860–861; Nr. 3067 (7 December 1421), 861; Nr. 3068 (7 December 1421), 862; Nr. 3069 (7 December 1421), 862; Nr. 3070 (7 December 1421), 862ff.

28. Cf. Jörg Rogge, "Gefängnis, Flucht und Liebeszauber: Ursachen und Verlaufsformen von Geschlechterkonflikten im hohen Adel des deutschen Reiches im späten Mittelalter," *Zeitschrift für historische Forschung* 28 (2001): 487–511, 504ff. Concerning the interrogation, see Demandt, *Regesten*, Nr. 4425 (28 July 1446), 1237–1241.

29. Bernd Breyvogel, article: "Anna von Württemberg," in *Das Haus Württemberg: Ein biographisches Lexikon*, ed. Sönke Lorenz (Stuttgart, 1997), 79–80.

30. For the separation of bed and board, see Demandt, *Regesten*, Nr. 4914 (1 January 1456), 1376. Concerning the life of Anna after the separation, see Spieß, *Familie*, 180.

31. Bernd Breyvogel, "Die Rolle Henriettes von Mömpelgard in der württembergischen Geschichte und Geschichtsschreibung," in *Württemberg und Mömpelgard. 600 Jahre*

Begegnung, ed. Sönke Lorenz and Peter Rückert (Leinfelden-Echterdingen, 1999), 47–76, 53–54.

32. Ibid., "Henriette," 49.

33. Concerning the historiography on Countess Henriette, see Gerhard Raff, *Hie gut Wirtemberg allwege: Das Haus Württemberg von Graf Ulrich dem Stifter bis Herzog Ludwig* (Stuttgart, 1988), 238–250.

34. Dieter Mertens, article: "Württemberg," in *Handbuch der baden-württembergischen Geschichte*, ed. Meinrad Schaab and Hansmartin Schwarzmaier, vol. 2 (Stuttgart, 1995), 1–99, here 53–55.

35. Cf. Pauline Puppel, *Die Regentin: Vormundschaftliche Herrschaft in Hessen 1500–1700* (Frankfurt a. M., 2004).

36. See Michaela Hohkamp, "Marital affairs as a Public Matter within the Holy Roman Empire: The Case of Duke Ulrich of Württemberg and his wife Sabine at the Beginning of the 16th Century," in Jason Coy, Benjamin Marschke, and David Warren Sabean, eds., (New York and Oxford, 2010).

37. Cf. Monika Mommertz, "'Imaginative Gewalt' – praxe(n)ologische Überlegungen zu einer vernachlässigten Gewaltform," in Michaela Hohkamp and Claudia Ulbrich, eds., *Gewalt in der Frühen Neuzeit: Beiträge zur 5. Tagung der Arbeitsgemeinschaft Frühe Neuzeit im VHD* (Berlin, 2005), 343–357.

38. Johannes Merkel, "Die Irrungen zwischen Herzog Erich II. und seiner Gemahlin Sidonie (1545–1575)," *Zeitschrift des Historischen Vereins für Niedersachsen* (1899): 11–101; see also Andrea Lilienthal, *Die Fürstin und die Macht. Welfische Herzoginnen im 16. Jahrhundert: Elisabeth, Sidonia, Sophia* (Hanover, 2007).

39. Raff, *Hie gut Wirtenberg*, 261, 258.

40. Concerning the marriage between Anna of Habsburg and William the Brave, see Rogge, "Gefängnis," 496–497, and also Herbert Koch, "Herzog Wilhelms von Sachsen erste Hochzeit vom 20. Juni 1446. Nach den Akten dargestellt," *Zeitschrift des Vereins für Thüringische Geschichte und Altertumskunde*, 30 (1915): 293–326.

41. Cf. Georg Spalatin [Georgii Spalatini Historici Saxonici], *Vitae aliquot electorum et ducum saxoniae inde A. Fridrico I. usque ad JO. Fridericum …, in: Scriptores rerum Germanicarum, praecipue Saxonicarum, in quibus scripta et monumenta illustria. Pleraque hactenus inedita, tum ad historiam germaniae generatim, tum speciatim saxoniae svp. misniae, thuringiae et varisciae spectantia....* (Leipzig, 1728), col. 1080ff.

42. Cf. Otto Posse, *Die Hausgesetze der Wettiner bis zum Jahre 1486: Festgabe der Redaktion des Codex Diplomaticus Saxoniae Reiae zum 800-jährigen Regierungsjubiläum des Hauses Wettin mit 109 Tafeln in Lichtdruck* (Leipzig, 1889), table 37 (25 November 1373) and table 86 (25 April 1459).

43. Rogge, "Gefängnis," 496–497.

Chapter 4

Subordinates, Patrons, and Most Beloved

Sibling Relationships in Seventeenth-Century German Court Society

Sophie Ruppel

"Siblingship is not a well established, clear-cut universal category, but rather a question to be put to each culture to be answered in that culture's own terms," writes the anthropologist David Schneider.[1] His comment was directed to ethnology, a discipline that has described a variety of forms of sibling relationship in different parts of the world.[2] Historians have only recently discovered sibling relationships as a topic that can provide new perspectives on different periods of the past.

We obviously cannot know what it meant to be a "brother" or "sister" unless we describe the phenomenon carefully within its own cultural (historical) framework. In this contribution, I would like to present a very specific type of sibling relationship: the structure and meaning of siblings in seventeenth-century German court society. Here, both hierarchies within families and normative ideas about roles, rights, and duties shaped individual relationships to a considerable degree. Dynastic networks and the dynamics of court society as a whole influenced relationships as well.[3] Adding a perspective from inside the aristocratic family to recent research on aristocratic social and political networks puts into question traditional ideas about the family as much as it does ideas about the functioning of early modern politics. Sibling relations were fundamentally important in court society—for the functioning of the dynasty as a whole as well as for the individual life course of its family members.

The source material on which the following analysis is based consists of the large quantities of correspondence between siblings from the second half of the seventeenth century, strictly speaking, from four series of siblings. One stems from the electorate Palatine (Karl Ludwig, elector Palatine, and his brothers and sisters).[4] The second is from the later electorate Hannover (Christian Ludwig von Braunschweig-Lüneburg and his brothers and sisters).[5] The third family came from Kurbrandenburg (Friedrich Wilhelm I and his brothers and sisters).[6] And the fourth example comes from the principality of Hessen-Kassel (Wilhelm and his brothers and sisters).[7] These families, a sample of about twenty persons, belonged to the circle of powerful northern Protestant principalities. Their correspondence—a vivid documentation of interaction—is ideal for dealing with questions of relationships in general, and the floods of aristocratic letters found in the archives allow a close look at conduct, cooperation, and conflict among the protagonists.

Sibling Communication in Court Society

The second half of the seventeenth century, after the Peace of Westphalia, was a period of relative political stability and saw an extension of the postal service—of individual postal systems of the principals as well as of imperial post services.[8] Nevertheless it could not be taken for granted that every letter arrived at its destination, and many of the siblings confirm this in their answers; for example: "I have received your letter dated the …"[9] Sometimes even the content is repeated to make sure the addressee knows the context of the letter.

How large and diversified—and even complicated—letter writing was in this period can easily be imagined by examining the so-called *Briefsteller* (writing manuals), which were very fashionable at the time. Letter writing in this period was determined by the specific needs of aristocratic society and thus was shaped by a complex letter ceremonial. How to address a person of rank, how to sign a letter, what size of envelope might be appropriate, etc. could be very difficult to decide. Letter writing was the most important way to exchange information, to negotiate, and to bring about any interaction between European dynasties, residing, as they did, far away from each other. In that respect, a "letter" is much more than what we subsume under this term. In court society, where public and private spheres were not separated, it combined political, social, familial, and personal functions and offered a whole range of features. It could be formal and simply informative as well as expressing emotions; most often it combined both.

Aristocrats seem to have spent most of their time writing letters. They corresponded with other members of the aristocracy, family members, artists, philosophers, diplomats, and all kinds of persons of rank. Siblings were particularly favored correspondents, many siblings writing to one another every week or even more often. Sophie von der Pfalz, for example, wrote to her brother Karl Ludwig as well as to her sister Luise Hollandine twice a week, and the sisters of Hessen-Kassel wrote to their brother Wilhelm weekly.[10] Frequent exchange of letters was encouraged by the very fact that siblings were dispersed throughout the courts of Europe. There even seem to have been implicit rules for the frequency of letter writing, for if a sister failed to write back in a week's time she apologized, as did Elisabeth von der Pfalz to her sister Sophie: "I have been so busy last week that I could not answer your letter as I should have done."[11] Nevertheless, it is not possible to get a clear picture of the frequency of correspondence, since letters have been stored in archives all over Europe and many were lost or even burned by the writers themselves. Sophie, for example, later electress of Hannover, promised her brother Karl Ludwig, elector Palatine, that she would destroy his letters to her. In the archive one finds letters that have been cut and partly destroyed—whether by the contemporaries themselves or by later hands is not possible to say.

The contents of the letters varied over a lifetime: whereas siblings in their childhood wrote about their adventures at court, young adults mostly exchanged sociopolitical information. After coming of age, they spoke of philosophical or theological matters or increasingly discussed medical questions. The length of the letters varies a great deal, from short notices, for example announcing a safe return from a journey, to letters up to ten or fifteen pages, full of information. Letters were often read aloud to other family members, copied, and forwarded. Thus news was spread, a whole communication circle was established, and siblings heard about (family) news from more than one side.

The Morphology of Aristocratic Sibling Relationships and Their Position in Dynasties

Whoever talks about siblings also has to consider family structures and the general functioning of the specific society. In the Holy Roman Empire of the seventeenth century, power was not yet institutionalized, and territories clung together through personal bonds. The empire was less an association of political systems and institutions than a compilation of kinship relations. The high aristocracy, composing the territorial rulers of the empire, constructed a web of closely interwoven dynasties. Although a northern, Protestant circle can be distinguished from a southern Catholic one, aristocrats were related in so many ways that nearly everybody could find a cousin or an aunt at the court of another territory. Dynasties extended across large spaces, as did broad, open networks of relatives, for which notions of a "nuclear family" cannot usefully be applied. The ruling elite could even be described as one large family, with the emperor as the symbolic father of his princes. On the one hand, these families (if this term can be used at all) were determined by competition as each aristocratic dynasty struggled to maintain or enhance its power. On the other hand, peace and stability were founded on the alliance of dynasties and a proper balance among them. The preservation of the peace and the status quo, which was laboriously negotiated at the conclusion of the Thirty Years' War in the Treaty of Westphalia, remained the aim of all estates of the empire throughout the second half of the century. As any shift in power had an effect on nearly every relationship within the aristocratic network, it was in everyone's interest to keep careful watch over the balance of power. This resulted in—from our point of view—a confusing web of alliances, mutual guarantees, marriage unions, or, sometimes, local running feuds. One important means of stabilization, of course, was the interweaving of dynasties via kinship relations. In effect, one could say that the structure of competition was counterbalanced by a densely woven kin network.

In this situation of balance and competition, the preservation of status was crucial, and that, in turn, necessitated continuity through male succession to preserve the property, offices, and prestige of the dynasty. It also meant insuring the effective positioning of a dynasty within the network of high aristocracy and the securing of strong allies. For all these aims, children were necessary, and as many fathers died early (frequently, for this and also for subsequent generations, in war), they also needed siblings. In this structure, actions that we today would classify as "private" appear more or less as public through the effect they had on the whole dynastic web. The fact that family structure and politics were closely interwoven thus generated a specific type of familial and sibling relationship.

Within this network, it is very difficult in some cases for the historian to sort out the relationship of two people, as the semantic use of familial terms differs from our ideas of "brothers" and "sisters" and other kinship terminology. If someone addressed his correspondent as follows: "Hochgeehrter lieber Herr Vetter, Schwager, Bruder und Gevatter"—"Most venerable dear cousin, brother-in-law, brother and godfather"—the historian is, understandably, confused. But once the system behind these terms is analyzed, it becomes clear how it worked. First of all there was no semantic separation between the family and high aristocracy at all— all principals and members of this circle were in any case to be called "cousins." A second element is combined with that: the words "brother" or "sister" are also applied to non-relatives. Terms that we now use only for the nuclear family (like "mother," "father," "daughter," "son," "brother," or "sister") were used to express a special friendship. Reading just the address of a letter therefore often does not help to determine whether a biological brother is meant or not. In fact, accepting somebody as a "sister," "father," or "daughter" was even accompanied with a ceremonial act, confirmed with three kisses (when persons met the next time).

This terminology of friendship, which is found very often in the sources, could even overcome differences in rank. Whether "brother/ sister" or "father/mother" or "son/daughter" was chosen was mostly determined by age differences, sometimes by rank—and of course gender. Examples here might be Karl Ludwig von der Pfalz's friendship with Kaspar von Ampringen, in which the former accepted the name of "father" to the latter, or Prince Ruprecht's friendship with Wilhelm VI von Hessen-Kassel, who was, like the prince, interested in all kinds of experiments, and whom Ruprecht accepted as a "son."[12] That rank could be secondary to age shows in the example of Elizabeth Stuart, who, being the daughter of a king, accepted a minor German princess, the Landgräfin Juliane von Hessen-Kassel, as her "mum."[13] This relationship also implied that ceremonial addresses, among other things, could be left out. So Elizabeth would, for example, simply address her as "Hochgeehrte Fraw Mutter" at the beginning of a letter instead of giving the whole name, which would require naming all the different territories that belonged to that Landgrafschaft at that time.

In this society built on relationships and networks, people thought in terms of multiple ties, which could be expressed in the way they addressed each other in their letters. The more kinds of relationships shared with another person, the more that person might be a trustworthy ally in difficult times. In the example of the person addressed above as "Hochgeehrter Herr Vetter, Schwager, Bruder und Gevatter," it is probable that he was (a) a member of the high aristocracy and therefore a peer, (b) a special friend, (c) a "real" brother-in-law, and (d) related to the writer's family (his child or himself) in a spiritual relationship as godparent. In fact this is the case: here Christian Ludwig von Braunschweig-Lüneburg was writing to his brother-in-law Frederic of Denmark, married to his sister Sophie Amalie, a friend, godfather, and, of course, fellow member of aristocracy.[14]

On a semantic level, in this respect, the empire appears as one big family branching out in all directions. This already hints at a permeability of the boundaries between the nuclear family and the wider branches of kinship and aristocracy. There was no semantic concept that drew a sharp line between what we would call family or nuclear family, and the broader dynasty or even aristocratic network. Because of their exclusive marriage circle, those in the high aristocracy were nearly all related to one another. The big barrier lay not (as was the case in the bourgeoisie) between family and society, but rather between the large extended family of European high aristocracy and the more restricted bourgeois family circles.

The nature of the high aristocratic family system affects the definition of a group of "siblings." Did "siblings" as a special group exist in dynasties, and might they still have been important? No doubt, we are applying a modern term to this part of the family; people of the seventeenth century seldom used such a group-term at all, usually talking instead of their "herren brüder and frawen schwestern," their "sir brothers and lady sisters." Rather than raising the much discussed topic of the appropriateness of the term "nuclear" for aristocratic families, perhaps the more interesting question engages the problem of how high or low the barriers were between family and society and how the distinctions compare to modern concepts of the family. There was still something which distinguished a "real" brother from a so-called brother. There were still certain features that made siblings specifically important people for the family members, though in another way than we might expect. Biological relations alone did not necessarily define siblingship: for example, half-siblings springing from relationships with someone of lower rank were not "siblings" at all, whereas children of equal birth from successive marriages were. Also, misbehaving children could be dropped as children or siblings. It was more or less the legitimate inner-familial rank that established siblingship and at the same time defined the specific positions or hierarchies among aristocratic siblings. In the following, I will try briefly to characterize sibling relationships within their position in the dynasty.

Childhood and Careers in the High Aristocracy

Aristocratic childhood differed remarkably from bourgeois or peasant childhood. Governesses, instructors, aunts, and uncles were involved in

the education and supervision of children. And the birth rate of aristocratic families was remarkably high, with ten to thirteen children not
unusual.[15] Historical research has usually found that the necessity of
securing succession explains the high birth rate. But this is only one argument among many, since it does not account for those having seven,
eight, and more sons in some families. In fact, there was more to it, as
siblings fulfilled certain functions for a dynasty and contributed to its
welfare—which will be explained later on.

High birth rates and long periods of childbearing, as well as successive legitimate marriages, first of all resulted, from the point of view of
the individual sibling, in extreme differences of age. When there were
twelve, thirteen, or even more siblings in a row, there were considerable
differences in age. For example, in Hessen-Kassel a mother (Amalie Elisabeth) was eighteen years older than her daughter Agnes, who herself was
sixteen years older than her youngest sister Louisa. This suggests that it
is not quite correct to speak of siblings as a peer group, or to set a group
of parents on the one side against the group of children on the other.
There were generations in between. This, of course, had consequences
for relations among siblings. Symbolically, for instance, it became obvious when much younger sisters addressed their oldest brother as "vatter"
("father"), as Sophie von Hannover did in her early letters to her brother
Karl Ludwig von der Pfalz.[16] In childhood, age differences also brought
about the supervision of younger siblings by older ones. Siblings controlled the behavior of their younger brothers and sisters or even took
decisions for them—if they grew up together. But in fact, this was not
very often the case, as children frequently spent their childhoods separated from their parents and their own siblings at the courts of aunts and
uncles, which can be seen in children's letters to their parents.[17]

In my sample, nearly all children spent a couple of years at the courts
of their parents' brothers and sisters. At the same time their aunts' and
uncles' children came to their parents' court, which resulted more or
less in an exchange of children among adult siblings. Liselotte von der
Pfalz, the daughter of Karl Ludwig, elector Palatine, who spent four years
with her aunt Sophie at Hannover, is a prominent example, but one
among many. This case illustrates the close relationship that could be established in these relations and how siblings of the parents were responsible to a considerable degree for their nephews and nieces.[18] Aunts and
uncles (i.e., parents' siblings) often integrated their nephews and nieces
at court, acted as instructors, arranged their marriages, or looked out for
other (e.g., clerical) careers for their protégés. Growing up at a foreign
court also prepared the children, especially the younger siblings, at an
early age for the tasks they would fulfill throughout their lives. Aunts

and uncles sometimes advanced to proper "substitute" parents. The four brothers of Braunschweig-Lüneburg (Christian Ludwig and his brothers), for example, on their educational journey in 1640, sent their regular reports about their studies to their uncle Friedrich, although their father was still alive at that time.[19] Especially when younger brothers and sisters of a successor were not married or had followed a clerical career, they were—like the Friedrich mentioned above—predestined to act as instructors of their nephews and nieces. Brothers of the father were usually guardians (*Vormünder*) of the oldest son anyway, a precaution in case of the early death of the father. In the case of early deaths of the parents, the siblings of the parents acted as substitute parents. Charles I of England, for example, explained after the death of his brother-in-law (Friedrich V von der Pfalz) to his nephews that they had "exchanged a father," and he assured them of his "fatherly care and affection."[20]

While child exchange can be seen as a strategy of networking within dynasties, sending children to other courts at an early age also served to help them find suitable marriage partners or to establish careers at foreign courts. Siblings almost never stayed at their home court in later life. Consequently, family members living at the other courts were instructed to write letters to their siblings at a very early age. Twelve-year-old Charlotte von Hessen-Kassel, for example, wrote to her brother about what happened at court, about a parrot that had flown away, or about how she missed him: "Gestern seindt es zwey jahr gewesen, das wir von E.L. (Ewer Liebden, S.R.) abgescheiden worden. Ist lange genug. Es ist uns nicht möglich lenger von E.L. abzuesein" (Yesterday it was two years that we have been separated from you. This is long enough. It is not possible for us to bear this any longer).[21]

Educational journeys and long stays at various European courts were very common. This was not only an experience of young boys, but also of young girls. Although girls did not go to study at a university and did not travel as much as their male counterparts, they nevertheless lived, especially as adolescents, at their aunts', uncles', and other relatives' courts for extended periods. Quite often two of them were at the same place, like Elisabeth von der Pfalz and her younger sister Henriette Marie, who stayed at their aunt's court in Berlin until Henriette Marie was married to the prince of Transylvania.

What for us seems to be an important feature of sibling relationships, a shared childhood, was in fact not very often the case in seventeenth-century court society. But that does not mean that siblings did not have close relationships. On the contrary, their connections grew stronger during adulthood as they bonded together by belonging to the same dynasty, their shared source of economic security and status. The different careers that siblings followed were seldom independent of one another. Through-out life an individual sibling remained part of the dynastic group and was positioned in relation to the family. To begin with, the oldest brother had no choice at all: as the successor to the throne, he was the one to take over power after the death of the father. This principle, that the eldest son inherited the territory as successor—the rule of primogeniture—is found in nearly all the ruling dynasties of the empire. Primogeniture was obligatory for the four secular electoral principalities, those princes ruling the larger territories and electing—or confirming—the emperor of the Holy Roman Empire. This had been laid down in the "Goldene Bulle" of Karl IV in 1356. If the eldest son died without any children, the second-eldest was to take his place and so on. In the seventeenth-century Empire, nearly all dynasties in the high aristocracy were structured by this principle of primogeniture. If the successor or an heir to a territory tried to evade his fate, which was sometimes seen as a burden, it could result in conflicts and instability, as the example of Georg Wilhelm von Braunschweig-Lüneburg illustrates. Handing over his already affianced bride to his youngest brother Ernst August, he resigned from his rights and ruled that Ernst August's children should follow him onto the throne after his death. This resulted in many negotiations and ruptures among the four brothers, which destabilized the dynasty as a whole.

Younger siblings could find several positions befitting their rank. One possibility was to marry into an allied dynasty. Although this was not only a choice for sisters—for example, younger brother Eduard von der Pfalz married Anna Gonzaga and lived at the Parisian Court—sisters were more likely to climb up the rank ladder via marriage and find their way into the center of another dynasty. Sophie Amalie, a sister of the brothers in Braunschweig-Lüneburg, is an example: she became queen of Denmark when her husband inherited the throne. Younger brothers, if they married at all, usually married someone of a lower rank. In fact, more younger brothers than sisters did not marry and simply stayed at the various European courts as courtiers or went into military service. One example was Ruprecht, the younger brother of Karl Ludwig, elec-tor Palatine, who became a famous figure in British history, playing a prominent role in the English Civil War as "Rupert of the Rhine."

One career open to both sexes was a life in the church. A leading posi-tion in a monastery or cathedral chapter, among other possibilities, was an acceptable position for younger sisters as well as brothers.[22] Abbesses, sometimes rulers of small territories, could lead very independent lives. Elisabeth von der Pfalz, for instance, became abbess of Herford and turned this abbey into an intellectual center of her time. Her territory was independent and subordinate only to the empire. But very often it took a long time for younger brothers and sisters to find an adequate position, and quite often they stayed at various courts for long years, searching for a place to live. Remaining at their home court seems not to have been an alternative at all. Although siblings might stay with their oldest brothers for short periods of time, none of them settled there for long.

Structures Determining Sibling Relationships in the High Aristocracy

Nowadays siblings are more or less seen as peers, as equals with the same rights within the family structure. Historically this was not always the case: the most striking characteristic of aristocratic sibling relationships is that they were determined by birth order and inner hierarchies within the sibling sequence. Very prominent in the sources are the terms *ius aetatis* or *praerogativa aetatis*.[23] These prerogatives of age were probably the most fundamental difference between modern ideas of siblingship and those in early modern aristocratic society. The prerogatives of age describe the explicit establishment of hierarchies of siblings according to the order of birth. This had a major impact on an individual's life. "In domo gehet es nach dem altter"—"in the house age is decisive"—is a line that appears in many variations and in many situations. It not only implies the dominant role of the firstborn brother, and the difference between the heir and the later-born siblings, but also a rank order among the later-born themselves.

To begin with, rank order by birth resulted in older siblings bearing responsibility for the careers of their younger brothers and sisters. For example, in the sibling group of the Palatine, the oldest sister, Elisabeth, first tried to find suitable positions or marriage partners for her younger sisters before placing herself. In some cases, these activities clearly went beyond offering help, and younger siblings could easily become subject to directives of their older brothers or sisters. Elisabeth, for example, organized her younger sister Henriette Marie's marriage with the Transylvanian prince against Henriette's wishes.[24] Here it is important to note that it was not only the oldest brother who, after the death of the parents, held the parental position who acted in these situations, but also older sisters.

Younger siblings owed respect to the older ones because of their earlier birth. Very young sisters even addressed the eldest brother as "father" (as mentioned above) and used very respectful language when writing to him. Sophie von Hannover wrote in her memoirs about her older brother Karl Ludwig: "I have always submitted to him, whom I considered to be my father."[25] To the contrary Elisabeth, the oldest sister, even reprimanded him and sometimes explicitly disagreed with his actions. In this respect, birth order determined behavior. Belonging to the older set in the sequence gave higher rank, which had to be respected by younger siblings. This hierarchy is found among brothers and sisters alike, although in mixed couples male siblings usually came before sisters.

The prerogatives of age can also be found on a symbolic level. Older siblings, for example, were due what was called *precedence*. This meant that younger siblings had to give way to older ones when entering a room, or be seated behind them at a meeting. Precedence applied to all kinds of situations—like affixing one's seal on a contract after the older sibling, signing a letter after the older one, or voting after the older one at any conference of the dynasty. Here, once again, public and private could not be separated in this society; these rules of precedence applied both inside and outside the court. Of course, such rules could easily cause conflicts between siblings when rank according to birth order collided with rank hierarchies of court society. When, for example, Ernst August von Braunschweig-Lüneburg became bishop of Osnabrück, he argued that as a cleric he should precede his older brother Johann Friedrich, who, of course, did not agree. The whole issue became a long-lasting conflict between the brothers and was finally solved in a complicated compromise defining different procedures for various situations. [26]

Even financial allowances, the appanages, were distributed according to birth order. If the father's testament did not fix the amount of the appanage of the younger siblings, it was distributed according to birth order. Older siblings usually got higher annual allowances than younger ones. In the Palatine set of siblings, it is obvious that younger brothers received less money than older ones: the second oldest brother, Ruprecht, for example, was paid 4,000 Reichstaler per year, and a younger one, Eduard, only 3,000. Sisters generally received less than their respective brothers in the birth order. In the Palatine sequence, the eldest sister Elisabeth was awarded 1,650 Reichstaler per year, the younger sister Luise Hollandine only 900 per year. The appanage was paid only to the unmarried, since dowry functioned as the final compensation and usually was accompanied by a formal renunciation of all other claims. All the women who married received a dowry, usually a fixed amount of money according to family traditions. Although quite often a fairly large sum, it frequently caused trouble with the rest of the family because it was not paid in advance but existed as a debt the oldest brother had to pay off and the other dynasty had to claim. All unmarried aristocratic women could rely on a lifelong appanage.

Both birth order and gender determined what one could expect from an eldest brother. Clearly, superior age structured sibling relationships in the high aristocracy to a great extent. The factor of age, however, was relevant not only among siblings but also between relatives in general. Its consequences for the practices of rank in daily life have been neglected and should be further scrutinized. Meanwhile, the question of how gender hierarchies could be affected by age differences in this society is not yet clear. To be sure, there were rules along which hierarchies were established—including gender—but in every situation, concrete hierarchies and precedence were negotiated while taking into account all the various categories of gender, rank, prestige, and age. Certain rank categories, however, are clearly marked. For example, when Sophie Amalie, a sister of the princes of Braunschweig-Lüneburg, became queen of Denmark through the succession of her husband, she had obviously climbed high on the hierarchical ladder. As queen, she without any doubt "preceded" her brothers and therefore, for example, put her name first when she wrote a letter to her brothers in Braunschweig-Lüneburg.

Along with the inner-familial hierarchies and roles, one finds a specific distribution of rights and duties among the siblings. The eldest brother had a lifelong responsibility for the welfare of his siblings. This duty was usually fixed in the testament of the father, sometimes naming a concrete amount of money that the eldest was to pay out, sometimes stating generally that he should provide enough for a life befitting his siblings' rank. To treat them adequately meant to provide a sufficient dowry for those sisters who married and to pay appropriate allowances to those siblings who lived as courtiers at other courts, entered convents, or joined the military. He was obliged to guarantee them financial support to allow a living according to their rank, unless poverty of the country precluded adequate payment. As it was phrased in the testament of Georg von Braunschweig-Lüneburg, the father of the Brunswick-Luneburgian sibling set: "besides, those of our sons who will govern the country are obliged to give a princely appanage to the others and they should not be short of anything … unless, which the merciful GOD may prevent, the whole country should be so miserable that these payments are impossible. In that case they should accept this."[27]

Adequate support could prove quite a problem if the country and its households were not well off—or if the successor refused to spend fortunes on his younger siblings. In that respect, the oldest brother had a double task: to govern the territory and lead it to prosperity, and to take care of the members of his dynasty. When, after the Treaty of Westphalia, Karl Ludwig von der Pfalz reestablished his devastated territory, he definitely struggled to reorganize, repopulate, and generally rebuild his country and tried to cut down the allowances for his own court and for his younger siblings. Consequently he faced problems not only with his sister Elisabeth but also with his brother Ruprecht (Rupert of the Rhine), who fervently fought for his rights. When Ruprecht came back to Germany in 1654 after years in the English military, he pleaded with his brother Karl Ludwig to help him as there was no chance to find an adequate place at the Stuart court. Charles I had mistrusted him after the surrender of Bristol and then Charles II, being exiled, himself depended on financial support from the continental aristocracy. But the elector Palatine denied Rupert's claims to payment for the years past and argued he could not increase the appanage because of the miserable state of his territory. The conflict reached its climax in 1656, when Ruprecht came to the Heidelberg castle and was not allowed to enter the ancestral seat.

Ruprecht's case reveals another interesting characteristic of dynastic relationships. When Ruprecht's pleas to his brother proved unsuccessful, he implemented a backup plan: in 1656 he wrote several letters to the emperor, Ferdinand, and complained about his brother's behavior, explaining that Karl Ludwig had withheld what he owed him. He described his own situation, included excerpts from the father's testament, and argued that he had been mistreated by his brother. To Wilhelm VI of Hessen-Kassel he further explained that Karl Ludwig had offered him only a poor village called Laubach, "a damned wet place, where no man can live healthily, so that I am forced to use other means if the electoral prince does not give in, so that I have to look out for a judge who would fight for my rights so that I would get what should be mine by nature and the will of God."[28] And a year later he threatened public exposure: "I will make a last try to find a compromise with my brother, if that is not successful, I will complain to everybody."[29] This was exactly what he soon did, communicating his situation to all the princes. They offered their mediation, and the emperor finally appointed a "Committee for the Reestablishment of Brotherly Unity."[30] The conflict lingered for years, but finally under the pressure of "public opinion" and the emperor's demand, Karl Ludwig had to give in. As the majority of the princes agreed that he had to provide an adequate appanage for his brother, he realized that he could not withhold it without damaging his and his dynasty's honor in court society as a whole. In this respect one could say that the whole of the aristocracy functioned as an institution of control for the behavior of the eldest brother towards his younger siblings. Here again it becomes obvious how intertwined family, dynasty, and the high aristocratic public were. Court society kept watch over its members, using the concept of honor as a counterbalance to enforce normative rules of behavior. If the eldest failed to treat his siblings adequately, it could result in a loss of honor or even in political problems.

From the examples we have seen so far, it is clear that the responsibility of the heir for the welfare of his younger brothers and sisters was a task he had to take seriously. He was not the absolute ruler of the dynasty but owed aid to those belonging to his house. For women, he was obliged to provide dowries or appanages. In any case where a position—like the admission to a convent—was linked with financial transfers, he bore the responsibility. Karl Ludwig, for example, contributed to the admission fees his sister Elisabeth had to pay when she entered the convent in Herford.

But this system of rights and duties had two sides. The view that younger siblings only presented a financial burden to the dynasty does not describe the situation adequately. On the contrary, younger siblings were seen as the living potential of a dynasty and thus were called upon to fulfill a whole spectrum of obligations. First of all, they were expected to lead a life in honor, which meant their behavior and way of life should not damage the dynastic reputation, or better still, should increase it and contribute to the collective prestige of the house. Otherwise they might lose their right to maintenance. When Luise Hollandine, another sister of Karl Ludwig, converted to Catholicism, she lost this status for a couple of years.

Educated in Leiden at a special court that the parents had established for the education of some of their children, Luise then lived for a long time at her mother's court. Neither marriage arrangements nor applications to Protestant convents were successful. However, she was given the possibility to learn the art of painting, taught by one of the most prominent Dutch painters of the period, Gerard van Honthorst (1590–1656). Her life at her mother's court seemed to have no future, so in 1657, already thirty-five years old, she secretly fled to France, where her brother Eduard lived. There she converted to Catholicism, having left a note for her mother explaining that she would have to follow her conscience and asking for forgiveness.[31] In 1659 she entered a convent in Maubuisson, where she became abbess in 1664. She led a very secluded life and spent most of her time painting. In the letters of her siblings, it becomes clear that she had damaged the dynastic honor by converting and especially by fleeing from her mother's court. She lost the support of her mother, who dropped her (not even mentioning her in her testament as a daughter), as well as the support of Karl Ludwig, the oldest brother reigning in Heidelberg.

Although Luise Hollandine was even supported by the English king and queen, she was abandoned by the most important figures of her dynasty. But she had another accomplice, who helped her in France: her brother Eduard, who himself had converted to Catholicism upon his marriage and resided at the French court. He was probably the one who helped her to be admitted to the abbey of Maubuisson and who arranged the pension she got from Louis XIV. That she had lost the favor of her oldest brother Karl Ludwig is not only seen in his initial refusal to pay her any appanage, but also in the fact that he did not correspond with her at all. So she tried to negotiate with him through her brother Eduard, who fervently took her side. Through Eduard's letters, Luise Hollandine begged for forgiveness, and for the restitution of favor. After she had become a respected abbess who had good contacts to the French Court, Karl Ludwig came around slowly, finally reestablishing their correspondence after Eduard's death.

Karl Ludwig's brother Eduard exemplifies further the tasks of younger siblings, who were residing at various courts all over Europe. They rendered useful services to their eldest brother and their home dynasty, most importantly informing the eldest brother about what was happening at the courts. In an age when newspapers did not yet exist, reliable information was a valuable commodity. Knowledge about what was happening at different courts determined the politics of a prince. The duty to provide such news was seen as a natural task of the siblings. In the sources there is a phrase for it: "to render one's duty" ("rendre ses devoirs"). Eduard von der Pfalz, for example, residing at the French court in Paris, regularly reported to his brother at Heidelberg. Sometimes he even waited for certain events to happen, in order to include the necessary details. He explained, for instance: "I did not answer your letter last week because the court was to arrive soon and I thought it might be much better to await its arrival."[32] Then he gave an extensive report on the arrival of Cardinal Mazarin, the king and the queen, what the people told him, how he paid the cardinal a "compliment" just as Karl Ludwig had instructed him, and so forth.

The function of news reporting could be fulfilled by all younger siblings, whether they reported from the court where they lived or from way stations on journeys they undertook. Page after page, the letters of younger siblings brought the reader news about court life, relating who had the king's favor, who lost it, who arrived, who departed; and describing rumors spreading, intrigues, deaths, births, marriage plans, etc. Such information—even on ballets or operas or the new fashions in clothing, dining, or dancing—was more or less political in a broad sense, especially in the case of Eduard, as the French Court functioned as the model for many of the small German courts. If there was a war going on siblings also reported military news; for example, Elisabeth von der Pfalz reported to her brother about the invasion of the French army. In a world in which letters were the only source of reliable information, correspondence from loyal siblings was of inestimable value to the ruling brother.

In the writing manuals of the time, the term for letters of information was "Kommunikationsschreiben," communication letters. Quite often they were copied and sent to other princes as well. Of course, it was not only the siblings who provided such letters; other relatives who lived at the various courts did so as well. Nevertheless, siblings were especially destined for this task, as they often depended financially on their home dynasty and owed this duty to their eldest brother. Additionally, their honor as a son or a daughter of that dynasty was based on the prestige of the dynasty. They remained connected to the dynasty of origin throughout their life, which strengthened their interest in its status. How highly political letters could be and how extremely dangerous it was if they were intercepted by a hostile party can be seen in the widespread coding of letters. To make sure the information did not fall into the wrong hands, Eduard, for example, left out the signature, or addressed letters to his brother ostensibly to other persons at the Heidelberg Court. Sometimes letters were written in numeric codes, like some of the letters of the brothers in Braunschweig-Lüneburg, which today are impossible to decipher.[33] (At some courts, cryptographers were in charge of deciphering the letters of enemies.) In very dangerous cases, a courier could be sent, equipped with a "*creditiv*," a letter attesting that he could be trusted. He would then get an audience, talk about the issues, and bring back the answer. But this precaution was only used in extreme situations.

Siblings not only provided information but also acted as negotiators and envoys at foreign courts. They were, in a way, part of both courts, the court of origin and the court that they resided at or had married into. Thus they bridged relationships between the dynasties. They often talked in their letters about commissions they fulfilled, about business they undertook for their brother, or about talks they had had with a king or other important figures of the political elite. In these negotiations, sisters as well as brothers could be involved. Karl Ludwig, after the death of Eduard, asked his sister Luise Hollandine to undertake certain diplomatic tasks at the French Court for him, and she wrote back to him, "I am very much obliged that you do me the honor of thinking of me and sending me some of your work; I hope I deserve it through my obedient service."[34]

Sisters married to a governing prince could be especially helpful to the head of the dynasty. Sophie von Hannover, for example, successfully connected the Palatinate and the Braunschweig-Lüneburgian principalities, arranging political cooperation and even encouraging their military cooperation. This proved very efficient when her brother faced a dispute with his neighbors in 1665 and especially in 1675, when French troops invaded Karl Ludwig's territory. His brother-in-law, Sophie's husband Ernst August (and especially Georg Wilhelm von Braunschweig-Lüneburg, Ernst August's brother), supported him militarily, gaining a spectacular victory over the French Marshal Crequi. In this respect, siblings can be seen as "envoys in residence" of an early modern type, before official civil servants took over this task and before state formation created institutionalized positions for this. Whether aristocratic sibling relationships in fact suffered a loss of function through the process of bureaucratization and nationalization, as institutionalized ambassadors came to fulfill tasks that had earlier been taken care of by siblings, still is subject to discussion.

To sum up: the most effective connection the head of a dynasty could establish was to marry his sister to the governing prince of another dynasty. It becomes obvious now why aristocratic families tended to distribute their children and their siblings all over Europe and why these can be seen as the living potential of a dynasty: younger siblings could be effective agents within the foreign courts. This again sheds new light on the high birth numbers of aristocratic families. Siblings functioned as bridges to other dynasties; they were major nodes within the net of alliances and dynastic relations. They linked various courts together by marrying into other courts (which also holds true for male siblings, as the example of Eduard von der Pfalz illustrates) or simply by staying at a court as courtier or entering into military service.

Karl Ludwig von der Pfalz had far-reaching contacts through his siblings: his brothers Rupert and Moritz lived at the English court, Philipp, before he died on the battlefield, established himself at the Oranian court, Luise Hollandine finally became an abbess in France, Elisabeth was an abbess in the small independent territory at Herford, Sophie became electress in Hannover, Eduard, married to Anna Gonzaga, lived at the French court, and Henriette Marie was married to the governing Transylvanian prince. This scheme can be found in all of the families in the high aristocracy—it was the same in the Braunschwieg-Lüneburgian dynasty, in the electorate of Brandenburg, or in Hessen-Kassel. They all tried to establish or stabilize the interdynastic connections via siblings—more or less successfully.

Women played an important role in building the dynastic networks, as they were the ones mostly concerned with marriage arrangements—not only as the ones to be married, but also as organizers of marriages. Although their names were seldom shown on the marriage contracts themselves, in the correspondence it becomes evident that aunts were especially involved in their nephews' and nieces' marriage arrangements. Often responsible for educating their siblings' offspring at their courts, they also searched for possible, dynastically advantageous marriages and often traveled to the various courts, taking the portraits of their protégés with them. In considering all these strategies of networking, of spreading ones' relatives all over the map, we gain insight into the functioning of this small, interwoven society, its more or less closed marriage circles and interconnectedness via siblings, aunts, and uncles, its functioning via personal relationships, and its massive use of letter writing to keep up the network.

The Structure of the Family as a Framework for Possible Cooperation, Conflict, and Affection

The behavior and the form of sibling relationships were very much determined by the structures mentioned above: by the application of the *ius aetatis*, the prerogatives of age, or by the rights and duties of the older with respect to the younger siblings and vice versa. The latter phenomenon has prompted Linda Pollock, who did research on aristocratic families in England, to suggest that this form of inner-familial relationship should perhaps be seen in the light of the broader system of patronage.[35] Analogous to patronage, both parties agreed on certain duties: while the oldest brother provided the financial or territorial resources, his younger siblings owed him help and loyalty. Pollock contradicts the widespread assumption that younger brothers in early modern aristocracy were more or less superfluous, powerless, and without any rights, and shows that although the heir was certainly privileged, younger brothers were also sent to university and had a right to participate in the dynasties' resources. On the other hand, the heir—and this too reminds one of patronage—helped the later-born siblings find adequate positions within aristocratic society. Pollock therefore concluded that from a younger brother's perspective, being a member of a well-established landed family gave him a ready-made patron within a reciprocal relationship.[36] This view is certainly correct and shows how the generally predominating ideas of possible relationships appeared outside and inside the family in aristocratic society. The overall present patterns of relationships structured micro- as well as macro-society. Just as the dynastic family was not clearly distinguishable from the surrounding dynasty, meaning that it is hardly possible to talk about a "nuclear family" here, sibling relationships and ideas of patronage certainly did not exclude each other. The oldest brother might even be seen as the administrator of the dynasties' resources upon which all the siblings depend. He owed them financial support befitting their rank. Still, it remains questionable that this can be regarded as patronage, as it was established via birth and as sibling-ship involves additional dimensions of rights and duties—not to mention emotional bonds and other personal aspects.

Despite the prerogatives of age, siblings were interdependent to a considerable degree: the heir was dependent on the cooperation of his younger brothers and sisters; the later-born depended on the wealth of the dynasty and its distribution by the governing brother. This interde-pendency was fertile ground for cooperation and conflict alike. It allowed for companionship as well as for a competitive struggle for a livelihood. The system itself structured any relationship. A sister living in an unhappy marriage could easily find in the oldest brother the person to whom she related most closely. The death of an oldest brother might offer the only chance for the next-oldest brother to find a prominent position in the aristocratic world and to inherit a whole territory.

The set of Palatinate siblings shows how the birth order could form the basis of affective bonds. Their emotional support for one another can be traced both in the letter exchanges and in the actions of the siblings. Among the Palatinate set of siblings there were two kinds of friendship: between later-born siblings whose situation was more or less alike, and between the heir of the dynasty and a younger sister. The first holds true for Ruprecht and Moritz, the two brothers who joined the English mili-tary together and who went to sea—until Moritz's boat sank in a storm in the Caribbean, an event that turned Ruprecht's life upside down and resulted in his journey home to Europe. Both later-born, both trying to establish themselves in English court society, they shared common inter-ests and seem to have established a close relationship. The same pattern can be applied to Eduard and Luise Hollandine, the two siblings who wound up residing at or near the French court, both of whom turned to Catholicism to accomplish their careers—which naturally created dis-cord with the oldest brother, Karl Ludwig, although both were reestab-lished in his "favor" as they served him well at the French court.

The special friendship between Karl Ludwig and Sophie, thirteen years younger, had a different basis. After the death of Friedrich V Sophie quickly accepted Karl Ludwig as her "vatter."[37] Although her friendship with him was very intense in her younger years—Karl Ludwig's wife, Charlotte von Hessen-Kassel, even accused her of an incestuous relation-ship with her brother[38]— it intensified even more over the years. From an heir's perspective, her career as electress of Hannover was very use-ful in any event, so there was no potential for conflict at all. Even more important might be that both were quite unhappy with their marriage partners for several years, so that the sibling obviously became the most important person in life. They seem to have written to each other with every mail service, and despite their own request that letters be burned, the remaining correspondence comprises at least four volumes in the Hanovarian archive.[39] His death in 1680 triggered the writing of her memoirs, where she explains: "Because soon after our arrival, when I least expected it, I learned that I had lost the elector, my brother, who was taken away by a fever which lasted for eight days, this affected me to an extent that I cannot express. He always loved me as his daughter and honored me by trusting me so much that he wrote to me with every mail service. And this he did with such an impassioned and charming style that this correspondence was one of the greatest pleasures in my life. This loss has enhanced my sufferings so much, that now, being 50 years old, I won't wait long until I follow my sister [Elisabeth, who also died in 1680] and my brother."[40]

Because marriages were always arranged, sibling relationships easily moved into the center of individual lives. Precisely because marriages were calculated along political lines, the relationship to a sibling—a brother or a sister—could often become the most important relationship. For all of the sibling sets here under study, a large letter exchange has been found. To write once or twice a week to a sister or brother was not unusual. Because siblings usually did not live together at the same court, visiting a sibling or traveling together with a sibling was quite common. Especially interesting is the expression of emotion found in letters: it is not only marked by minimal deviation from Baroque rhetoric as one might imagine, considering the conventions of that time. Siblings wrote in a very emotional way about sadness after the death of a brother or a sister, about fraternal confidence, about their sorrows and fears, and over and over again about their hope of seeing each other again. Some of the letters are truly astonishing and in their extreme emotionality remind the reader of letters from a much later period when a premium was put on sentimentality. The letters from the sibling set from Hessen-Kassel are packed with emotions as the sisters give free expression to their feelings. Thus Charlotte von Hessen-Kassel, openly describing how she suffered in her marriage, called her brother "allerliebster außerwählter Engels herr bruder"—"most beloved and exceptional angel of a brother"—and continuously lamented how she missed him. In fact, these letters are quite reminiscent of love letters.

Certain combinations of siblings were likely to be conflict-laden: relationships between the eldest brother and the second-oldest, or the eldest brother and the oldest sister (as the leading figure among the sisters), could be centers of conflict. There was often a lifelong dispute over financial matters between the eldest and the second-oldest brother or the eldest sister, which could result in a flood of contracts, negotiations, and renegotiations about financial or territorial matters, all carefully preserved in the archives. Both Ruprecht, the second-oldest son, and Elisabeth, the eldest sister, quarreled bitterly with their eldest brother Karl Ludwig about financial issues throughout their lives. Elisabeth, who organized a younger sister's marriage against the will of her brother the elector and therefore quarreled with him, often expressed herself in very harsh terms in order to establish her claims. Nevertheless, she still passed all the news on to him and thus upheld the usual system of rights and duties.

Ruprecht's case is even more complicated. Having been well established at the Stuart court, he was very much in need of money during the exile of Charles II and the rule of Cromwell. When Karl Ludwig refused to help him out, a lifelong conflict arose between the brothers, who had formerly been on good terms and even fought side by side to win back their Palatine territory in 1638. With the restoration of the Stuarts, Ruprecht went back to England, although as we have seen, Karl Ludwig finally had to give in. Ruprecht more or less abandoned all his ties to his home dynasty and relied on his English relatives, who showed more loyalty to him than did his brother. In fact, this conflict had bitter political consequences for Karl Ludwig because he lost the support of the English king, who took sides with Ruprecht in the end. England had been an important ally but now even threatened serious consequences if the elector Palatine refused to give in.

That Ruprecht had "changed" dynasty is finally illustrated by his refusal to return to the Palatinate when the aged Karl Ludwig, left with a sole sickly and weak son, needed him to marry to secure the succession of the dynasty. In the end, Karl Ludwig's son died soon after his father and the whole territory fell to a collateral line of the family. The consequences of "changing" dynasty are well illustrated here: the heir no longer had his relative as a source of information, which opened the way to serious political consequences for the position of the dynasty within the context of the aristocratic network. The fact that the relationship between the two oldest brothers was potentially so rich in conflict can be seen in many aristocratic families, where even in some cases they led armies against each other.

There were many causes of conflict among siblings: precedence, the distribution of resources, testamentary provisions, inheritance and succession, alliances with other dynasties, honor and status, disgraceful behavior, and religious conversion. Turning to different allies could be especially dangerous, since a brother allied with another court could provide important information to the enemy. The Braunschweig-Lüneburgian dynasty was very much weakened by this problem in the 1670s: one of the brothers was an ally of Louis XIV and the other of the emperor. However, conflicts did not typically arise (as far as we can see through their letters) because of character traits. Misbehavior was measured by the ruling normative ideas, which determined what kind of action was to be deemed dishonorable action or what constituted the failure to fulfil expected roles. Furthermore, a conflict was never only between two individuals but was, as in Ruprecht's fight for his appanages, interwoven with the network of political players.

Such a conflict concerned a dynasty as a whole as well as the wider high aristocratic network. Within the large family of the high aristocracy, mediation was the necessary instrument for handling conflicts. Mediation was brought into play to handle conflicts between political opponents, but it was also very useful to manage tensions between siblings, as in the case of Karl Ludwig and Rupert. Mediation meant that the quarreling parties did not argue among themselves, but through a third party, the mediator, who tried to negotiate a compromise acceptable to both disputing parties. Sometimes a sibling who was not involved acted as mediator, but most of the time this role was taken by a prince from another court. Successful mediation increased the prestige and honor of the mediator. Sometimes even the emperor was called upon as mediator between brothers—which illustrates again that the aristocratic family cannot really be considered as belonging to the private sphere.

Conclusion

While sibling relationships within the high German aristocracy during the Early Modern Period cannot be understood as rigidly determined by the structures in which they were embedded, still the normative ideas about privileges and responsibilities provided interpretive models for the roles to be played by the eldest brother, the younger brothers, and the sisters. It was within these roles that siblings shaped their individual relations. Within the frame of culturally defined expectations, siblings argued about their rights and duties and acted out aspects of enmity and friendship. Hans Medick and David Sabean have argued that interest and emotion cannot be separated,[41] and in the example of aristocratic sibling relationships this becomes very obvious.

Familial solidarity did not come about automatically but depended on the equilibrium of rights and duties. That people were well aware that the order of sibling relationships was precarious can be seen in the provisions of numerous wills and contracts. Many of the fathers' testaments contain passages beseeching sons and daughters to keep peace and unity. In the Braunschweig-Lüneburgian case, where two brothers governed two parts of the territory, they confirmed in a *Hausvertrag*, a contract laying down the rules of their dynasty, that "[w]e and our descendants decree … in important issues … as God has made us rulers of one Fatherland and as we sprang from one grandfather, to endeavor to act well-measured, everything coming from one heart, spoken from one mouth, written with one quill, and without special cause there shall be no dissonance between us, our civil servants, and servants. We want and shall not leave one another alone, but in all distress which happens to be we will faithfully support each other with advice, assistance and a helping hand."[42]

No doubt, the risk of conflict was high in a family structure determined by a highly uneven distribution of goods and by the interdependency of siblings in social, economic, and political life. But this potential for conflict was counterbalanced by the dense network among the princes of the empire. The collective watch over moral standards and the collective effort to keep the peace after the Thirty Years' War resulted in an ambitious attempt to keep up the newly established order among the princes of the empire. Violent contention or even war between brothers had to be carefully avoided, because within this network an "inner-familial" conflict could easily set fire to the whole of Europe.

The specific form of sibling relationships in the high aristocracy in the seventeenth-century Holy Roman Empire was marked by an interrelatedness that was fertile ground for cooperation and conflict alike. Though this interdependence took many forms, siblings were usually physically separated and distributed throughout the courts of Europe. Both the successor and his later-born siblings had certain rights and took over specialized tasks for the dynasty at the various courts. Younger brothers and sisters acted more or less as "envoys in residence" for their home dynasties. Even with all the tensions and disputes among them, their cooperation should not be underestimated.

The stratification of aristocratic society at large continued within the bosom of the dynasties themselves, establishing a hierarchy among the siblings according to birth order. It was believed that just as God placed a person on a certain spot or within a certain rank in society, He also placed a child in a carefully chosen position within a sequence of siblings. And He expected the individual to fulfill the roles and tasks consonant with this specific place within His well-ordered society.

While seventeenth-century aristocratic society had its own specificity, it is remarkable that there are significant parallels with various non-

Western societies, both in the language of kinship and in social interactions. For example, anthropologists working in South Asia have found semantic codes, resource allocation, and principles of seniority among adult siblings that provide interesting comparative perspectives. The general high esteem in which sibling relationships are held is part of a cultural system where siblings can have greater significance for each other than do husbands and wives.[43] Whatever the difficulties involved in the comparison of these two cultures, it can throw light on variations in, and the logics of, sibling relationships.

The English King Charles I penned a sentence that goes to the heart of Early Modern aristocratic understandings of sibling relationships: the loss of a sibling was irreparable and more significant than other losses. After the death of Friedrich V, Charles I (who was not even his biological brother, but his brother-in-law) wrote to his Palatine nephews: "I may truelie challenge a greater losse by his death than you: for you have but exchanged a father (I cumming in his roome) but I, have irrecoverablie lost a brother."[44]

Notes

1. David M. Schneider, "Conclusions," in *Siblingship in Oceania: Studies in the Meaning of Kin Relations*, ed. Mac Marshall (Lanham, New York, and London, 1981), 392.
2. Circirelli gives a survey on this in Victor G. Circirelli, "Sibling Relationships in Cross-Cultural Perspective," *Journal of Marriage and the Family* 56 (1994): 7–20. Also, Patricia Goldring-Zukow, ed., *Sibling Interaction Across Cultures: Theoretical and Methodological Issues* (New York, 1989).
3. This essay looks at some aspects of sibling relationships. For further reading one might turn to my study: Sophie Ruppel, *Verbündete Rivalen: Geschwisterbeziehungen im Hochadel des 17. Jahrhunderts* (Cologne, 2006).
4. Heinrich 1614–1629 (died early), Karl Ludwig 1617–1680, Elisabeth 1618–1680, Ruprecht 1619–1682, Moritz 1621–1654, Luise Hollandine 1622–1709, Ludwig 1623–1624, Eduard 1624–1683, Henriette Marie 1626–1651, Philipp 1627–1650, Sophie 1630–1714, Gustav 1632–1641, Charlotte 1628–1631.
5. Magdalena 1618–1618, Christian Ludwig 1622–1665, Georg Wilhelm 1624–1705, Johann Friedrich 1625–1679, Sophie Amalie 1628–1685, Ernst August 1629–1698, Dorothea Magdalena 1629–1630, Anna 1630–1636.
6. Luise Charlotte 1617–1676, Friedrich Wilhelm 1620–1688, Hedwig Sophie 1623–1683, Johann Sigismund 1624–1624.
7. Agnes 1620–1626, Moritz 1621–1621, Elisabeth 1623–1624, Wilhelm 1625–1626, Emilie 1626–1693, Charlotte 1627–1686, Wilhelm 1629–1663, Philipp 1630–1638, Adolf 1631–1632, Karl 1633–1635, Elisabeth 1634–1688, Louisa 1636–1638.
8. See: Wolfgang Behringer, *Thurn und Taxis: Die Geschichte der Post und ihrer Unternehmen* (München, Zürich, 1990).
9. For example Ruprecht (Rupert Prince Palatine) writes to his sister Sophie, the later Electress of Hannover: "Jay resu chere seur la vostre datee le…" Rupert's letters to

Sophie in Niedersächsisches Hauptstaatsarchiv Hannover (hereafter NHStA), Hannover 91, Kurfürstin Sophie, Nr. 15, folio 3. Note: Original spelling is used in all quotations that follow.

10. This can be reconstructed in various archives, e.g., for Charlotte of Hessen-Kassel in Staatsarchiv Marburg (hereafter StAM) 4a or for Sophie von Hannover in NHStA, Hannover 91 Kurfürstin Sophie, e.g., no. 37a or 39a.

11. "Je suis si pressé la semaine passée que je nay point fait reponce a votre derniere come ie dois." Elisabeth von der Pfalz to Sophie von Hannover on 9 April 1661; in NHStA, Hannover 91, Kurfürstin Sophie no. 36 folio 289.

12. See the publication by Karl Hauck, ed., *Die Briefe der Kinder des Winterkönigs* (Heidelberg, 1908).

13. See Margaret Lemberg, *Eine Königin ohne Reich: Das Leben der Winterkönigin Elisabeth Stuart und ihre Briefe nach Hessen* (Marburg, 1996).

14. See NHStA, Cal. Br. 24 Nr. 1315.

15. Cf. Detlev Schwennicke, *Europäische Stammtafeln, neue Folge*, vols. I.1–I.3 (Frankfurt a. M., 1998).

16. See: NHStA, Hannover 91 Kurfürstin Sophie Nr. 36.

17. E.g., letters of the young Wilhelm VII von Hessen-Kassel to his parents in StAM, no. 4a 54, 3.

18. See the correspondence in Eduard Bodemann, ed., *Aus den Briefen der Herzogin Elisabeth Charlotte von Orléans an die Kurfürstin Sophie von Hannover: Ein Beitrag zur Kulturgeschichte des 17. und 18. Jahrhunderts*, 2 vols. (Hanover, 1891).

19. See NHStA, Dep. 84 B Nr. 529 et al.

20. See Bayerisches Hauptstaatsarchiv (hereafter BayHStA) GHA Korrespondenzakten Nr. 1032.

21. Charlotte von Hessen-Kassel to her brother Wilhelm on 15 July 1639; in Erwin Bettenhäuser, ed., *Familienbriefe der Landgräfin Amalie von Hessen-Kassel und ihrer Kinder* (Marburg, 1994) 34.

22. See also Karl-Heinz Spieß, *Familie und Verwandtschaft im deutschen Hochadel des Spätmittelalters* (Stuttgart, 1993).

23. See Ruppel, *Verbündete Rivalen*, chap. 3, 5.

24. See the letters in NHStA, Hannover 91, Kurfürstin Sophie, Nr. 36.

25. "Je me remettois entierement à luy que je considérois comme mon père," in Adolf Köcher, ed., *Memoiren der Herzogin Sophie nachmals Kurfürstin von Hannover*, vol. 4 (Leipzig, 1879), 59.

26. See NHStA, Cal. Br. 22 Nr. 643 et al.

27. "Daneben sollen aber die, welche von unsern Söhnen zur Regierung gelangen werden, angehalten seyn, denen übrigen ihren fürstlichen Unterhalt die Zeit ihres Lebens zu schaffen...und darunter gar kein Mangel passieret werden," in the testament of Georg of Braunschweig-Lüneburg of 1641, in NHStA, Cal. Br. 22 Nr. 1708, or Philipp Rehtmeier, *Braunschweig-Lüneburgische Chronica Oder Historische Beschreibung der Durchlauchtigsten Herzogen zu Braunschweig und Lüneburg...zum Erstenmal in dreyen Theilen ans Licht gestellet von Philippo Julio Rehtmeier* (Braunschweig, 1722), 1653ff.

28. "ein verdampt wässeriges ohrt, da kein mensch gesundt leben kann, also dass ich meine sache gezwungen werde anders anzugreifen und dieweil der Churfürst nicht anders will, einen richter zu suchen, der mir das meinige, so mir von Gott und der natur zukomet, zuspricht und zu eygnet." Ruprecht to Wilhelm von Hessen-Kassel on 31 October/10 November in the new calender 1657; in Hauck, *Briefe der Kinder*, 128.

29. "Und bin ich willens widrumb zum letzten ein versuch zu thun, ob mein herr brueder der Churfürst sich mit mir zu vergleichen begeret, wohe nicht, so werde ich mich bey wem ich kann beklagen," Ruprecht to Wilhelm von Hessen-Kassel on 2 January 1658, in ibid., 133.

30. A "Commission zur Herstellung brüderlicher Einigkeit."

31. A copy of this note still exists in NHStA, Hannover 91, Kurfürstin Sophie, Nr. 34 d.

32. "Je nay pas repondu la semaine passé a VAE [Votre Altesse Electorale] parce que la Cour estoit si prest a venir que jay creu quil estoit plus appropos de remettre ma depesche jusques a cellecy." See Eduard von der Pfalz to Karl Ludwig von der Pfalz on 31 January 1654, in NHStA, Hannover 91, Kurfürstin Sophie nr. 36 fol. 217.

33. See NHStA, Dep. 84 B.

34. "Ich bin E.G. [Euer Gnaden] hochlich verobligirt, das sie mihr die ehr thun meiner zu gedencken und mich dar neben von ihrer arbeitt schicken...wolt wünschen durch meine gehorsame dinst solches von E.G. zu meritiren." See Luise Hollandine to her brother Karl Ludwig of Palatine, 23 May (year not readable), NHStA, Hannover 91 Kurfürstin Sophie Nr. 42, folio 10.

35. Linda Pollock, "Younger Sons in Tudor and Stuart England," *History Today* 39 (1989): 23–29.

36. Ibid., 26, 29.

37. This is how she addresses him in her early letters. See NHStA, Hannover 91, Kurfürstin Sophie Nr. 36.

38. See letters of Charlotte to her brother Wilhelm; StAM, no. 4 a 49, 11.

39. See NHStA, Hannover 91, Kurfürstin Sophie, Nr. 37 und 39 a et al.

40. "Car j'appris peu de jours après nostre retour, comme j'y pensois le moins, que j'avois perdu M. l'électeur mon frère, et qu'une fièvre de 8 jours l'avoit emporté, ce qui m'affligea à un point que je ne scaurios exprimer. Il m'avoit toujours cherie comme sa fille et me faisoit l'honneur d'avoir une si grande confiance en moy qu'il m'écrivoit tous les ordinaires et cela d'un stile si plein de geu et d'agrément, que cette correspondance faisioit un des plus grands plaisirs de ma vie. Cette perte a si fort augmenté mon mal de ratte que je songe toujours qu'à présent que j'ay 50 ans, je ne tarderay pas long temps à suivre ma soeur et mon frère," in Köcher, ed., *Memoiren der Herzogin Sophie*, 137.

41. Hans Medick and David Warren Sabean, "Interest and Emotion in Family and Kinship Studies: A Critique of Social History and Anthropology," in *Interest and Emotion: Essays on the Study of Family and Kinship*, ed. Medick and Sabean (Cambridge, 1984), 9–27.

42. "Deßgleichen sollen und wollen Wir und Unsere Nachkommen...in wichtigen Sachen...gleich uns Gott zu Herrn eines Vaterlandes gesezet und von einem Großvater entsprießen laßen, Unß sambt und sonders eußerst angelegen sein laßen, daß alles woll gegründeter Maßen, gleich auß Einem Herzen herfließend, aus Einem Munde geredet, mit einer Feder geschrieben, daher gehen, und ohne sonderbahre große Erheblichkeit gar keine Dissonantz zwischen unß, Unsern Rathschlägen und Dienern gefunden werden. Wollen und sollen...einer den ander nicht verlaßen, sondern in allen begebenden Nöhten mit Raht, Hülff und That trewlich beistehen." Adolf Köcher, *Geschichte von Hannover und Braunschweig von 1648 bis 1714*, vol 1 (Leipzig, 1884), 605.

43. Jane C. Goodale, "Siblings as Spouses: The Reproduction and Replacement of Kaulong Society," in Mac Marshall, *Siblingship*, 275–306.

44. See BayHStA, GHA Korrespondenzakten Nr. 1032.

Chapter 5

The Crown Prince's Brothers and Sisters

Succession and Inheritance Problems and Solutions among the Hohenzollerns, from the Great Elector to Frederick the Great

Benjamin Marschke

Introduction

The rulers of Brandenburg-Prussia have long been assumed to have had unproblematic successions. The seemingly smooth successions through primogeniture have even been widely credited as a contributing factor in the rise of Brandenburg-Prussia in the seventeenth and eighteenth centuries. Indeed, the "canon" of Hohenzollern rulers has been viewed as almost predestined since the eighteenth century: the "Great Elector" Frederick William (1640–1688), Elector/King Frederick III/I (1688–1701–1713), King Frederick William I (1713–1740), and King Frederick II, "the Great" (1740–1786).[1] In reality, each of the Hohenzollern rulers faced serious kinship and succession problems typical of the time.[2]

As in most Protestant territories of the Holy Roman Empire, primogeniture was not firmly established in Brandenburg-Prussia during this period, and the Hohenzollerns' recurring and earnest considerations of successions by alternative unigenitures and even partitions of the Hohenzollern lands resulted in crises.[3] Additionally, the Hohenzollern successions were repeatedly and seriously complicated by the threat of "reversionary" politics, i.e., the opposition to the ruling monarch posed by (or coalescing around) his own heir apparent. The term originally derives from the frequent "reversionary" agreements (or "reverses") that prospective successors made with foreign powers or subjects, in which they promised to grant favors or compensation once they took the throne in return for financial or political support or protection while still crown prince.[4] The threat posed by the "crown prince's party" was a dire problem for many "absolute" monarchs in early modern Europe.[5] Finally, the Brandenburg-Prussian monarchy was forced to arrange suitable marriages and/or otherwise appropriately provide for each of the crown prince's brothers and sisters. Dealing with the monarchy's "biological reserve" of heirs who would not succeed was a problem virtually everywhere in Europe at the time, and the Hohenzollerns were no exception.[6]

The case of the Hohenzollerns from the Great Elector to Frederick the Great is especially interesting because it offers vivid examples of the wide range of kinship and succession problems (and potential solutions) facing European monarchies at the time. Furthermore, the mistaken notion that the Hohenzollerns' successions were secure and smooth has distorted our perception of Brandenburg-Prussian history. By better understanding the Hohenzollerns' kinship and succession problems (and their solutions), I propose an alternative framework to the development of Brandenburg-Prussia.

Background

There were proclamations of primogeniture from the Hohenzollerns going back to the fifteenth century. When the Hohenzollerns succeeded to the electorate of Brandenburg in the early fifteenth century, they became subject to the Golden Bull of 1356, which imposed primogeniture on electorates. Elector Albrecht Achilles' *Dispositio Achillae*, issued in 1473, declared that the *Kürwurde* was to be indivisible and was to be passed down by primogeniture.[7] However, this proclamation did not mean that the Hohenzollern lands would not be divided in the future. On the contrary, Joachim I (reigned 1499–1534) acknowledged the *Dispositio Achillae* but ordered the electorate divided between his two sons at his death in 1534. His eldest son, Joachim II (1534–1571), inherited the electoral title and the Alt-, Mittel-, and Uckermark, but his younger son, Johann (1534–1571), inherited the Neumark.[8] The younger son, "Hans von der

Neumark," died childless in 1571, and the Kurmark was reunited under Joachim II's sole surviving son, Johann Georg (1571–1598). Johann Georg then ordered that the reunited Hohenzollern lands be partitioned among his seven sons upon his death.[9] Upon Johann Georg's death in 1598, his eldest son, Joachim Friedrich (1598–1608), rejected the testament and excluded his six half brothers from the succession. Joachim Friedrich claimed sole succession to all of the Hohenzollern lands and issued the *Geraischen Hausvertrag*, which not only reiterated the *Dispositio Achillae*'s declaration of primogeniture and the impartibility of the Hohenzollern lands, but also declared that all new acquisitions would become part of the indivisible inheritance.[10] However, in light of the Hohenzollerns' kinship and succession problems in the seventeenth and eighteenth centuries, these declarations counted for little.

Elector Georg Wilhelm and Frederick William

Elector Frederick William, "the Great Elector," was the only surviving son of his father, and he married off his two sisters during his own reign.[11] However, his succession in 1640 was extremely problematic due to "reversionary" politics. Frederick William, born in 1620, wound up at odds with his father, Elector Georg Wilhelm (ruled 1619–1640), and especially with his father's favorite, Count Adam von Schwarzenberg.[12] The crown prince became a figure around whom discontented subjects and allies could rally. At issue were prospective marriage partners for the crown prince, Brandenburg-Prussia's diplomacy in the midst of the Thirty Years' War (1618–1648), and especially Schwarzenberg's dominant role in the government. Georg Wilhelm and Schwarzenberg favored an Austrian bride for Frederick William and an Austrian alliance for Brandenburg-Prussia, both of which Frederick William rejected. While visiting the Hohenzollerns' Rhineland territories and the Netherlands in 1636, Frederick William began negotiating with the local estates and the Dutch to declare his rule over the Hohenzollern's Rhineland territories and declare their neutrality.[13] The crown prince was also rumored to be considering various alternative marriage plans. Georg Wilhelm rejected these plans and demanded that Frederick William return to Brandenburg. The crown prince stalled, and instead continued to negotiate independently.[14] After being repeatedly ordered to return, Frederick William ultimately refused. Only in 1638, once he was assured that he would not be forced into a marriage against his will, did the crown prince return.[15]

After his return his relationship with his father, both political and personal, did not improve.[16] On the contrary, Frederick William feuded with Schwarzenberg and accused him of poisoning him—if Georg Wilhelm were to die without an heir, then Schwarzenberg would have been able to establish his own dynasty in Brandenburg.[17] The crown prince remained estranged from his father and was purposefully excluded from any involvement in governmental affairs and forbidden to travel, presumably to prevent him from subverting his father's (and Schwarzenberg's) authority.[18]

Frederick William's sole succession as ruler of the Hohenzollern lands was uncomplicated by brothers. Nonetheless, the certainty of his sole succession and his political differences with his father (and his father's favorite) meant that as crown prince he was a figure around whom discontents gathered (or was an instrument that discontents utilized), and he thereby undermined the authority of the sitting ruler of Brandenburg-Prussia. His exclusion from the government and his ongoing feud with Schwarzenberg meant that his succession in 1640 was anything but unproblematic.

Elector Frederick William and Elector/King Frederick III/I

The Great Elector is the subject of a comprehensive historiography centered on his role as the founder of Brandenburg-Prussia as a rising power. Much has been made of Frederick William's administrative unification of the far-flung Hohenzollern territories, and descriptions of him such as *"Der Mann, der Preußen schuf"* are common.[19] The Great Elector's role in the 1688 succession is made only more problematic by this historiography. The historiography surrounding Frederick III/I is quite limited and has been dominated by King Frederick II's harsh judgment of his grandfather in his *Memoirs of the House of Brandenburg* since its publication in the eighteenth century. The 300-year anniversary of Frederick's crowning as the first Prussian king was a chance for revision (and rehabilitation), but it is still common to begin with Frederick II's evaluation.[20]

The principle problem with the succession of 1688 was providing for Crown Prince Frederick's brothers and half brothers. Three of the Great Elector's sons from his first marriage and four of his sons from his second marriage survived to adulthood.[21] Complicating matters further was Frederick William's stormy relationship with his eldest surviving son. Frederick William's favorite son had been the firstborn, Karl Emil

(1655–1674), and Frederick, born 1657 and crown prince after 1674, was increasingly estranged from his father after his older brother died. Frederick ultimately blamed his stepmother, Dorothea, for his worsening relationship with his father, but Frederick's physical deformities and mental weakness seem to have been the root of his father's dislike of him.[22] The mutual hostility between the ruler of Brandenburg-Prussia and his heir apparent was public, and Frederick William openly cast doubt on Frederick's capacity to rule.[23]

Equally at issue was reversionary politics. Frederick had reached his majority by the time of his elder brother's death, and from then until his father's death he and the "crown prince's party" were the greatest threat to Frederick William's authority. From the late 1670s until 1688, conflicts revolved around the succession and foreign policy. Basically, Frederick William, Dorothea, and their favorites chose an alliance with France and a partition of the Hohenzollern lands among the male heirs, while Frederick and his party favored an alliance with the emperor and primogeniture. Frederick's stepmother Dorothea accepted money from the French to sway Frederick William, and she pushed him to accept the Peace of St. Germain in 1679, ending Brandenburg-Prussia's role in the Dutch War (1672–1679).[24] The following year, Louis XIV was made guarantor of Frederick William's testament, which would have partitioned the Hohenzollern lands among Frederick, his younger brother, and Dorothea's four sons. Frederick believed that his stepmother was behind the planned partition, as did most of his contemporaries.[25]

Faced with the pro-French sentiments of Brandenburg-Prussia's ruler, the emperor's agents sought to win over the crown prince.[26] Because Louis XIV was guarantor of the 1680 testament, which Frederick assumed would partition the Hohenzollern lands, Frederick was naturally inclined toward the emperor.[27] Frederick, then, wound up the head of the pro-Empire party at court.[28] After the revocation of the Edict of Nantes in 1685 and during the buildup to the Nine Years' War (1688–1697), Frederick William shifted back to an alliance with the emperor. A new testament issued in 1686 was guaranteed by the emperor, not Louis XIV.[29] Crown Prince Frederick was not told the terms of the testament, but it was assumed, again, that Frederick William was ordering a partition of the Hohenzollern lands upon his death.[30]

Frederick anticipated a dispute over any claim as sole successor.[31] In the midst of this court intrigue, the emperor offered Frederick his recognition of Frederick's succession to all of the Hohenzollern lands. In a classic case of reversionary politics, the quid pro quo was the "Schwiebus reversion" negotiated between Crown Prince Frederick and the emperor in 1686.[32] Frederick undercut his father's negotiations with the emperor and promised to return the contested province of Schwiebus to the emperor upon his succession in return for the emperor's recognition of him as sole successor.[33] The Schwiebus reversion gave the emperor a stake in Frederick's survival and his ascension to the throne, and even the vague promise of asylum should Frederick's precarious situation at his father's court become untenable.[34]

Crown Prince Frederick thought that he was in danger at his father's court because he believed that his stepmother was trying to circumvent primogeniture through poison.[35] Frederick and many others blamed Dorothea for his older brother's death.[36] Karl Emil had fallen ill and died while on campaign with Frederick William during the Dutch War, and Dorothea had coincidentally been visiting their camp at the time.[37] In the context of a hysteria regarding poisoning gripping Europe in the mid-1670s, it was readily assumed that Dorothea had poisoned Karl Emil.[38] Her hyperbolic mourning at the crown prince's death was viewed as crocodile tears.[39] Repeated suspicions that she poisoned family members ultimately earned Dorothea the moniker "Agrippina of Berlin."[40]

In 1679, Frederick fled to Kassel and took refuge with Elector Frederick William's younger sister Hedwig Sophie of Hessen-Kassel (1623–1683), who was his aunt—and his prospective mother-in-law, as Crown Prince Frederick's fiancée was his first cousin, Elisabeth Henriette of Hessen-Kassel (1661–1683). The elector demanded that the crown prince be returned, but his sister in Kassel refused to turn over her nephew and future son-in-law.[41] The Great Elector threatened to disinherit Frederick entirely, and indeed the 1680 testament guaranteed by Louis XIV left only a bare core of the Hohenzollern lands to Frederick, partitioning the remainder among his brother and half brothers.[42] In return for permission to marry and establish his own household, Frederick returned to Berlin and vowed never again to leave the Hohenzollern lands without permission.

The drama at court was far from over, though. The following year Frederick was given what was believed to have been poisoned coffee at a party hosted by his stepmother Dorothea.[43] Supposedly only the swift administration of a purgative by one of his favorites saved the crown prince—Frederick's aunt and mother-in-law in Kassel had given him the purgative as an antidote to poison.[44] The poor health of the Elector, the sickly nature of the crown prince, and the suspicious deaths of members of the royal family only increased the tensions at court and heightened the stakes of the brewing succession crisis. By 1683 Frederick William's health was visibly failing, and he was not expected to live much longer.[45] At the same time, Crown Prince Frederick, who had always been sickly, was also not expected to live more than three or four more years.[46]

When Frederick's first wife, Elisabeth Henriette, fell ill and died in 1683, Frederick openly accused Dorothea of poisoning her, and the elector actually ordered a commission to investigate the crown princess's death.[47] No evidence of poison was found, but suspicions remained. Frederick remarried, to Sophie Charlotte of Hannover (1668–1705), and when his new wife became pregnant, they fled to his in-laws in Hannover. A son was born on the way to Hannover, but died within several months.[48] Frederick and his wife returned once more to Berlin. Accusations that Dorothea was trying to poison Frederick continued. While visiting his father in early 1686, Frederick was supposedly given poisoned coffee by his "evil step-mother," and again his life was saved only by the quick action of one of his favorites.[49]

The following summer the Great Elector traveled to the Netherlands, and he did not allow Frederick or his younger brother Ludwig (1666–1687) to accompany him but instead took along their eldest half brother, Dorothea's son Philip Wilhelm (1669–1711). William III of Orange was expected to die without a direct heir, and the Great Elector's sons by his first marriage should have had a claim to the succession through their mother. Yet they were left in Berlin, while Philip Wilhelm was ceremoniously presented in the Netherlands.[50] It seemed clear that Philip Wilhelm was being groomed to succeed William III of Orange. Meanwhile, the problems at court continued. In December 1686, Frederick fell deathly ill again, supposedly again a victim of poison.[51] Shortly thereafter, in February 1687, the Great Elector, his health failing, announced that he was dying. The succession seemed to be at hand—but then Frederick William recovered.

The climax of the crisis followed. Frederick's younger brother Ludwig fell ill in March and died in April 1687, presumably poisoned by an orange given to him at a party hosted by Dorothea.[52] As in the case of the suspicious death of Frederick's first wife, an official inquiry was launched, and its findings were inconclusive—it did not rule out poison.[53] With his brother dead and no heir of his own, only Frederick stood between Dorothea's sons and the throne.

When Frederick fell ill again in April 1687, shortly after his brother's death, it was again assumed that he had been poisoned. Frederick and Sophie Charlotte fled to Karlsbad, where they were guests of the emperor.[54] Frederick William demanded that Crown Prince Frederick return, but Frederick refused and then threatened to move on to the Hohenzollern Rhineland duchy of Cleves, where he was governor (just as the Great Elector had done to his own father).[55] This was the nadir of the relationship between the ruler and the crown prince of Brandenburg-Prussia, and the moment of truth in the succession crisis. Frederick demanded that his brother's murderer be brought to justice and claimed that he feared for his life at his father's court.[56] For his part, the Great Elector openly questioned the paternity of Sophie Charlotte's new pregnancy.[57] Frederick William not only labeled the crown prince a "deserter" and cut off his funds,[58] but he also threatened to grant the duchy of East Prussia to Frederick's half brother Philip Wilhelm and even to disinherit Frederick entirely.[59] Only in November 1687, with the intervention of the emperor and the Dutch, did the ruler and crown prince of Branden-burg-Prussia finally reconcile their differences.[60] Frederick and Sophie Charlotte finally returned to Brandenburg only six months before the death of Elector Frederick William.

It is ironic that the Great Elector Frederick William, best known as the founder of the unified Brandenburg-Prussian state, always planned for it to be broken up after he died. Early on, Frederick William's testament of 1664 would have left Karl Emil's younger brothers their own territorial states; second-born Frederick was to succeed to newly ac-quired Halberstadt.[61] Frederick William excused the partition by only splitting off lands acquired during his reign and not dividing the lands he had inherited.[62] Even as he again ordered a partition in his 1667 testa-ment, Frederick William admonished his successor to make no further partitions.[63] Later, if Frederick William had been ceded Pomerania at the Peace of St. Germain in 1679, then he intended to leave it to Philip Wilhelm, his eldest son with Dorothea.[64] He thereby obeyed the letter, if not the spirit, of the dynasty's declarations of primogeniture.[65]

The Great Elector's testaments of 1680 and 1686, on the other hand, were clear breaks with the Hohenzollern's proclamations of primogeni-ture. Frederick was right to suspect that the 1680 testament was unfa-vorable to him. His father left to Frederick's younger brother and half brothers not just newly acquired territories, but large parts of the Ho-henzollern lands.[66] Most problematic was Frederick William's last testa-ment, of January 1686, which was still valid when he died in May 1688 and in which the Great Elector disregarded all thoughts of primogeni-ture, leaving the crown prince little more than Brandenburg and East Prussia.[67] It might have been worse: at the height of the crisis in 1687 Frederick's father had threatened to disinherit him entirely.

This succession crisis is quite often skipped over entirely, because the dire kinship and succession problems of the last years of the Great Elec-tor's reign are overshadowed by the Turks' advance to Vienna and the outbreak of the Nine Years' War. Others deal with these problems only anecdotally, subsuming them in a section with a title like "Dispute in the Family," the focus of which is on the familial human-interest aspects, not the implications for dynastic politics.[68] In these works there is virtually no recognition that this crisis threatened the dynasty. When historians have dealt with the Great Elector's conflicts with his heir and his plans to partition Brandenburg-Prussia, they have typically viewed these as aberrations. The 1680 testament is viewed as "a very difficult step to understand" and the "inexplicable expression of an unpredictable individuality."[69] It is assumed that Frederick William, deathly ill and under the influence of the court, made a mistake.[70] Moreover, the scholarship commonly asserts that the Great Elector acted only at the prompting of his wife, and that Dorothea was the victim of "motherly weakness" in this regard.[71] It would be better to understand that it is anachronistic to project "state-centered" thinking (and the rationality of primogeniture) onto the seventeenth-century, and the Great Elector was simply (quite rationally) prioritizing the survival of his dynasty over the unity of his territories, as was quite typical of the time.[72]

Regardless of the historiography's relative neglect and denial of the Great Elector's plans to partition Brandenburg-Prussia, after his father's death Frederick declared the testaments null and void.[73] Frederick attained the assent of his father's chief ministers,[74] and perhaps just as importantly, he had the acquiescence of the executor of his father's testament, the emperor, in return for Schwiebus.[75] In anticipation of resistance from his stepmother and his half brothers, Frederick's ascension to the throne better resembled a coup d'état than an orderly succession. To prevent word of the Great Elector's death from getting out, the city gates were closed with the explanation that a murder had occurred.[76] Frederick demanded that the military governors and government officials throughout Brandenburg-Prussia immediately swear an oath to him before news of his father's death became public.[77]

Frederick quickly followed up his ascension to the throne with two magnificent fêtes, for the birth of a son (the future King Frederick William I) and the funeral of his father. To cement his seizure of power, Frederick III proclaimed primogeniture for the Hohenzollerns, again, in 1690.[78] Only after several years of negotiations did Frederick and his half brothers agree in 1692 to a *Hausvertrag* settling their claims to the succession. Frederick granted his half brothers pensions and titles as princes of Prussia and margraves of Brandenburg, but he alone succeeded to rule all of the Hohenzollern territories.[79] Frederick granted an appanage at Schwedt to his eldest half brother, Philip Wilhelm, but only as a nonsovereign source of income. This was not a partition, as was done at the time in Thuringia, Saxony, Hessen, or Anhalt.[80] Instead, the "Schwedt" Hohenzollerns remained part of the main line and did not constitute a separate dynasty—they were only first referred to as the "Brandenburg-Schwedt" line in the nineteenth century.[81]

The Brandenburg-Schwedt Agnates

Frederick's material provisions for his half brothers did not eliminate the kinship and succession problem that they posed. His eldest two half brothers, Philip Wilhelm and Albrecht Friedrich (1682–1731) founded their own lines of princes of the blood, which continued on for another generation.[82] Philip Wilhelm's sons, Friedrich Wilhelm (1700–1771) and Heinrich Friedrich (1709–1788), became the heads of the Schwedt branch of the dynasty in turn.[83]

As was common elsewhere in Europe at the time, the Schwedt agnates were potential frondeurs.[84] Frederick's half brother Philip Wilhelm was a major force at court until his death in 1711. He had a position akin to that of crown prince—should anything have happened to Frederick III/I, then Philip Wilhelm would have presumably served as regent for Crown Prince Frederick William.[85] Philip Wilhelm not only was a potential successor to the throne but also was regarded by contemporary observers at court as a power player.[86] His marriage in 1699 to a sister of Leopold "der Alte Dessauer" von Anhalt-Dessau (1676–1747), confirmed and reinforced his prominence.[87] Philip Wilhelm became the nucleus of the "opposition party" at court and in the military, and he was eclipsed only by Crown Prince Frederick William as the center of opposition to Frederick III/I.[88]

Problems with the Schwedt agnates continued under King Frederick William I's reign. Frederick William tried to establish his tutelage over the Schwedt margraves more firmly, and they resisted in kind. Upon taking the throne, Frederick William insisted that his eldest uncle, Albrecht Friedrich, be forced to subject himself formally and publicly as a vassal.[89] Frederick William established guardianship over Philip Wilhelm's sons during their minority as well.[90] In return, the king's uncle and cousins resisted royal orders and fostered their own foreign contacts. Fearing secret political activities by the agnate branch of the dynasty, Frederick William sent spies and observers to Schwedt to find out who met with the agnates.[91]

Meanwhile, the agnate branch of the Hohenzollerns led the main line in terms of monarchical splendor in Brandenburg-Prussia under Frederick William I. Philip Wilhelm had collected tall soldiers for his regiment before Frederick William began doing so, and Philip Wilhelm's descendents continued to collect tall soldiers and Moor musicians: their "giants" rivaled those of the king's regiment.[92] The agnates built and expanded a baroque palace and baroque gardens in Schwedt, and they even designed and built a representative cityscape in Schwedt that anticipated

Frederick William's expansions of Berlin and Potsdam.[93] In economic terms, the Schwedt branch of the dynasty expanded the estates originally granted to it by Frederick III/I through the purchase of more estates so dramatically that Frederick William forbade them to acquire any more—they were directly competing with the king's own similarly cameralist agenda, which involved expanding the crown's domains by buying up estates.[94]

The agnates' marriage strategies were quite endogamous, as was dictated by the king as head of the dynasty. King Frederick William did not allow Philip Wilhelm's eldest son, also named Friedrich Wilhelm, to marry until he was in his early thirties, and then the king married Margrave Friedrich Wilhelm to one of his own daughters.[95] The king's half-cousin, then, became his son-in-law as well, which further established the Schwedt branch as part of the main Hohenzollern line.[96] During King Frederick II's reign, Margrave Friedrich Wilhelm married off his three daughters more ambitiously: the eldest and youngest were married into the houses of Württemburg and Hessen-Kassel, respectively.[97] However, Margrave Friedrich Wilhelm's middle daughter was married to another child of King Frederick William I: King Frederick II's youngest brother (and her uncle) Ferdinand.[98] Philip Wilhelm's younger son, Heinrich Friedrich, further entwined the Schwedt agnates with the Anhalt-Dessau line and enraged King Frederick William by clandestinely marrying a daughter of "der Alte Dessauer" (and his own first cousin).[99] One of their daughters then married into the Anhalt-Dessau line once more (again to a first cousin).[100]

The agnate branch of the Hohenzollern dynasty still posed a problem during the reign of King Frederick II—Frederick's notorious warnings to his successor about princes of the blood may have been directed at the Schwedt margraves.[101] In turn, Frederick humiliated the agnates at every chance. He demanded that they submit themselves to him as vassals upon his ascension to the throne, as his father had done.[102] In Berlin, Frederick made sure that the agnates were unwelcome at court.[103] Perhaps most mortifyingly, Frederick minimized his cousins' role in the army, and he removed Margrave Friedrich Wilhelm from command—a denigration to which the king subjected his own younger brothers as well.[104] Frederick undermined the authority of his cousins on their own estates by readily entertaining complaints and lawsuits against them from their subjects and neighbors.[105]

Though typically relegated to only the footnotes of the history of Brandenburg-Prussia, Frederick III/I's half brothers represented a major kinship problem (and potentially, a succession problem) for the Hohenzollerns during his reign. Although nothing ever came of the threat that the Schwedt agnates posed to the ruling Hohenzollerns, they undeniably did pose one.

Elector/King Frederick III/I and King Frederick William I

Not only did Frederick III/I have to continue to deal with the problem of his half brothers after he ascended the throne, but he also was confronted with a series of legitimacy and succession issues. The greatest legitimacy problem for the first Prussian king was undoubtedly his royal status itself.

We should view Frederick's royal ambitions as part of a wave of aspirations to royal status across Europe at the turn of the eighteenth century.[106] In the late 1690s, Brandenburg-Prussia and Bavaria agreed to support each other's quest for recognition as royalty.[107] Quickly the Hohenzollerns were eclipsed by the Saxon Wettins, when August the Strong became king of Poland in 1697. At the same time, the elector of the Pfalz aspired to become king of Armenia.[108] When the War of Spanish Succession broke out only months after Frederick III's coronation in January 1701, "King Frederick I" became one of many monarchs aspiring to royal status, most of whom were ultimately unsuccessful. King Philip V of Spain was eventually accepted as such, but "James III" of England and "Charles III" of Spain both failed to force acceptance of their claims. Duke Max Emanuel of Bavaria's hopes of becoming king of Sardinia or Naples also came to naught. Duke Victor Amadeus II of Savoy was ultimately recognized as king of Sardinia in 1720, but only after making him king of Lombardy during the war proved diplomatically impossible and only as recompense after Spain successfully ousted him as king of Sicily.

We should view Frederick's coronation in the context of this free-for-all of claims: it would be an error to think it was "unproblematic," "accepted," and "irreversible."[109] Indeed, Frederick's coronation was done at the last minute, during a very brief window of opportunity. Frederick was only able to secure the emperor's tentative promise to recognize him as king at the end of 1700, on the eve of the impending general European war in which the emperor would need Brandenburg-Prussian troops.[110] What resulted was a hastily planned and executed coronation, based on little more than the emperor's tacit approval of Frederick's aspirations.[111] Despite its budget-busting cost, the Prussian coronation did not make the impact that Frederick had hoped it would. It was hardly noticed in France, for example, and even where it was publicized, the media of the day were oblivious to its subtleties.[112] The result was a "failed tradition" that did not take hold—no Prussian king repeated Frederick's coronation ceremony.[113]

Acceptance of Frederick's claim to be a king by the other rulers of Europe was tentative, limited, and belated. The emperor, whose recognition was key to the implementation of Frederick's plans, would acknowledge Frederick only as king *in* Prussia and would continue to disparage Frederick's claims to sovereignty as elector of Brandenburg. William III, Stadtholder of the Netherlands, king of England, and another of Frederick's allies in the coming war, confirmed that he would recognize Frederick's coronation only a couple of weeks beforehand. Saxony-Poland made its recognition contingent upon Brandenburg-Prussia joining the Great Northern War (1700–1721) against Sweden—Frederick did not join the war, and the Polish envoys were conspicuously absent at his coronation.[114] Sweden, for its part, did not recognize Frederick as royalty for over two years.[115] France and Spain, against whom Frederick fought in the War of Spanish Succession, never recognized him as king in his lifetime and recognized Prussia as a kingdom only at the signing of the Peace of Utrecht, two months after his death in 1713.

Frederick William I was the only son of Frederick III/I to survive to adulthood, but it would be wrong to think that the succession was therefore unproblematic. No later than his return from the Rhine front in 1709 did Crown Prince Frederick William become the center of the "crown prince's party" opposing Frederick III/I and his favorite ministers, Johann Casimir Reichsgraf Colbe von Wartenberg and Augustus Reichsgraf von Wittgenstein.[116] Opposition to them had as much to do with personality as policy,[117] but the "reform party" also pushed for changes in royal finances, foreign policy, and the military.[118] As early as 1707 the crown prince's secretary, Ehrenreich Bogislav von Creutz, had been made a member of the king's privy council.[119] In December 1709 Ernst Bogislav von Kameke, another favorite of the crown prince, was pushed into the inner circle of the royal government as "real privy councilor."[120] His appointment was the beginning of the end of Wartenberg and Wittgenstein's (and Frederick III/I's) hold on power in Brandenburg-Prussia.

By the time of Kameke's appointment, the crown prince was the nucleus of a group of officials and generals that opposed the policies of Frederick III/I and his favorites.[121] Throughout 1710, the crown prince's party grew only stronger as the deficiencies of Frederick III/I's regime became more apparent, and, presumably, as the inevitability of the succession made reversionary politics—currying favor with the crown prince—more important.[122] In the autumn and winter of 1710, domestic crises racked Brandenburg-Prussia. A catastrophic outbreak of the plague and poor harvests were depopulating East Prussia, and the royal response had been bungled by Wartenberg and Wittgenstein.[123] Perhaps even worse, the royal finances were in such disarray that Brandenburg-Prussia was nearly bankrupt.[124] The dire situation presented the opportunity and the impetus for Crown Prince Frederick William's party to make sweeping changes.

Crown Prince Frederick William demanded a survey of the government in late summer 1710.[125] Royal officials throughout Brandenburg-Prussia were to report on the conditions in the provinces and make suggestions for improvements. Reports were submitted in early September. In late September, Wittgenstein responded with an improbable report that claimed a dramatic increase in revenues and a tremendous budget surplus.[126] On 1 November 1710 the crown prince's "opposition party" released a memorandum regarding the royal finances.[127] The memorandum foreshadowed the cameralist policies of Frederick William I's reign and aimed at rebuilding the rural economy. Specifically, it focused on the tax burden and the management of the crown's lands. Most importantly, it condemned the work of Frederick III/I's favorites in these regards.[128]

In mid November, Frederick William demanded an investigation of Wittgenstein's claims regarding the royal revenues and budget. The crown prince's insistence on an assessment of Wittgenstein's policies was an accusation of mismanagement against Wartenberg and even against Frederick III/I. The king appointed a favorite of Frederick William to head a commission to investigate the accusations.[129] By late December the commission had uncovered extensive incompetence and widespread corruption. The commission's report condemned Wittgenstein, and by corollary, Wartenberg.[130] Wittgenstein, who was preparing to flee the country, was arrested and paraded through the streets of Berlin to the prison at Spandau.[131] Wartenberg was forced to resign the same day and was immediately relieved of his seal and removed from his quarters in the royal palace.[132] The end of 1710, then, was effectively the end of Frederick III/I's reign. The crown prince and his party had successfully seized power.[133] Deprived of his favorite ministers, Frederick III/I had no one to whom he could turn, and he was forced into quasi-abdication.[134] Essentially, Crown Prince Frederick William set the agenda and ran the day-to-day government in a publicly acknowledged "co-rulership."[135] Contemporary observers could readily see that Frederick III/I ruled in name only.[136]

It was at this point that the radical reforms associated with Frederick William I's reign began, not when he ascended to the throne over two years later.[137] Most conspicuously, expenditures for Frederick III/I's

lavish court were curtailed.[138] Within days of Wittgenstein and Wartenberg's arrest and dismissal, Frederick William's favorites were ordered to
investigate the court's expenses.[139] A reduced budget for the court for
1711 was then issued, followed by a further reduced budget for 1712—
more importantly, the court's expenses were actually limited to the bud-
gets.[140] The other hallmarks of Frederick William I's reign also appeared
before he took the throne. The royal finances were overhauled, and tax
collection was made more efficient.[141] A puritanical program of church
visitations and social policing was also instituted.[142] Furthermore, Frederick William took an active hand in foreign policy matters. As he had
previously argued should have been done, he withdrew Brandenburg-
Prussian troops from the Rhine front of the ongoing War of Spanish
Succession to secure Brandenburg against potential depredations related
to the Great Northern War.[143]

The historiography surrounding the reigns of Frederick III/I and Frederick William I has either ignored the latter's coup against the former
or viewed it as a great step forward. It is not impossible to gloss over
"Wartenberg's fall" completely.[144] Otherwise, the victory of the crown
prince's party has been viewed overwhelmingly positively.[145] Generally,
the crown prince and his "reform party" have been judged much more
capable than Frederick III/I of running Brandenburg-Prussia. The ouster
of the king's favorites and the relegation of the king to comfortable ir-
relevance have been portrayed as a major step toward the development
of the cameralistic bureaucratic state that characterized Frederick William I's reign. The implications for the authority and stability of the
monarchy have been neglected—the sitting king had lost control of his
own court and his own government.

King Frederick William I and King Frederick II

As the only surviving son of Frederick III/I, Frederick William I faced
none of the issues with siblings that his predecessor had. His stepmother
had never had children and had never played an important role at court,
and she had even been sent back to Mecklenburg shortly before Frederick III/I's death.[146] The most serious threats to Frederick William I's
reign from within his own dynasty were the machinations of his queen,
Sophie Dorothea of Braunschweig-Hannover (1687–1757) and later
those of his son. Frederick William I ultimately encountered the same
problem that Frederick III/I did: an aggressively dissenting crown prince.
Historians have generally regarded the notoriously bad relationship between King Frederick William I and Crown Prince Frederick as a tragic

case of bad parenting. At best, there is recognition that Frederick William was concerned for the well-being of the state in the hands of his successor, and that he was frustrated with his eldest son because he feared that as king Frederick would undo his work.[147] In reality, Frederick William feared Frederick's intrigues while he was still crown prince.[148]

Frederick, born in 1712, reached his majority midway through Frederick William I's reign, and the king was a "lame duck" early on because his health was visibly failing by the early 1730s.[149] It was obvious to contemporaries, too, that Frederick's succession to the throne would again bring dramatic changes in Hohenzollern policy, both foreign and domestic. The stark contrast between the cultured, philosophical, and liberal Frederick and his crude, pious, and severe father is well known. Regarding foreign policy, Frederick and his mother were the core of the "English party," which actively opposed the "Austrian party" dominant at Frederick William's court.[150] As in the case of Frederick William and his own father, it was abundantly clear that the crown prince would take things in a very different direction upon his succession.

Frederick's openly critical stance toward his father's rule and the virtual inevitability of the succession meant that an opposition coalesced around him.[151] By 1728 Frederick had his own entourage, and he was meeting with British and French diplomats and discussing the prospect of an "early succession."[152] Although historians have usually treated Frederick William's famously harsh treatment of Frederick only anecdotally, as an impatient and brutal father dealing poorly with his teenaged son, we should understand their problematic relationship as a political conflict within the Hohenzollern dynasty.[153] Frederick William's repeated public denigrations of the crown prince—ordering him to kiss his boots in public, for example—should be viewed as the outward signs of a power struggle between king and crown prince at the Prussian court.[154]

When Crown Prince Frederick began plotting to flee the Hohenzollern lands (and his father's authority) in 1730, the king became aware of his plans but let them proceed.[155] Frederick's plan was doomed, and he was caught immediately. Frederick's attempted escape was not merely a case of a teenager running away from home (as it has often been regarded since), but a preliminary step toward a palace coup.[156] Once outside Brandenburg-Prussia and his father's control, Frederick would have had more leverage politically. It would have been possible to negotiate a reversion with an outside power (as his grandfather had done, unbeknownst to his great-grandfather), potentially adding the threat of foreign intervention to the threat of an early succession.[157]

Frederick William's humiliation and imprisonment of Crown Prince Frederick (and his execution of Frederick's friend and co-conspirator,

Hans Hermann von Katte, for desertion) should be understood as squelch-
ing the opposition party at court, not as merely disciplining a rebellious
adolescent.[158] A primary goal of the many arrests and interrogations following Frederick's arrest was to root out the crown prince's party.[159] Contrary to the Prussian legends, Frederick William dealt with his son coolly
after his capture, and he probably never seriously intended to have Frederick executed for desertion.[160] The real threat that Frederick William
could wield against Frederick was that he would disinherit him and have
him imprisoned for life, and his interrogations of the crown prince seem
to have been conducted with this goal in mind.[161] Despite the proclamation of Frederick III/I that supposedly instituted primogeniture, primogeniture was still not firmly established in Brandenburg-Prussia in the
early eighteenth century.[162] Second-born August Wilhelm (1722–1758)
was Frederick William I's favorite son, and disinheriting Crown Prince
Frederick would have solved several problems for the king.

The reconciliation between Frederick William I and Crown Prince
Frederick followed quickly: after a year under house arrest, Frederick was
rehabilitated.[163] The crown prince was essentially eliminated as a threat
to the king's authority.[164] Frederick was sent to Neuruppin and then
married (to a bride of his father's choosing, see below) and allowed
to establish his own household in Rheinsberg.[165] The stationing of the
crown prince in remote towns meant that he was removed from the
centers of power, Potsdam and Berlin.[166] Once reconciled, Frederick William confirmed Frederick as his sole heir in his testament of 1733, thus
proclaiming primogeniture. Frederick's three younger brothers were
provided with small estates as appanages.[167] Like the Schwedt agnates,
their estates were not sovereign, but income-producing.[168]

In the midst of all this, Frederick William married off four of his
daughters. These marriages were all endogamous, and none of them
was especially prestigious. Three were to other branches of the Hohenzollerns, and the fourth was the other half of crown prince Frederick's
double marriage.[169] Frederick William's marriages for his children have
been the subject of some speculation in the historiography surrounding him. One view is that Frederick William's dynastic strategy was to
keep his children strictly "Prussian," without any conflict of interest, by
marrying them to relatives in minor neighboring principalities.[170] Alter-
natively, Frederick William's "failure" to contract better marriages has
been regarded as a symptom of his general failure to win recognition
on the European diplomatic stage.[171] Given Brandenburg-Prussia's low
ranking among European powers, and given his diplomatic alienation
from the Protestant great power, Britain, it is doubtful that Frederick
William could have done much better for his children, had he wanted

to.[172] More likely, Frederick William's marriage strategy was to dispose of the "biological reserve" that the crown prince's brothers and sisters represented as simply, quickly, and cheaply as possible.[173] Because he had four sons by 1730, Frederick William was presumably confident that the dynastic succession was secure, and his daughters would have become irrelevant for dynastic politics. One of the royal princesses explained the king's marriage strategy: "[Frederick William] gave us to the first available suitors."[174]

Frederick II and His Siblings

Much has been made of the familial and anecdotal aspects of Frederick II's relationship with his siblings, and virtually everything written about his siblings views them in light of their relationships with Frederick. Wilhelmine, especially, has been regarded as Frederick's fellow traveler, perhaps even his female companion of choice (in lieu of his neglected wife).[175] Wilhelmine is best known for her memoirs of her early life, which are often used as a source regarding the reign of Frederick William I (and Frederick's time as crown prince).[176] In a similar way, Heinrich, Frederick's best-known brother, has been alternately ignored and vilified.[177] Just as Wilhelmine is always regarded as Frederick's sister, "one cannot speak of Heinrich without thinking of Frederick."[178] Heinrich has not only been eclipsed almost entirely by his eldest brother in the historiography, but to the extent that he has been considered at all, he has been stained by his opposition to Frederick.[179] The only other sibling of Frederick to receive significant attention has been "the forgotten prince," August Wilhelm.[180]

The rest of Frederick's nine siblings who survived to adulthood are virtually unknown. Despite the historiography's relative neglect, Frederick's siblings posed a number of kinship and succession problems that demanded a variety of solutions. More than anything else, Frederick's handling of his siblings was analogous to his father's handling of him, and comparison of the parallels is a common theme in the historiography.[181] In turn, the king's brothers and sisters responded much as Frederick had responded to Frederick William I: they grew to dislike and oppose him and allied together against him.[182]

The marriages that Frederick contracted for his younger siblings were no great departure from his father's marriage strategy. The best result of this was the marriage of one of Frederick's two unmarried sisters to the future king of Sweden,[183] but his youngest sister never married at all.[184] Frederick contracted marriages for his brothers that would be as unhappy as the marriage that his father had contracted for him.[185] The marriages that Frederick arranged (or allowed) were mostly endogamous. First, he forced Crown Prince August Wilhelm to marry his sister-in-law, which added a third marriage to Frederick and his sister's double marriages to sibling scions of Braunschweig.[186] In 1752 Heinrich, too, was forced into a marriage of Frederick's choice.[187] As had Frederick, Heinrich consented to marry in return for his own household: "I put on the chains of marriage in order to win my freedom."[188] Heinrich ultimately became totally and publicly estranged from his wife, who became part of the queen's court (the queen was already totally and publicly estranged from the king).[189] Frederick would not allow Heinrich a divorce, and the two brothers supposedly competed for same-sex lovers.[190] Frederick allowed his youngest brother, Ferdinand, to marry their niece in 1755—she was the daughter of their sister Sophie and the Schwedt Margrave Friedrich Wilhelm.[191]

Frederick not only continued Frederick William I's marriage "strategy" for his children, but he also provided for his brothers as his father had provided for him. In 1743–1744 Frederick granted each a private estate as an appanage, including an appropriate residence, outside Berlin.[192] August Wilhelm was given Oranienburg, but in the case of Heinrich and Ferdinand, Frederick provided for them exactly as his father had provided for him as crown prince, granting them his own former homes at Rheinsberg and Neuruppin, respectively. Despite their appanage estates, Frederick's younger brothers remained part of his household (and under his tutelage), and they gained their independence only upon their marriages.[193] Because his brothers posed the same threat to him that he had posed to Frederick William I, Frederick's treatment of his brothers was bullying and despotic, as his father's treatment of him had been. As a matter of principle, Frederick did not let his brothers play any role in the state whatsoever.[194] Faced with the threat of opposition centered around his brothers, Frederick struck back.

Early on, denigration at the hands of Frederick prompted Heinrich to threaten to leave Brandenburg-Prussia to enter foreign military service in 1746.[195] When Heinrich's insubordination became a problem, Frederick threatened to remove him from command of his regiment in 1749.[196] Heinrich yielded but had to demonstrate that he was "reasonable" by accepting a bride of his brother's choice.[197] Heinrich anonymously published satiric criticism of Frederick through the 1750s.[198] Frederick's deprecating and suspicious remarks about "princes of the blood" in his political testament of 1752 are often assumed to be aimed at Heinrich.[199]

It was not Heinrich but rather August Wilhelm who was crown prince.[200] Any opposition to Frederick's rule based on reversionary politics would have coalesced around him, and August Wilhelm's criticisms of Frederick's foreign policy in the 1750s provoked the harsh response that he should mind his own affairs.[201] Early in the Seven Years' War (1756–1763), Frederick blamed August Wilhelm for the military debacle following the battle of Kolin, and the crown prince was publicly removed from command and humiliated.[202] Presumably Frederick's dismissal and degradation of his heir apparent destroyed any "crown prince's party," and August Wilhelm died the following year. The year after that, Frederick's youngest brother Ferdinand left the army for "health reasons" and retired from public life.[203]

Heinrich, then, became an opposition figure in the Brandenburg-Prussia of Frederick II after the death of August Wilhelm. Frederick's persecution of August Wilhelm had alienated Heinrich even further—Heinrich wrote to Ferdinand that both August Wilhelm and Frederick were dead to him.[204] Heinrich also found himself in a position akin to that of crown prince during this period. Should Frederick have died or become incapacitated, Heinrich would have become regent for their nephew (August Wilhelm's son), the future King Frederick William II (1744–1797, reigned 1786–1797).[205] Heinrich continued to openly criticize his older brother's conduct of the Seven Years' War, and the resonance of his criticisms among the Prussian officer corps have been viewed by the historiography as putting him at the head of a potential Fronde against Frederick II.[206] Heinrich was well known as an able military commander, the Prussian soldiery was tremendously fond of him, and even foreigners seem to have preferred him to Frederick, so it may well have been that Heinrich was too popular for Frederick to disgrace.[207] By the early 1760s the Seven Years' War was over, the future Frederick William II had reached his majority, and any potential threat to Frederick II's authority had passed.

Conclusion

In retrospect, the spectacular success of the Hohenzollerns and the "rise" of Brandenburg-Prussia have generally obscured the recurring succession crises and the sustained threats to the authority of the "absolute" Hohenzollern rulers from within their own dynasty. The Hohenzollerns were not exempt from the variety of kinship and succession difficulties that vexed other European monarchies from the mid seventeenth to the mid eighteenth century—in fact, the Hohenzollerns seem to have had at least their share. These issues should not be regarded as anecdotal family history, but rather as serious dynastic political problems.

A central issue for the Hohenzollerns (and for each European state during this period) was whether the dynastic lands should be partitioned among the legitimate heirs or kept indivisible at the succession. Although the Hohenzollerns' lands were ultimately passed down through primogeniture at every succession, the options of partitioning the lands (in 1688) or selecting an alternate unigeniture (in Frederick III/I's half brother Philip Wilhelm, or in Frederick II's brother August Wilhelm) existed, and the now familiar "canon" of Brandenburg-Prussian rulers was hardly preordained.

If primogeniture was an answer to one succession problem, then it also created a number of kinship problems for the monarchy.[208] Primogeniture was unpopular among the heirs excluded from the succession, and it created the potential for a power struggle over the succession—hence Frederick III/I's dramatic seizure of power in 1688. A more common concern was that if the crown prince's brothers and sisters were to be excluded from the succession, then they somehow had to be provided for suitably in terms of social status and material well-being. Daughters and sisters had to be married off appropriately, and appanages and suitable marriages arranged for sons and brothers.

Although the coming of age of the Hohenzollern crown prince well before each succession did spare the dynasty the problems of a regency, a chronic issue for the Hohenzollerns (and many other European monarchies during this time) was reversionary politics—the threat posed to the authority and power of the sitting monarch by his own crown prince. The Hohenzollerns' kinship and succession crises reached their climaxes years before the death of each reigning ruler and made the successions themselves anti-climatic. Even the succession in 1688, when Frederick III/I seized power after the Great Elector's death, was less climactic than the preceding crises. Frederick William I had displaced his father already in 1710–1711, rather than in 1713. Frederick II's status as sole successor was already settled by 1733, rather than in 1740. That the successions of Frederick William I and Frederick II were uncontested by 1713 and 1740 does not mean that there had not been critical problems among the Hohenzollerns regarding them.

Avoiding being undermined by one's own heir apparent and the opposition that coalesced around him was a concern for every ruler of Brandenburg-Prussia during this period. Additionally, younger brothers who would have become regents in the case of the death or incapacitation of the ruler became loci of opposition in a similar way (Philip Wilhelm under Frederick III/I, and Heinrich under Frederick II). The success of the rulers of Brandenburg-Prussia in managing (or eliminating) the threat of the "crown prince's party" varied widely. The Great Elector was repeatedly stymied by his crown prince's defiance and his ability to take refuge outside his jurisdiction, and his foreign policy and his orders regarding the succession were critically undermined by his successor. Frederick III/I faced down the threat that his half brother Philip Wilhelm posed as the center of the opposition party at his court, but he ultimately allowed his rule to be completely usurped by his son. Frederick William I's heavy-handed response to the threat to his authority posed by his own son may have effectively solved the immediate problem, but the spectacular imprisonment of the crown prince was hardly an ideal solution to the dilemma of reversionary politics. Frederick's similarly harsh treatment of his younger brothers as potential frondeurs, especially his public degradation of August Wilhelm, should be understood similarly.

Finally, the Hohenzollern dynasty during this period was hardly as stable as has often been assumed. The failure to recognize the tremendous kinship and succession problems that the Hohenzollerns faced during the period commonly thought of as the "rise of Prussia" has skewed our understanding of the development of Brandenburg-Prussia. The notion that successions proceeded smoothly and that kinship problems did not exist has led to a dramatic overestimation of each Hohenzollern ruler's legitimacy and authority on the throne, and a distorted perception of the nature and development of monarchical power in Brandenburg-Prussia.

I owe special thanks to Julia Graham and her staff in the Humboldt State University Library Interlibrary Loan Service for their exertions (and successes) in finding the materials vital for this essay. Special thanks, too, to Dakota Hamilton and John Mangum for reading and critiquing an earlier version of this piece.

Notes

1. I refer to the four rulers of Brandenburg-Prussia on whom I am focusing by their familiar anglicized names (Frederick/Frederick William), but I refer to all other historical figures by their original German names (Johann, Friedrich, Heinrich, etc.).
2. This has not gone entirely unnoticed. Christopher Clark and Peter Baumgart point out the recurring conflicts between fathers and sons, but neglect the relationships (and conflicts) between siblings. See Clark, *The Iron Kingdom: The Rise and Downfall of Prussia, 1600–1947* (Cambridge, MA, 2006), 101; and Peter Baumgart, "Kronprinzenopposition: Friedrich und Friedrich Wilhelm I.," in *Friedrich der Große in seiner Zeit* (*Neue Forschungen zur Brandenburgisch-Preussischen Geschichte 8*), ed. Oswald Hauser (Cologne and Vienna, 1987), 1–16, here 2.
3. Regarding the late and tentative adoption of primogeniture in Protestant Germany especially, see Paula Sutter Fichtner, *Protestantism and Primogeniture in Early Modern Germany* (New Haven, 1989).

4. See Romney Sedgwick, "Introduction," in *Letters from George III to Lord Bute, 1756–1766*, ed. Romney Sedgwick (London, 1939), vii–lxviii.

5. A disadvantage of the early and unambiguous designation of a successor in familial dynasties (as was typical in early modern Europe) was the virtually inevitable tension or conflict between the incumbent ruler and his/her successor. Jack Goody, "Introduction," in *Succession to High Office*, ed. Jack Goody (Cambridge, 1966), 1–56, here 14–15, 45.

6. Karl-Heinz Spieß, "Lordship, Kinship, and Inheritance among the German High Nobility in the Middle Ages and Early Modern Period," in *Kinship in Europe: Approaches to the Long-Term Development (1300–1900)*, ed. David Warren Sabean, Simon Teuscher, and Jon Mathieu (Oxford and New York, 2007), 57–75. It can be debated whether a crown prince's brothers and sisters were assets or liabilities to their dynasty. Fichtner generally describes non-succeeding children as a burden; see Fichtner, *Protestantism and Primogeniture*. Sophie Ruppel generally portrays non-succeeding siblings as useful; see Ruppel's article in this volume and Ruppel, *Verbündete Rivalen: Geschwisterbeziehungen im Hochadel des 17. Jahrhunderts* (Cologne, 2006).

7. See Stefan Hartmann, "Der Thronwechsel als Krise und Entwicklungschance am Beispiel des Kurfürstentums Brandenburg," in *Aus der Arbeit des Geheimen Staatsarchivs Preußischer Kulturbesitz* ed. Jürgen Kloosterhuis (Berlin, 1996), 3–15, here 6.

8. Because this did not divide the Kurmark (the lands associated with the electoral title), this partition did not run afoul of the Golden Bull of 1356, which declared primogeniture in the electoral territories. Spieß, "Lordship, Kinship, and Inheritance."

9. Johann Georg had one son from his first marriage and six more sons from his third marriage.

10. Hartmann, "Der Thronwechsel als Krise," 6–8.

11. Frederick William's younger brother, Johann Sigismund (1624–1624), died as an infant. Regarding his sisters and his relationships with them, see Sophie Ruppel's contribution to this volume and Ruppel, *Verbündete Rivalen*. His older sister, Luise Charlotte (1617–1676), was married to the Duke of Courland (Jakob, 1610–1681) in 1645. His younger sister, Hedwig Sophie (1623–1683), was married to the Landgraf (Earl) of Hesse (William VI, "The Just," 1629–1663) in 1649.

12. Regarding Schwarzenberg (1583–1641), see Ernst Opgenoorth, *Friedrich Wilhelm: Der Große Kurfürst von Brandenburg. Eine politische Biographie*, vol. 1: *1620–1660* (Göttingen, 1971), 80–88.

13. Ibid., 39–41.

14. Ibid., 41–44.

15. Ibid., 50.

16. Suffice it to say that in this case, as in all of the cases discussed here, the emotional and political relationships and conflicts between family members were intertwined and interconnected. See Hans Medick and David Sabean, "Emotionen und materielle Interessen in Familie und Verwandtschaft: Überlegungen zu neuen Wegen und Bereichen einer historischen und sozialanthropologischen Familienforschung," in *Emotionen und materielle Interessen: Sozialanthropologische und historische Beiträge zur Familienforschung*, ed. Medick and Sabean (Göttingen, 1984), 27–54.

17. Leopold von Ranke, *Preußische Geschichte, 1415–1871*, ed. Hans-Joachim Shoeps (Mühltal, 1981), 70.

18. Clark, *Iron Kingdom*, 101. After his return Frederick William became, in a sense, the "banished heir," whose involvement (and interference) in government was disallowed in order to lessen tensions between the incumbent and successor. See Goody, *Succession to High Office*, 23.

19. Barbara Beuys, *Der Große Kurfürst: Der Mann, der Preußen schuf. Biographie* (Reinbek bei Hamburg, 1979).

20. For example, Linda Frey and Marsha Frey, *Frederick I: The Man and His Times* (Boulder, 1984), 1–2; Heinz Duchhardt, "'Petite Majesté' oder unterschätzter Architekt? Ein Barockfürst in seiner Zeit," in Deutsches Historisches Musem (Katalog), *Preußen 1701: Eine Europäische Geschichte*, vol. 2 (Berlin, 2001), 47–56, here 47; Peter Baumgart, "Ein neuer König in Europa: Interne Planung, diplomatische Vorbereitung und internationale Anerkennung der Standeserhöhung des brandenburgischen Kurfürsten" in *Preußen 1701*, vol. 2, 166–176, here 166; and especially Johannes Kunisch, "Friedrich der Große und die preußische Königskrönung von 1701" (Paderborn, 2002), reprinted in *Dreihundert Jahre Preußische Königskrönung: Eine Tagungsdokumentation*, ed. Kunisch (Berlin, 2002), 265–284.

21. Frederick William married his first wife, Louise of Orange (1627–1667), in 1646, and his second wife, Dorothea of Holstein (1636–1689), in 1667.

22. See Julius Großmann, "Jugendgeschichte Friedrich I.: Erste König in Preußen," *Hohenzollern Jahrbuch* 4 (1900): 19–59, here 48–50. Heinrich Jobst Graf von Wintzingerode's forthcoming doctoral dissertation will address this issue specifically in a section titled "Giftmischerin und böse Stiefmutter?" He will convincingly argue that Crown Prince Frederick had an amicable relationship with his stepmother early on, and that he even appealed to her to smooth over his relationship with his father. Graf von Wintzingerode, "Preussens Erste Prinzen von Geblüt: Die Markgrafen von Brandenburg-Schwedt" (PhD Dissertation, Freie Universität Berlin, forthcoming, 2009). Again, it is clear that the conflict between father and son defies categorization as either emotional or political. See Medick and Sabean, "Emotionen und materiellen Interessen."

23. Johann Gustav Droyson, *Friedrich I., König in Preußen* (Berlin and New York, 2001), 14; and Ernst Opgenoorth, *Friedrich Wilhelm: Der Große Kurfürst von Brandenburg. Eine politische Biographie*, vol. 2: *1660–1688* (Göttingen, 1978), 319.

24. Frey and Frey, *Frederick I*, 43; and Ernst Daniel Martin Kirchner, "Dorothea von Holstein-Glücksburg, zweite Gemahlin des grossen Churfürsten Friedrich Wilhelm, geb. 1636, verm. 1668, X 1689," in Ernst Daniel Martin Kirchner, *Die Churfürstinnen und Königinnen auf dem Throne der Hohenzollern: im Zusammenhang mit ihren Familien- und Zeit-Verhältnissen; aus dem Quellen.* vol. 2 (Berlin, 1866), 302–340, here 330.

25. Werner Schmidt, *Friedrich I., Kurfürst von Brandenburg, König in Preußen* (Munich, 1996), 61–62; Derek McKay, *The Great Elector* (Harlow, 2001), 262; and Hans-Joachim Neumann, *Friedrich I.: Der erste König der Preußen* (Berlin, 2001), 49.

26. Ludwig Hüttl, *Friedrich Wilhelm von Brandenburg: der Große Kurfürst, 1620–1688. Eine politische Biographie* (Munich, 1981), 479.

27. Kirchner, "Dorothea," 330; and Schmidt, *Friedrich I.*, 64, 74.

28. Opgenoorth, *Friedrich Wilhelm, Zweiter Teil*, 319; and Frey and Frey, *Frederick I*, 43.

29. Kirchner, "Dorothea," 331.

30. McKay, *The Great Elector*, 238–239.

31. Schmidt, *Friedrich I.*, 75.

32. Ibid.

33. Opgenoorth, *Friedrich Wilhelm, Zweiter Teil*, 319; Schmidt, *Friedrich I.*, 73–74; McKay, *The Great Elector*, 255.

34. Schmidt, *Friedrich I.*, 74.

35. There is no credible evidence that Dorothea actually poisoned anyone (quite the contrary), but the fact remains that she was undeniably suspected of having done so. Graf von Wintzingerode, "Preussens Erste Prinzen von Geblüt."

36. McKay, *The Great Elector*, 238; Hüttl, *Friedrich Wilhelm von Brandenburg*, 478; and F. R. Paulig, *Friedrich I., König in Preußen: Ein Beitrag zur Geschichte seines Lebens, seines Hofes und seiner Zeit* (Frankfurt an der Oder, 1887), 10.

37. Kirchner, "Dorothea," 315.

38. Cases of poisoning in Paris and Versailles involving the French court in the mid to late 1670s, including the conviction and execution of serial poisoners, were well publicized. See Schmidt, *Friedrich I.*, 58.

39. Paulig, *Friedrich I.*, 10.

40. Neumann, *Friedrich I.*, 39; Frey and Frey, *Frederick I*, 37; and Schmidt, *Friedrich I.*, 58.

41. Though Ruppel does note that the correspondence between Frederick William and Hedwig Sophie was "not personal," she does not address this episode of their relationship in *Verbundete Rivalen*, 307–308.

42. Kirchner, "Dorothea," 329.

43. Paulig, *Friedrich I.*, 19; Kirchner, "Dorothea," 330; Frey and Frey, *Frederick I*, 32; and Neumann, *Friedrich I.*, 38.

44. Hüttl, *Friedrich Wilhelm von Brandenburg*, 480; Frey and Frey, *Frederick I*, 32; and Kirchner, "Dorothea," 330.

45. McKay, *The Great Elector*, 236.

46. Neumann, *Friedrich I.*, 45; and Schmidt, *Friedrich I.*, 63.

47. Hüttl, *Friedrich Wilhelm von Brandenburg*, 480; Paulig, *Friedrich I.*, 20; and Frey and Frey, *Frederick I*, 33.

48. This was Friedrich August, who died in January 1686.

49. Paulig, *Friedrich I.*, 33–35; and Frey and Frey, *Frederick I*, 36.

50. Opgenoorth, *Friedrich Wilhelm, Zweiter Teil*, 321.

51. Bruno Gloger, *Friedrich Wilhelm, Kurfürst von Brandenburg. Biografie* (Berlin, 1985), 342.

52. Paulig, *Friedrich I.*, 36.

53. Opgenoorth, *Friedrich Wilhelm, Zweiter Teil*, 322; and Neumann, *Friedrich I.*, 53. It has been explained that the medical doctors in whose care Ludwig died did not want to admit to malpractice and therefore blamed poison for his death. Beuys, *Der Große Kurfürst*, 396.

54. Beuys, *Der Große Kurfürst*, 396.

55. Instead, Frederick and Sophie Charlotte took refuge in Kassel.

56. Opgenoorth, *Friedrich Wilhelm, Zweiter Teil*, 323; and Beuys, *Der Große Kurfürst*, 397.

57. Sophie Charlotte gave birth to an unnamed stillborn son in October 1687. Opgenoorth, *Friedrich Wilhelm, Zweiter Teil*, 322–323; Gloger, *Friedrich Wilhelm*, 342; Beuys, *Der Große Kurfürst*, 397; and Neumann, *Friedrich I.*, 55. The Great Elector and his wife had never liked Frederick's second wife, and Dorothea had scandalously questioned her virginity at the time of their marriage. Frey and Frey, *Frederick I*, 36.

58. Gloger, *Friedrich Wilhelm*, 344; and Neumann, *Friedrich I.*, 54.

59. Gerhard Oestreich, *Friedrich Wilhelm, Der Große Kurfürst* (Göttingen, 1971), 97; Gloger, *Friedrich Wilhelm*, 344; McKay, *The Great Elector*, 240; and Neumann, *Friedrich I.*, 54.

60. Clark, *Iron Kingdom*, 102.

61. Hans Hallmann, "Die letztwillige Verfügung im Hause Brandenburg 1415–1740," *Forschungen zur brandenburgischen und preussischen Geschichte* 37 (1925): 1–30, here 20.

62. Opgenoorth, *Friedrich Wilhelm, Zweiter Teil*, 317; and Frey and Frey, *Frederick I*, 41.

63. Thomas Fuchs, "Dynastische Politik, symbolische Repräsentation und Standeserhöhung. Die preußische Königskrönung 1701," in *Von Kurfürstentum zum "Königreich*

der Landstriche." Brandenburg-Preußen im Zeitalter von Absolutismus und Aufklärung, ed. Günther Lottes (Berlin, 2004), 15–35, here 31; and Schmidt, *Friedrich I.,* 59.

64. Kirchner, "Dorothea," 319.

65. Schmidt, *Friedrich I.,* 59; and Hartmann, "Der Thronwechsel als Krise," 11.

66. Not just Halberstadt but also Minden and Ravensberg would have been left to Frederick's younger brother and half brothers. Hallmann, "Die letzzwillige Verfügung," 22.

67. Schmidt, *Friedrich I.,* 60; and Frey and Frey, *Frederick I,* 40.

68. *"Streit in der Familie"* is the title of Gloger's section. Conflict and reconciliation among family members is a constant theme. Great emphasis is laid on Ludwig's last hours, in which he begged his father to visit him but Frederick William, believing Ludwig was improving, refused to see him.

69. "… ein schwer verständlicher Schritt, letzten Endes eine Äusserung der unausrechenbaren Individualität, die man nur feststellen, nicht mehr erklären kann." Hallmann, "Die letzzwillige Verfügung," 22.

70. Hans-Joachim Neumann, *Friedrich Wilhelm der Große Kurfürst: Der Sieger von Fehrbellin, mit 63 Abbildungen* (Berlin, 1995), 172.

71. *"Mütterliche Schwäche"* is Kirchner's term, see Kirchner, "Dorothea," 328. See also Gloger, *Friedrich Wilhelm,* 340; Hüttl, *Friedrich Wilhelm von Brandenburg,* 478; Opgenoorth, *Friedrich Wilhelm, Zweiter Teil,* 318; Oestreich, *Friedrich Wilhelm,* 96–97; and Clark, *Iron Kingdom,* 102. The "revision" of this view is to point out that Frederick William's 1664 testament was already going to divide his lands among his sons from his first marriage, before he married Dorothea or had sons with her. Hence it was not the "motherly weakness" of Dorothea, but rather that of his first wife, Louise of Orange. Frey and Frey, *Frederick I,* 39; and Schmidt, *Friedrich I.,* 59. In a notable exception to the above excuses, Paulig attempts to rehabilitate the Great Elector by arguing that the "partition" was not a partition at all. Arguing from the perspective that Frederick William "the state-builder" would never have destroyed it with a partition, he asserts that primogeniture would have been in effect, and that the secondogeniture territories would not have been sovereign, but merely appanages. Paulig, *Friedrich I.,* 25–26. Paulig's argument has been effectively refuted by Opgenoorth, who explains that the younger brothers would have ruled in their own names and received oaths from the officials in their territories. Opgenoorth, *Friedrich Wilhelm, Zweiter Teil,* 318.

72. See Spieß, "Lordship, Kinship, and Inheritance."

73. It seems more reasonable to attribute this to Frederick's unwillingness to share the succession with his half brothers than to claim that Frederick was the inventor of the modern concept of the indivisible state, as Hallmann does: see Hallmann, "Die letztwillige Verfügung," 24.

74. Neumann, *Friedrich I.,* 58; and Oestreich, *Friedrich Wilhelm,* 98.

75. Frederick tried to wriggle out of the Schwiebus reversion after he successfully ascended the throne. This was not a pressing issue during the Nine Years' War, while the emperor was dependent on Prussian troops. Only in 1695 did Frederick turn over Schwiebus and the emperor officially recognize Frederick's primogeniture. Paulig, *Friedrich I.,* 30–31.

76. Beuys, *Der Große Kurfurst,* 403. Concealing the death of a ruler until his successor can consolidate his own rule is not uncommon, see Goody, *Succession to Higher Office,* 10, 19.

77. Paulig, *Friedrich I.,* 41; Beuys, *Der Große Kurfurst,* 403; and Neumann, *Friedrich I.,* 58.

78. McKay, *The Great Elector*, 262.
79. This was the Abkommen von Potsdam, 13 March 1692. Graf Wintzingerode's forth-coming doctoral dissertation will address this specifically in a section titled "Der Rezeß von 1692: Grundgesetz der Schwedter Hohenzollern?" Graf Wintzingerode, "Preussens Erste Prinzen von Geblüt." This kind of disposal of non-succeeding broth-ers is common; see Goody, *Succession to High Office*, 29–31.
80. Fichtner, *Protestantism and Primogeniture*, passim.
81. Udo Geiseler, "'Daß ich nicht allein sein Vater, sondern auch sein König und Herr sey.' — Die Beziehungen der Margraves von Brandenburg-Schwedt zu den Hohen-zollernkönigen im 18. Jahrhundert," in *Pracht und Herrlichkeit: Adlig-fürstliche Leb-ensstile im 17. und 18. Jahrhundert*, ed. Peter-Michael Hahn and Hellmut Lorenz (Potsdam, 1998), 45–93, here 49.
82. Philip Wilhelm and Albrecht's sons were the "Philippine" and "Albertine" lines of Markgräfen. Albrecht's two sons who survived to adulthood died in the 1740s with-out producing male heirs. Frederick III/I's younger half brothers, Karl Philip (1673–1695) and Christian Ludwig (1677–1734), produced no male heirs. Karl Philip was killed by agents of Frederick. Karl Philip, campaigning in Italy during the Nine Years' War, eloped with an Italian princess. Frederick did not approve of Karl's marriage and ordered his arrest. Karl was mortally wounded in the ensuing scuffle. Paulig, *Friedrich I.*, 48–49.
83. The agnate line died out in 1788 with the last male heir, Heinrich Friedrich, and Schwedt reverted to the main Hohenzollern line.
84. Geiseler, "Daß ich nicht allein sein Vater," 45–46, 73.
85. Goody, *Succession to High Office*, 34.
86. Geiseler, "Daß ich nicht allein sein Vater," 50.
87. Johanna Charlotte von Anhalt-Dessau (1682–1750). "Alt Dessau" was a Branden-burg-Prussian general (later field marshall) who became a major force at court. Friedrich von Oppeln-Bronikowski, *Der Alte Dessauer: Fürst Leopold von Anhalt-Dessau: Eine Studie seines Lebens und Wirkens* (Potsdam, 1936).
88. Geiseler, "Daß ich nicht allein sein Vater," 54–56.
89. Ibid., 58. Frederick William I's grasp of the value of ceremony has been greatly un-derestimated. See Marschke, "'Von dem am Königl. Preußischen Hofe abgeschafften *Ceremoniel*': Monarchical Representation and Court Ceremony in Frederick William I's Prussia," in *Orthodoxies and Diversity in Early Modern Germany*, ed. Randolph C. Head and Daniel Christensen (Boston, 2007), 227–252.
90. Geiseler, "Daß ich nicht allein sein Vater," 57–59.
91. Ibid., 64–65. That there was no evidence of any political activities is not as impor-tant as Frederick William's clear understanding that such activities would pose a threat.
92. Ibid., 60, 77.
93. Ibid., 76.
94. Ibid., 69, 74.
95. Margrave Friedrich Wilhelm married Princess Sophie Dorothea Marie (1719–1765). Ibid., 61–62.
96. Marrying one's daughters to agnates was common in early modern Europe as a means of ensuring that should the succession fall to the agnate line, then one's grandchild could ultimately succeed to the throne. Spieß, "Lordship, Kinship, and Inheritance." This arrangement would have meant that should the succession have somehow fallen to the Schwedt line, then it could have ultimately been a grandson of Frederick William (by his daughter) who would succeed to the throne.

97. Friederike Dorothee Sophie (1736–1798) married Friedrich Eugen of Würtemburg (1732–1797), and Philippine Auguste Amalie (1745–1800) married Friedrich II of Hessen-Kassel (1720–1785, reigned 1760–1785). Geiseler, "Daß ich nicht allein sein Vater," 63.
98. Anna Elisabeth Luise (1738–1820) married Ferdinand (1730–1813). Ibid., 63.
99. Heinrich Friedrich married Leopoldine Marie of Anhalt-Dessau (1716–1782). This clandestine "alliance" enraged King Frederick William I because he saw in Heinrich Friedrich's marriage a willful defiance of his own authority as Heinrich Friedrich's military commander and head of the house of Hohenzollern. "Der alte Dessauer," head of the Prussian infantry and a favorite of the king, presented the news of his daughter's marriage to his nephew to the king as a fait accompli. Ibid., 62–63. The grounds for the king's displeasure was not the union of the Anhalt-Dessau and Brandenburg-Schwedt lines, but rather the low status of Leopoldine Marie, who was a commoner. Graf von Wintzingerode, "Preussens Erste Prinzen von Geblüt."
100. Geiseler, "Daß ich nicht allein sein Vater," 81. Luise Henriette Wilhelmine (1750–1811) married Leopold III of Anhalt-Dessau (1740–1817, reigned 1751–1817).
101. Regarding Frederick's comments, see below. Ibid., 47.
102. Ibid., 58.
103. Ibid., 65–66.
104. Ibid., 67–68.
105. Frederick II created a royal judicial council specifically to deal with the endemic legal issues in Schwedt in 1755. When Margrave Friedrich Wilhelm protested at the intrusion of the royal judicial apparatus in his estates, Frederick II made it even worse: he ordered that the council be housed in the margrave's palace in Schwedt and paid for by the margrave. When the margrave initially refused to cooperate, Frederick threatened to send Prussian troops to carry out his orders. Ibid., 71–72.
106. Baumgart, "Ein neuer König in Europa," 166; and Marschke, "Von dem am Königl. Preußischen Hofe abgeschafften Ceremoniel."
107. Fuchs, "Dynastische Politik," 33.
108. Ibid.
109. Duchhardt incorrectly describes the coronation this way. Heinz Duchhardt, "Die preußischen Nicht-Krönungen nach 1701," in Dreihundert Jahre Preußische Königskrönung: Eine Tagungsdokumentation, ed. Johannes Kunisch (Berlin, 2002), 257–263, here 261. Instead, see Barbara Stollberg-Rilinger, "Höfische Öffentlichkeit: Zur zeremoniellen Selbstdarstellung des brandenburgischen Hofes vor dem europäischen Publikum," Forschungen zur brandenburgischen-preußischen Geschichte, Neue Folge 7, no. 2 (1997): 145–176, here 172–173.
110. Baumgart, "Ein neuer König in Europa," 171–172.
111. Ibid., 173.
112. See Christophe Duhamelle, "Die Krönung von 1701 und ihre Wahrnehmung in Frankreich," in Preußen 1701: Eine Europäische Geschichte, vol. 2 (Berlin, 2001), 240–246; and Manfred Wichmann, "Die Rezeption der Krönungsfeiern 1701 in der Zeitgenössischen Presse," in Preußen 1701, 237–239, here 239.
113. Sebastian Olden-Jørgensen, "Ceremonial Interaction across the Baltic around 1700: The 'Coronations' of Charles XII (1697), Frederick IV (1700) and Frederick III/I (1701)," Scandinavian Journal of History 28, no. 3/4 (December 2004): 243–251; and Duchhardt, "Die preußischen Nicht-Krönungen nach 1701."
114. Baumgart, "Ein neuer König in Europa," 174–175.
115. Ibid., 175.

116. Friedrich von Oppeln-Bronikowski actually titles this section of his biography of Frederick William I "Der Kronprinz und die Kronprinzenpartei." Oppeln-Bronikowski, *Der Baumeister des preussischen Staates: Leben und Wirken des Soldatenkönigs Friedrich Wilhelms I.* (Jena, 1934), 47–65. Carl Hinrichs titles this section of his biography of Frederick William I "Der Kronprinz im Mittelpunkt der Opposition." Hinrichs, *Friedrich Wilhelm I., König in Preußen: Eine Biographie, Jugend und Aufstieg,* 2nd ed. (Hamburg, 1941), 454–457. Wartenberg (1643–1712) and Wittgenstein (1663–1735) functioned as prime minister and as general director of the royal domains, respectively. See especially Hinrichs, *Friedrich Wilhelm I.,* 454ff.

117. Hinrichs, *Friedrich Wilhelm I.,* 454.

118. *Reformpartei* is Oppeln-Bronikowski's term. Oppeln-Bronikowski, *Der Baumeister des preussischen Staates,* 58.

119. Creutz (1670–1733) became a *Rat* in the *Geheime Hofkammer.* Hinrichs, *Friedrich Wilhelm I.,* 455.

120. Kameke (1664–1726) became a *wirkliche Geheime Rat.* Kameke was an enemy of Wartenberg and would later become a major figure in Frederick William's government. Ibid., 455.

121. This included not only Creutz and Kameke, but also Marquard Ludwig von Printz (1675–1725), Werner Wilhelm von Blaspil (d. 18th century), and General Friedrich Wilhelm von Grumbkow (1678–1739), all of whom would play major roles in Frederick William I's government. Ibid., 456.

122. Especially important was the addition of Heinrich Rüdiger von Ilgen (1654–1735), a member of the privy council for war (Geheime Kriegsrat). Ibid., 454–455.

123. A third of the population of East Prussia died in the catastrophe of 1709–1710. Ibid., 457.

124. The tax burden on the peasantry was crushing, and the rents on the royal domains did not even cover the cost of administering them. Ibid., 458–459.

125. Droyson, *Friedrich I.,* 245.

126. Ibid., 245; and Hinrichs, *Friedrich Wilhelm I.,* 473.

127. Hinrichs also uses the term *Gegenpartei.* Hinrichs, *Friedrich Wilhelm I.,* 475.

128. Ibid., 475–476.

129. Ilgen selected Creutz and Blaspil to be part of the commission, and Creutz wrote the commission's report. Ibid., 478.

130. Ibid., 481.

131. Ibid., 482. The following May Wittgenstein paid a heavy fine and was banished to his remote estates. Ibid., 486–487.

132. It was Ilgen who asked Wartenberg to resign, relieved him of his seal, and removed him from his quarters in the palace. He, too, was released and banished from Berlin. Ibid., 482–486.

133. Ibid., 491; Oppeln-Bronikowski, *Der Baumeister des preussischen Staates,* 58; and Heinz Kathe, *Der "Soldatenkönig": Friedrich Wilhelm I, 1688–1740. König in Preußen — Eine Biographie* (Cologne, 1981), 28.

134. Oppeln-Bronikowski, *Der Baumeister des preussischen Staates,* 58.

135. *"Mitherrschaft"* is Hinrichs's term. Hinrichs, *Friedrich Wilhelm I.,* 491. It is common in such arrangements that the successor edges out the incumbent; see Goody, *Succession to High Office,* 13, 24.

136. Hinrichs says that Frederick III/I enjoyed only a *"unmerklichen Bevormundung."* Hinrichs, *Friedrich Wilhelm I.,* 492. This is more accurate than Baumgart's portrayal of Frederick William's *"in loyaler Opposition ausgetragenen Dissens."* Baumgart, "Kronprinzenopposition," 2.

137. Droyson, *Friedrich I.*, 249; and Hinrichs, *Friedrich Wilhelm I.*, 492.
138. Oppeln-Bronikowski, *Der Baumeister des preussischen Staates*, 57.
139. Kameke and Printz were assigned to do this. Hinrichs, *Friedrich Wilhelm I.*, 494.
140. Hinrichs, *Friedrich Wilhelm I.*, 494–495.
141. Oppeln-Bronikowski, *Der Baumeister des preussischen Staates*, 57; and Hinrichs, *Friedrich Wilhelm I.*, 499–501.
142. Oppeln-Bronikowski, *Der Baumeister des preussischen Staates*, 57.
143. Hinrichs, *Friedrich Wilhelm I.*, 511–513.
144. For example, Friedrich Christoph Förster, in his foundational three-volume biography of Frederick William I, never mentions this at all. Much later, Robert Ergang and Hans-Joachim Neumann's biographies never mention it, either. Wolfgang Venohr's biography of Frederick William only mentions that Wartenberg was forced to resign—in one line. See Förster, *Friedrich Wilhelm I., König von Preußen*, 3 vols. (Potsdam, 1834–1835); Ergang, *The Potsdam Führer: Frederick William I, Father of Prussian Militarism* (New York, 1941); Neumann, *Friedrich Wilhelm I.: Leben und Leiden des Soldatenkönigs* (Berlin, 1993); Venohr, *Friedrich Wilhelm I.: Preußens Soldatenkönig* (Munich, 2001), previously published as Venohr, *Der Soldatenkönig: Revolutionär auf dem Thron* (Frankfurt am Main, 1988), 93.
145. See especially Droyson, *Friedrich I.*; Hinrichs, *Friedrich Wilhelm I.*; and Oppeln-Bronikowski, *Der Baumeister des preussischen Staates*.
146. Frederick William I was the son of Frederick III/I's second wife, Sophie Charlotte of Hannover. After her death in 1705, Frederick married a third time to Sophie Luise of Mecklenburg-Schwerin (1685–1735). Sophie Luise's mental illness was the reason for her return to Mecklenburg.
147. Hinrichs, "Der Konflict zwischen Friedrich Wilhelm I. und Kronprinz Friedrich," in *Preussen als historisches Problem: Gesammelte Abhandlungen*, ed. Gerhard Oestreich (Berlin, 1964), 185–202, here 189ff.; reprinted from Hinrichs, *Der Kronprinzenprozeß: Friedrich und Katte* (Hamburg, 1936), 5–20.
148. Baumgart, "Kronprinzenopposition," 6–7; and Detlef Merten, *Der Katte-Prozeß: Vortrag gehalten vor der Berliner Juristischen Gesellschaft am 14. February 1979*. Schriftenreihe der juristische Gesellschaft e.V., no. 62 (Berlin and New York, 1980), 11–12.
149. Frederick William first experienced an attack of porphyria, the disease that would ultimately kill him, in 1729. During an attack of the disease in 1734, even Frederick William thought that his death was imminent; he had a mausoleum built for himself in the Potsdam Garrison Church. Regarding the king's worsening health and porphyria, see Ida MacAlpine, Richard Hunter, and C. Rimington, "Porphyria in the Royal Houses of Stuart, Hanover, and Prussia: A Follow-up Study of George III's Illness," *British Medical Journal* 5583 (6 January 1968): 7–18; and Claus A. Pierach and Erich Jennewein, "Friedrich Wilhelm I. und Porphyrie," *Sudhoffs Archiv* 83, no. 1 (1999): 50–66.
150. See Wilhelm Oncken, "Sir Charles Hotham und Friedrich Wilhelm I. im Jahre 1730: Urkundliche Ausschlüsse aus den Archiven zu London und Wien," *Forschungen zur Brandenburgischen und Preußischen Geschichte* 7 (1894): 377–407; and Gerhard Simon, "Der Prozeß gegen den Thronfolger in Rußland (1718) and in Preußen (1730): Carevic Aleksej und Kronprinz Friedrich," *Jahrbücher für Geschichte Osteuropas* 36, no. 2 (1988), 218–247, here 231.
151. Hinrichs, "Der Konflikt," 195–196; and Simon, "Der Prozeß," 229–230.
152. Merten, "Der Katte-Prozeß," 23, 26.
153. Once again, political interest and emotion seem to have been intertwined and interconnected. See Medick and Sabean, "Emotionen und materielle Interessen."

154. Simon, "Der Prozeß," 230–231. Ironically, Frederick William seems to have tried to represent his relationship with his own father as ideal by repeatedly contrasting his supposed obedience and veneration of Frederick III/I with Crown Prince Frederick's insubordination and contempt toward him.

155. Simon, " Der Prozeß," 232; Merten, "Der Katte-Prozeß," 9.

156. Merten, "Der Katte-Prozeß," 23–24.

157. Hinrichs, "Der Konflikt," 200; Merten, "Der Katte-Prozeß," 23. Peter I of Russia dealt with a similar situation in 1718 by imprisoning, torturing, and ultimately killing his eldest son for having fled abroad. Simon, "Der Prozeß."

158. Frederick William seems to have concluded that the only appropriate punishment for Katte (1704–1730) was execution. A "lifelong" imprisonment or exile would have lasted only until the succession of the crown prince, as in the case of another of Frederick's co-conspirators, Peter Christoph Karl von Keith. Keith fled to England in 1730, was tried *in absentia* and executed in effigy, but then promptly returned to Prussia in 1740. Merten, "Der Katte-Prozeß," 9–10, 40, 43.

159. Simon, "Der Prozeß," 240; Merten, "Der Katte-Prozeß," 11–12, 23–24, 40.

160. Even the execution of Katte had been quite unpopular within the officer corps of Frederick William I's army. The crown prince's execution would have had serious negative repercussions for Brandenburg-Prussia's image. Simon, "Der Prozeß," 242–244.

161. Merten, "Der Katte-Prozeß," 44; and Gerhard Ritter, *Frederick the Great: A Historical Profile*, trans. Peter Paret (Berkeley, 1968), 29–30.

162. Frederick II's lengthy arguments in favor of primogeniture in his *Mémoires pour servir à l'Histoire de la Maison de Brandenbourg* make this clear. See Brunhilde Wehinger, "Denkwürdigkeiten des Hauses Brandenburg. Friedrich der Große als Autor der Geschichte seiner Dynastie," in *Von Kurfürstentum zum "Königreich der Landstriche": Brandenburg-Preußen im Zeitalter von Absolutismus und Aufklärung*, ed. Günther Lottes (Berlin, 2004), 137–174, here 156.

163. Frederick ran away and was captured and imprisoned at Kustrin in August 1730. Katte was executed in November. Frederick returned to Berlin for the first time in November 1731 for the marriage of his sister Wilhelmina (1709–1758).

164. Frederick William kept Frederick under surveillance for the remainder of his reign, but Frederick never presented a serious threat again. Ritter, *Frederick the Great*, 37–38.

165. Frederick and his sister, Philippine Charlotte (1717–1801) both married into the ruling house of Braunschweig-Lüneburg in 1733. Frederick married Elisabeth Christina (1715–1797) and Philippine Charlotte married Karl (1713–1780). By all accounts these were not prestigious marriages for Brandenburg-Prussia.

166. This is another instance of the "banished heir," wherein the heir apparent's involvement (and interference) in government is disallowed in order to lessen tensions between ruler and successor. See Goody, *Succession to High Office*, 23. In this case, even Frederick's "banishment" could not entirely eliminate reversionary politics. Frederick William's foremost minister, Friedrich Wilhelm von Grumbkow (1678–1739), carried on a secret correspondence with the crown prince, and the Holy Roman emperor selected envoys to Prussia who might appeal to the crown prince. See Frederick II, King of Prussia, *Briefwechsel Friedrichs des Grossen mit Grumbkow und Maupertius, 1731–1759*, ed. Reinhold Koser [1898] (Osnabrück, 1966); and Gustav Berthold Volz, "Die Politik Friedrichs des Großen vor und nach seiner Thronbesteigung," *Historische Zeitschrift* 151 (1935): 486–527.

167. This is another instance of the disposal of non-succeeding brothers. Goody, *Succession to High Office*, 29–31.

168. August Wilhelm was to inherit Wusterhausen, Heinrich (1726–1802) was to inherit Niegripp, and Ferdinand (1730–1813) was to inherit the Mansfeldischen *Güter*. Each princess was left 30,000 Rthl. Geheimes Staatsarchiv Preussischer Kulturbesitz (GStA PK) Brandenburg-Preußisches Haus (BPH), Repository 46, File K 14b, "Rein Concepte der Donations Urkunden d.d. 1. Septbr. 1733 für die nachgeborenen Königl. Prinzen…"
169. In 1729 Friederike Luise (1714–1784) was married to Margrave Karl of Brandenburg-Ansbach (1712–1757). In 1731 Wilhelmine (1709–1758) was married to Friedrich of Brandenburg-Bayreuth (1711–1763). In 1733 Philippine Charlotte was married off as half of the aforementioned double marriage to Karl of Braunschweig. In 1734 Sophie (1719–1765) was married to the aforementioned Schwedt margrave, Friedrich Wilhelm.
170. Ritter, *Frederick the Great*, 35.
171. Peter-Michael Hahn, "Pracht und Selbstinszenierung. Die Hofhaltung Friedrich Wilhelms I. von Preußen," in *Der Soldatenkönig: Friedrich Wilhelm I. in seiner Zeit*, ed. Friedrich Beck and Julius H. Schoeps (Potsdam, 2003), 69–98, here 87.
172. On Brandenburg-Prussia's status among other European states, see Duhamelle, "Die Krönung von 1701," 244. Especially the crushing of the (entirely unrealistic) hopes for a double marriage between the crown princes of Prussia and Great Britain and each other's sisters has been misjudged a failure of Frederick William's international diplomacy. See Oncken, "Sir Charles Hotham," passim.
173. This disposal of the sisters of the crown prince, especially, stands in marked contrast to the "usefulness" of siblings that Ruppel postulates. See Ruppel, *Verbundete Rivalen*. The endogamous marriage of daughters, again, would have been good dynastic politics, because it would have ensured that if the main Hohenzollern line did die out and an agnate line ascended to the throne, then ultimately a descendent of Frederick William would rule again. See Spieß, "Lordship, Kinship, and Inheritance."
174. "… hat [Frederick William I] uns dem ersten Besten gegeben." Quoted by Eva Ziebura, "Prinz Heinrich und seine Schwestern," in *Prinz Heinrich von Preußen: Ein Europäer in Rheinsberg*, ed. Generaldirektion der Stiftung Preußische Schlößer und Gärten (Munich, 2002), 58–62, here 59. Indeed, except for his eldest daughter, Wilhelmina, who was 22 years old when married, Frederick William married off his daughters while they were still quite young (at 14, 15, and 16 years old).
175. Typical of the genre are Constance Wright, *A Royal Affinity: The Story of Frederick the Great and His Sister, Wilhelmina of Bayreuth* (New York, 1965); and Jürgen Walter, *Wilhelmine von Bayreuth: Die Lieblingsschwester Friedrichs der Grossen* (Munich, 1981). For a revision and rehabilitation of Wilhelmina, see Marilyn Roberts, "The Memoirs of Wilhelmina of Bayreuth: A Story of Her Own," in *Eighteenth-Century Women, Studies in Their Lives, Work, and Culture*, ed. Linda Troost (New York, 2001), 129–164, here 129.
176. Wilhelmine's memoirs, written while she was alienated from both her philandering husband and her famed brother, have also been denounced as bitter and mendacious. See Leopold von Ranke, "Zur Kritik Preußischer Memoiren," in *Abhandlungen und Versuche, Erste Sammlung. Leopold von Ranke's Sämmtliche Werke*, vol. 24 (Leipzig, 1872), 41–70. Roberts quotes Droyson denouncing Wilhelmine's memoirs as "totally lacking in historical merit." Roberts, "The Memoirs of Wilhelmina," 134.
177. Jürgen Luh, "Frondeur, Feldherr, Diplomat — Das Bild des Prinzen Heinrich in Wissenschaft und Öffentlichkeit des späten 19. und 20. Jahrhunderts," in Generaldirektion, *Prinz Heinrich von Preußen*, 543–546, here 543.

178. "Man kann nicht über Heinrich reden, ohne Friedrich mitzudenken." Annette Dorgerloh, "'Mon autre moi-même' — Zum Verhältnis der Brüder Heinrich und Friedrich," in Generaldirektion, *Prinz Heinrich von Preußen*, 49–51, here 49. Typical of the genre is Christian, Graf von Krockow, *Die preußischen Brüder: Prinz Heinrich und Friedrich der Große. Ein Doppelportrait* (Stuttgart, 1996).
179. Luh, "Frondeur, Feldherr, Diplomat," 543.
180. Mary Lavater-Sloman, *Der vergessene Prinz: August Wilhelm, Prinz von Preussen, Bruder Friedrichs des Grossen* (Zürich, 1973); and Wilhelm Moritz Pantenius, *Der Prinz von Preussen, August Wilhelm als Politiker.* Historische Studien 108 (1913; reprinted Vaduz, 1965). Unfortunately I was unable to obtain Ziebura's *Prinz August Wilhelm von Preußen* (Berlin, 2006) before this essay was submitted.
181. See, for example, Pantenius, *Der Prinz von Preussen*, 2; Dorgerloh, "Mon autre moi-même," 49; Bernhard Mundt, *Prinz Heinrich von Preussen 1726–1802: Die Entwicklung zur politischen und militärischen Führungspersönlichkeit (1726–1763)* (Hamburg, 2002), 90; and Gerhard Knoll, "Prinz Heinrich im Urteil seiner Zeitgenossen," in Generaldirektion, *Prinz Heinrich von Preußen*, 20–26, here 20.
182. Dorgerloh, "Mon autre moi-même," 49–50.
183. In 1744 Luise Ulrike (1720–1782) was married to Adolf Friedrich of Holstein-Gottorp (1710–1771), who had already been elected to succeed to the throne of Sweden. This was not an entirely exogamous marriage, either. Adolf Friedrich's right to the throne of Sweden was through his uncle, King Friedrich I (1676–1751, reigned 1720–1751). Friedrich was a great-grandson of Elector Georg Friedrich, a grandson of Hedwig Sophie (the Great Elector's sister), and a nephew of Elisabeth Henriette (Frederick III/I's first wife).
184. Amalie (1723–1787) stayed at the Prussian court as one of the highest-ranked females (Frederick gave his own sisters precedence over his brothers' wives) well into her thirties. She became abbess of Quedlinburg in 1756, which was an appropriate appanage. See Ziebura, "Prinz Heinrich," 61.
185. Pantenius, *Der Prinz von Preussen*, 2.
186. In 1742 August Wilhelm married Luise Amalie of Braunschweig (1722–1780), a sister of Elisabeth Christina, Frederick's queen. Luise Amalie was Frederick's choice for August Wilhelm, not August Wilhelm's choice. See Pantenius, *Der Prinz von Preussen*, 2; and Ziebura, "'Das göttliche Trio': Die Prinzen Heinrich, August Wilhelm und Ferdinand von Preußen," in Generaldirektion, *Prinz Heinrich von Preußen*, 55–58, here 55.
187. Heinrich was married to Wilhelmine of Hessen (1726–1808). She was daughter of a younger (non-succeeding) son of the Hessen-Kassel (Maximillian, 1689–1751). Like Heinrich, she was also a great-great-grandchild of Elector Georg Friedrich, through Hedwig Sophie (the Great Elector's sister). See Rudolf G. Scharmann, "'Ich habe mir die Ketten der Ehe anlegen lassen, um meine Freiheit zu gewinnen.' Prinz Heinrich und Wilhelmine von Hessen-Kassel," in Generaldirektion, *Prinz Heinrich von Preußen*, 65–68.
188. Scharmann's title is a quote from Heinrich: "Ich habe mir die Ketten der Ehe anlegen lassen, um meine Freiheit zu gewinnen." See also Ziebura, "Das göttliche Trio," 56.
189. Scharmann, "Ich habe mir die Ketten," 67.
190. Ibid., 67; and Ziebura, "Das göttliche Trio," 56.
191. This was Luise of Brandenburg-Schwedt (1738–1820).
192. This is another instance of the common disposal of non-succeeding brothers. See Goody, *Succession to High Office*, 29–31.

193. Mundt, *Prinz Heinrich*, 96–97.
194. Ibid., 84. As in the case of the exclusion from governmental affairs of Elector Frederick William before his succession to the throne, or King Frederick II's enforced sequestration in Ruppin and Rheinsberg before his succession, this is an example of the "banished heir." Goody, *Succession to High Office*, 23.
195. Mundt, *Prinz Heinrich*, 85.
196. Ibid., 88.
197. Ibid., 109; and Klaus Dorst und Stefan Schimmel, "'Sibi et urbi': Die Berliner Residenz des Prinzen Heinrich," in Generaldirektion, *Prinz Heinrich von Preußen*, 265–272, here 265.
198. Jürgen Luh, "Der Prinz und die Politik," in Generaldirektion, *Prinz Heinrich von Preußen*, 123–125, here 123.
199. "Es gibt eine Art Zwitterwesen, die weder Herrscher noch Privatleute sind und die sich bisweilen sehr schwer regieren lassen: das sind die Prinzen von Geblüt. Ihre hohe Abstammung flößt ihnen einen gewissen Hochmut ein, den sie Adel nennen. Er macht ihnen den Gehorsam unerträglich und jede Unterwerfung verhaßt. Sind irgendwelche Intrigen, Kabalen oder Ränke zu befürchten, von ihnen können sie ausgehen. In Preußen haben sie weniger Macht als irgendwo sonst. Aber das beste Verfahren ihnen gegenüber besteht darin, daß man den ersten, der die Fahne der Unabhängigkeit erhebt, energisch in seine Schranken weist, alle mit der ihrer hohen Herkunft gebührenden Auszeichnung behandelt, sie mit allen äußeren Ehren überhäuft, von den Staatsgeschäften aber fernhält und ihnen nur bei genügender Sicherheit ein militärisches Kommando anvertraut, das heißt, wenn sie Talent und einen zuverlässigen Charakter besitzen." Quoted in Gerhard Knoll, "Prinz Heinrich," 20.
200. August Wilhelm was named "Prince of Prussia" in 1744. Pantenius, *Der Prinz von Preussen*, 2.
201. Ziebura, "Das göttliche Trio," 57.
202. August Wilhelm's dismissal and degradation was a spectacle at court at the time. Peter-Michael Hahn, "Prinz Heinrich von Preußen: Ein königlicher Prinz ohne Herrschaft," in Generaldirektion, *Prinz Heinrich von Preußen*, 15–19, here 17.
203. Ziebura, "Das göttliche Trio," 57.
204. Ibid., 57.
205. Jürgen Luh, "Der Prinz und die Politik," 123. Goody, *Succession to High Office*, 34.
206. Luh, "Frondeur, Feldherr, Diplomat," 543–545; and Hahn, "Prinz Heinrich," 17.
207. Knoll, "Prinz Heinrich," 21–22.
208. These were nearly universal problems. See Fichtner, *Protestantism and Primogeniture*; and Goody, *Succession to High Office*.

Chapter 6

Evolution within Sibling Groups from One Kinship System to Another (Sixteenth to Nineteenth Centuries)

Gérard Delille

Both relative status and social interaction among brothers and sisters have long been considered essential to understanding the fundamental mechanisms that "structure" a society at any given moment. For anthropologists, the study of these relationships constitutes a necessary starting point for approaching any society.[1] In Western history, it has made all the difference to the supporting framework of the social orders whether it was characterized by strict equality between genders and older and younger siblings, with an equitable sharing of goods, or by strict male primogeniture and exclusion of daughters and younger males from inheritance. Indeed in the latter system, celibacy was frequently the lot of younger sons, and there is no need to insist on the central importance this played in Catholic societies for the recruitment of celibate priests or on the extent of the revolution in this regard brought by the Protestant Reformation in any of its variations.

An extraordinary number of studies deal with the role, place, and destiny of children within groups of siblings, but they frequently consider these only as aspects of a more general situation. More specific studies, at least by historians, are much rarer—those that have attempted to take into account the totality of elements that characterize variations in brother-sister or elder-younger sibling relations (birth order, identity of different members of the family in relation to each other and to those outside the family, access to inheritance or succession and to marriage, dowries, kinship terminology, and so forth), together with their attendant consequences (the local multiplication of collateral lineages, a single lineage accompanied by the expulsion of younger siblings, migration). One of the most interesting recent studies—adopting an ethno-historical approach—is *Les cadets*, edited by Segalen and Ravis-Giordani.[2] This work highlights, for Europe as a whole, juridical distinctions earlier brought to light for France by the legal historian Jean Yver, distinctions that characterize whole regions, such as those with a "house" (maison) system (Catalonia, French Pyrenees), inheritance shared equally among brothers, or strict egalitarianism, the latter sometimes limiting the possible advantage for a particular child (Paris Basin) and sometimes devolving property only to those children who have not already been placed.[3] For the Middle Ages, Georges Duby, in a series of works, has provided rich detail on the restructuring of relationships within noble sibling groups between older and younger siblings that accompanied the social transformations from the twelfth to thirteenth centuries.[4]

Two essential factors work together to determine a situation at a given moment: the respective place of men and women and of older and younger children within a sibling group Hence, we are dealing with a "double entry system" involving a limited number of combinations, which should not, however, lead us to simplify things, since considerable ingenuity could be deployed in different circumstances. For example, in ancient Judaism, brothers were considered identical (but not necessarily "equal"—we can find numerous examples in the Old Testament of "the privilege of the elder sibling"), but sisters were neither identical to their brothers nor identical among themselves. Thus sororate marriage was permitted (a man marrying the sister of a deceased first wife was considered to be marrying a different "flesh"), while levirate marriage was prohibited (a woman marrying her first husband's brother was marrying the same "flesh"). There exists, as we know, an exception to this prohibition: when the brother has not had any offspring, his widow may marry his brother. The two future spouses accept a precise legal fiction: the new groom takes the role of his deceased brother, and his children will be legally considered his brother's children. Sometimes this transfer of identity is so difficult to endure that the brother refuses and submits to the ritual ceremony of "the shoe."

The problem of position or status within a group of siblings is further compounded by the nature of alliance with other groups of siblings. Must an eldest male sibling necessarily marry an eldest female sibling, or, as was the case in the houses of eighteenth-century Gévaudan, a younger female sibling, precisely one who was not an heir?[5] Should one be vigilant about status-equal marriages (homogamy) within social orders and oblige, for example, a count to marry only a countess, or might one play with birth order by allowing a non-inheriting younger noble to marry the elder, rich daughter of commoners, opening the door to hypo- and hypergamy?

Beyond considerations of social and economic status, the relative positioning and opportunities of brothers and sisters within a sibling group can have considerable structural consequences for the nature of matrimonial exchanges themselves. If all the brothers and sisters marry, they will be the source of diverging lines of descent, which might eventually proliferate enough to open the way for an interplay of exchanges, systematic or not, between the different lineages. If, on the other hand, younger siblings are condemned to a state of celibacy, or if they have to migrate in order to get married, only single lines of descent will remain, and the interplay of exchanges will not be able draw on collateral lines, since they are unable to develop. This is precisely what occurred in many regions of Western Europe with the widespread adoption of primogeniture among the ruling classes between the end of the sixteenth and the end of the eighteenth centuries. In the great noble families, which were often organized between the fourteenth and sixteenth centuries into lineages that could even have several dozen branches (for example, the Caracciolo of southern Italy), the adoption of primogeniture (allowing not only the marriage of only the eldest male sibling, but also only that of the eldest female sibling) in the seventeenth and eighteenth centuries led to a reduction in the number of lineages and sometimes to the extinction of families. Each generation of siblings found itself a little further removed and a little more cut off from an increasingly remote kinship. At the end of this process, the recognition of common kinship, with its ties of solidarity as well as its supragenerational conflicts, completely disappeared. What remained were single lineages with isolated sets of siblings, profoundly affecting the mechanisms of matrimonial exchange. Later we shall return to this problem.

Compression of lineages and isolation of sets of siblings were the outcome of deep social and cultural transformations, but they might also be more simply occasioned by demographic accidents (interruptions in lines of descent, single children, and the like) or by particular social and economic circumstances (poverty encourages emigration, a successful lineage fails to recognize poorer cousins). Situations such as these were frequent in every period, but it is important to consider the context in which they occurred. In the fifteenth and sixteenth centuries, they contrasted sharply with the great groups of lineages common on the continent (England was very different), while during the eighteenth century they tended to blend into a general pattern of lineage concentration and discontinuity.

To understand how practices were configured in such different periods, I have chosen to analyze two precise examples that are quite unlike each other geographically and socially and have different religious characteristics (each one unfolded in its own peculiar narrative structure). Setting these two examples side by side will enable us to get a clearer view of the deep-rooted mechanisms at work and the transformations that affected the entire system of kinship and marriage between the sixteenth and eighteenth centuries.

Isolated Groups of Siblings: Manduria (Sixteenth and Seventeenth Centuries)

In Manduria, a large agricultural community in southern Italy (province of Tarentum), the dominant pattern of familial organization was the coalescence of large groups of male descendants. Some of these groups, such as the Dimitri, the Micella, the Stratea, and the Di Noe, could comprise several dozen lines and in the same generation contain as many as twenty or thirty conjugal families or more.[6] Unlike neighboring Campania, these groups had no geographical center but were dispersed throughout the villages without forming "lineage districts" similar to the ones I have earlier described for villages in the region of Salerno.[7] Nonetheless, cohesion and solidarity conjoining the different lineages were no less strong than elsewhere. At the level of marriage alliances, these groups as a whole acted as exogamous units, entering into exchanges with other such groups. From the beginning of the sixteenth to the beginning of the eighteenth century, the Dimitri celebrated 390 marriages, but only two of these were within their own group. From a total of 324 unions, no Mera ever married another Mera. Taking all of the evidence together, it is clear that people did not marry within their own agnatic descent group.

On the other hand, it was quite possible to enter into repeated alliance with other lineage groups, sometimes over centuries, simply by taking care not to marry into the same lineage branch as before, but only into a collateral branch at least "four times removed" from the previous one—that is, to ensure that a new spouse was at least a third cousin of a previous spouse. This mechanism of exchange, alternating systematically between different lines of descent, though still within the framework of the larger, more encompassing lineage, I have dealt with at length in other works.[8] It was one of the keystones to the organization of "complex" and "semi-complex" systems of kinship and alliance (described in note 1 below) that were found everywhere in Western Europe, from Italy to Spain, from northern and southern France to the Netherlands and Germany, in high proportions with respect to the total number of marriages.[9] To find even partial "exceptions" one has to go to England and Northern Europe.

By constantly constructing alliances with spouses chosen from lines different from previous ones, but still within a larger agnatic lineage, in little over a century the d'Agostina of Manduria married 7 times with the Mera and 4 times with the Pasanisa. The D'Alemma, for their part, celebrated 7 alternate line marriages to the Piccinna, 6 with the Ricchiuta, 6 with the Micella, and 4 with the Mera. If to this we add direct exchanges (brother/sister exchange or the marriage of two brothers with two sisters) as well as other "short" exchanges (marriages of a widower and a widow together with children from their first marriages), we may conclude that approximately 60–70 percent of marriages obeyed the laws of collateral exchange. This does not mean that there were no consanguineal closures. In fact, almost all of these marriages were "consanguine," but they were beyond the degrees of consanguinity prohibited by canon law, in other words, to the fourth/fifth and fifth degree, and through chains of descendants that passed through several women, so as to avoid the male kin of each spouse's father and mother.[10]

However, alongside these great family groups there also existed isolated sets of siblings and single lines unrelated to any consanguineal collateral branch, often threatened with rapid extinction. What types of alliances could such tenuous family groups generate? In theory, nothing barred them from practicing direct exchanges of sisters, or exchanges with alternate lines, if the other exchange unit contained a large enough number of lines. For example, in Manduria, the Giustiniani, who regularly married with the Pasanisa, deployed only two lines during the course of the seventeenth century and then only one line in the eighteenth. In the latter case, this meant each time resorting to the larger "lineage" of one's own mother (Carlo Giustiniani, son of Camilla Pasanisa, married Caterina and, in a second marriage, Donat'Antonia Pasanisa, who were related in the fourth and fifth degree) or to that of one's grandmother (Angelo Domenico Giustinani, grandson of Camilla Pasanisa, married Benedetta Pasanisa). Such marriages violated unwritten prohibitions, widely respected by the entire group of families (one did not marry with the paternal kin of one's mother or grandmother). Such an expedient could only be occasional and limited in scope. Must we therefore conclude from this that isolated sets of siblings and lines could not apply a systematic principle for marriages, if not the "play of love and chance"?

In an attempt to understand how smaller groups developed their own practices in a culture with "rules" of reciprocity favoring larger descent groups, I selected a substantial sample (approximately 200 cases) of siblings and male lines that never generated collateral branches. Here I did not include larger descent groups, like the Giustiniani, that for a variety of reasons dwindled down to a single line. In all the examples, there were maternal uncles and possibly paternal uncles, but they were without descendants. Most of these families were, in fact, originally from outside the region and had established themselves in Manduria through marriage with a woman from the village. The "life expectancy" of such lines was generally short: two or three generations before extinguishing physically or migrating to other locations. The men were generally agricultural laborers, but one also encounters the occasional doctor or lawyer who had come to live in the village for a time. Not all of these people were, therefore, poor in the economic sense, though they were poor in terms of their "biology" and lineage. Even if their numbers might seem elevated, all these disarticulated groups represented only a tiny fraction of the population of Manduria.

I shall begin by taking a simple example, chosen by chance from our sample of sixteenth-century families. Domitio Reggi, a native of Arnesano in the region of Otranto, settled down in Manduria around 1555–1560, probably as a result of his marriage with Ambrosina Puglia, daughter of Urso Puglia and Montagna Mera. The descent of this couple is brief and includes a limited number of persons (Figure 6.1):

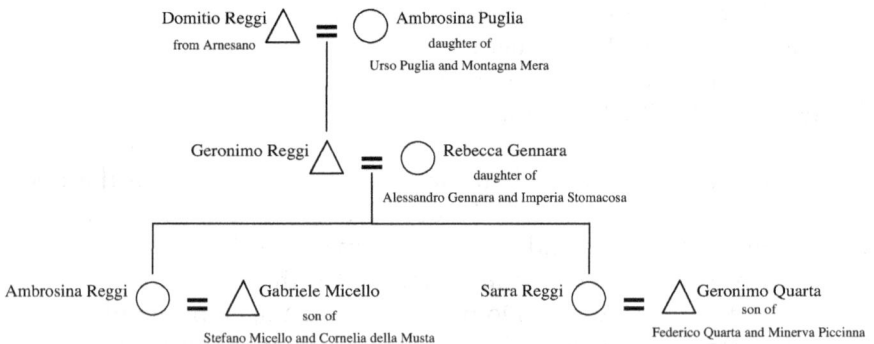

Figure 6.1. Descent of Domitio Reggi and Ambrosina Puglia Manduria, Sixteenth Century

The simplicity of this genealogical development, its isolation, the diversity of the families with which alliances are formed: all this points to a system of random relationships that were built up in answer to an immediate and ever changing set of contingencies. We observe no trace of exchange between alternate lines: Geronimo Reggi did not marry within the lineage of his mother, and his two daughters, Ambrosina and Sarra, followed his example. To know whether their alliances were constructed or not, we need to proceed in systematic fashion.

Unlike their son-in-law, Ambrosina Puglia's parents (Urso Puglia and Montagna Mera) both belonged to lineages that activated mechanisms of alternate exchange. From one line to another, the Mera regularly married with the Eraria, while the Puglia turned freely to the Modea or the Di Falco. On the side of Urso Puglia we can find alliances made with the Nigra, the Mancosa, and the Eraria, names that reappear through relations that are often very close to the side of Montagna Mera, Ambrosina's mother, and describe "classic" closures in the collaterality of the two spouses.

Domitio Reggi's wife brought him a dowry, including perhaps a house that permitted him to settle in Manduria. She also provided him with access to networks and exchange practices, which he was able to activate and to use in order to integrate himself more permanently into the village. Among Ambrosina Puglia's brothers and sisters—that is, Geronimo Reggi's uncles and aunts—we find a Rita Puglia who married Donato de Lorenzo, and a Troziana who married Hortentio Mognia. Nothing in the siblings of Donato and Hortentio or in their immediate descent leads us to the Reggi or to families allied with the Reggi. The same observation can be made with regard to Ambrosina's elder brother, Loiso Puglia, who married a Perna de Stratis. On the other hand, his younger brother Lillo Puglia married a Pellegrina della Porta, one of whose brothers, Baldassare, took Flandina Gennera as a wife, who was none other than the aunt of Rebecca Gennara, wife of Geronimo Reggi, the son of Ambrosina Puglia—which results in the following chart (Figure 6.2):

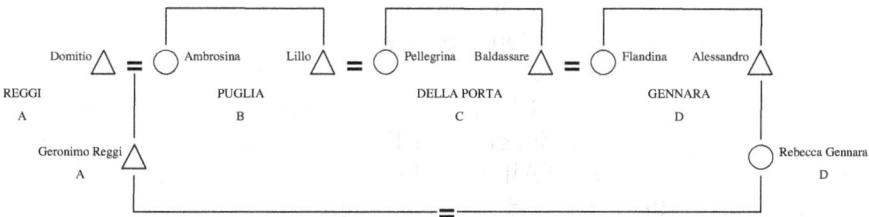

Figure 6.2. An Example of Generalized Exchange. Manduria, Sixteenth Century: Reggi/Gennara Families

In other words, we have here a "classical" example of "generalized ex-change" in which A (Reggi) marries B (Puglia) who marries C (Della Porta) who marries D (Gennera) who marries A. The birth order of the different characters involved in this cycle emphasizes to what extent we are dealing with a conscious and coherent strategy: starting from Ambrosina, the entire chain of alliances, at the first level, is formed by third- and fourth-born siblings, in order to later unite two elder siblings in the following generation. We know how important the sequencing of birth orders is in the construction of generalized chains of exchange. Franciscus A. E. Van Wouden has shown, for example, in the case of the Kei and Tanimbar islands (eastern Indonesia), that the exclusive and compulsory marriage of cross-cousins is reserved only for elder sons, and in Kei, such a marriage is positively prohibited to other sons.[11]

We can find in the daily practice of a large village in southern Italy an alliance mechanism that is identical to that described in Cervantes' novel *The Illustrious Kitchen-Maid*.[12] The generalized exchange plan is presented to us as the final and unexpected result of the peregrinations of two gentlemen from Burgos, Don Diego de Carriazo and Don Thomas de Avendaño, who under assumed names and disguised as vagabonds have left home to take up the life of *Picaros* in the tuna fisheries of Zahara. In an inn in Toledo, Don Thomas falls in love with Costanza, the scullery maid who is also being courted by Don Phaedrus de Punonrostro, son of Toledo's *corregidor,* or chief magistrate. Once the identities and kinships of the two gentlemen from Toledo have been revealed, the solution is a generalized exchange that includes the sisters of the three main charac-ters. This literary transposition does a remarkable job of translating what was probably no more than an alliance mechanism connected to the fact of isolation, that is, the "vagabondage" of the initial sibling groups: it stresses how frequent the practice was, but also the rational perception that the protagonists themselves had of it.

The same principle may be applied to all the other marriages in our little genealogy of the Reggi. Thus, the collaterals and then the allies of Rebecca Gennara's collaterals lead us to the union between Ambro-sina Reggi and Gabriele Micello and, by another route, to that between Sarra Reggi and Geronimo Quarto. This marriage is also consanguineal to the fifth degree: Sarra is daughter of Rebecca Gennara, daughter of Alessandro Gennaro, son of Fiore, son of Alfonso; Geronimo Quarto is son of Minerva Piccinna, daughter of Francesco, son of Lorenzo, son of Reminia Gennara, sister of Alfonso. Here we find a criss-crossing and ac-cumulation of alliances—and ultimately closure—through generalized exchange[13] as the generations advance: A (Reggi) marries B who marries C who marries D who marries A, then other D (Gennara) who marries

E who marries F who marries G (Micello) who in turn again marries A. The double relation between horizontal (generalized exchange) and vertical intergenerational chains (consanguineal marriages) allowed a diminished and fragile family group to "latch on" to an organized ensemble and then to structure its relations over time, and finally to integrate itself within the village community.

This initial analysis of the behaviors of isolated groups opens the way to a preliminary interpretation: while the large descent groups developed exchange systems between alternate lines (in this case agnatic lines) characteristic of complex and semi-complex alliance structures, modest lineages only constructed chains of alliance based on principles of generalized exchange, which—like direct brother-sister, sister-brother exchange—could be understood as elementary structures of kinship. Thus, complex and elementary mechanisms coexisted within the same society, and the different use that was made of them depended on the social context in which the players deployed their strategies. This hypothesis holds true only if we admit the dissimilarity and autonomy of these different circuits of alliance. But is this "generalized exchange," such as can be seen in the case of the Reggi family, the very same thing as a generalized *elementary* exchange able to constitute the fundamental skeleton or supporting framework?

For nineteenth-century Bigouden in the region of Brittany, Martine Segalen has speculated whether the system of "re-linkage," which in many respects was similar to the generalized marriage exchange structure we have been analyzing for sixteenth-century Manduria, except for the fact that in Bigouden such marriages were in the majority, can be viewed as a "variation of generalized exchange."[14] She observed how in the Breton case, "the strictest bilaterality" and non-differentiation of the sexes prevented the identification of lines that could serve as a skeleton for the system of spousal circulation.[15] "Exchanges are, thus, not oriented; as a result, the notions of cycle or closure are foreign to the Breton system."[16] Yet despite this fact, we can still speak of exchange because the dense overlapping of kinship ties structured the system, allowing patrimonies to circulate without escaping family control: "it matters little what sex the spouse is, it matters little that this patrimony is circulating. ... Reciprocity must be maintained for a time."[17] This explanation cannot be applied to the case of Manduria and numerous other regions in Europe where the great patrilinear lineages were dominant and behaved as groups of exchangers—not as a block, but following precise internal hierarchies and divisions. The re-linkages, "generalized exchanges," or direct exchanges were also widely active within these great ensembles but did not express a system of relations different from the dominant one of exchanges between alternate lines. They seem rather to have completed or complemented them and to have strengthened them, deriving as they did from the same logic of exchange.

Another point also has to be made: generalized exchanges, direct exchanges, and the like were not the decisive elements that organized or "structured" the totality of exchanges. But they were nonetheless important "accessory" mechanisms for making the initial steps to allow isolated lines and sets of siblings to be integrated into a more complex and elaborate system of relations before merging completely if they, in turn, developed their own complex lineage structures through the proliferation of lines. Conversely, these mechanisms also permitted the great groups of descent to "correct" certain demographic or economic "accidents" or take advantage of particular situations, such as to absorb a family dying out in the male line. The most recent studies on the financial bourgeoisie in seventeenth-century Paris have shown how this group systematically privileged generalized types of exchanges that guaranteed considerable freedom of choice and action.

Isolation of Sibling Groups in the Eighteenth-Century Nobility

In the eighteenth and nineteenth centuries, things changed radically: exchanges between alternate lineages, which had ensured the general ordering of the system, and generalized exchanges and direct exchanges, which had supported these whenever the need arose, gradually tended to lose their importance and disappear. Although the process was a slow one, obeying different chronologies that varied from region to region, it occurred throughout the entire continent. England—excluding Scotland, Ireland, and Wales—had a different system (in the sixteenth and seventeenth centuries one can detect almost everywhere a practice, which had the ultimate effect of isolating family lineages from each other, of excluding exchanges among alternate lines and limiting direct exchanges or "short" exchanges such as uncle/nephew with aunt/niece) and experienced little change (from the sixteenth and seventeenth centuries onward the renewal of alliances appears to be very rapid, and we do not see the same names constantly recurring, as we do in Manduria).

In the eighteenth century the population of Europe grew considerably, but this did not affect all classes equally. On the one hand, the "popular" classes, for whom infant mortality was beginning to decline, underwent rapid expansion, while on the other, the "ruling" classes, practicing primogeniture, tended to stagnate demographically and die out.

For example, in the kingdom of Naples the great noble lineage of the Acquaviva, which had counted 12 lines around 1580, was left with only one by the end of the eighteenth century. During the same period the Caracciolo de Martina went from 12 to 4 lines, while the Imperiali, of Genoese origin, dropped from 10 lines in 1630 to 3 by the end of the eighteenth century.[18] Local ruling classes were not spared in the process: in Manduria between the end of the sixteenth and end of the eighteenth centuries, the Pasanisa went from 14 lines to 3 and the Giustiniani from 7 to 1 before finally dying out. Here was one of the causes of the serious crisis that beset the kingdom's municipal administrations during the eighteenth century. Generally speaking, the disastrous demographic trends affecting the ruling classes had considerable political consequences. In Venice, by the end of the eighteenth century there were no longer enough nobles to exercise all the offices of the Republic, and Napoleon had no difficulty knocking down the worm-eaten state edifice.

In all the great Milanese noble families the process of transition from "lineage" to line was complete by the first half of the eighteenth century. The Archinto, who numbered 4 lines around 1650, had only 2 by 1750; the Barbiano, who numbered 5 in 1600, were down to one by 1750.[19] Thus, things appear simple: the spread of the practice of primogeniture hindered the proliferation of family lineages and imposed single line descent, which led to the gradual disappearance of exchanges between alternate lines and the grave crisis that affected the whole ancient system of kinship and alliance.

The return to a more or less generalized policy of marriage for all siblings would reappear only at the end or, in the best of cases, toward the middle of the eighteenth century, but it would not lead to the reconstitution of a "lineage" system, since by that time all the family, matrimonial, and patrimonial mechanisms of solidarity between the lines had definitively vanished—a situation that was sanctioned by new family and marriage legislation that appeared at the end of the eighteenth century (laws of Joseph II in Austria, revolutionary laws and later *Code Civil* in France), which considerably reduced the field of prohibited consanguinity and affinity. Whatever the family's new demographic situation, each family would continue to play its own game.

However, this explanation is valid only for the nobility and the local ruling classes. The "popular" classes, which had undergone considerable demographic expansion and thus had multiplied the number of lines of descent, ought, in theory, to have continued and to have reinforced the practice of exchanges between alternate lines. But this was not the case. Society as a whole, in different ways and at different speeds, followed a fundamental trend that was characterized by a proliferation of ever more closely related consanguineal marriages and a simultaneous rising number of totally exogamous marriages. Behaviors traceable to the internal transformations occurring within the nobility gradually spread to the other social classes, as Sabean and Tassin have shown.[20] There appeared highly endogamous forms of alliance, such as the levirate and sororate, which had never previously existed, at least in Catholic countries.[21] While in the past it might have been possible to "recover" a daughter who was an heiress by marrying her with a distantly related line or a traditionally allied family group, once these networks disappeared she had no alternative to "save" her family other than to marry her closest cousin, if one existed, or an uncle who had remained unmarried until that time. Dispensation for these types of marriages became more frequent during the second half of the eighteenth century.

But what happened in those regions where the great noble families did not practice primogeniture or did so only intermittently? Here, in theory, the nobility should have provided no "model," no new system of kinship and alliance. To get a more precise view of this question, I shall turn to examples that, at least in the geographic sense, are very distant from the kingdom of Naples or southern Europe. Of a very ancient origin (the tenth century), the Ysenburg rapidly divided into numerous branches, most of which were settled in Hessen and in Sachsen. One of the branches, the Budingen, which first emerged in the thirteenth century, asserted itself as the most economically, politically, and demographically important. The only branch to continue on into the sixteenth century, it later split up into numerous lines (Ronneburg, Offenbach und Birstein, and Philippseich, among others), some of which are still in existence today.[22] During the seventeenth and eighteenth centuries, this Protestant family did not practice primogeniture: at the very most a few younger sons and daughters were forced to remain celibate, but on the whole marriages remained numerous, and the extinction of lines was amply compensated by the appearance of collateral offshoots.

From the 1530–1540s until the middle of the eighteenth century, the Budingen formed repeated alliances with another great aristocratic "lineage," the Nassau, by means of the well-tried mechanism of alternate lines. After an initial marriage with a Nassau-Weilberg, collateral lines united in the next generation with the Nassau-Idstein, Nassau-Dillenburg, Nassau-Saarbrucken, and then again with the Nassau-Weilburg. Thereafter, they turned to the Nassau-Wiesbaden, still through the collateral line (involving the sons-in-law of a previous remarriage with a Dillenberg), and again to the Nassau-Dillenburg, and in the following generation again to the Nassau-Dillenburg but through a collateral line. Thus, these marriages avoided consanguineal relatives that were too close.

In the second half of the seventeenth century, things changed: ties with the Nassau gradually disappeared for reasons that I will not go into here, except to note that they depended in part on the evolution of the internal structure of these "lineages." Conversely, the number of internal marriages (an Ysenberg with an Ysenberg), hitherto very rare, increased in number and then literally exploded during the first half of the eighteenth century. Here we have a situation that appears to be very different from that of many Italian or French noble families (and different from that of the "popular" families that multiplied marriages among people with the same name), which, after being reduced to a single line, could not activate ties such as these. However, a closer look at this retreat into endogamy reveals a new strategy for the construction of alliances around a much-reduced number of lines.

The sequence of close consanguineal marriages in the lines of Georg Albrecht/Carl August and Wilhelm Moritz/Johann Phillip Ysenberg is very significant in this respect (Figure 6.3). In 1733, Luise Charlotte, an only daughter and heiress, married her closest patrilateral cousin, Friederich Ernst. Previously, in 1713, Ernst Carl had married his own patrilinear cousin, Charlotte Amalie, who in 1725, after she was widowed,

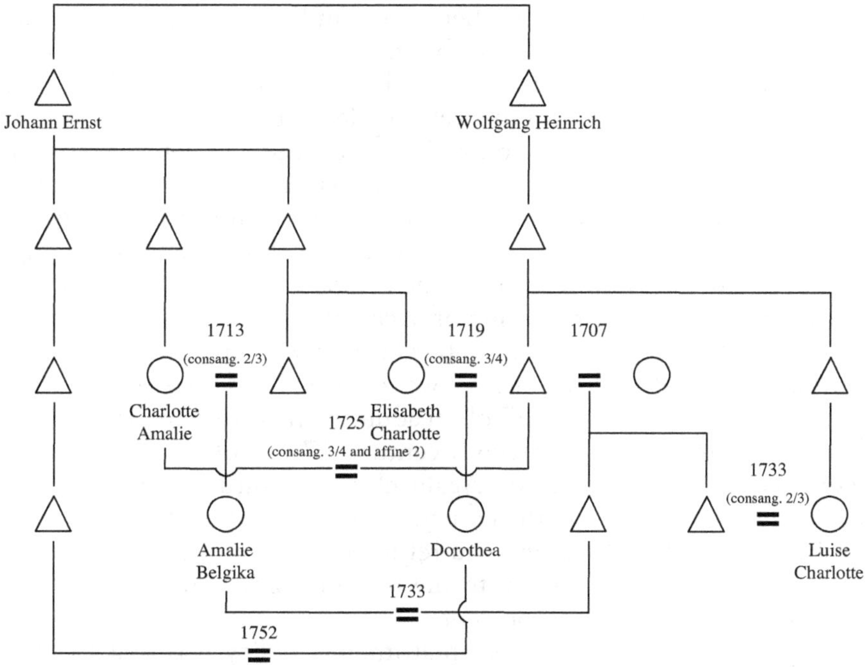

Figure 6.3. The Ysenberg-Budingen Family: Consanguineal Marriages in the Lines of Johann Ernst (Marienborn) and Wolfgang Heinrich (Offenbach)

married her cousin of the third/fourth degree, Wolfgang Ernst, himself the widower of Elisabeth Charlotte, who was cousin both to Wolfgang and Amalie. This form of reinforcement would only increase during the second half of the eighteenth and the first half of the nineteenth centuries. What clearly emerges from this example is the precise intention (unlike that governing the alternate line exchanges practiced by past generations) to quickly close the entire group of matrimonial circuits by means of very short routes, in this case patrilinear ones. The remarkable consequence of these behaviors was that the lines that were furthest removed from the Ysenberg quickly found themselves "sidelined" and had to construct their own independent network of alliances, which, even when primogeniture was not practiced, had the ultimate effect of "breaking up" the group of descendants. In this case, the reduced frequency of celibacy simply made it easier (in contrast to noble Milanese or Neapolitan families) to activate consanguineal marriages, while it limited totally exogamous marriages. The longer-lasting openness that resulted from this rupture of the "lineage system" appeared much later in the Ysenberg than in other noble European families, which could be what accounts for their "conservatism" (the persistence of ancient exchange systems) throughout the entire nineteenth century.

Among the Hohenlohe, another great family that adopted behaviors very similar to those of the Ysenburg, entry into the religious orders, which had been very numerous up until the end of the fifteenth century, came to a brusque halt with the Reformation.[23] From that time onward, the proportion of children destined for marriage and celibacy appears to have remained relatively stable. In the sixteenth century, 7 out of 10 adult men were married and 3 celibate; in the seventeenth century, out of 33 adult men 26 married and 7 remained celibate; and in the eighteenth century, 24 out of 33 adult men were married and 9 unmarried. For every period, the proportion of bachelors remained near or slightly under one-third of the total. In the case of women, in the sixteenth century out of 18 adult women 12 were married and 6 were unmarried; in the seventeenth century 37 of 56 adult women were married and 19 unmarried; and in the eighteenth century, 17 out of 26 adult women were married and 9 unmarried. Again, close to a third of the women did not marry. In the eighteenth century, some branches of the family that, probably for political reasons, had returned to Catholicism, again committed some of their children to the religious orders: immediately the celibacy rate shot up to 50 percent.

The result of this "reformed" matrimonial policy was that the Hohenlohe, who counted 2–3 branches from the fifteenth to the beginning of the sixteenth centuries, numbered 4 branches by the second half of the sixteenth century, 7 or 8 by the seventeenth century, and 8 to 9 in the eighteenth century. This family was by no means an exception. We are far from the Neapolitan, Milanese, or French families, which from the second half of the seventeenth century were constantly threatened with extinction. In contrast to Southern Europe, this multiplication of lines involved neither an extension nor even a simple maintenance of the number of matrimonial exchanges between alternate lines. As in the case of the Ysenberg, the number of patrilateral parallel marriages multiplied from the second half of the seventeenth century on. Such marriages had been totally absent in the fifteenth and sixteenth centuries, and while there were still only 2 in the first half of the seventeenth century, they rose sharply to 5 in the second half of the seventeenth century and to 12 in the eighteenth century (until 1815). Furthermore, these marriages were increasingly close in consanguinity.[24] Conversely, at the other "extremity," allied families tended to diversify. But whether these strategies were endogamous or exogamous, from the second half of the seventeenth century onward marriages came increasingly to be conducted with Hohenlohe lines that were closer and closer, or more independent and isolated with respect to the remoter lines.

In the families of peasants and artisans of the Protestant regions, the trends (taking into account variable demographic parameters such as high mortality rates) appear to be very close to those found among the nobility. David Sabean's excellent study on Neckarhausen in the eighteenth and nineteenth centuries leaves hardly any room for doubt: marital exchanges between a very limited number of very closely related—isolated— lines appear very marked; the number of consanguineal or affinal marriages, as in Catholic regions, shot up from the 1740s; and marital partners became increasingly closely related.[25] Paradoxically, between this small Protestant village in Württemberg where the economy was rapidly expanding and social mobility was accelerating, and Casalnuovo, a large Catholic village in Apulia where agricultural yields did not begin to improve until the 1880s, differences with regard to the structural mechanisms of exchanges and the construction of matrimonial alliance networks do not appear to have been very great. This is a problem of considerable proportions that requires a great deal of reflection.

This rapid comparative study has allowed us to draw a certain number of important conclusions:

1) The practice of primogeniture was certainly not the main cause of the rupture of the "lineage system" and the circuits of alliances that characterized it from the middle of the seventeenth century. The system "broke

down" even when families continued to be characterized by large numbers of lines, since these lines became gradually more autonomous and behaved more like isolated lines. Hence, the need to turn to explanations that take into account the interplay of more complex sets of relations and behaviors that were at once social, political, and cultural. If the line took the place of the "lineage," it was perhaps also because new types of power relationships were becoming established at every level of the social hierarchy. Monarchy and other centralized forms of power, which had previously relied on the great family groups to provide middlemen between the central power and local populations, began increasingly to favor "functionaries," power technicians who were directly under their orders. The nobility was without a doubt the first "victim" of this new order. During the nineteenth and twentieth centuries, the gradual but total transition to the category of individual-functionary resulted in the complete disappearance of the line itself, sweeping away the last traces of "dynastic" organization, not only in the great families but also in the families of notaries, doctors, professors, and diplomats. Their place was taken by isolated nuclear families, which, during the course of the twentieth century, gradually evolved toward an increasingly "shattered" structure and toward marriages that were resolutely exogamous.

This is one explanation, but others are also possible. The most traditional of these, formerly proposed by Sutter and Tabah, established a relationship between the frequency of consanguineal marriages and the demographic growth of the population.[26] The probability of endogamic marriages increases when a population is rapidly expanding: if all my uncles and aunts have had twenty children, all of whom are my first cousins, it will be easier for me to choose a spouse from among them than if I only had only three or four cousins. The situation of German families is by and a large an illustration of the former case, while Milanese families are an example of the latter. But it seems to me that this explanation does not take into account other essential aspects, in particular, qualitative changes in consanguineal and affinal marriages, which were becoming increasingly close during the course of the eighteenth and nineteenth centuries, and the coincidence that became established between near endogamy and remote exogamy, which can be found both among both German and Milanese families.

2) Between the seventeenth and eighteenth centuries in the nobility—and the same may also be observed for the other social classes—no progressive, linear transition occurred from a more or less closed or endogamous matrimonial exchange system to a more open system. There was a break with the strategies and mechanisms of closure. Unions be-

tween alternate lines constructed along the entire breadth of the descent group for many generations gave way to unions that were either very close or very remote and were increasingly ego-centered. Paradoxically, the matrimonial behaviors of the nobility in the eighteenth century more closely resemble certain ancient traditional models, such as Jewish marriage (uncle/patrilinear niece) or Arab marriage (patrilinear cousins), which led to demographic imbalances (two fathers are needed to marry a daughter) and to alliances external to the group. In any event, the change was a qualitative one and not quantitative.

3) During the course of the seventeenth and eighteenth centuries, the fact or not of marrying all the members of a group of siblings did not translate into differentiated changes in the system of matrimonial exchanges; it did, however, considerably alter the contexts in which the new alliance "rules" would take effect. By the presence or absence of close cousin lines, the systematic practice of primogeniture (or its nonpractice) was for a time able to swing the balance in favor of close endogamous unions (the German case) or, on the other hand, in favor of exogamous unions (the Milanese case). At the social, economic, political, and cultural levels (continuity of noble families, social renewal, economic clout of the nobility, devolution of property to the state, control of political offices, liberalism or authoritarianism, cultural traditions), the difference was by no means insignificant. With regard to the European nobilities of the eighteenth and nineteenth centuries, this area of enquiry has received little attention and would no doubt be rewarding to pursue.

4) In restructuring itself on isolated lines or relations that were either very close or very remote, kinship and alliance conferred to the political domain a new freedom and autonomy that it had hardly known before. In the eighteenth, and later in the nineteenth century, alliances and political parties were increasingly built independently of marriage alliances, though these could prove to be useful. Other players, who were by no means previously absent but who had been necessarily obliged to come to terms with the consequences of solidarities and "rules" within descent groups, now began to play an increasingly preponderant role. Economic and ideological relationships substituted those of kinship and alliance. In Casalnuovo, a veritable seizure of power was made in 1740–1741 by a new and heterogeneous group of persons motivated by a highly anti-feudal program. But in the council, most assessors and councilors entertained "business" relations (financial relations were the most obvious) with a very limited ruling nucleus composed of the mayor and the

two first assessors, who were themselves (and they were the only ones) united by relations of matrimonial alliance (the first assessor, Giuseppe Maria Barci, was the brother-in-law of the mayor, Domenico Nicola Schiavone).[27]

Kinship and alliance no longer played, or did so only in a very limited manner, a mediating role between politics and economic and ideological considerations. The process imposed itself in different ways and at different speeds that varied with the country and cultural and social contexts. But it is important to emphasize that this political "openness" appeared as a structural fact connected to transformations in the system of kinship and alliance.

Notes

1. The latest research has added, to the traditional distinction between elementary societies with rules for matrimonial exchanges of a prescriptive type (where one has to marry a specified person, for example, a female cousin on the mother's side), and complex or semi-complex societies with negative rules (one can not marry certain people: for example, all the relatives of both the male and female line to the fourth degree), distinctions based on the diverse nature of the siblings and the matrimonial exchanges that are then possible. So in a complex society one can find both two brothers who marry two sisters and a brother and sister who marry a sister and a brother, while in an elementary or semi-complex society only one of the exchanges is possible. It can result each time in quite different social structures. See Claude Lévi-Strauss, *Les structures élémentaires de la parenté* (Paris, 1949; 2nd ed., 1968) and Françoise Héritier, *L'exercice de la parenté* (Paris, 1981). This chapter is an attempt to explore further the problem of such differences and variations and their evolution as regards the siblings situation in a complex society—that of Western Europe.
2. Georges Ravis-Giordani and Martine Segalen, eds., *Les cadets* (Paris, 1994).
3. Jean Yver, *Egalité entre héritiers et exclusion des enfants dotés: Essai de géographie coutumière* (Paris, 1966). Emmanuel Le Roy Ladurie, "Système de la coutume: Structures familiales et coutume d'héritage en France au XVI siècle," *Annales ESC* 27 (1972): 825–846.
4. Georges Duby, *Le chevalier, la femme et le prêtre* (Paris, 1981).
5. Elisabeth Claverie and Pierre Lamaison, *L'impossible marriage: Violence et parenté en Gévaudan, XVIIe, XVIIIe et XIXe siècles* (Paris, 1982).
6. Manduria Municipal Library, *Libro Magno delle famiglie di Manduria.*(3 volumes in folio, 1582 ff, compilation begun by Archiprete Lupo Donato Bruno in 1582).
7. Gérard Delille, *Famille et propriété dans le royaume de Naples* (Rome and Paris, 1985).
8. Gérard Delille, "Échanges matrimoniaux entre lignées alternées et système européen de l'alliance: une première approche," in *En substances: Textes pour Françoise Héritier*, ed. Jean-Luc Jamard, Emmanuel Terray, and Margarita Xanthakou (Paris, 2000), 219–252.
9. Héritier, *L'exercice de la parenté*.
10. In the case of complex or semi-complex societies, "des bouclages consanguins peuvent avoir lieu, avec des cheminements préférentiels, dès que les interdits cessent de

s'exercer" (consanguine closures may occur, along preferential pathways, as soon as the prohibitions against them cease to be applied): Héritier, *L'exercice de la parenté*, 114.
11. Cited by Francis Zimmerman, *Enquête sur la parenté* (Paris, 1993), 84–85.
12. The text is analyzed in Delille, *Famille et proprieté*, 217–220. The simplified chart of alliances is as follows :

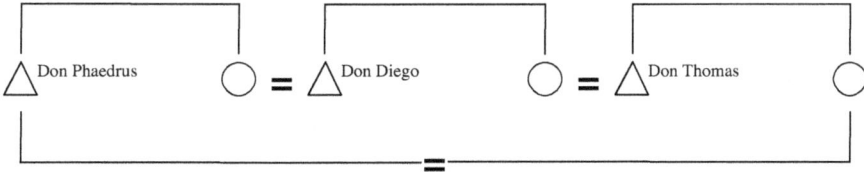

13. The generalized matrimonial exchange (A marries B who marries C who marries A) connects three or more family groups and is opposed to the limited exchange that involves only two groups (A marries B who marries A); see Claude Lévi-Straus, *Les structures élémentaires*. It is a matrimonial device that is frequently found both in elementary and complex societies. In the latter, generalized exchange is often permitted, as in the examples we analyzed, for isolated lineages to organize their alliance before possibly moving on to more complex and durable systems of relations.
14. Martine Segalen, "Mariage et parentèle dans le pays bigouden sud: un exemple de renchaînement d'alliance," in *Les complexités de l'alliance*, vol. 2: *Les systèmes complexes d'alliance matrimoniale*, ed. and intro. Françoise Héritier-Augé and Elisabeth Copet-Rougier (Paris, 1991), 177–205.
15. Ibid., 202.
16. Ibid.
17. Ibid.
18. Gérard Delille, *Le maire et le prieur: Pouvoir central et pouvoir local en Méditerranée occidentale (XVe–XVIII siècle)* (Paris and Rome, 2003).
19. Dante E. Zanetti, *La Demografia del patriziato milanese nei secoli XVII, XVIII, XIX. Con una appendice genealogica di franco Arese Lucini* (Pavia, 1972).
20. David Warren Sabean, *Kinship in Neckarhausen 1700–1870* (Cambridge, 1998); Guy Tassin, *Mariages, ménages au XVIIIe siècle: Alliances et parentés à Haveluy* (Paris, 2001).
21. Jean-Marie Gouesse, "Mariages de proches parents (XVIe–XXe siècle): Esquisse d'une conjonture," in *Le modèle familial européen: Normes, déviances, contrôle du pouvoir*, ed. Gérard Delille and Franco Rizzi (Rome, 1986), 31–61.
22. Genealogy of Ysenburg family as in Detlev Schwennicke, ed., *Europaische Stammtafeln, neue Folge*, vol. 17: *Hessen und das Stammes-herzogtum Sachsen* (Frankfurt am Main, 1998), 59–76.
23. *Europäische Stammtafeln*, vol. 17 (1998), 1–23.
24. Generally speaking, this period was characterized by a drastic reduction in, that is to say, the disappearance of, this type of alliance. This meant a return to strictly exogamous male descent groups of the "lineage" type. This fact is of major importance but is still widely unknown in the history of European kinship and alliances.
25. Sabean, *Kinship*, 208–216 and Table A. 25, 531.
26. Jean Sutter, "Fréquence de l'endogamie et ses facteurs au XIXe siècle," *Population* 23 (1968): 303–324; Jean Sutter and Léon Tabah, "Fréquence des mariages consanguins en France," *Population* 3–4 (1948): 607–630.
27. Delille, *Le maire*, 335.

PART TWO

SIBLING RELATIONS, CLOSE MARRIAGE, AND HORIZONTAL KINSHIP, 1750–1900

Chapter 7

Brother Trouble

Murder and Incest in Scottish Ballads

Ruth Perry

Ballads—those beautiful sung narratives that flourished in the British Isles in the seventeenth and eighteenth centuries—can reveal to the cultural historian something about the social attitudes and psychological cast of the people who sang, listened, and daydreamed to them. But the critic who wants to read them as historical evidence must handle their texts carefully, because they are received literature, not usually written by the people who sang them, and each set of words is just one version among many variants that have evolved over time in the hands of different performers. What a single version that happened to be collected at a particular time and place might reveal about that singer, or that culture, is difficult to say with absolute certainty. On the other hand, ballads were a significant part of the popular culture in early modern England and Scotland. People committed them to memory and sang them over and over in their cottages and communities, bought them by the thousands in broadsides and chapbooks, and wherever they were literate, jotted them down in commonplace books.

This chapter briefly sketches this centrality of ballads in Anglo-Scottish culture in the early modern period and tracks the changes over time in two related Scottish ballads dealing with brother-sister incest. Although we cannot claim as definitive the particular variants examined for this change, a literary analysis of the differences between two ballads collected two centuries apart corroborates some of what we know about changes in the family from other sources. A comparison of these two ballads shows a marked change in the quality of brother-sister relationships in the course of 150 years, resulting in a diminution of the sister's agency in the later period as well as a starker, more tragic outcome to their story of illicit incest.

Ballads were a crucial cultural phenomenon in eighteenth-century society, a common experience of rich and poor, so embedded in the soundscape as not to be remarked, any more than the air people breathed. Ballads were many people's first literary experience in eighteenth-century England and Scotland, whether simple broadsides from which they learned to read or the earliest sung stories that moved them to tears or ignited their imaginations. Oliver Goldsmith loved ballads, and several find their way into *The Vicar of Wakefield* (1766). He wrote in his essay "Happiness" (1759), "The music of Mattei [the Neapolitan singer La Colonna[1]] is dissonance to what I felt when our old dairymaid sung me into tears with 'Johnny Armstrong's Last Good Night', or the cruelty of 'Barbara Allen'."[2]

Ballads were more present in eighteenth-century Great Britain than literary critics and historians tend to remember. We are so used to making our way in the world with our eyes that we forget what Walter Ong calls the "lifeworld of the oral/aural past"[3]—an environment, in the city at least, of street cries and rhymes, bells ringing and chants, work songs and lullabies, an environment in which rags were sought and strawberries sold to the accompaniment of words and musical phrases so familiar that the hearer did not have to be able to understand the words to recognize which peddler was abroad exercising his or her lungs. Ballads were sung in taverns and camps, in dimly lit laborer's cottages as well as in the blazing halls of the wealthy; they were memorized and transmitted orally by ordinary people and professional singers and actors alike. They were printed on broadsides and in chapbooks and garlands and often circulated from print to oral transmission and back again. A ballad might be learned by ear and then written down to save or to remember; or it might be learned from a broadside, remembered, and then passed along orally.

From the earliest dawn of printing, broadsides were the comic books and the poster art of the poor: single sheets decorated with woodcuts on which were printed the texts of ballads with the title of the familiar tune to which those words could be sung. Between the middle of the sixteenth century and the beginning of the seventeenth century, more than 3,000 broadsides were officially entered in the Stationer's Register, although it is likely that five times as many were printed and sold in that period.[4] The walls of taverns and cottages were pasted up with as many as twenty, thirty, or more of these productions for decoration and quick reference as *aides memoires*. However ballads were composed, however far back they go historically speaking, our earliest printed record of them has often been in the form of a broadside.

Scholars have disputed the origins of English ballads.[5] Biblical themes, romance themes, and carols furnish the materials for the oldest of them. Some scholars believe that ballads were the work of professional min-strels, skilled musicians and poets who entertained in the great baronial halls of the Middle Ages. Others claim that they were the art of the com-mon people, polished by countless renditions and the exacting responses of their unlettered audiences. But all agree that when they began to be collected by the literati in the late eighteenth century, they were no lon-ger a proliferating genre but variously in decline.

Nevertheless, ballads continued to be sung and chanted in homes, fields, and the streets through the nineteenth century and to be bought and sold at fairs and in the cities of England and Scotland. Peddlers car-ried them the length and breadth of these countries in their packs, along with cloth, thread, needles, thimbles and other household goods. Bal-lads were the literary art of the common people and, more than novels, the popular culture of all classes. To examine a ballad that was circu-lating in eighteenth-century Scotland as cultural evidence of attitudes toward sex, self, and society is therefore not an empty exercise. What complicates the use of ballads as cultural evidence is that there is never one single definitive text but many variants, so that one has to refer to themes, episodes, formulas, and storylines rather than precise sequences of words.

The ballad I want to examine here is "Sheath and Knife," known to Robert Burns (at least a few verses of it) and its melody notated by him in the *Scots Musical Museum* (1787–1803), which he compiled with James Johnson. It was subsequently collected by William Motherwell from the recitation of Mrs. King of Kilbarchan parish on 9 February 1825 and appears in his *Minstrelsy: Ancient and Modern* (1827). Sir Wal-ter Scott also remembered this ballad from his childhood: "I have heard the 'Broom blooms bonnie' sung by our poor old nursery-maid as often as I have teeth in my head, but after cudgelling my memory I can make no more than the following stanzas."[6] Scott puts a ballad in the mouth of his character Effie Deans in *The Heart of Midlothian* (1818). She sings a stanza that appears to be a composite of several songs, with the two refrain lines: "The broom grows bonny, the broom grows fair" and "And we daurna gang down to the broom nae mair." She is just coming back from seeing her lover when she sings it, defying her sister's inquiries. For her, it marks an end of innocence and the beginning of suffering. Ironically, the illegitimate child that Effie bears from this affair returns at the end of the novel—like the repressed impulse he represents—to kill his father, imbricating sex and blood and murder like the ballad that this refrain alludes to.

Here, then, is the text as Motherwell collected it.

Sheath and Knife (Child 16)[7]

> It is talked the warld all over
> The brume blooms bonnie and says it is fair
> That the king's dochter gaes wi child to her brither.
> And we'll never gang doun to the brume onie mair.
>
> He's taen his sister doun to her father's deer park,
> The brume blooms bonnie, etc.
> Wi his yew-tree bow and arrow fast slung to his back
> And we'll never, etc.
>
> 'Now when that ye hear me gie a loud cry
> The brume blooms bonnie, etc.
> Shoot frae thy bow an arrow and there let me lye.
> And we'll never, etc.
>
> 'And when that ye see that I am lying dead
> The brume blooms bonnie, etc.
> Then ye'll put me in a grave, wi a turf at my head
> And we'll never, etc.
>
> Now when he heard her gie a loud cry
> The brume blooms bonnie, etc.
> His silver arrow frae his bow he suddenly let fly
> Now they'll never, etc.
>
> He has made a grave that was lang and was deep,
> The brume blooms bonnie, etc.
> And he has buried his sister, wi her babe at her feet.
> And they'll never, etc.
>
> And when he came to his father's court hall,
> And the brume blooms bonnie, etc.
> There was music and minstrels and dancing and all
> But they'll never, etc.
>
> 'O Willie, O Willie, what makes thee in pain,
> The brume blooms bonnie, etc.

'I have lost a sheath and knife that I'll never see again.'
For we'll never, etc.

'There is ships o your father's sailing on the seas
The brume blooms bonnie, etc.
That will bring as good a sheath and knife unto thee.'
And we'll never, etc.

'There is ships o my father's sailing on the sea
The brume blooms bonnie, etc.
But sic a sheath and a knife they can never bring to me.'
Now we'll never, etc.

Like most other Scottish or English ballads, this one has all the hall-marks of oral composition: repetitive textual, metrical, and melodic structures; patterned arrangements of narrative; recurrent formulaic phrases and epithets (a grave that is "long and deep"; a "yew-tree bow"); conceptual parallelism and incremental repetition (in one verse she tells him to put her in a grave; in the next verse he digs a grave and buries her in it); and formalized refrain lines: "the brume blooms bonnie" and "we'll never go doun to the brume onie mair."[8] The repetitions not only serve the memory of the singer, but they permit the listener to think about what has gone before, to let his/her attention lapse for a moment, to sink into fantasy, to paint some pictures in the mind. They pace the story.

The action usually unfolds in event and speech—sometimes dia-logue—without narrative comment and begins somewhere in the mid-dle. Historical time is irrelevant; what happens in ballads is timeless or out of time. "It is talked the warld all over." Ballad tone is neither senti-mental nor moralizing but stark and ritualistic; there is little or no sub-jective consciousness behind it. This creates the distance necessary for the powerful and tragic events of ballads to be safely shared by narrator and audience. The rhythm of the episodic structure of ballads has been described as "leaping and lingering"—that is, as leaping instantaneously, with no attempt at realism, over great swathes of time and space and then lingering in a single moment, letting its complications sink in. In this episodic structure, focusing on vivid scenes that appear and disap-pear according to some familiar logic of the mind, ballads are like noth-ing so much as dreams.

In "Sheath and Knife" we move effortlessly from one scene to an-other—the deer park, the grave, walking in the broom, the court hall filled with merriment; even the enigmatic but suggestive reference to the sheath and knife springs forth as from intuition rather than reasoned thought. The action feels symbolic rather than literal, represented im-

personally from the outside rather than narrated subjectively; the stark-
ness of the narration together with the horror of the situation is what
moves us. We do not know how the sister feels, but she seems to be
cooperating in her own death when she tells her brother to shoot an arrow from his bow when he hears her give a loud cry, which is apparently
the cry of childbirth.

On the other hand, the brother has staged this tragedy. "He has taen
his sister down to her father's deer park. … With his yew-tree bow and
arrow slung fast to his back." Yew trees are associated with death and
sorrow in the folklore of Great Britain, and with graveyards, where they
are often planted. Moreover, he has brought with him a silver arrow, a
special, precious arrow, the instrument of execution for a woman who is
a king's daughter—and his only sister. It may also be that the silver acts
as a charm against evil or retribution. When he returns to his father's
court hall, he finds himself in the midst of festivities. The music and
dancing are evocative of sexuality and bodily pleasure—music always
signifies passion and the lapsing of reason. The pleasure around him sets
off his sadness in contrastive relief; he seems all the more alone because
everyone around him is gay. And when he invokes the phallic imagery
of a knife inside a sheath, we know that he is speaking of his sister both
as his lost sexual partner, unique among women and specially suited to
him—nowhere in the whole world where those ships of his father's are
sailing will there be another like her—and also as the carrier, the sheath,
of his child.

This brother and sister are two parts of one whole; they could not be
closer. Their bodies belong together as intimately as a fetal child within
its mother's womb. They are made for each other in the way they are
presented in the ballad, siblings with the same father, interchangeable
and identical so far as the description goes, except that one is male and
one is female. Their sexual interests are mirrored in each other; they
begin and end in one another. Male and female, they are not opposed or
different but positioned as two interlocking parts. The problem is that
as a woman, the sister's body shows the evidence of their congress, and
they both seem to understand with an unspoken accord that she must
be made to disappear. The reasons are not specified, but one knows that
the world, which is already gossiping about them, will not tolerate this
incestuous, too-close union any more. The offspring of their illicit union
cannot be allowed to see the light of day.

There is no reference to consequences—no sense of what will happen when the "king's dochter" is found missing—only the brother's deep
sense of bereavement after the killing, as if half of him has been shot
away, removed, irretrievably lost, and he will never be the same. The

brother expresses no guilt—which is, after all, an emotion about the self. The pain of loss he feels and expresses with this haunting metaphor is all the more terrible and unrelieved for his lack of guilt. The chorus lines, too, underscore the sense of ritual and irretrievable loss. An eighteenth-century audience in a social situation, having heard this song many times, might have joined in on these lines, participating in the story and giving vent to their feelings. In a village this song might have been the property of a local singer, and when people gathered to work or to talk in the evening, the person who knew "Sheath and Knife" might have been prodded to sing it and these chorus lines caroled back by those listening.

"The broom blooms bonnie and they say it is fair" obviously puns on the word "fair"—the blooming broom is so beautiful and life is so unjust and so tragic. The broom, a yellow-flowering shrub that grows in the margins of cultivation, like the "greenwood," marks a liminal place outside the established limits of society, outside the law, in the bushes, so to speak, where illicit sex always takes place.[9] In Scots ballads, people always lie down in the broom, away from prying eyes.[10] And not only is broom beautiful, bonnie, but its blooming is of short duration. The poignant "And we'll never go down to the broom any more" signals the end of innocence for us as well as for the principals in the story—and also the end of sexual pleasure and of companionable strolling for the brother and sister.

This is how the ballad was known at the end of the eighteenth century, and how Francis James Child copied it from Motherwell and Scott, the great collectors of the Romantic period. More recently, evidence has surfaced of a much earlier version of this ballad, which poses some puzzling questions. This much earlier version of "Sheath and Knife" was written down in the commonplace book of Robert Edwards, along with other poems and musical examples. Robert Edwards, born in 1617, was a minister of Murroes parish near Dundee, in eastern Scotland. His commonplace book dates to about 1630. He titles this entry "The Sheath and the Knife or Leesome Brand"—Leesome Brand being someone's name—and his text is a variant that includes some of the features of Child 15, "Leesome Brand," which is an entirely separate ballad from "Sheath and Knife" in the Child canon.[11] In "Leesome Brand," in the version collected by Peter Buchan and published in his *Ancient Ballads and Songs of North of Scotland*—the version Child included in his collection—the speaker's son, a ten-year-old boy named Leesome Brand, comes to an "unco" land and falls in love with a gay lady at court who is roughly his age.[12]

> This ladye was scarce eleven years old,
> When on her love she was right bauld;

> She was scarce up to my right knee,
> When oft in bed wi men I'm tauld.

When "nine months have come and gone" this lady turns "pale and wane" and says to Leesome Brand, "In this place I can nae mair stay." She sends him to her father's stable for horses for them both and to her mother's coffers for her tocher or dowry. It is she who has parents at court—not he—and she who provides the means for their escape. He follows her instructions and they mount and ride; but after a while his "true love then began to fail" and she tells him that she feels as if her back is breaking. She wishes she had a midwife, but he tells her that they are far from any midwife. He offers to do for her what a man can do, but she rejects his offers of assistance and sends him away to hunt while she gives birth. She dies in childbirth and so does her baby. After he finds her lying there dead, he returns to his own home to his mother (his father in other versions), who questions him about his sadness. He replies that he has lost a golden knife and a gilded sheath. When his mother asks if there are not goldsmiths "here in Fife" who can make another knife and another sheath, he replies "I've lost my ladye I lov'd sae dear, / Likeways the son she did me bear."

According to Child, versions of "Leesome Brand" have been found throughout Scandinavia (there are versions in Norwegian, Swedish, Danish, Finnish, and Icelandic), and there are also variants in German, French, and Dutch. The Danish ballad "Redselille og Medelvold" (Rose-lilly and Ole) is a variant of "Leesome Brand" about unlucky lovers who are not siblings. It begins when a mother discovers that her daughter's breasts run with milk and extorts from the girl a confession that she has been beguiled by a man. The mother then threatens various punishments for both of them. The girl tells her lover, and they take two horses and ride away together. After they have ridden awhile, the girl finds that her time has come, and her lover lifts her off her horse and spreads his cloak for her. He offers to bandage his eyes and render such service as a man may, but she does not want him to know the pangs a woman suffers and sends him off to hunt. He comes back to find her dead with two sons dead too; he buries them all and then falls on his sword.

What is interesting about the ballad "Sheath and Knife or Leesome Brand" found in Robert Edwards's 1630 commonplace book—a variant not known by Child when he compiled his groundbreaking *The English and Scottish Popular Ballads*—is that it combines elements from both "Sheath and Knife" and "Leesome Brand" to create an incest ballad with very different affective qualities than either of the two contributory ballads as they were collected separately two centuries later. What follows is a transcription of the variant in Robert Edwards' 1630 manuscript book.

The Sheath and the Knife or Leesome Brand

Ther was a sister and a brother
the sun gois to under the wood
who most intirelie lovid othir
god give we had nevir beine sib.

Sayes "sister I wald lay the by
the sun gois to etc.
and thou wald not my deuds cry"
god give we, etc.

"Alas brother wald ye doe so
the sun gois to etc.
I rathir nou death undergoe
alas give we had newer bein sib

the morrne is my fathirs feast
the sun etc.
Weil in my clothis I most be least
god give we had newir bein sib.

When they conwining al at ons
to royal feasting in the hal
it me behovith them amongs
ge dekit in a goun of pa;

and when I lout me to my to
the sun etc.
my lesse wil brak and go in tuo
god give etc.
and when I lout me to my kni
the sun etc.
my lesse will brak and go in thrie
god give etc.

and it wil go from on to uthir
the sun etc.
until it come to Jhon my brother
lord give etc.

and Jhon my brothir is most il
the sun etc.

he wil hus both burne on a hil.
lord god we had etc.

I sal go to my fathirs stable
the sun etc.
and tak a stid both wight and able
lord give etc.

and we sal ryd til tym we spend
the sun etc.
until we see our trystis end."
lord give etc.

She had not riden a myle but ane
the sun etc.
when she gan quaking gran and gran
lord give etc.

"Is ther water in your shoes
or comes the wind into your glowes

Or think ye me to simple a knight
to ryd or go with you alnyght?"

"and when ye heire me loud loud cry
ye bend your bow and ran tharby

and when ye se my ly ful stil
so souing your horne come me til.

I wald give al my fathirs land
for on woman at my command."

when that he cam soon hir besead
[the bab was borne the lady dead.]

Ther he has tain his yong yong sonne
and borne to a milk womane.

he dreu his suord him wonding sore
from this tyme to wrid newir more.

"mother" quoth he "can so mak my bed
can se mak it long and nothing bread.

mother alas I tint my knife
I lovid better then my lyffe.

mother I have als tint my shead
I lovid better then them bead.

ther is no cutlar in this land
can make a kniffe so at my command."

he turned his faced to the wa
gave up the goast and gaid his way.

the on was layid in Marie Kirk
othir in Marie Queire
out throch the on there greu a birke
and out throch hir a breir.
ye may knou surlie by their signes
They wer tuo lowirs neire.[13]

The most stunning difference between the Robert Edwards's 1630 "Sheath and Knife" and the one sung by Mrs. King of Kilbarchan in 1825 is that the infant lives and is given up to "a milk woman"—a wet nurse. Thus the incestuous relationship is not simply damned in this variant: something living and hopeful comes from it. Furthermore, the refrain lines of the Edwards variant, while very different from the refrain lines Mrs. King sang in 1825, are also meaningful. The repeated second line, "The sun gois to under the wood," evokes the hour of sunset, the hour that daylight ceases and darkness covers all, like the hour before death. This refrain line is very old; it appears in a four-line anonymous, medieval lyric of the thirteenth century:[14] "Nou goth sonne under wode"—the "sonne" being Christ, the son of God, as well as the sun, and "wode" being the wood of the cross as well as a stand of trees. It evokes both a simple sunset and the crucifixion, the loss of light from the world. The fourth line of every stanza of Roberts Edwards's "Sheath and Knife," also repeated throughout the ballad, is "God give we had nevir bein sib." "God give" means "God grant," an invocation unusual in ballads, which rarely have Christian sentiments. "Sib" is a capacious word in Middle English, denoting many different kinds of blood kinship as well as non-biological relatedness. It connotes very special closeness and intimacy. Best friends might be "sib." But siblings are the most "sib" of all because of their special relationship in the English kinship system—a point to which I will return.

Another major difference between the Motherwell variant collected from Mrs. King in 1825 and this older version of the ballad found in Robert Edwards's commonplace book is that the brother-sister relationship represented is much more egalitarian in the older 1630 version.

"Ther was a sister and a brother / the sun gois to under the wood / who most intirelie lovid [each] other / god give we had nevir beine sib." Rather than "He takes his sister down to her father's deer park," as in the eighteenth-century variant, in the 1630 version we are told that "they most intirely" loved one another. He then says "sister I wald lay the by [sister I would lay thee by] … and thou wold not my deuds cry"—that is, sister I would hide thee so that you, i.e. your pregnancy, would not proclaim my deeds to the world. And she replies: "Alas, brother wald ye doe so / The sun gois to under the wood / I rathir nou death undergoe / God give we had nevir been sib." Then she says it is her father's feast day and she must be laced in her clothes and join the guests. When she bends over, her laces will break, presumably because of her pregnant girth. She says that *she* will go to her father's stable and get a horse for them to ride away on.

They have not ridden but a mile when her waters break and he asks if he is too simple, or lowly, to ride or stay with her all night. She tells him that when he hears her loud cry to bend his bow and run to the sound; and when he sees her lying still to sound his horn—or, rather, to make his horn sigh—and to come to her. She says "I wald give al my fathirs land / for on woman at my command," a poignant reminder that their sexual relations have dissevered her from her natural gender group. One assumes that he does as she tells him, but

> When that he cam soon hir besead,
> The sun gois to under the wood
> The bab was borne the lady dead
> God give we had nevir been sib.

So in this earlier version he does not kill her—does not use his yew-tree bow to shoot a silver arrow at her—but is perhaps hunting, as in "Leesome Brand," when she delivers her baby and dies in the attempt. Then comes the verse about the living offspring:

> Ther he has tain his yong yong sonne
> The sun gois to under the wood
> And borne to a milk womane
> God give we had nevir beine sib.

After that he draws his sword and wounds himself sore and asks his mother to make his bed for him.

> Mother alas I tint my knife
> The sun gois to under the wood

> I lovid better than my lyffe.
> God give we had nevir beine sib.
>
> Mothir I have als tint my shead
> The sun goes to under the wood
> I lovid better than them bead.
> God give we had nevir beine sib.

Then he turns his face to the wall and gives up the ghost. The ballad ends with the familiar formula about true lovers: one was laid in the church and the other in the choir, and out of one grows a birch and out of the other a briar.

> Ye may knou surlie by thir signes
> The sun goes to under the wood
> They wer tuo lowirs neire.
> God give we have nevir beine sib.

This is an interesting early variant of the "Sheath and Knife" ballad circulating at the end of the eighteenth century. Although the biological weight of the liaison falls on the woman, and although the brother speaks of wanting to keep "his" deeds from being known in the world, we are told in the first verse that these two love each other entirely and equally. Rather than the brother simply taking his sister to the woods and killing and burying her, these two try to run away together. Moreover, when she is gone he wounds himself with his sword and dies, rather than just standing around in his father's hall with music and minstrels, muttering enigmatically about losing a sheath and knife. Most significantly, in this version their child is alive with a wet nurse at the end, not dead and buried with the mother. It is an altogether more positive vision of their connection both in terms of their love, their death, and the lament in which they wish that they were not sib, which means more than wishing they were not siblings. It also means "I wish we were not related" or "I wish we were not so close or intimate."

This earlier version has a more fluid, continuous narrative line rather than being made up of disjoint, symbolic episodes. From the moment the brother worries about the world finding out about them until the birch and the briar grow from their graves, the sequence is clear. In the eighteenth-century/early nineteenth-century variant of "Sheath and Knife" the story ends elliptically with the brother's sadness in the midst of court revelry, and the sexual connection of the brother and sister is foregrounded with the enigmatic phrase "sheath and knife," repeated three times. This figure for a set of genitals that go together—but whose perfect fit is irreplaceably lost—ends the ballad; this haunting image still resonates when the song is over. The 1630 variant, by contrast, finishes with the familiar trope of the birch and briar, telling us that these familiar symbolic plants marked two "lovers neire." That appears to be more significant than the brother's lament that "no cutlar in this land/ can make a kniffe so at my command," a complaint that also confounds the sexual figuration, since it is his sister who has died and their child who is living. In the 1630 variant, the incestuous sex matters less than their tragic relationship; they are star-crossed lovers who happen to be brother and sister rather than a brother and his sister, the king's daughter, who has been having illicit sex with her brother and must pay with her life for it.

In the eighteenth-century version collected in the nineteenth century, the woman is much more passive and she alone must die—the weight of the sexual transgression falls on her. The sister in the seventeenth-century version has a great deal more agency: she is the one who goes to the stable and gets a horse for them to ride; she tells her lover what to do; and when she dies with tragic inevitability her brother no longer wants to live but takes his own life. The drama is told entirely from the outside: what happens, what he says, what she says. That impassivity still marks the later eighteenth-century version, but all sense of the particularity of the woman has disappeared, for she says almost nothing. She is there as the cause of the brother's distress, but one knows nothing about her. Insofar as anyone is affected by this drama, the only self that matters in the late eighteenth-century version is the brother's self.

What are we to make of the change in the ballad "Sheath and Knife" over the course of two centuries? Does it mean anything at all? Can we interpret the changes in it as signifying changes in society? These are only variants, after all, and there is no way of knowing if there were others circulating that make this way of reading them moot. Extrapolating from a single variant found in a 1630 commonplace book must be tentative and provisional. Nevertheless, the cultural critic cannot resist asking whether these differences signify changes in attitudes toward incest, or sex, or brother-sister relations. In interpreting texts from an oral tradition, it is worth remembering Walter Ong's dictum that "oral traditions reflect a society's present cultural values" rather than preserving its past. "The integrity of the past [is] subordinate to the integrity of the present" in any oral tradition, he writes.[15] In other words, oral transmission tends to update texts; what is no longer relevant drops out of an oral repertoire. So the change in this ballad, the breaking apart of "Sheath and Knife" and "Leesome Brand" into two separate ballads in the course of a century and a half, probably does tell us something about a shift in cultural attitudes between 1630, when Robert Edwards compiled his manuscript book, and the later eighteenth century, when Walter Scott's nursemaid sang "Sheath and Knife" to him and more or less when Mrs. King learned it, while Agnes Lyle learned "Leesome Brand" as a separate ballad.[16]

Quite a few other ballads about incest were collected in eighteenth-century Scotland, and all of them—and there are six in Child's canon—are about brother-sister incest.[17] Not one of them is about intergenerational incest between fathers and daughters or uncles and nieces. Nor is that because brother-sister incest was the only kind of incest that occurred in the British Isles. Court records—in England at least—provide plenty of evidence of the garden-variety intergenerational father-daughter and uncle-niece incest, although none of it seems to have been memorialized in ballads. There were, in addition, several notorious cases of sibling incest in eighteenth-century England where the principals flouted convention and lived together, generating plenty of horrified gossip.[18]

It is unlikely that the exclusive reference to brother-sister incest in Scottish and Irish ballads reflects the reality of sexual practice in the period. It may reflect, instead, the lines of transmission for this form of literature, and the fact that women tended to be the carriers of the old ballads; women may have found it too upsetting to sing about intergenerational incest.[19] Even ballads about the less threatening and more egalitarian form of brother-sister incest were undoubtedly painful to remember and to sing. Indeed, when one of these incest ballads was collected from Irish traveling people in the twentieth century, the collector noted that it was considered an "unlucky" or "forbidden" song. And Sara Cleveland, an American singer who learned one of these brother-sister incest ballads from her mother, reported that her mother rarely sang it and then only when alone or working around the house.[20] So it is possible that the exclusive focus on brother-sister incest in orally transmitted ballads is an artifact of the gendered patterns of transmission of these ballads.

But it is also possible that these incest ballads all focus on a similar form of sibling incest because they all come out of one cultural moment, traceable to roughly the same period and location—northern Scotland in the late eighteenth/early nineteenth century. One can only speculate about what they might reveal about kinship, siblings, self, or society at this particular historical juncture.

In four of seven brother-sister incest ballads (listed in n. 17), the incest is committed knowingly,[21] and in "Sheath and Knife," "Lizie Wan," and "The Rich Man's Daughter," the brother kills the sister when he discovers that she is pregnant. In "Brown Robyn's Confession," the erring brother goes to sea and then suddenly neither the sun nor moon nor stars are visible. The other sailors are sure that someone on board among them is evil and decide to cast lots to determine who is bringing them bad luck and needs to be cast out. When the lot falls to Brown Robyn, he confesses to incest with his mother *and* his sister, and he bids his fellow sailors bind him to a plank and throw him overboard, which they do.

In the other three incest ballads, "The Bonny Hind," "The King's Dochter Jean,"[22] and "Babylon," the brother—who, having been abroad for many years, does not recognize his sister and is himself unrecognizable—assaults and rapes her, not knowing that she is her brother. When he learns what he has done, he kills himself or she kills herself. It has also been suggested that incest is at the root of the murderous rage between brothers in "Two Brothers" and in "Edward." The incestuous desire of one brother for their sister—"a little bush that might have been a tree"—and the protective resistance of the other brother are what ignites the struggle between them that leads to the fratricidal murder of one brother by the other.

Nor is outright incest the only form of "brother trouble" associated with sexual conduct in ballads collected in the eighteenth-century British Isles. Brothers in ballads often seek to control their sisters' sexuality by determining who they can and cannot marry. And when a sister is not obedient to her brother's wishes, he kills her or kills her lover. In "Bonnie Susie Cleveland," the brother lights the fire under the pyre to which his sister is tied. In "Andrew Lammie," the girl's mother and father beat her full sore, but it is her brother who breaks her back for loving Andrew Lammie. In the "Cruel Brother," the brother kills his sister with a little penknife because although her lover has asked permission of all her kin to marry her—her mother, her father, and her sisters—he neglects to ask her brother's permission.[23] In "Dowie Dens of Yarrow" and in "Clerk Saunders," the brothers kill their sister's lover because he comes from the wrong class.

Sibling solidarity is a hallmark of the British kinship system, in which lineage is traced through both the mother and the father. Siblings are the closest of all kin in a bilateral, cognatic system because only siblings have identical consanguineal kin. Through their common mother, they are uniquely related to a set of maternal relatives in addition to their paternal relatives. Furthermore, siblings are the only link between these sets of maternal and paternal relatives because although marriage binds their parents together, it creates no recognized connection between the blood relations of the two spouses: the mother's sisters are not related to the father's brothers, but both are related to the children of the union.

Siblings thus create a significant link in the chain of kinship. One linguistic trace of the significance of siblings in the British kinship system is the fact that the terms for nieces and nephews—the children of one's siblings—often meant "grandchild" as well. In other words, the children of one's siblings were like one's own grandchildren, as significant to oneself intergenerationally as the direct line through one's own progeny.[24] Socially and psychologically, brothers and sisters were often each others' earliest sustained cross-sex relationship and childhood companions as well.

In the course of the eighteenth century, the primacy of this brother-sister relation changed in relation to a number of factors—among them the development of capitalism, the drive to accumulate property, and changes in inheritance law.[25] Less and less were sisters considered equal members with their brothers of their clans or kin groups, less and less were they thought to be female versions of their brothers, but increasingly "chickens raised for other men's tables" as James Harlowe so eloquently puts it in Richardson's novel, *Clarissa* (1748). The social expectation that sisters would be protected and cherished by their brothers, and the expectation that brothers would be responsible for their sisters, diminished in the course of the eighteenth century.[26] These ballads about brothers who kill their sisters, who rape them violently, or who kill their lovers—that is, who appropriate, direct, or terminate their sexuality—all register the sense that brothers own their sisters. Their cruelty is magnified by the betrayal of the closeness expected between a brother and a sister, a betrayal of the protection a brother once owed his sister, and a betrayal of the sibling love that once distinguished the British kinship system.[27] By the eighteenth century brothers are represented in ballads as dangerous to the interests of their sisters, whether because of biology (female pregnancy revealing sexual relations in "Sheath and Knife"), character (the aggressive stance of the brother in "Babylon" and "The Bonny Hind"), or evolving male privilege ("The Cruel Brother")—or some combination of all three.

When "Sheath and Knife or Leesome Brand" was divided into two separate ballads—one in which two lovers come to grief and one in which a brother kills his sister because she carries his child and he wants to hide the evidence of his incest—it signals a new economy in the relations between brothers and sisters. Brothers seem to have significantly more power than their sisters; they keep a tight rein on their sister's sexual favors—whether for themselves or by choosing their sisters' lovers. Rather than being tragic for both lovers, incest has become dangerous for a woman in this later world because her pregnancy reveals it. The story has changed from being a story of star-crossed lovers to a story in which the woman must be sacrificed. Incestuous sex has become so shameful that it must be hidden at all costs. The ballad focuses on the brother's acts and feelings and we hardly hear from the sister in the later variant "Sheath and Knife"; in the earlier version, however, she has a lot more to say.

The Romantic period, the early nineteenth century, is of course the period associated with brother-sister incest, conceived as refusing to accommodate to a genuinely alternative other, instead preferring an insistent narcissistic mirroring in a loved second self. The sheath-and-knife trope for brother-sister incest in ballads collected at the turn of the century might also be seen as a figure for the intense, solipsistic enthusiasm for the self in its context—an emphasis that privileges the alter ego of the sibling rather than seeking farther afield for a love object.

Juliet Mitchell, analyzing brother-sister incest in our own society, notes that the mother is usually absent in the clinical configuration of sibling incest.[28] Writing psychoanalytically about sibling incest, she describes the "narcissistic love-of-the-other-as-the-self," which can explode into murderous hatred because of the threat of self-annihilation if there is no mother present to supervise her children and to keep familial relationships in order. According to Mitchell, brothers and sisters drawn to one another both love one another as versions of themselves, alter egos, and at the same time hate each other for supplanting each other in their families. When the mother is absent, there is no one to reinforce the differentiation between mothers and sisters, making sure that mothers and sisters do not become confused.[29] The confusion that results when incest issues in pregnancy is that a man becomes a father/brother and a woman becomes a mother/sister.

According to Mitchell, love and hate, sexual attraction and murderous rivalry coexist in modern-day sibling relationships. "Siblings provide a way of learning to love and hate the same person," she says;[30] this is one of the truths that still resonates for contemporary audiences of this ballad. The later version of "Sheath and Knife" is too abbreviated to identify any elements of hate or rivalry in it—but there is also no mention of the true love that so dominates the 1630 version of the ballad. However, the mother is certainly missing (as she is from much of the fiction of the end of the eighteenth century).[31] Although there is a father with a court and ships sailing on the seas, there is no mother in the ballad. The brother-sister mirroring is figured in the repeated image of the sheath and knife as well as the dangerousness of their closeness. Sex and death are inextricably entwined in this ballad in the killing of the sister the moment after she gives birth, and in the burial of the infant with the sister/mother.

I have been arguing that "Sheath and Knife," a ballad that Sir Walter Scott heard as a young boy and that William Motherwell collected from an "old singing woman" in 1825, carries cultural attitudes of the eighteenth century toward the self, sexuality, and the family—and that these cultural attitudes come into sharper focus when compared with a variant of the ballad in circulation two centuries before. The way the brother controls his sister's fate, her relative silence, his isolation and self-regarding misery, the way the death punishment is dealt to the woman of the couple who engage in transgressive sex, the stillborn infant, the absence of the mother in this tragedy—all of these elements bespeak a configuration of kinship and sexuality familiar to us from other sources.[32] The ballad illustrates women's sexual victimization, a focus on male subjectivity—even a kind of pre-Romantic narcissism—the absence of adult women, and bodies that are not polymorphously pleasurable but that are formally male and female, designed functionally to fit together like a sheath and knife, by a kind of divine workmanship. The loss of one half renders the other incomplete. But the perfect fit—and indeed sexuality itself—is unholy in the ballad, because the incest tinges it with horror and it is not romanticized with love. That these meanings were available in ballads sung by ordinary people in the period suggests that they were not confined to the novel-reading literate classes but permeated all levels of society. The ballad form itself is a testimony to the human capacity to wrest beauty out of tragedy—and to create art with nothing more than the human voice and mind.

Notes

This chapter is a revised version of an article previously published as "Brother Trouble: Incest Ballads of the British Isles," *The Eighteenth Century* 47.2 (2006): 289–307. It appears here with the permission of the author, who holds the copyright.

1. Maria Colomba Mattei Trombetta di Roma, called la Romaninia or La Colonna or Signora Mattei. Her career began in Naples in 1743, and she sang in numerous Italian cities before reaching London in 1754–1755. She returned to London and finished her career there, in 1758–1762. Philip H. Highfill, Kalman A. Burnim, and Edward A. Langhans, *A Biographical Dictionary of Actors, Actresses, Musicians, Dancers, Managers & Other Stage Personnel in London, 1660–1800*, vol. 10 (Carbondale, IL, 1973), 137–138. Thanks to Lowell Lindgren for this reference.
2. Published 13 October 1759 in *The Bee*.
3. Walter J. Ong, *Orality and Literacy* (London, 1988), 43.
4. Claude M. Simpson, *The British Broadside Ballad and Its Music* (New Brunswick, 1966), xi.
5. Albert B. Friedman supposes that many of them might have been in existence as early as 1100, but points out that Child's oldest example ["Judas," Child #23] dates

from the late thirteenth century and that there are only half a dozen ballads in Child's collection from manuscripts older than 1500. Friedman, *The Ballad Revival* (Chicago, 1961), 15.

6. Charles Kirkpatrick Sharpe, *A Ballad Book* (Edinburgh, 1880), 159, cited in Francis James Child, *The English and Scottish Popular Ballads*, 5 vols. [1882–1898] (Northfield, MN, 2001), vol. 1, 259.

7. Francis James Child's monumental collection of *The English and Scottish Popular Ballads* was published in ten volumes between 1882 and 1898. He included 305 ballads in his collection, and they are still referred to by the numbers he gave them.

8. These elements of oral composition are listed by (among others) David Atkinson, *The English Traditional Ballad* (Burlington, VT, 2002), 12.

9. Atkinson, *Traditional Ballad*, 148.

10. A further association between broom and sexuality is suggested by the folk marriage custom of jumping over a broom—an implement originally made of broom, whence its name.

11. A version of "Leesome Brand" was collected by Motherwell from Agnes Lyle of Kilbarchan parish at about the same time as he collected "Sheath and Knife" from Mrs. King of the same parish. It is very similar to "Sheath and Knife," except that the lovers are not said to be brother and sister and they have with them a child—his "auld son"—whom he carries in his "coat lap." This child, too, is killed when he shoots his arrow.

12. Buchan, *Ancient Ballads and Songs of North of Scotland*, 2 vols. (Edinburgh, 1828).

13. Helena Mennie Shire, "Introduction," in *Poems from Panmure House*, ed. Helena Mennie Shire (Cambridge, 1960), 13–19. Shire observes on 22–23 that at the same time this ballad was circulating, Ford's play "'Tis Pity She's a Whore" was on the stage. The similarities of incident and atmosphere between that play and the ballad lead her to conjecture that "Ford may have had a version of this ballad running in his head" when he wrote the play.

14. See *The Norton Anthology of Literature*. Thanks to Alan Levitan for this reference.

15. Ong, *Orality and Literacy*, 48.

16. Motherwell collected these ballads in 1825, but by then both these women were elderly—he called them "old singing women"—and had learned their repertoires many years earlier. All of these ballads were collected in Scotland. See Mary Ellen Brown, *William Motherwell's Cultural Politics* (Lexington, KY, 2001), Appendix 1, 161–170.

17. "Babylon" (Child 14), "Sheath and Knife" (Child 16), "The Bonny Hind" (Child 50), "Lizie Wan" (Child 51), "The King's Dochter Lady Jean" (Child 52), "Brown Robyn's Confession" (Child 57). There is another brother-sister incest ballad from Ireland sung by Peta Webb called "The Rich Man's Daughter" that is not a Child ballad but follows this pattern. The brother kills the sister when she is about to give birth to their child.

18. Frances Burney's oldest brother, James, eloped with his half sister Sarah Harriet in 1798 and lived with her for the next five years. For this and other known cases of incest in eighteenth-century England, see my *Novel Relations: The Transformation of Kinship in English Literature and Culture 1748–1818* (Cambridge, 2004), 381–387, here 383–384. Horace Walpole reported that William Pitt's sister Elizabeth, who had numerous and public liaisons, including one with Lord Talbot, was launched on her scandalous career by an affair with her brother Tom. *The Correspondence of Horace Walpole*, compiled by Edwin M. Martz with Ruth K. McClure and William T. LaMay (New Haven, 1983), vol. 20, 411. Lord Bolingbroke is also supposed to

have an incestuous affair with his sister, Miss Beauclerk, in 1788 or 1789. See William F. LeFanu, ed., *Betsy Sheridan's Journal* (New Brunswick, 1960), 176–177. I am indebted to Betty Rizzo for these last two references.

19. For a discussion of women as the transmitters of ballads, see my "'The Finest Ballads': Women's Oral Traditions in Eighteenth-Century Scotland," *Eighteenth-Century Life* 32, no. 2 (2008): 81–97.

20. Sara Cleveland sings "Queen Jane" on her Folk Legacy CD, the only published American version of "The King's Dochter Lady Jean." This feeling about the song is reported by Kenneth Goldstein in his notes to the CD and reported by David Atkinson in *The English Traditional Ballad*, 113.

21. "Sheath and Knife" (Child 16), "Lizie Wan" (Child 51), and "Brown Robyn's Confession" (Child 57). For a more elaborate treatment of this theme in folksong, see P. G. Brewster, "The Incest Theme in Folksong," *FF Communication* 80, no. 212 (1972): 3–36.

22. Including the version sung by Sara Cleveland, "Queen Jane."

23. It has also been suggested that if her brother kills her before she consummates her marriage and conceives an heir, he will not have to share their inheritance with her.

24. Naomi Tadmor, *Family and Friends in Eighteenth-Century England* (Cambridge, 2001), 121.

25. I do not have space in this essay to expand on this shorthand. But for a fuller treatment of the reasons for this changed relationship see my *Novel Relations*, especially chapter 4, "Brotherly Love in Life and Literature."

26. Eileen Spring traces the visible beginnings of this change to the use of the "strict settlement" in inheritance law in the late seventeenth century. See Eileen Spring, *Law, Land and Family: Aristocratic Inheritance in England 1300–1800* (Chapel Hill, 1993), 10–15.

27. See, for example, the examples of supportive seventeenth-century brother-sister relationships given in *Novel Relations*, 158–159.

28. Juliet Mitchell, *Siblings: Sex and Violence* (Cambridge, 2003).

29. Ibid., 29.

30. Ibid., 225. In a successful resolution of this tension, continues Mitchell, a person learns to transform narcissistic love into "object-love and murderousness into objective hatred for what is wrong or evil in the self and other."

31. The absence of the mother in the later version of this ballad is another sign of its eighteenth-century provenance, as those familiar with the literature of this period will recognize. Mothers begin to disappear from English novels by the second half of the eighteenth century. See my *Novel Relations*, especially chapter 8, "The Importance of Aunts."

32. Again, see my *Novel Relations*. But there is plenty of other work on gender relations and sexuality in the eighteenth-century British Isles that could account for these particulars.

Siblinghood and the Emotional Dimensions of the New Kinship System, 1800–1850

A French Example

Christopher H. Johnson

For a half-century, French historians and demographers have been documenting the marked shift in marriage patterns in France (and beyond) toward consanguinity, including widespread first-cousin marriage, that occurred during the later eighteenth and nineteenth centuries. Some, like Jean Sutter—the pioneer in such studies—attribute the change simply to large families and rapid population growth, hence the greater availability of consanguines, while others emphasize secularization and the declining concern with regard to the "incest" prohibitions of the church. The large-scale study by Jean-Louis Gouesse was content to demonstrate the phenomenon without searching for explanations. Neither larger changes in kinship structures nor analysis of internal family life figured significantly in the discussion.[1] At the same time, some attention was given by French writers (though on nothing like the scale of the English or Germans) to the appearance in literature, and among the literati themselves, of intense brother-sister love often bordering on incest and of the centrality of siblings within social and cultural intercourse in general during the same era. Indeed, this phenomenon was one of the elements most clearly defining Romanticism.[2] Although the connection between the new affective world of siblings and the rise of consanguineous marriage might seem obvious—close siblings produce children who are likely to be close cousins—analysis along these lines, certainly for France, has been rare.[3]

The reason for this lies in an inadequate understanding of the larger picture of what happened to the practices and structure of kinship from 1750 to 1850. That picture is now in place thanks mainly to the pioneering efforts of David Sabean in *Kinship in Neckarhausen* and in the flurry of conferences and publications that have occurred under his leadership since 2000.[4] The key characteristics of the new kinship regime of the nineteenth century and the place of siblings within it are presented in the introduction to this volume. What occurred in the overall kinship system was a shift from vertical to horizontal structures and kin reckoning. Within the family, the nature of authority transformed. Patriarchy of the older sort—what Carole Patemen called "father-right," in which the father ruled a descent system geared to the maintenance of the dynastic "bloodline"—gave way to greater equality among children, whatever their birth order, reflected in both inheritance and power. But a new kind of male authority nevertheless came to be established, described by Juliet MacCannell as "the regime of the brother" and by Pateman as the establishment of "husband-right," though in reality it was both.[5]

In France, a brief moment of potential familial and gender equality in the first year of the Republic was rapidly extinguished as "fraternity" came to be sharply defined as male in the streets and in the Convention during the Year II, a process best captured by Lynn Hunt's examination of the political culture brewed by parricide, guilt-ridden association of all evil with the queen, become harlot *and* lesbian, and the shadow of Armageddon cast across *la patrie en danger*.[6] Several years would pass before the Napoleonic Code fully inscribed husband-right, but in the meantime the courts consistently diminished wives' rights in divorce and, as Susanne Desan has shown brilliantly, favored brothers in conflicts with sisters over inheritance. The family had been substantially deregulated, which often meant that past protections (such as the right of an unmarried pregnant woman to charge her partner before the law) were lost, while unprecedented private authority was placed in the hands of the head of household, usually the husband, brother, or guardian.[7]

But still, an enormous change had taken place. Parental authority in matters of marriage had been severely shaken. Although fathers never could simply dictate whom (or whether) their children should marry (thanks to the Council of Trent), their power over dowry and inheritance gave them leverage that only the most daring or love-struck child could ignore. By the mid eighteenth century, however, families were already practicing a much more open and sensitive approach to matrimony, where the children were exposed to options in ways that gave them (or appeared to give them) greater freedom of choice. Other well-documented developments placed the child, then the courting couple, then loving spouses at center stage. Younger sons and daughters sought and won greater recognition. They, tyrannized lovers, objects of forced courtships, abused wives, and other victims of patriarchal authority had their day in court, or at least before the commissaires of the Châtelet and provincial Présidial tribunals, and were received with sympathy.[8] Revolutionary legislation sought to instantiate this developing familial culture before falling back to the compromises demanded by the "band of brothers." But even so, things could never be the same, and sisters, wives, mothers, and aunts found that unregulated familial liberty and privacy gave them pathways to autonomy and influence that had not previously existed. Above all, they became the arbiters of the culture of love and mutual respect that came to define proper family life. This authority in the private sphere spilled over in many ways into the public, certainly having something to do with the explosion of feminist politics during the Second Republic.[9] Central to all this were the relationships among brothers and sisters, and at one remove, among cousins.

Much scholarly study of the affective universe of families (and the role of siblings within them) in the eighteenth and nineteenth centuries has been based in fiction and poetry and rooted in an assumption of "the decline of kinship," which had been supposedly superseded by the "modern" nuclear family, the self-motivated individual, and modern capitalism (as if these could not operate within a kinship system). Nevertheless, important insights can be drawn from this literature because it focuses on the internal emotional dynamics of families. Michel Foucault argues that the eighteenth century saw a momentous transformation in "Western societies" in which a "new apparatus," sexuality, was "deployed" under the impulsion of "economic processes and political structures" that could no longer rely on the system of "alliance" that had served to regulate "relations of sex" via rules of marriage and kinship set by church and state to maintain a relative "homeostasis of the social body." The nuclear family became the crucible of sexuality, extolling its pleasures and bearing its burdens. "Its role was to anchor sexuality and provide it with a permanent support." Alliance and its elements hardly disappeared, but the nature of its regulation shifted. "The deployment of alliance is built around a system of rules defining the permitted and the forbidden, the licit and the illicit, whereas the deployment of sexuality operates according to mobile, polymorphous, and contingent techniques of power." For Foucault, these techniques developed over the nineteenth century via the "psychologization" and the "psychiatrization" of sexuality, culminating in Charcot and Freud, who effectively revitalized the system of alliance by "discovering" the rules of sexuality and defining as "normal" the male-centered heterosexual nuclear family that overcame ominous "complexes" via psychoanalysis.[10]

But the interesting hypothesis for the purposes of this essay, which Foucault does not focus on, is that the era in which sexuality with its various manifestations—romantic love, the rise of the "couple," familial intimacy, "sensibility," and a fascination with "perversions," so lovingly chronicled by literary critics and historians[11]—came to be "deployed" in Western culture, roughly 1750–1850, was also one in which the new techniques of power were in their *infancy*. In their stead, as we have noted, deregulation of the family was the rule, and literature, art, music, and philosophy everywhere reflected a vortex of emotions liberated from the system of alliance. Sade obviously represented the extreme, but no theme of sexuality and emotional introspection was beyond exploration.[12] Internal family life was minutely dissected, laying bare the joys and tensions, the conflicts of the young harbingers of the new regime with the defenders of the old, and all the rest.

Central to this discourse was incest. Foucault makes perhaps his most telling point when he writes:

> Since the eighteenth century, the family has become an obligatory locus of affects, feelings, love; [and] for this reason sexuality is 'incestuous' from the start; … [incest] is constantly being solicited and refused; it is an object of obsession and attraction; a dreadful secret and a pivot. It is manifested as a thing that is strictly forbidden in the family insofar as it functions as a deployment of alliance; but it is also a thing that is continuously demanded in order for the family to be a hotbed of constant sexual enticement.[13]

Foucault was referring to the entire sweep of modern history, but at no time was all this truer than in the Revolutionary age. He also pays no attention to the *type* of incest rising to prominence in specific historical eras. But the discourse of this same period privileged the brother-sister relationship in an unprecedented manner, supplanting the classic intergenerational themes of the seventeenth century.[14] At the same time, a highly charged, sexualized bond of militaristic fraternity pervaded the language of politics: love of brothers and love of nation became conflated.[15] Added together, then, siblinghood experienced an unprecedented intensity in the late eighteenth and nineteenth centuries that corresponded directly with the advent of Foucault's "sexuality" and operated more or less "freely" before being reined in by the disciplinary powers of modern science. It was thus in the fertile soil of sibling emotions that the new family and kinship regime of the nineteenth century took root.

This essay explores these emotions via a collection of letters and journals authored by ordinary bourgeois and bourgeoises whose families achieved local elite status during the half-century spanning the year 1800.[16] Such materials are exceedingly rare, especially for France. They confirm—on the ground level, so to speak—the discourses of siblinghood evident in the world of literature and among intellectuals as well as the political rhetoric of the day. They also open the way toward a systematic understanding of the functions of siblings in the creation of the new kinship system and their relevance to the larger social, economic, and political forces of emergent modernity.

Sexuality

The Galles, Jollivet, and Le Ridant families of Vannes (Morbihan), long culturally French though of Welsh and Breton origins, came together in a double wedding of 1787 and were further bound in a Jollivet-Le Ridant marriage a decade later. The Galles owned one of the premier publishing houses in Brittany and, despite their moderate royalism, continued to publish official documents and educational textbooks, along with their usual range of popular literary, philosophical, and historical works, during the Revolution. The Jollivets and Le Ridants came from independent farming stock in the Vannetais hinterland whose sons established themselves as *notaires* in the city in the mid eighteenth century, producing lawyers and military officers in the next generation. One, Jean-Marie Le Ridant (who married Marie Jollivet in 1797), joined the counterrevolutionary Chouannerie but fought for France during the empire until 1812, when he chose prison over joining the Russian invasion. He and his brother-in-law, notaire and lawyer René Jollivet, led Vannes's royalist resistance to the One Hundred Days and emerged (significantly through the work of Marie Jollivet Le Ridant, who had forged ties with the Bourbon court in exile) as the families' main players on the national stage.[17]

The next generation, the main focus here, arrived in profusion during the Revolution and empire, typical of burgeoning bourgeois families of the age.[18] Marc Galles and Adelaïde Jollivet produced six children—Jean-Marie, Fanny, Bertin, Eugène, Aimée, and Cécile—before the post-childbirth death of Adelaïde in 1797. Marc followed her four years later. René Jollivet and Jeanne Le Ridant lost no children either, baptizing François, Jean-Baptiste, and Yves, but Jeanne did not long survive the birth of "Yvon." René Jollivet remarried quickly, his young bride, Cécile

Marquer, coming from a line of notaires in nearby Auray, a conserva-
tive Catholic stronghold with a famous shrine. Adèle, named to honor
her aunt, and René II were her only children, as she too passed on after
the loss of her third child in 1801. Jollivet soon married again, drawing
upon a wealthy landowning family with (former) aristocratic connections from La Roche-Bernard, the Thomas-Kercados. Désirée, who lived
a full life, provided six more Jollivets: Stanislas, Eugène, Marie-Louise,
Jenny, Fanny, and Marie-Elizabeth, the last arriving in 1814.

The prevalence of maternal death and orphanhood for the Galles children is excessive but not extreme in this age when male physicians were
replacing (or outranking) midwives at the upper-class birthing bed.[19]
Stepmothers and half siblings generally were loved as one's own. Désirée
would occasionally irritate the adult Adèle, but the latter loved all of her
"brothers and sisters" without distinction, although she and René II did
have a special bond, revealed by our correspondence, due to the disappearance of their mother when they were three and four.[20] René Jollivet
I became the guardian of "les enfants Galles" (whose grandmother—one
of several great women of the older generations—ran the firm that took
that name), creating an enormous brood of sixteen children whose birth
dates ranged from 1788 to 1814. Cousins were little differentiated from
siblings, and the two families lived around the corner from each other
in the heart of Vannes. Marie Jollivet and Jean-Marie Le Ridant, who divided their time between Paris and their country house near Auray, were
childless, but, because of their prestige, she emerged as the crucial force
in the oversight of the families' destinies—the charismatic aunt with
intelligence, wit, and connections to which all of the next generation
deferred, though not always without heartache.[21]

The core of this sibling archipelago, where our correspondence is the
most intense, formed around Eugène Galles (born 1794) and Adèle Jollivet (1796), who would marry, the first of many cousins to do so in these
families, in 1818. Jean-Marie Galles (1790) took over management of the
publishing house when he was eighteen, and sister Fanny (1788) married
a tax official and family confidant, moving to Redon in 1811. They and
the two oldest Jollivet sons, François (1788), who entered public administration, and Baptiste (1790), who followed a military career, remained
close to their younger siblings throughout their lives and were almost
substitute parents in the presence of so many deaths.[22] The Jollivet children of René's third marriage delighted the older siblings in the middle,
figuring extensively in their correspondence, but they too stood away
from the emotional fervor that marked this cohort's relationships. Bertin
Galles (1792), who became a naval officer in 1812; Eugène, who followed him to Saint-Cyr, but went to the infantry in 1813; Yvon Jollivet

(1794), who took over his father's notarial étude in 1816; Aimée Galles (1793); Adèle and René Jollivet II (1797), who also chose a career in the navy; and finally Cécile Galles (1796), a wonderfully opinionated but sickly friend to all who would die at thirty without marrying: these formed an incredibly tight-knit group of siblings/cousins with almost identical experiences, educations (and the girls were remarkably well trained), and interests, both cultural and political. Separated by only six years, they (though Yvon and René mainly by reference) interacted in letters that allow us to penetrate their hearts.[23]

This family correspondence comes down to us thanks to the eldest son of Adèle Jollivet and Eugène Galles, General René Galles, who in his later years gathered reams of family letters to guide him in the preparation of his "Journal," the story of his parents, his aunts and uncles, and his youth through his graduation from the Ecole Polytechnique in 1839.[24] Although he sorted out a few, many of these letters are remarkable in their intimacy and frankness, revealing emotional dynamics usually only found in fiction.[25] His memoir and that of his cousin Jules Jollivet (also a general), along with several dozen letters preserved in the Papiers Jollivet at the Morbihan archives, supplement this vast collection.[26] Several dozen letters from the older generation were included, allowing some interesting comparisons. Adèle's and her siblings' letters to young René while in school comprise a hefty file, and aunt Marie Jollivet Le Ridant's correspondence with Adèle has been preserved as well. Altogether, we are in a position to plumb deeply into the affective dimensions of siblinghood over three generations and its articulation with the emergent consanguineous kinship system of the Revolutionary age.

At the core of this correspondence are the letters exchanged by Adèle and Eugène before and after their marriage and those between them and their siblings/cousins. Although two dozen date from the last years of the empire, the rest (some 327 letters and notes) were written between 1815 and 1825, the year of Eugène's tragic death from yellow fever while on duty as an army captain in Guadeloupe. His "semesters" on duty, starting on Belle Ile off the Morbihan coast in 1816 and then taking him all over the northern half of France, explain the volume of the correspondence, while his shocking end explains their meticulous preservation.[27] Let us begin with the romance of Adèle and Eugène and the new family of the nineteenth century, that incestuous "hotbed of constant sexual enticement."

Our first introduction to their love, tellingly, comes from their sisters/cousins writing to Eugène upon his arrival on Belle Ile. Cécile Galles wrote (17 January 1816): "we were so worried about not hearing of your safe passage that every time a knock came at the door, Adèle and I froze with fear." What a relief it was when his first letter came. Cécile celebrated by redecorating his room, which she knew he would find "charming." Aimée Galles then wrote on Ash Wednesday about the delightful Carnival she had spent, culminating in a grand turkey dinner chez Maman Jollivet. It seems that Adèle was not at home, but rather had visited Eugène, for Aimée jokes about him dancing with "ta Ménagère" on Mardi Gras. She then goes on, in a serious vein: "You tell me not to be jealous of Adèle. Well, that's a fault I'd never have toward her, for the greater her affection is for you, the more it gives me pleasure, since I take joy in seeing you happy together. I only ask that you save a portion of your affection for a sister who loves you most tenderly."[28]

Aimée's next letter (3 April) introduces a new wrinkle, her own courtship, opening a parallel (surrogate?) relationship and a remarkably revealing discourse on the affective universe of siblings in the early nineteenth century.

> My aunt [Marie] and my uncle Jollivet [René] are very happy with the party who presents himself for me. They know the individual, who is a man of quite agreeable outward appearance, having wit, means, and a very good demeanor, and good prospects for advancement. My aunt has obtained information about his reputation within the [fiscal] administration, and he is highly regarded. It is said that he might be placed in Redon, thus near us all. It is now for me to decide, and that's most difficult. Here, only Adèle gave me a real hearing. But my relatives in the big city say yes; it is now a question of saying it too. Give me your approbation—aunt will write you for it.

So it was that Aimée was "courted." André Savantier was born in Auray of a bourgeois family with a history of friendship, if not kinship, with the Jollivets. If Aimée had ever met him, it was so long ago that her aunt felt obliged to comment on his appearance. Although her marriage had no doubt been a subject of family discussion, she might have expected that the usual round of social events would produce a range of potential partners. At twenty-three, she was hardly ancient. Thus, such an arrangement seems surprising. But if her true love could not be hers, perhaps she did not care.

She was in fact much more interested in the developing relationship between her brother and their cousin. Living side by side, the young women in Vannes spent most of their waking hours together. Adèle was simply regarded as Aimée's and Cécile's "sister." The courtship between the two cousins occurred *among* the four of them. Nothing pleased Aimée more than to write to "their" brother Eugène about Adèle's love for him and the delight their relationship had engendered among their siblings, as on 29 April 1816:

Do you know that I'm your agent for hugs and kisses, and I also own a stock of them to sell to you, although my neck's not long enough to hold them all. Otherwise, I already would have sold a hundred. I'm right here with our sister, the charming Adèle, who is also writing you and, I believe, making jokes at my expense, because I believe a certain person has beautiful eyes that I'd tear mine out for and as beautiful as yours, but she believes none in the world could match yours. ... [Don't forget that] I'm your best friend.

Sibling ties, close and more distant, are in evidence everywhere. In a month, Aimée remarks, she would go off to Redon to be with eldest sister Fanny during the later stages of her most recent pregnancy. On 12 May, she wrote that Eugène had better write to staunch her loneliness, and should he come to Vannes, "come get me. We certainly don't want Adèle to be by herself." There was nothing to say "concerning myself," without a line from Aunt Marie or "the individual. They must be dead." A tax inspector's position may open for Savantier "somewhere in Brittany." So much for that. She reported family news and told about making sugar almonds to "cure your cold." About his last letter: "Adèle never found you so silly, nor I so rude when you compared her to a diamond and me to an uncut stone—hardly flattering, but I forgive you, for love is blind."

Cécile, Adèle's "best friend," was also captivated by the budding romance. To Eugène on 1 June:

[I] talk about you very often with our dear Adèle. And it's not necessary, I assure you, to make her think about you. She's only happy when she thinks that she will see you soon and she counts the days. The places where she can view the sea are those that please her the most. Her favorite turnips are those that come from Belle Ile. What more can one say?

Two weeks later, pouting a bit because Eugène has not written, she urged him to "pursue your conquest, but I pray you not to forget that love ought not neglect friendship." A second sister was pining as well.

Alas, Eugène's visit in early July visit went badly for the young lovers. Miserable, he sought solace from Aimée, who was delighted that he would "choose me to soothe your oppressed heart."

Calm your anxieties, my friend. You must believe that you still hold her affection and if possible it is even greater than before. I have studied Adèle in depth for a long time—and you as well, good Eugène. I have known your inclination toward her from the beginning. I saw with some pain you become attached to her, and her thoughtlessness [ses étourderies] made me fear that you would experience a bottomless pool of sorrows. But now consider how happy I am, since I believe that I have had a small part in the transformation of your destinies. You know that as soon as my aunt returned, I went to stay at Pont Sal. Seeing the interest that this good aunt took in Adèle, whose thoughtlessness pained her, I pleaded her cause and assured my aunt that counsel gently given would quickly bring Adèle back to reason. ... I shared with [Aunt Marie] my sense of your inclination toward Adèle. This good aunt immediately thought of making a happy couple. It didn't take long for Adèle to become herself again and value your affection. ... I can thus tell you that Adèle loves you more each day [and] labors to give you proofs of it. A solid and rational mind is replacing lightness and thoughtlessness. [T]he time is coming when she will have fully developed sound and amiable qualities. ... She makes it her project to embellish her mind and her heart ... by reading instructive and interesting books. Her goal is that her Eugène will find his happiness with her and he will always hold her dear.

Eugène, do not doubt her love for you. ... You have nothing but happiness to look forward to. Tell me, my friend, that you are content, for I am miserable when my good brothers are not.

Thus did Aimée cure the mal de coeur of her brother on behalf of her cousin-sister. The overlapping lines of emotional connection revealed here are striking and speak to the heart of the new sibling-based kinship universe of the age. Aunt Marie, the key sibling of the previous generation, was now drawn in, but it was Aimée the loving sister who implemented it and who also convinced Adèle that intellectual self-improvement was a desirable quality in a prospective wife.[29]

Most remarkable of all, perhaps, is that Aimée had her own problems with "love," to which she devoted a mere seventeen lines of this eighty-line letter.

We have written each other once, Monsieur S. and me, since you left. He has asked my aunt Ridant, every time he writes to her, to pass along his news to me, but since she only writes on the 32nd of the month, our correspondence by commission moves along rather slowly. ... We are quite patient lovers—and quite rational—aren't we?[30]

The business-like nature of Aimée's approaching engagement contrasts sharply with the romance of Eugène and Adèle. Two different marital regimes are simultaneously at work here. Aimée's is an arranged marriage, the "deployment of alliance." Her aunt located an appropriate match, and she was to respond without an enormous amount of soul-searching. It appears that while her passions flamed for her dashing brother and that she could satisfy them to an acceptable extent by entering the heart of the affair between Eugène and Adèle, the Savantier marriage provided a safe haven where illicit love, aroused in "deployment of sexuality," might cool.

Aimée Galles and André Savantier wed on 10 December 1816. Her dowry was modest, and other gifts followed suit. The whole family, save Bertin, gathered for the affair and saw the couple off to the site of André's new post, Châteaulin in far-western Brittany. On 30 December, Aimée wrote from her new home:

> Mon cher Eugène, here we are still separated, and, instead of ten leagues apart, it's forty. I hope that our distance will not change the affection we have for each other, that you will always love your Aimée as she loves you. Write me, send me your news often as well as that of our sister Adèle. Make me part of all that concerns you. You know how interested I am in seeing you happy and what pleasure it gives me when you are; continue forever to regard me as your friend and be assured that, even though I am farther than you from the one you love, when you need my services in her regard, my pen and even my feet ... are at your beck and call.

Aimée's anxiety about somehow losing her closeness to Eugène and her role as go-between was heightened by deep concerns for the safety of both her brothers in the horrible winter of 1816–1817 and the unpleasantness of her new surroundings. She hopes that she can

> bear the burden of being separated from my own. You have no idea of what a place I live in. This is the ugliest hole I've ever seen. But the social life is just fine and compensates a little. ... Meanwhile, *je me désennui près de mon mari* [I find amusement with *or* kill time with my husband], who is a right good boy and can only bring happiness to your sister.

Her letter needs little commentary, but perfectly illustrates the stresses as well as the expectations of arranged marriages. Aimée's heart remained in Vannes with her siblings. Yet she coped sufficiently with ennui to become pregnant almost immediately. We learn of it under the most tragic of circumstances, for Bertin had died in a shipwreck off the African coast. Cécile came to be with Aimée and was heartened by what she saw, remarking that "her husband has excellent qualities and loves her very much." So there was warmth where there might have been only rectitude.

In April 1817, Aimée could be found with "her own" in Vannes. On the afternoon of the seventeenth, the three "sisters" wrote Eugène together. After reporting to him that the paperwork for his promotion to captain has arrived, Cécile turned the letter over to Adèle and Aimée, "your true beloveds." Adèle's note was brief, as she was feeling blue, and she ceded the stage to Aimée, who in effect wrote for her and finally said it: "she loves you so much, my friend, but I doubt if she could have greater affection for you than your Aimée." She closed with exactly the same song of love as had Adèle: "je t'embrasse et t'aime de tout mon coeur."

Aimée would stay in Vannes until June. Eugène came home for an extended visit, and in the course of the late spring and summer, he and Adèle decided to marry. If Aimée and her brother verged on loving each other as lovers, he and his acceptably distant cousin were perfectly content to think of themselves as brother and sister. If Eugène called her "mon Adèle," "ma chérie," "ma bonne femme," and "ma chère cousine," she was also "ma très chère soeur." And she, on several occasions, followed suit. Aunt Marie was delighted that they had loved each other as "brother and sister" since the days when they played together at Pont Sal. It was Aimée, as usual, who offered the greatest insight: theirs would not in fact be a "love match," but something more. She wrote Eugène on 29 August 1817:

> The affection you have one for the other with Adèle cannot be extinguished, as often happens in *mariages d'inclination* (love matches), since it does not go back only a few years, but all your lives. Accustomed from your childhood to your chérie as a sister and she loving you as a brother, you have contracted an affection that will die only with life itself.

Consanguinity from this perspective is thus a positive force for lasting happiness in marriage, just as it had been in the long years of growing up together. Aimée was exhibiting nothing aberrant or even unusual in her love for her brother, as earlier recounted, nor was she now in her formula for lifetime happiness.

She reveals in fact the core of a now-maturing set of values that honored close marriage. It was not only respectable, but desirable. What joy in living one's entire existence in the warmth and familiarity of "one's own"! And Aimée knew all too well, because she, consigned to a marriage of the older sort, would not experience the same delight. Hers was one, practically speaking, that widened the net of contacts and created loyal clients among the Savantiers' circle and potential positions down the line in the tax administration. And certainly such marriages would not disappear in the nineteenth century. But within a bourgeoisie of sufficient significance and wealth, a culture of endogamy was emerging. On the practical level, clientage was less the issue than consolidation of power, prestige, and assets already gained, so close marriage made sense.

What was the nature of the interaction between interest and emotion in the emergence of this new marital regime? Letters among all the family during the second half of 1817 help us appreciate the complexity of the problem. While Aimée, Cécile, and Aunt Marie were privy to our couple's plans early on, "Pape Jollivet" had been left in the dark. Slightly peeved when the request from Eugène finally arrived in June, he nevertheless immediately gave his approbation, though he was a bit concerned about their youth, if not at all about their close kinship. Aunt Marie had encouraged the relationship from the beginning. Both pronounced it a "good match" (meaning socially and financially advantageous for their families), but above all their "hearts were warmed" to see children raised as siblings united. They took the practical steps to smooth the way, Marie introducing Adèle and Eugène in Parisian society[31] and Deputy Jollivet then pressing forward Eugène's appointment to Colonel Le Ridant's command in Orléans. Jollivet also "took care of" the dispensation for kinship from the church, a mere formality even in the eyes of these good Catholics.[32] A momentary crisis, in which the young couple's failure to consult with Aunt Marie over a minor manner caused her to "withdraw her support," was overcome, characteristically, by a flurry of letters to her from their siblings.[33]

The marriage was set for 10 June 1818. The wedding was the event of the season in Vannes, and the family's position was reflected by the two dozen signatories, ranging from Joachim Oillic, a modest pharmacist and second cousin still living on the small Cathedral Square, to General Bonté, an imperial noble of enormous landed wealth. This marriage began a landslide of consanguineous unions within these families. Eight out of twenty-three marriages in the next two generations would be with first cousins. Among the Vannes bourgeoisie generally, roughly a quarter of marriages in the first half of the nineteenth century were between first and second cousins.[34]

The terms of Adèle and Eugène's marriage contract illustrate the economic characteristics of cousin marriage. Adèle's dowry was a relatively modest 2,400 francs. Typically, it consisted of "assets that came from her mother," thus keeping the Marquer property in the family.[35] Eugène Galles's *apport* comprised his inheritance from his mother (Adelaïde Jollivet) and his father. The sum was not given, but since his 10,000-franc share of the publishing house was excluded from the marital *communauté*, the bulk of this portion came from his mother and therefore reconsolidated property that also might have been lost to the Jollivets.[36] It is easy to see why cousin marriage was tempting, from a financial point of view, for families that were already rather well off: although the potential growth from an exogamous marriage (which the Galles had earlier enjoyed) was foregone, acquired assets were protected, and growth could occur through the hard work of a solidly established couple in cooperation with a loving and supportive family, above all one's brothers and sisters.

Crisis

The affective dimensions of siblinghood went far beyond sexuality, of course. Sisters and brothers, the children of sisters and brothers, and one's cousins, along with their parents, figured centrally in one's life at every turn. Adèle Jollivet Galles made this clear when she reassured her son René, far away in Nantes for his first year at the Collège Royale in 1829, that his family was always with him (and that he needed to write!), reminding him: "never forget those most important to you, your brother and sister, your uncles and aunts, and your cher Papa."[37] The last was his grandfather, René Jollivet, and "uncles and aunts" definitely included siblings of his generation, Marie and Jean-Marie Le Ridant as well as the latter's youngest brother and his wife, Alexis and Virginie Le Ridant, major landowners in the Vannetais who lived across the street from Adèle and her children. Their son Jules was René's "best friend" and would marry his sister Cécile.

Siblings could always be counted upon in times of trial. Although friendships with non-relatives (or at least people who were not reckoned as such in this world of increasingly interlocking families) could be very strong—Adèle and Cécile had a coterie of *amies* in Auray who loved to discuss politics—it was siblings who did duty in crisis. Birth, sickness, and death naturally led the list. We have already seen Aimée repair to Redon for the last weeks of Fanny's pregnancy, and Cécile did the same for Aimée when the first Savantier was on the way in Châteaulin two years later. Cécile had made the trip previously, to carry the news of brother Bertin's death personally in order to allay the shock to the pregnant Aimée. Eugène also visited her during this dark hour. Cécile, as the single sister/cousin, was always at home with Adèle. She held her hand when Adèle miscarried her first pregnancy, she walked with her for air and exercise in the park when she became "big as a house" with her second (René), she attended at all Adèle's births along with sister-in-law Zuma Jollivet and Aunt Virginie Le Ridant, and she wrote to Eugène of the births of both her namesake Cécile and Félix because he could not obtain leaves for either.[38]

Births, in the absence of the father, were almost always registered with the state (a male-only duty) by an uncle of the newborn, while death certificates were generally signed by brothers or nephews of the deceased. Our correspondence, however, allows us to witness death vigils and watch the family gather around the bereaved. Let us take two examples.

Jean-Marie Galles ("Galles" to the family because of his leadership role in family, business, and community) headed the household in the ancestral home attached to the printworks and bookshop on the town's main square. Adèle and Eugène had their own quarters in the rear of the second floor, while Cécile and her domestic occupied rooms elsewhere in the sprawling dwelling.[39] Galles delayed marriage until January 1822, when he was thirty-four. His wife, Josephine Le Monnier, was a distant relative from the upper bourgeoisie of Auray with strong connections in Liberal politics, a tendency in marital choice already begun earlier among these moderate monarchists.[40] The joy accompanying the approaching birth of their first child was clouded by illness that soon turned to death. Their correspondence tells the story.

In September, a letter from Aimée to Eugène describes a household besieged by a "fever" of "epidemic" proportions in Vannes. She had come from Châteaulin to nurse them. Adéle was improving, taking quinine, but still was too ill to write her husband. Josephine remained gravely stricken, and they worried about the effects on her unborn child, due in two months. But "Galles is the sickest of all" and found it impossible to work with other officials (he was first deputy mayor) to stem the disease in the city. Only the children seemed immune, and "we keep house and home together."[41] Although everyone weathered the storm, Jean-Marie was still bedridden two months later, for his daughter Marie-Thérèse was registered at the Mairie by brother-in-law Yves Jollivet. It was also clear that the birth had severely weakened Josephine.

The correspondence picked up again in February 1823 after Eugène returned to duty in the north. Adèle, already depressed by his departure, wrote on the twenty-sixth: "Josephine gets worse and worse, and despite her youth and the early spring, I have little hope for her recovery. Her struggle to sustain her happy life is a drama that wounds the heart. Her poor husband is much changed since you left, hoping against hope." The epidemic of 1822–1823 was cholera, and the symptoms lead one to suspect it. As if this were not enough, Adèle was sick with worry about "my dear brother, my dear René," whose ship carrying four hundred men from Toulon to Rochefort had encountered a terrible storm off the coast of Portugal and had not yet been heard from. Memories of Bertin Galles haunted them. Eugène had not received her letter when he wrote his first on 27 February, but his news was almost as depressing, as the "fever" had overtaken his regiment. He consoled himself with talk of family: regret at having missed his "brother" René Jollivet (he assumed René was safely home); hope of seeing her more elusive brother Baptiste, now stationed at Sedan; and above all the joy of spending long hours with their Uncle Le Ridant. He expressed his concern for Josephine and Galles but did not know how grim things had become. He also stressed the strategic significance of their union: "I wish with all my heart that this succession will come to pass," because it bridged many past political barriers.

A birth cemented the ties that marriage created and promised future expansion of the kin network. The death of a child, while traumatic, usually would be offset by a new birth. But the death of a spouse irrevocably ruptured the kinship grid that had been achieved by the marriage, especially in the Christian West, where the most powerful of the church prohibitions concerned marriage to a dead spouse's sibling (there was only one such marriage in Vannes before 1852), sending the families involved reeling into double despair—for the loss of a loved one and for the loss of the alliance. If the dead spouse left a child or children, however, the connections among the families, as we have seen in great detail with the Galles, Jollivets, and Le Ridants, remained strong and the political and economic consequences of the new kin tie more or less intact. But with the loss of both parent and only child, the links were severely weakened if not broken altogether. This was the tragedy of Jean-Marie Galles, Josephine Le Monnier, and "Résia" Galles. On 12 March 1823, Adèle bore the news: "My beloved Eugène, since my last letter I have beheld an excruciating scene that has rent my heart. Josephine is no more. Poor Galles is beside himself with grief." She and her siblings/cousins persuaded him to go his closest sister Fanny's house (now in Vannes) and with her to the Ridant country house of Pont Sal. Adèle took charge of Résia, but Josephine's mother, after a "scene" and in the absence of Galles, took the baby to her family home. In fact, Adèle was relieved, having never been so "distressed even for my own children, as I am for this poor little one whose frail existence is so precious for her father."

Eugène's long response (20 March 1823) offered a wide range of counsel and consolation. Though his letter to his brother has been lost, we gain some insight into their relationship and his sense of Jean-Marie. "Galles, with a character seemingly reserved, has an excellent heart and will repress his sorrow; but he will deeply appreciate the sympathy of all of his own [tous les siens], the only thing that will comfort him." Surround him with sibling and cousin love, Eugène urged, writing that they must now focus everything on the survival of Résia. "My poor brother has tasted only a spark of happiness and experienced all the horrors of misfortune. What compensation providence owes him! He will henceforth find it only in his daughter—provided that he preserve this dear child." Even from afar, brother Eugène offered advice: place Résia with a wet nurse in a nearby hamlet, close enough to visit but away from the city and "above all out of the hands of Madame Le Monnier." If he preferred to keep her at home, "there is no question that you [Adèle] can care for her as for your own children." Jean-Marie chose the latter: who better than the cousin-sister and his regular consort at public events in happier days?

But it was all in vain. On 18 April 1823, Adèle wrote to her husband: "I had no hope that our dear little Résia could resist so much pain. She died last night. To think that it has been fifteen months to the day since her star-crossed father was married and that she was his last ray of happiness." Adèle shudders at the thought that this might have happened to them. "My heart is in knots. I can't eat." Jean-Marie went this time to Truhélin, the country house of René Jollivet, accompanied by sister Cécile, to be among the younger cousins and to breathe the sea air of Arridon. "The idea of seeing him return here paralyzes me [*me glace*]; with the death of his wife, we had consolation to offer, but now, my love, we have nothing at all." Later correspondence, however, shows that Galles allowed his emotions to flow in the midst of overwhelming support from his sibling archipelago (and that of his parents) and slowly returned to the world of the living. Three years later he married again. Marie-Louise Saint (and "a saint she was," wrote nephew René Galles), also of Auray, was a second cousin—far enough removed—of Josephine and kept the Liberal alliance intact. That same year, 1826, Jean-Marie Galles, whose passion for paleography had rekindled in the interim, founded the Société Polymathique du Morbihan, which became one of the leading regional learned societies in France. A year later, his son Louis, the first of five children with Louise, was born healthy. He, along with several cousins, would follow his father in uncovering the distant past of the Morbihan.[42]

Our second example was the pivotal moment in these families' epic: the death of Eugène Galles. Eugène had become the shining knight of this generation after the loss of his brother Bertin in 1817 and the dashing of his cousin/brother François's career in the administration of the interior (he had become a Sous-Préfet at the age of thirty) by an early death in 1821. Aunt Marie and Uncle Le Ridant were grooming Eugène—he was only twenty-nine at the time of Jean-Marie's disasters—for elevation to the highest levels of the army. His promotion to Chef de Bataillon was pending when the regiment of Colonel Le Ridant was called upon to bolster the troop concentration in the Caribbean due to the ongoing tensions with Spain and Britain after the Ultras had broken the Congress system by invading Spain in 1823. The hectic days before his departure had given Eugène only a moment to kiss Adèle and their three little ones goodbye before reporting to Brest. It would be the only time that he saw the newborn Félix. Eugène shipped out for Guadeloupe on 3 December 1823.

Although he missed his family terribly, Eugène's correspondence reported his many adventures, as well as his disdain for French colonialism and slavery, in as interesting a manner as possible, keeping the appropriate stiff upper lip. There was no indication of the disquiet that had settled over Guadeloupe in the summer of 1825 in the wake of a major hurricane. The mosquito-borne pestilence known as yellow fever arrived at the base at Basse-Terre in August. In the end, it carried away more than half of the 48th of the line—657 men, of whom twenty-two were officers. Captain Eugène Galles was among them. He had been informed shortly before he fell ill that his promotion to Chef de Bataillon had been approved.[43] The official date of death was 7 October 1825.

The arrival of the unthinkable news in Vannes, shortly before Christmas, came first in letters from Aunt Marie Le Ridant (who was with her husband, the regiment's commander) to Jean-Marie Galles and from René Jollivet to his brother Yvon. It was a day René Galles, then seven, would never forget.

> My sister Cécile and I were at dinner [across the street] chez l'excellent Madame Virginie Le Ridant. Though only a child, I noticed that the dinner, usually so gay, was sad; Mr. Alexis and his wife looked at each other from time to time in silence and their eyes … seemed wet with tears. Suddenly the dining room door opened and a servant from our house … said: "Madame, I've come to get the children for, you know, Monsieur is dead."
>
> Ah! how well I understood the horrible truth immediately! I cried out "Papa, Papa!"
>
> Ah! I can still see my stricken mother, her long hair undone, on the floor of her bedroom. My uncle Galles and my uncle Yvon were there. They had come together to announce the terrible and crushing news. My aunt Cécile led me away.[44]

Aunt Marie now had to write Adèle, but she waited long enough to make certain that the news had already been broken to her by her cousins-brothers. Her letter, dated 22 October, is from a mother to her daughter.

> Weep, my child, weep! You have lost the best husband who ever existed, perhaps, on this earth. You were the soul of his thoughts; he spoke this dear name with an air so tender, so sweet that it seemed to console his poor heart. My own was torn to shreds, my dear Adèle, but in my deepest grief, I still gave thanks to heaven that his death came so quickly and without great suffering.

Marie said that they all had taken the precautions counseled by the attending physicians, but both Eugène and her husband came down with the fever. Jean-Marie Le Ridant recovered after "eight days of misery." One can imagine her state of mind during those long hours, but she did not remark on it. Instead, she wrote only about their rage over the loss of their hero: "I can hardly find the words to tell you of my profound sorrow, but to paint for you that of your uncle would be infinitely more difficult." He had lost "his son" and wept for days.[45]

Marie's letter also contained something besides consolation. Though she asked Adèle to keep it a secret (from the children as well), she and her husband had decided to leave all their assets to René, Cécile, and Félix and to look after the children's education during their own lifetimes (Marie would live until 1840). In a later letter (24 February 1826), written after she had received one from Adèle in which her desolation was apparently total and her mood suicidal, she reminded her niece that Eugène lived on in the children and it was for them that she must "reclaim her courage." Eugène watched over them and would expect no less. "He counts on you to raise them" and thus we must "imitate the peace within souls of the departed and find the will to conquer such paralyzing grief."

Although Marie might not have known about it, Adèle had once condemned a man who committed suicide after the death of his wife precisely on the grounds of abandoning their children, and her aunt's words no doubt reminded her of that moment five years before. Indeed, Marie recounts the story of a widowed free black woman of Guadeloupe, a mother of three whose husband had been a musician. Her will was almost broken by his loss, but she persevered and, with the help of her extended family, was now doing well as a retail merchant. This clearly was an object lesson (again we must be amazed at the total lack of racism in her tone), especially since "your children are not as badly off." Uncle Le Ridant added a rare note at the end, saying simply: "preserve yourself for [your children], for you are more necessary to them than ever before. I embrace them as well as you, whom I love and will love forever most affectionately." This letter also invited Adèle to go to live at Pont Sal whenever she felt ready. The children loved it and would be able to romp and play in the fresh air. Moreover, she could sublet the apartment in the maison Chalmel without having to return to her quarters chez Galles, which would be filled with so many memories of her Eugène.

But memories also console, and none were more precious than those preserved in his hand. As time passed, Adèle would often reread those letters from "mon amant, mon frère," which she felt blessed to possess—letters where his humor, his talent as a raconteur, his political insight, his ethics, his detailed suggestions on prenatal care and child-rearing, his engagement of her interests, his willingness to share his disappointments and misgivings about himself, his ability to caress her with words of solace when she was depressed, and his boundless love for *son Adèle* would speak to her every day. Thus might she survive. And once again, among the living, that survival—from the moment of Eugène's death until her own, twenty-five years later, after raising three brilliant children who would expand the family's honor—owed everything to this two-generation sibling archipelago.

Family

But brothers and sisters, aunts and uncles meant much more than aid and comfort (along with stern advice) in moments of crisis. They animated the much more numerous times of pleasure and were the core of social life, where frivolity mixed with serious purpose in ways taken for granted by the participants. "Promenades" along the beautiful city walls of Vannes and in the adjoining parks were obligatory on Sunday afternoon, but recommended daily. Married couples and their children of course predominated, but they were rarely alone. Family legions turned out, chatting in the shade with "their own" as well as this or that contingent of friends with whom they shared memories and interests (and often ancestors) or might in the future share marriage beds. More intimate strolls allowed not only lovers to work through their tribulations, but sisters and cousins to make their plans (or fortify their unborn).

Rare was the week that passed without a big Sunday or holiday dinner chez Maman (Kercado) Jollivet, Fanny Galles Pavin, or Zuma Kerviche Jollivet, then chez Virginie Danet Le Ridant, Louise Saint Galles, or "Juliette" Le Bouhéllec Jollivet. Evening dinner parties always included relatives, but also brought together friends and associates in business, politics, or voluntary associations. These soirées were commanded by the mistress of the house (one always dined chez Madame so-and-so), and discussions of everything included the women at the table, for how could one exclude "one's own"? Here too the business of courtship and marriage took place within the nonchalance of casual conversation. The social calendar was also dotted with major banquets sponsored by public officials to which the urban notables were invited. Adèle and Cécile were usually among the guests, accompanied by an unmarried brother or cousin. As everywhere in Europe, Vannes had its round of balls, for the most part connected to holidays seasons, where the whirlwinds of courtship unfolded. Brothers and cousins invariably escorted sisters and cousins as they tested the waters of love. The eyes of the latter, as the statistics show, often turned back on "those closest to them," habituated to them "since childhood."[46]

The prime locale of familial social intercourse, however, was the country house, bearing its distinctive name by which it was always identified. Marie and Jean-Marie Le Ridant were the first in the families to own a château, a charming eighteenth-century structure with its attendant lands at the bridge to Auray over the Sal estuary (hence "Pont Sal"), purchased at auction in 1803. "Truhélin" in lovely and much closer Arradon came to notaire René Jollivet a few years later in the rapid turnover of emigré lands. His son René the naval officer became its proprietor after his death in 1830. In the 1830s and 1840s, Truhélin welcomed dozens of young relatives and their school friends for summers of boating, fishing, lawn games, luncheons, and evening intimacies where the marriages of René Galles's cohort were forged. His cousin Jules Jollivet (the son of Captain René) remembered these days with joy, enumerating all the uncles and aunts who came with their children to Truhélin and who eventually purchased their own Valhallas nearby, eight different families in all by 1850.[47]

Another measure of the centrality of siblings in this era are naming practices, which in our families (and in random surveys of others) strongly follow the axis of aunt/niece, uncle/nephew and are usually accompanied by godparentage, though that responsibility, in many large families, also fell to the oldest siblings. It begins after the marriages of 1787 and does not obtain before that. And so we have:

Generation I: François/François Jollivet; Adelaïde Jollivet Galles/Adelaïde [Adèle] Jollivet; Cécile Marquer Jollivet/Cécile Galles; Jean-Marie Galles/Jean-Marie Galles; Jean-Baptiste-Marc Galles/Jean-Baptiste Jollivet (though he may have been named for his grandfather Le Ridant); Eugène Jollivet/Eugène Galles; Jean-Marie/Jean-Marie [Alexis] Le Ridant; Louis Le Ridant/Louis [Alexis] Le Ridant; Marie Jollivet Le Ridant/Marie Jollivet. This was not a hard and fast rule; Bertin Galles was given the maiden name of his grandmother, the stalwart who really ran the Galles printworks from 1763, when she became a widow, until her death in 1807. Fanny and Aimée Galles seem to have had no ascending namesake. Yves Jollivet was named after his grandfather and René Jollivet II after his father. Only one of the later Jollivet children was named from within the three families. It is possible that their names came from the Kercados, about whom I have little information. Thus, this transition is marked by a mixture of the more traditional remembrance of the vertical line and the valuation of the horizontal sibling connection.

Generation II: Fanny Galles Pavin/Fanny Prud'homme; Fanny/Fanny [Félix] Galles; Eugène Galles/Eugène [Yves] Jollivet; Eugène Galles/Eugène Savantier; Bertin Galles/Bertin Savantier; Aimée Galles Savantier/Aimée Pavin; Cécile Galles/Cécile [Eugène] Galles; Adèle Jollivet

Galles/Adèle Pavin; Adèle/Adèle [Jean-Marie] Galles; René Jollivet II/ René Galles; Félix Jollivet (great-uncle)/Félix Galles; Jules [Alexis] Le Ridant/Jules Jollivet. In this generation, Jean-Marie Galles and Yves Jollivet did not have namesakes, though both assumed godfather roles for nephews, and several new names appeared, but the aunt/niece, uncle/ nephew link predominated, and godparentage usually accompanied naming. There was no father/son naming, and only René Galles shared both an uncle's and a grandfather's name. Although only a thorough analysis (and another essay) could broaden this thesis, this is impressive evidence of a clear shift toward honoring and claiming service from siblings and a break with the past.[48]

Mobility

On the practical level, siblings assisted at every turn. Intra-familial loans dot our correspondence. Although notarized arrangements were made to turn the management and the profits of the Galles publishing house over to the eldest male, Jean-Marie, each of his siblings owned an equal share of the business's assets. True, the Jollivet notarial étude was Yves's alone, made so via its sale to him by his father before the latter's death in 1831, but in accordance with the law, all his many heirs shared equally in René Jollivet's substantial property holdings, simply drawing rentier income from them. Truhélin and its adjacent farm, however, came under the consolidated ownership of René Jollivet II through the consent and compensation of his siblings. There is no evidence of conflict over property settlements within these families. A perusal of inheritance tax records for Vannes generally reveals very few contested successions during the first half of the nineteenth century.[49]

In general, however, these families' career trajectories were toward public service, as was the case for many of their class in Vannes and numerous weakly commercial towns like it across the nation, and it was here that sibling aid was crucial. As I have shown in detail elsewhere, the careers of Adèle Jollivet Galles's generation and that of her children's were assisted at crucial moments in their careers—early on by uncles and aunts, later by their own brothers and sisters.[50] Marie Le Ridant, because of special connections at court and her standing in Parisian "society" during the Restoration, made many a "*démarche*" on behalf of her nephews, especially Eugène Galles and René Jollivet II, both *militaires*, and made certain that her brother met the right people in Paris when he was a moderate royalist deputy. She also introduced Eugène in high society, not only in Paris but wherever in France he was stationed. Aunt

Marie also financed the education of her grand-nephews René and Félix Galles (but refused to pay for art lessons for their sister!). Her husband, a long-time officer (rising to Maréchal de Camp in 1830), was influential in the admission of several nephews into prestigious secondary military schools and to Saint-Cyr. René Galles, the only member of the immediate tri-family to graduate from the Ecole Polytechique, the pinnacle of the French education system at the time, would not have made it without the influential recommendation and personal contacts of M. Erdevan, a high official in the Parisian police and a close friend of Yves Jollivet, that assured his admission to the Pension Bourdon, a preparatory school for the Ecole that gave advanced training to promising boys like René who had not had high enough scores for admission the previous year.

Siblings also played a powerful role in marriage alliances. Obviously, as we have seen, they were central influences in creating the atmosphere and animating the settings in which love bloomed among cousins and intimate friends, but they also did important service as go-betweens in the exogamous marriages that complemented close unions in most families.[51] Both Yves Jollivet and Jean-Marie Galles, the scions of their generation, had married local women who came from families that had been at odds politically with their kin's older generation, staunch royalists all. But the two of them had joined Vannes's Masonic lodge in 1816, exposing themselves to more liberal ideas and creating bonds of mystic brotherhood with many republicans and Bonapartists, who had long dominated it.[52] Moreover, in 1811 Uncle Le Ridant's youngest brother Alexis had married Virginie Danet, who came from one of the most powerful and loyal families of the empire, with his brother's blessing.[53] Yves and Jean-Marie, having married into the Masonic milieu, now influenced the politically exogamous marriage decisions of two other Jollivet brothers. In 1831 Captain René wed Julienne Le Bouhéllec, the daughter of a revolutionary and imperial politician, who as mistress of château Truhélin would oversee the activities of this wondrous courtship mill. Stanislas took Marie Thubé, the daughter of a military supply chief held over from the empire, as his bride in 1830.

In the next generation, Stanislas and Marie orchestrated one of the family's most advantageous alliances in 1848, when Félix Galles, to the delight of Adèle, married Aimée Taslé, daughter of the chief judge of the court of appeals in Rennes (and niece of a former mayor of Vannes). Stanislas Jollivet, at the Avocat Général of the same court, had taken Félix under his wing, launching a career that would lead to a Procureur Generalship and a seat on the Cour de Cassation in Paris. His brother René, in 1848 a captain in the artillery, was the original candidate for Aimée's hand but had backed away, probably because he was in love with his cousin Marie Le Montagner, now in Hennebont where her father was a physician, whom he would marry in 1850. The Taslé connection was reinforced—another nineteenth-century commonplace—when, through the good offices of his cousin Félix, Louis Galles, Jean-Marie's only son and future leader of the regional learned society, married Aimée's sister Monique in 1856.[54] Such stories were repeated many times throughout the Vannetais elite (though without the specificity that correspondence provides) as multiple networks of siblings did their work.[55]

Nineteenth-Century Kinship

The magnitude of the roles and functions of siblings in the nineteenth century can be appreciated by thinking about the prior generations of these families.[56] All three families had followed classic paths in which talented men married women from families with established roots, honor, and assets in the city, so that when they came together in 1787 all stood toward the top of the Third Estate socially and economically. Past marriages had been far outside the prohibitions of the church, and while couples said they loved each other, practical considerations (e.g., absorbing a print shop or taking over an étude from a childless uncle-in-law) dominated the decisions. Brothers and cousins had tried to raid children's inheritances, and one uncle-guardian had to be taken to court to relinquish control of the printing business. Even the two brothers Nicolas and Jean-Nicolas Galles, who won the suit, had a nasty squabble over the disposition of the inheritance from Nicolas's deceased wife in 1748 and did not get on well thereafter, though Nicolas pulled back and left the operation to his brother and Jacquette Bertin, his enterprising wife.

The next generation seemed genuinely positive toward their siblings and was the first to begin *tutoyer* (to use the familiar second person) with one another, though not with their parents. Still, their language largely lacked warmth and their concerns remained practical. Jean-Marie Galles, Nicolas's only child and the firm's agent in Paris, wrote the cousins he was raised with, Perrine and Marc, only about marriage prospects and business, while Perrine railed at him about not marrying. The large Jollivet contingent was broken by the emigration of the three eldest males to the colonies, and the little correspondence that we have indicates that it was like pulling teeth to get them to write. René Jollivet, in his correspondence with his father, hardly mentions his siblings, whether present or absent. Still, as noted above, brothers and sisters were chosen as namesakes for the next generation, and when they did write to each other they spoke with affection, though not in anything like the playful and sensitive language of Aimée or Cécile Galles thirty years later.

A good example is a letter from Adelaïde Jollivet Galles to her brother in Martinique talking about siblings René, Marie-Joseph, and Félix: she delivered character assessments with some criticism, but fawning love was another matter, especially when compared with her passion for her husband, Marc. René, she wrote, "enjoys a reputation fit to satisfy the most ambitious of men of his status. He has worked very hard and continues to do so without relaxing. It is time that he gathers the fruits of it." Her youngest siblings were a bit mercurial and self-absorbed, but very bright. She then, typically, described the physical appearance of the "striking" nineteen-year-old Marie in some detail, having said nothing about Félix's. In general, then, it would appear that sibling relationships in this generation, while a step forward from previous antagonism or indifference, still lacked the emotional intimacy their children enjoyed. In that next generation only the eldest, Jean-Marie Galles and Yves Jollivet, both more reserved and businesslike, still smacked of their parents' demeanor.[57]

Although it would require a great deal more comparative research to approach definitive generalizations, the Galles-Jollivet archives and collateral research among the bourgeois elite of Vannes suggests that the "generation of 1820," which made such a striking impact on French society, politics, and intellectual life, also played a pivotal role in the history of kinship.[58] In Vannes, it was the cohort of Adèle Jollivet and Eugène Galles that initiated the vogue for cousin and other forms of close marriage that multiplied in the following cohort. They in turn significantly expanded what would become a nineteenth-century phenomenon (though reserving for at least one sibling an exogamous marriage) that carried the family into the national bourgeoisie and contributed to an ever-expanding intertwining network of class and kin.[59] The enhancement of the family's resources, honor, civic role, and power depended integrally on marriage choices guided into both sorts of unions by a wide new horizontal kinship system. At its heart were siblings and lots of them, in this heyday of large families—brothers and sisters bound by love who welcomed, in love, their in-laws, whether as cousins already close or those distant.

But love was one thing, power another. While an Aunt Marie or a sister Aimée or a cousin-mother Adèle were fundamental figures in forging the success of this system, the benefits and honors went largely to their brothers. The sibling archipelago provided the touchstone for the dynamic development of nineteenth-century bourgeois society, but like that society, it was gendered male.

1787 Marc Galles = Adelaïde Jollivet

1 Josephine Le Monnier ○ | 1822 = △ 1826 Jean-Marie | ○ Marie-Louise Saint | △ 1811 Fanny = Henri Pavin | △ Bertin navy | ○ Aimée | 1816 = △ André Savantier | △ Eugène | 1818 = ○ Adèle Jollivet | ○ Cécile

1787 Jeanne Le Ridant = René Jollivet | 1794 Cécile Marquer

Jean-Marie Le Ridant | 1797 = Marie Jollivet

Eugénie Castelot ○ | 1817 = △ François | △ Jean-Baptiste cavalry | ○ Zuma Kerviche | 1822 = △ Yves | △ René | 1830 = ○ Julienne Le Bouhéllec | ○ Adèle | 1818 = △ Eugène Galles

3 René Jollivet | 1801 = Désirée Kercado

Marie Thubé ○ | 1830 = △ Stanislas | △ Eugène | ○ Louise | 1822 = △ Augustin Le Montagner | ○ Jenny | ○ Fanny | ○ Marie-Elisabeth | 1837 = △ Alfred Lallemand

Augustin Le Montagner △ = ○ Louise Jollivet

Adèle Jollivet ○ = △ Eugène Galles

Alexis Le Ridant △ | 1811 = ○ Virginie Danet

Auguste infantry △ | ○ Marie Le Montagner (Hennebont) | 1850 = △ René Galles intendancy | △ Cécile | ○ | 1839 = △ Jules Le Ridant navy | △ Félix | 1848 = ○ Marie Taslé (Rennes) | ○ Cécile Galles | 1839 = △ | △ Jules | △ Jean-Marie | 1839 = ○ Marie Favin (Fontainbleau) | △ Louis (Paris)

François Jollivet △ = ○ Eugénie Castelot

Yves Jollivet △ = ○ Zuma Kerviche

René Jollivet △ = ○ Julienne Le Bouhéllec

François-Marie △ | 1839 = ○ Anne Pélauque (St. Gaudens) | △ Eugène | ○ Maria | 1848 = △ Ch. Avrouin (Paris) | △ René | △ Jules infantry | = ○ Anne Bonté

Fanny Galles ○ = △ Henri Pavin

Jean-Marie Galles △ | 2 = ○ Marie-Louise Saint

Adèle ○ | 1839 = △ Marius Charrier (Noirmoutier) | △ Henri infantry | ○ Monique Taslé | 1856 = △ Louis | ○ Louise (nun) | ○ Marie | ○ Adèle | ○ Anna

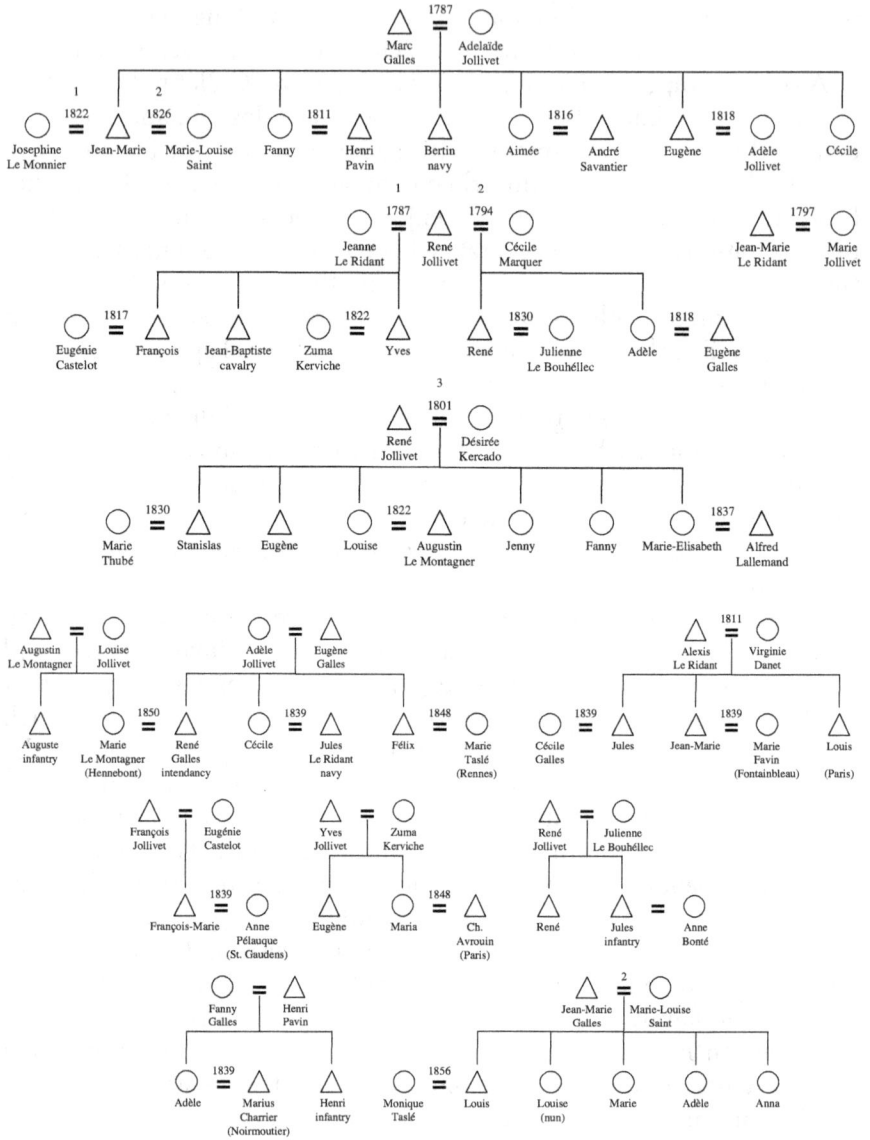

Figure 8.1. The Galles, Jollivet, and Le Ridant Families, 1787–1856: Genealogies I and II

Notes

1. Jean Sutter, "Fréquence de l'endogamie et ses facteurs au XIXe siècle," *Population* 23 (1968): 303–324; Jean-Marie Gouesse, "Mariages de proches parents (XVIe–XXe siècle): Esquisse d'une conjoncture," in *Le modèle familial européen: Normes, dévi-*

ances, contrôle du pouvoir, ed. Gérard Delille and Franco Rizzi (Rome, 1986), 31–61.
An exception is Françoise Zonabend, "Le très proche et le pas trop loin: Réflections sur l'organisation du champ matrimonial des sociétés à structures de parenté complexes," Ethnologie française 11 (1981): 311–317.

2. The place of brother-sister love and (usually) near-miss incest in Romantic literature (and artists' lives) is well known. The most famous French examples are Diderot's play Le fils retrouvé, Bernardin de Saint-Pierre's Paul et Virginie, and Chateaubriand's Atala and René, while the Shelleys, Wordsworth, and Byron top the English list, with Goethe the best known from across the Rhine. In a large literature, see Pierre Barbéris, A la recherche d'une écriture: Chateaubriand (Paris, 1974); René Chateaubriand, Atala/René, trans. and intro. Irving Putter (Berkeley and Los Angeles, 1980); Margaret Waller, in "Being René, Buying Atala: Alienated Subjects and Decorative Objects in Postrevolutionary France," in Rebel Daughters: Women and the French Revolution, ed. Sara E. Melzer and Leslie W. Rabine (Oxford, 1992), 157–177 underlines the vast and immediate readership acquired by both; James Twitchell, Forbidden Partners: The Incest Taboo in Modern Culture (New York, 1987); Glenda A. Hudson, Sibling Love and Incest in Jane Austen's Fiction (London, 1992; reprinted New York, 1999); Michael Minden, The German Bildungsroman: Incest and Inheritance (Cambridge, 1997); Evelyne Hesse-Fink, Etudes sur le thème de l'inceste dans la littérature française (Bern, 1972); and the classic by Otto Rank, The Incest Theme in Literature and Legend, trans. Gregory Richter (Baltimore, 1992). See also the recent study of Ellen Pollack, Incest and the English Novel, 1684–1814 (Baltimore, 2003), especially her analysis of Austen's Mansfield Park.

3. But see André Burguière, "'Cher cousin': les usages matrimoniaux de la parenté proche dans la France du 18e siècle," Annales HSS 55, no. 6 (1997): 1339–1360.

4. David Warren Sabean, Kinship in Neckarhausen, 1700–1870 (Cambridge, 1998); David Warren Sabean, Simon Teuscher, and Jon Mathieu. eds., Kinship in Europe: Approaches to Long-Term Development (1300–1900) (Oxford and New York, 2007); the Preface of this volume summarizes these initiatives; for an overview on the evolution of European kinship, see Sabean and Teuscher, chapter 1: "Kinship in Europe: A New Approach to Long Term Development."

5. Juliet Flower MacCannell, The Regime of the Brother: After the Patriarchy (London, 1991); Carol Pateman, The Sexual Contract (Stanford, 1988).

6. Lynn Hunt, The Family Romance of the French Revolution (Berkeley, 1993); Dominique Godineau, The Women of Paris and Their French Revolution, trans. Katherine Streip (Berkeley and Los Angeles, 1998).

7. Suzanne Desan, The Family on Trial in Revolutionary France (Berkeley, 2004); Jennifer Ngaire Heuer, The Family and the Nation in Revolutionary France, 1789–1830 (Ithaca, 2005).

8. Arlette Farge, La vie fragile: Violence, pouvoirs et solidarités à Paris au XVIIIe siècle (Paris 1986); David Garrioch, Neighbourhood and Community in Paris, 1740–1790 (Cambridge, 1986); Janine Lanza, From Wives to Widows in Early Modern Paris: Gender, Economy, and Law (Aldershot and Burlington, VT, 2007). This last is a problem that I have researched in great depth but set aside temporarily. I have presented several papers, among them "Marital Conflict in Eighteenth-Century France: Some Thoughts on Empowerment in the Age of the Enlightenment," that engage such themes as they arise from the study of family conflict observed in the papers of the Commissaires du Châtelet de Paris. On the broader issues of the shifting culture of family life and of interpersonal relationships in eighteenth- and nineteenth-century France, see François Ronsin, Le contrat sentimental: Débats sur le mariage, l'amour,

le divorce, de l'Ancien Régime à la Restauration (Paris, 1990); the works of novelist Stéphanie de Genlis that best portray internal family dynamics are *Les petits émigrés*, 2 vols. (Paris, 1798) and *Alphonse et Dalinde*, in her *Contes choisis des veillées du château* (London, 1828), 124–300; see also Gabriel de Broglie, *Madame de Genlis* (Paris, 2001); Philippe Ariès, *Centuries of Childhood*, trans. Robert Baldick (New York, 1962); Jean-Louis Flandrin, *Families in Former Times: Kinship, Household, and Sexuality*, trans. Richard Southern (Cambridge, 1979); François Lebrun, *La vie conjugale sous l'Ancien Régime* (Paris, 1985); Marie-Françoise Lévy, ed., *L'enfant, famille et la Révolution Française* (Paris, 1990); Maurice Daumas, *Le syndrome des Grieux: La relation père/fils au XVIIIe siècle* (Paris, 1990) and *La tendresse amoureuse XVIe–XIXe siècle* (Paris, 1997); Annik Pardaihle-Galabrun, *The Birth of Intimacy: Privacy and Domestic Life in Early Modern Paris*, trans. Jocelyn Phelps (Oxford, 1991); Richard Rand, ed., *Intimate Encounters: Love and Domesticity in Eighteenth-Century France* (Princeton, 1997); Christine Adams, *A Taste for Comfort and Status: A Bourgeois Family in Eighteenth-Century France* (University Park, PA, 2000); Anne-Vincent-Buffault, *Histoire des larmes: XVIIIe–XIXe siècles* (Paris, 1986) and *L'exercice de l'amité: Pour une histoire des pratiques amicales aux XVIIIe et XIXe siècles* (Paris, 1995); Gabrielle Houbre, *Le discipline de l'amour: L'éducation sentimentale des filles et des garçons à l'age du romanticisme* (Paris, 1997). On Great Britain: G. J. Barker-Benfield, *The Culture of Sensibility: Sex and Society in Eighteenth-Century Britain* (Chicago, 1992); Randolph Trumbach, *The Rise of the Egalitarian Family* (New York, 1978); Christopher Flint, *Family Fictions: Narrative and Domestic Relations in Britain, 1688–1798* (Stanford, 1998); Leonore Davidoff and Catherine Hall, *Family Fortunes: Men and Women of the English Middle Class, 1780–1850* (Chicago, 1987).

9. Whitney Walton, *Eve's Proud Descendants: Four Women Writers and Republican Politics in Nineteenth-Century France* (Stanford, 2000); Joan Scott, *Only Paradoxes to Offer: French Feminists and the Rights of Man* (Cambridge, MA, 1996), chap. 3; Karen Offen, *European Feminisms, 1700–1950: A Political History* (Stanford, 2000), chaps. 4–5.

10. Michel Foucault, *The History of Sexuality: An Introduction*, trans. Robert Hurley (New York, 1990), 105–107.

11. See note 8, especially the works of Daumas, Pardaihle-Galabrun, Rand, Houbre, Barker-Benfield, Trumbach, and Flint. For an exhaustive exploration of most of these themes from an original and critical perspective, see Ruth Perry, *Novel Relations: The Transformation of Kinship in English Literature and Culture, 1748–1818* (Cambridge, 2004).

12. Hunt, *Family Romance*, chap. 5; Ronald Hayman, *Marquis de Sade: Genius of Passion* (New York, 2003); Roland Barthes, *Sade, Fourier, Loyola* (Paris, 1971); Robert Darnton, *The Forbidden Bestsellers of Pre-Revolutionary France* (New York, 1995).

13. Foucault, *Sexuality*, 108–109. Pollack, *Incest and the English Novel*, 11–17, provides excellent commentary on this concept.

14. The enormous controversy that swirled around Racine's Phèdre, first presented in 1677 (including Jacques Pradon's counter-play *Hippolyte*, produced at the same time), symbolizes the preoccupation with intergenerational incest at the time. David Sabean, in "Inzestdiskurse vom Barock bis zur Romantik," *L'Homme: Zeitschrift für feministische Geschictswissenschaft* 13, no. 1 (2002): 7–28, puts the entire transition in perspective. Jean Racine, *Phèdre*, ed. and preface by Raymond Picard (Paris, 2000); Roland Barthes, *Sur Racine* (Paris, 1983), 115–122.

15. No one deals with this theme better than Lynn Hunt, *Family Romance*, chap. 3.

16. Fonds Galles, 2 J 1–262, Archives Départementales du Morbihan (ADM), includes over 1,600 letters, mainly from the first half of the nineteenth century, exchanged

by members of the three multiply intermarried families; many genealogies; and a detailed manuscript autobiography concentrating on his early years by General René Galles (1819–1889); and the Fonds Jollivet, which, though less extensive, includes earlier correspondence and the reminiscences of General René Jollivet, 1832–1895), and forms the foundation of my book *Becoming Bourgeois: Love, Kinship, and Power in Provincial France (1700–1880)*, in progress.

17. For details, see Christopher H. Johnson, "Into the World: Kinship and Nation-Building in France, 1750–1885," in *Trans-regional and Transnational Families in Europe and Beyond: Experiences since the Middle Ages*, ed. Christopher H. Johnson, David Warren Sabean, Simon Teuscher, and Francesca Trivellato (New York, 2011).

18. There is unfortunately no study I know of that deals specifically with the issue of family size by social class or income level in France during this era, but it is well known that fertility began its long decline in the first half of the nineteenth century and that peasant-proprietor family limitation was largely responsible for it. Meanwhile, evidence from local and family studies points to large and even growing numbers of (surviving) children among upper middle-class families. The young age of marriage for women (age twenty-two in my sample for Vannes) and shunning contraception (though the knowledge was certainly available), unlike small property owners, probably account for the phenomenon. My examination of genealogies and efforts at family reconstitution of the bourgeois elite of Vannes indicates that before mid-century most families had four or more children that lived to adulthood. Death of wives was a grim presence (see note 19), but men rapidly remarried, usually to younger women. Exact figures are hard to come by (and the issue does not arise in many studies due to the arduous research required to recompose families statistically), but Davidoff and Hall, in their classic work on English middle-class families, found that for their eighty-three families, "the average number of children was 7.4 with birth intervals from fourteen to twenty months." *Family Fortunes*, 223. The most important work on the general problem remains Charles Tilly, ed., *Historical Studies of Changing Fertility* (Princeton, 1978), which focuses above all on analyzing the relationship of fertility and family size to the general processes of industrialization, but only Etienne van de Walle broaches the issue of class differences, arguing from (not much) literary evidence that the bourgeoisie followed the aristocracy in the extensive practice of contraception, leading to a general decline in class fertility from the later eighteenth century on ("Alone in Europe: The French Fertility Decline until 1850," Tilly. ed., *Fertility*, here 264–66). But most of the literary evidence is not about *marital* contraception, which is the issue. The way families continued to control the division of the patrimony was by orienting some children toward nonmarriage, particularly by entering the church or, for men, the military (which had a disproportionate number of lifetime bachelors) and buying out their shares; cousin marriage could also be a means. In examining genealogies of family networks among the bourgeois elite of Vannes, I found that roughly one-fourth of the children who came of age between 1770 and 1820 did not marry, while their married brothers and sisters produced four or more surviving children (if not cut off by the death of the father). The following generations of the nineteenth century saw a marked increase in the number of unmarried siblings (especially women becoming nuns) *as well as* a decline in the number of children of married couples. Among the dozens of monographs on France providing evidence of a peak in bourgeois family size in the later eighteenth and early nineteenth centuries, see Jean-Pierre Chaline, *Les Bourgeois de Rouen: une élite urbaine au XIXe siècle* (Paris, 1982) (especially selected genealogies, 415ff.); Leon Rostaing, *La famille de Montgolfier, ses alliances, ses descendants* (Lyon,

1933); Roland Caty and Elaine Richard, *Armateurs marseillais au XIXe siècle* (Marseille, 1986); Dauphin et al., *Ces bonnes lettres*, chap. 1.

19. Sherwin B. Nuland, *The Doctors' Plague: Germs, Childbed Fever, and the Strange Story of Ignác Semmelweis* (New York, 2003); Irvine Loudon, *Death in Childbirth: An International Study of Maternal Care and Maternal Mortality, 1800–1950* (Oxford, 1992); Laurel Thatcher Ulrich, *A Midwife's Tale* (New York, 1990) shows the growing encroachment of male doctors on the midwives' domain and Martha Ballard's negative assessment of their competence.

20. Although there is a huge literature in the social sciences on contemporary stepfamilies, very little historical work has been done on the subject. But see Sylvie Perrier, "The Blended Family in Old-Regime France: A Dynamic Family Form," *History of the Family* 3, no. 4 (1998): 459–471, which stresses good internal relations. Lawrence Stone famously characterized marriage then and now as "serial polygamy," with divorce finally outpacing death in recent times.

21. David Sabean underlines the pivotal role of aunts and other older female kin in German upper middle-class families in his conclusion to *Kinship in Neckarhausen*, 502–506, as does Ruth Perry in assessing eighteenth-century literary representations of them, *Novel Relations*, chap. 8.

22. This is typical of large families, recorded throughout the social science literature—see Leonore Davidoff's chapter in this volume.

23. See genealogies, Figure 8.1 at end of text.

24. For more detail on René Galles, see Johnson, "Into the World."

25. This is not the place to debate the issue, but a good deal of historical analysis of eighteenth- and nineteenth-century letter-writing emphasizes a certain standardization of form and content based to a considerable extent on manuals written to assist the correspondent. In a growing literature, see especially Cécile Dauphin, Pierrette Lebrun-Pézerat, and Danielle Poubron, *La correspondance: les usages de la lettre au XIXe siècle* (Paris, 1991). There is no internal evidence at all of this practice in the letters examined here, which are enormously varied in tone and substance and speak of daily happenings with an air of complete authenticity.

26. See note 8.

27. Philippe Ariès, *Centuries of Childhood*, owed much of his pathbreaking "discovery" of childhood in the eighteenth century to such correspondence.

28. Aimée to Eugène, 23 February 1816, ADM, 2 J 79. Unless otherwise noted, further references are from this same source. The dates of the letters are noted in the text.

29. This is a fundamental theme in nineteenth-century bourgeois marriage, and one perhaps not emphasized enough in the literature. But see Davidoff and Hall, *Family Fortunes*, 273ff.

30. Aimée Galles to Eugène Galles, 30 July 1816, ADM 2 J 79.

31. Anne Martin-Fugier, *La vie élégante ou la formation du Tout-Paris, 1815–1848* (Paris, 1990). The story, including a comment by a woman at the opera that the handsome couple looked as if they were "in a novel," is from René Galles, "Journal," I, 11, 2 J 82, ADM.

32. R. Galles, "Journal," I, 13. On this issue, see André Burguière, who concludes: "But contrary to the assumption that the existence of an ecclesiastical prohibition aimed at marriages between kin to the third cousin degree (arriére-petits-cousins) would have an effect, *cousinage* in itself never constituted an obstacle either for the lovers themselves or even for those who sought to oppose their wish to marry." Burguière,

"'Cher cousin,'" 1360. His work is based on hundreds of applications for dispensations in Paris during the eighteenth century, where the numbers increased dramatically in the course of the century.

33. Letters from Aimée (23 August and 6 September 1817), Cécile (8 September), and Adèle (4, 10, and 20 September, 18 November, 3 December), who reports on the reactions of the older Jollivet brothers and Jean-Marie Galles as well as the discussions with Aunt Marie.

34. Johnson, "Kinship and Civil Society."

35. On the mother-to-daughter transmission of dowries in Old Regime France, see Bernard Derouet's chapter in this volume.

36. En Vannes, mariages, 10 juin 1818; En Vannes 3504, ADM.

37. 25 September 1829, ADM, 2 J 80.

38. Sister Cécile's charming letter to Eugène on 21 July 1824 tells of the arrival of Félix who, besides being more robust that his siblings at their birth and taking to the breast immediately, "gave me his first present in spraying me with full force." These and the stories that follow are drawn, unless otherwise noted, from the two-way correspondence between Adèle and Eugène Galles, 2 J 79, ADM.

39. René Galles, Journal I, 20–21, describes the house in detail.

40. For details, see Johnson, "Kinship and Civil Society."

41. Aimée to Eugène, undated (September 1822).

42. Johnson, "Kinship and Civil Society."

43. Marie Le Ridant to Jean-Marie Galles, 6 December 1825, 2 J 81, ADM.

44. "Journal," I, 42.

45. Marie Jollivet Le Ridant to Adèle Jollivet Galles, 25 October 1825, 2 J 81, ADM.

46. These comments are drawn from an array of letters, mostly between Eugène and Adèle Galles, 2 J 79, ADM. On the statistical incidence of close marriage among the Vannes bourgeois elite, see Johnson, "Kinship and Civil Society."

47. Jules Jollivet, "Mes souvenirs," Fonds Jollivet, ADM.

48. This parallels David Sabean's exhaustive investigation of naming practices around the same time in Neckarhausen, though he concentrates more on godparentage, a more significant role there than among the bourgeois of Vannes.

49. Although it is not the subject of this essay, a systematic comparison of the numbers and level of antagonism of succession conflicts among sibling heirs in this period as opposed to earlier times might be a statistical way to gauge changing valuation of sibling love and cooperation. Also see Desan, *The Family on Trial*, which focuses on succession battles.

50. Johnson, "Into the World."

51. This is a major theme in Johnson, "Into the World."

52. On the Masonic lodge of Vannes, see Michelle Le Fahler, *Recherche de documents maçonnique au XVIIIe–XIXe siècles: Mémoire de Maîtrise* (Rennes, 1976); Yannick Rome, *La Franc-maçonnerie à Vannes, Auray, Belle-Ile, Ploërmel au XVIIIe et XIXe siècle* (Vannes, n.d. [1985?]).

53. J. J. Danet, her father, was also a Mason. He was later disgraced, a result of prosecution for corruption as the department chief tax officer.

54. Johnson, "Into the World."

55. See the overview provided in ibid.

56. For the background, see Johnson, *Becoming Bourgeois*, Part I.

57. On Jean-Marie's personality, see above. Yves Jollivet went through the trauma of the death (tuberculosis) of his son Eugène with a similar stoicism. We sense more

respect than deep love in the correspondence of his siblings and even a certain antagonism toward his wife, Zuma Kerviche.

58. See Alan Spitzer, *The Generation of 1820* (Princeton, 1987).
59. Johnson, "Into the World."

Chapter 9

Kinship and Issues of the Self in Europe around 1800

David Warren Sabean

In this chapter I aim to explore a number of issues that have to do with the restructuring of kinship in Europe during the several decades be-fore and after 1800. In doing so I will concentrate mostly on texts that have to do with sibling relations and intense emotional ties between brothers and sisters, often imagined during that period as incestuous. I can only sketch in here a few salient features of the reconfiguration of kinship, contrasting what might be called "modern" kinship (begin-ning in the long nineteenth century) with its early modern form.[1] The coordinate set of structures that took form as of the late fifteenth cen-tury and reached its height in the early eighteenth century found fa-milial dynamics organized around the development and maintenance of "stable" properties—estates, farms, tenancies, prebends, monopolies, privileges, and offices. Emphasis was on lineal genealogical connection, that is, succession, devolution, and descent. The point to keep in mind is the long-term organization around inherited property rights, continuous exchanges, and memories built around succession and inheritance. This structure was characterized by vertical relationships, with most discus-sions about family ordered around paternal/filial relations and claims for property and solidarity embedded in a discourse about blood and descent. Another feature of the system was patron/client relations that linked families asymmetrically over several generations.

One of the key elements in formatting kinship in this earlier period was the absence of repeated marital exchanges between lines, families, lineages, clans, etc. In other words, a marriage contracted between two lines could not be replicated for many generations because of the state/ church prohibition of cousin marriages.[2] Marriages between close consanguineal kin reattach families already allied in a previous generation. They make in-laws of cousins and constantly make affinal relations out of consanguineal ones. A marriage to a first cousin repeats an alliance between two families or lines in the generation following the initial tie. Marriages between second cousins allow for alternate generation exchange—the marriages of grandparents being replicated or reciprocated by grandchildren. A system that allows or encourages endogamous, cousin marriages operates quite differently from an exogamous one that prohibits them.

There is considerable evidence that I will not go into here to show that a shift to endogamous marriage practices took place progressively after the mid eighteenth century throughout Europe.[3] By 1800, marriages previously thought to be incestuous—between first and second cousins, or to a relative of a deceased spouse—became frequent everywhere in Europe among all property-holding groups. Such marriages created interlocking kindred through repeated alliances over more than one, sometimes many, generations. In Baroque Europe, having to marry outward, away from the clan, always meant marriage with a "stranger." The marriage system that developed after 1750 involved alliances with the familiar, with "same" rather than with "other." I have to leave the reasons for the shift aside for now, but I can note that this massive alteration in kinship dynamics was related to a general shift in state, society, and economy whereby wealth and public office circulated through more fluid channels in ways that called for tighter coordination of allied kin—a strategy for operating in a market economy and a liberal state. Kinship was reconfigured away from the vertical toward the horizontal, from a structure characterized by inheritance to one characterized by alliance, from clan-like structures to more fluid, open-ended networks of kindred. Succession to office, for example, was effected no longer by real or quasi property rights and monopolies run by oligarchies, but through systematic promotion by horizontally linked kin (cousins, often far-flung, reckoned through both parents and coordinated sets of in-laws). In the new economy—to offer another example—capital was pieced together through networks of quite extensive kin.

In restructuring the alliance system, new mechanisms had to be put into place to channel familial energies and regulate socially sanctioned marital choices. There is a large literature to suggest that more choice was given to children in courtship—although one should never under-estimate the importance of parents' control in directing the decisions of their children throughout the nineteenth century. More importantly, families became the focal point for developing sentiment, managing cul-tural style, and directing erotic desires. Socialization into the aesthetics of choice was all the more important, given the fundamental problem of managing the flow of capital in the system of alliance. I want to sug-gest that the period from 1740 to 1840 was one where brothers and sisters schooled themselves in sentiment and developed for each other a language of pure affection and love.[4] Attachment to a future spouse grew out of feelings and moral style developed among siblings or sets of cousins who grew up together.[5] The incredible outpouring of cor-respondence among pairs of siblings during the period offers us insight into the practices of the new intimacy.[6] So too do the scads of novels, epic poems, plays, and theological treatises concerned with sorting out the legitimate and illegitimate feelings that brothers and sisters shared.[7]

Let me take two examples from late eighteenth-century German literature, novels by the popular but now obscure Friedrich Klinger and the not-so-obscure but widely unread Christoph Martin Wieland.[8] Klinger's novel, *Geschichte Giafers des Barmeciden* (1792–1794) (set in Persia), falls into two parts.[9] The first interweaves consideration of Kantian ethics into a wildly imaginative story concerning the chief char-acter, Giafer, and his emotional and moral development in conjunction with his "niece" Fatime. While the second part of the novel will intro-duce a brother-sister theme, here in the introductory half the uncle-niece relationship stands in for the most intimate familial connection of two children growing into adulthood. Like siblings, they are brought up in the same household. Klinger uses the intimacy of their emotional lives to explore issues of self construction as part of a larger consider-ation of human nature and moral action. Like many texts of the period, this one is concerned with how people become moral beings, and it probes interior domestic scenes for the origins of character, personal-ity, and temperament. Indeed, writes Klinger, "our ideas about God, the world, and men, moral and physical appearances, are formed through our first experiences, the voice of our soul, the power of our reason over our passions, and above all through the strength of our heart, the source of our moral sense."[10]

At the opening of the story, Giafer has to deal with the crisis of his father's execution, ordered by a caliph bored by the father's concern for his people. Subject to emotional storms, alienation, and doubt, Giafer puts himself back together piece by piece in intimate conversation with his niece. Here as in many other considerations of "sibling" intercourse, from the very beginning there is a definite undertone of eroticism that in many instances blossoms into full-fledged desire. It is easy to find this in correspondence from the period, as I shall show, but literary genres of all kinds explore this dimension as well. Giafer speaks of the soft heat from his (pubescent) niece that flows into his heart. She becomes the central figure for reintegrating his emotional life and clarifying his thoughts. And Klinger makes explicit the conjunction of the spiritual and sensual in an image of the young girl emerging into the first stirrings of sexuality.

> Only recently had she entered the period, in which the purpose (*Dasein*) of a young woman is revealed, the heart begins to open itself, and pregnant glances and powerful feelings of self-consciousness indicate changes in the inner nature. ... Fatime was just like the ethereal image that we imagine of Psyche, the bride of Amor, and her beautiful little body extended so gently around her beautiful soul as if they were made of the same material.[11]

The problem for Giafer is to sublimate his desire for Fatime as the precondition of his emergence into society. This takes place in two stages. The first involves a heightening (or discovery) of desire for his niece in a scene where a rainstorm plasters her light clothing against her body. The second is his undertaking to suppress (*Unterdrang*) her image, "in all the magic of her youthful fascination."[12] I am leaving out of this account a good deal of the story—Giafer's encounter with Ahmet (God? an angel?), who teaches him Kant; Ahmet's sending him out into the world; Giafer's turn away from good intentions to adultery and murder; the revelation that everything has been a dream to teach him what the human is capable of—in order to tease out the interwoven strand of the Giafer-Fatime relationship. His character has been formed in intimate intercourse with her—that goes with him into the world.[13] Even his first encounter with sensuality, the beautiful, and the erotic is mediated through his niece.[14] The next step in autonomy, however, is understood to be to leave home and leave his "sister" behind.[15]

After all the dream sequences, which are understood to be the equivalent of real experiences,[16] Giafer decides to return home and settle down with his niece: "in Fatime he viewed the most tender lover, the truest friend, the most reliable participant in his happiness and despair, in whose arms, he hoped to forget all the cares he could imagine."[17] The new caliph, Haroun, calls him to court and makes him the grand vizier, forbidding the marriage with Fatime on grounds of incest. It turns out that Fatime is only Giafer's mother's stepbrother's daughter (his step cousin; clearly Klinger changed the relationship in the middle of the story and did not go back to make it all consistent) and therefore not forbidden as a spouse in the Koran; nonetheless, the caliph puts an end to their relationship by marrying her himself. Here is where the plot gets complicated and develops a more direct brother-sister theme. Haroun himself is in love with his own sister, Abassa, who becomes the object of Giafer's desire once the relationship with Fatime is stymied. Haroun arranges their marriage, but because of his own feelings forbids consummation of the marriage on the pain of death. Giafer, meanwhile, finds it difficult to distinguish between Fatime and Abassa.[18] And Haroun, after he "robs" Giafer of his fiancée in the mistaken hope of forgetting Abassa by embracing Fatime, imagines himself embracing his own sister. Once the deception is no longer possible, the wife cannot continue to satisfy the desire for the sister.[19]

Much of the text revolves around the problem of the proper feelings of a brother for a sister. Haroun and Abassa continually argue about sentiment, love, and passion. For her, the relevant step to maturity is to leave the brother and transfer her sentiments to his friend and confidant. In a sense, Giafer is relevant precisely because he is *like* the brother and offers a *substitute* for the brother. The tragedy lies in the actual brother's inability to give up the sister and find a woman in her image, and Giafer tells him that his own love for Abassa is superior, purer, and nobler, because it goes beyond the incestuous.[20] Haroun's obsessive love for Abassa brings him to rail against the laws prohibiting brother/sister marriage: "she grew up on my bosom—I found her—awoke the first sentiments of her heart, developed with care the blossoming of the beauty of her body, her spirit. Mine were the first feelings which now flow more radiant, more beautiful in her heart. I heard my own thoughts again, ornamented and newly inspired."[21] He is describing here a commonplace motif of intrafamial discourses of the period, where the self was formed in an intimate dialectic with another beloved and where "same" and "other" became totally implicated in each other.

In some ways, the text is a debate about the distinction between sexual/passionate desire and sibling love. The same problem is handled in many novels—one of the earliest being Fürchtegott Gellert's 1739 *Schwedische Gräfin von O...*—by the ruse of a marriage between siblings ignorant of their relationship. While the feelings that first drew them together are understood to stem from their blood connection—their sameness—the moral/emotional issue is how to restructure their sentiments after the discovery. The other issue has to do with the emotional, moral, and intellectual formation of the self inside the dynamics of the family, but a family structure less dominated by vertical relationships than by horizontal ones. The sister is a reflecting mirror in which the brother comes to know himself. And this is precisely what Haroun finds himself unable to get over: in the end "I did not form her for me but cultivated the flower for someone else."[22]

Wieland's *Agathon* is a philosophical novel loaded with discussions of Plato. The author uses it to discuss Platonic philosophy, moral sentiment, political theory, and court society, which he comments on and criticizes at length. The original edition came out in 1766 and is strongly influenced by Rousseau.[23] In this story, the first love of the hero Agathon involves intense feeling and interminable caresses, such that he and "Psyche" find themselves to be an essential part of each other. Destiny separates them before they can consummate their relationship, and later on in the story they determine that they are actually brother and sister. Agathon's other great love is Danae, a woman trained for aesthetic pleasure and in all the sensual arts of seduction. Indeed, she is given the task at court to seduce Agathon, but her ambivalence is prompted by a developing interest in Agathon as an ideal lover and by her own desire to go beyond carnal pleasure. Although she and Agathon do end up having sex, both of them are more interested in pursuing an "ideal." In end she becomes Psyche's best friend and with sex only a memory, another sister to Agathon.

At the outset of the story, Agathon discovers Psyche after she has been abducted and washed up in Delphi, where he was raised: "their souls recognized each other immediately and seemed at one glance to flow into one another."[24] In this example of the brother/sister story, the two children develop their aesthetic capacities and moral virtue in an intense exchange with each other, even though they are unaware of the true nature of their relationship. The very fact that they are siblings determines the similarity of dispositions and characters, and the argument of the novel is that no one else could play the same role for each other. The development of selfhood, personality, identity is intimately bound up with the implicit and direct understanding that comes from sharing the same blood. And yet, there is no question that this also has an erotic dimension. The early stirrings of sexuality are experienced by the brother and sister, and in this kind of novel, only chance prevents the completion of their desire for one another. In this scenario, the feelings for one another are clearly incestuous, but the root of the incest lies in the drive to complete the self in a narcissistic coupling. "The use of speech ends when souls directly share, gaze at, and touch each other, and feel in one moment more than the tongues of the muses could express even in a whole year."[25] Psyche tells Agathon that she considers herself to be nothing but a part of his being.[26] What does he find in her? Nothing other than the eternal and infinite.[27] And he also develops his moral sense and his virtue (*Tugend*) in the hours spent in her arms. After they are parted, Agathon ends up in the home of a sophist, where young women are running around in transparent clothes and the possibilities of sexual encounter clearly arouse the young man. Here Wieland sets up the contrast between the sister and women of purely erotic attraction. Agathon readily admits his desire but counters it with his sense of morality—precisely that aspect of his character that was developed in the intimacy of sibling association.[28]

The point that is reiterated throughout the story is that the entire model of future possibility grows out of the relationship of brother to sister and that the moral character of a man is created in relationship to his sister. Agathon:

> I have thought, knowing so much about our souls, that with each of them, in their considerable development over time, I conceive progressively a specific ideal beauty, which unconsciously determines our taste and our moral judgment and which provides the general model by which our imagination projects those pictures that we call great, beautiful, and splendid.[29]

Trying to capture the way beginnings, rooted in sibling affection, determine the outcome of character, Agathon dismisses various other paths to self development:

> that spiritual beauty of the soul and this noble direction of its operation according to the intent of the law-giver of our being, I believed to find most certainly in the observation of nature, which I thought of as a mirror, from which the most essential, incorruptible, and divine is reflected back to our spirit.[30]

This does not work—at least directly—nor does the pursuit of friends or the counsel of priests offer him the possibility of self-directed moral development. Nature, of course, offers the possibility of contemplating beauty,

> but with the tender [gefühlvoll] Psyche it [nature] touched the most sensitive strings of her heart. The conversation, in which we fell into without noticing it, revealed an agreement in our taste and in our dispositions, which quite quickly brought about just as intimate a sympathy in our souls as if we had known each other for many years. It was as if everything that she said I read in direct contemplation of her soul and in return, what I said, was a pure echo of her own feelings or were the development of those ideas that lay in her soul as embryos.[31]

Being together, of course, pushes the two of them in the direction of sexual consummation, and I think it is important to understand here and in the discourse of the period that the sibling relationship was grasped as erotic and that the ethical had a deep association with the physical. A Freud growing up in this period would have understood the sexual dynamic not to inhere in mother and son but in brother and sister. One did not leave the mother in search of her replacement, but one left the sister to find her double: "the love of a brother and his sister is at once the strongest and purest of all attachments."[32] Playing with the idea of the intensity of brother and sister, Agathon says that in lieu of the fact that they did not know they were siblings, they talked a lot about the siblingship of their souls.[33]

A great deal of the story circles around the difference between ideal and erotic love and pits the (presocial) experience with Psyche against the out-in-the-world negotiation of new desires. Agathon's relationship with Danae undergoes a series of changes, in a kind of dialectic between his imagined picture of what she is or could be and his encounter with her reality. All along Psyche retains the first place in his heart and no one is able to replace her, "because the simple memories which remained of her gave him a far greater pleasure than the feelings that any other beauty was capable of arousing in him."[34] Even when Agathon later becomes attached to the erotically charged Danae, Psyche continues to leave an imprint on his emotional and aesthetic life. As Danae replaces Psyche as his object of love, he attempts to base the second experience on the first: "Indeed he loved her [Danae] with such an unselfish, so spiritual, so desire-free love, that his boldest wish went no further than to be with her in that sympathetic union of souls that Psyche had given him to experience."[35] Still not knowing the true relationship with Psyche and now fully engaged with Danae, Psyche comes to him in a dream. "It appeared, he thought, that their love had been that of a brother and sister, a love of souls, and not that which is normally called love. The picture he had of Psyche was inseparable from virtue, and he realized, that for a long time he had confused the two whenever he thought of her."[36]

At the end of the story, a number of fascinating shifts take place. Agathon ends up in the household where an old friend of his from Athens, the son of the house, has in fact married Psyche, who now reveals to her brother that they are indeed siblings.

> This love had always been more of that kind which nature establishes between siblings of harmonious temperaments, than that compared to common passion, which is founded on the magic of another instinct. Theirs had always remained free from the feverish symptoms of this last kind. They had found a special pleasure imagining that at least their souls were intimately connected [verschwistert—connected as brother and sister], since they had not had enough grounds (as much as they had wished it) to ascribe to a sympathy of blood the innocent pleasure that they felt for one another.[37]

Just as Agathon has searched for a replacement for Psyche, so now she finds in his friend a replacement for him—"in many ways a second Agathon."[38] And Agathon himself now discovers Danae living close by. She too has changed, now dedicating herself to virtue—precisely that thing that Agathon had found in himself through Psyche. His sister and former lover now develop the deep friendship of siblings for one another.[39] And Agathon and Danae develop a new love for each other, "healed by virtue."[40] Danae spends her time helping to raise Psyche's children, such that they come to think that they have two mothers—the two women call each other "sister."[41] Worried that his physical desire for Danae will overwhelm him (she is now sister to his sister, after all), Agathon leaves town for a while, returning to bathe in a love feast of friendship. "What their friends found so perfect [*Vollkommen*] was the observation that Agathon made no distinction between Psyche and Chariklea [Danae's new name] and seemed to have completely forgotten that the latter once had been Danae and what she had meant to him."[42] Having lost all sexual desire for Danae, Agathon has finally found in her a true sister—a resolution that suggests that a pure moral attachment can only be a sibling one. In a later poem, called "First Love," Wieland had Agathon address Psyche, his sister, ruminating on the meaning of one's first love for a sister:

> O Magic of first love!
> Now that my life
> Turns toward evening,
> Still you bless me.[43]

Quite a few commentators around 1800 tried to work out the differences in feelings toward the sister and the wife. Some put the issue in Kantian terms, suggesting that with one's wife there was always an objective moment that instrumentalized the relationship. And in a sense, that seems to be the position that Wieland was driven to in *Agathon*, in which the only solution he could find for his hero to see in his lover a true subject was to turn her into a sister. The theologian Carl Ludwig Nitzsch thought that sexuality inevitably led to objectification. But although the sexual drive was completely selfish, sexual desire itself developed only after a benevolent disposition was formed within the family—setting up proper objects of desire. And Nitzsch makes two further points that follow from the intimacy developed within the family. In order to reduce its instrumental core, marriage ought to consider how the alliance of two families binds together people from within the same cultural milieu. The point is that a person ought to be able to find in this manner a spouse as similar to a sibling as possible. Indeed this seems to be the foundation for the spurt of cousin marriages that can be observed around the turn of the nineteenth century and for the *frisson* of attaching oneself to the closest friend of a sister or brother. Secondly, whatever comes out of a marriage, the tenderness between spouses never attains the level of intensity characteristic of siblings. Love between a brother and a sister is the model of purity, of selflessness, of a relationship as end in itself.[44]

A crucial part of the new discourse about sentiment involves a consideration of marriage as something that takes place among people on the same cultural, class, and stylistic plane, a union of true equals and true intimates. If exogamy rules of the seventeenth century enforced marriage with the "stranger," the new dynamics involved a search for the familiar, an attachment to a mirroring self. The developing brother/ sister imaginary in the context of the shift in kin relations from vertical to horizontal underscored a system of marriage exchange that stressed homogamy—the search for the same rather than the other.[45] The intense structuring of new social milieus through reiterated social and cultural exchanges of allied families made cousins—often cousins raised in the same household—into objects of desire.

Recent work by Christopher Johnson on a large French bourgeois family network pushes the analysis in the same direction.[46] In the extended family he studied, the rise of close, erotically charged brother/sister ties provided a new central focal point for familial dynamics, and the language of cousinship became conflated with that of siblingship. One sister (whose letters of longing for her brother bordered on the incestuous, according to Johnson) wrote to her brother about his impending marriage to their cousin: "The affection you have one for the other with Adèle cannot be extinguished, as often happens in *mariages d'inclination*, since it does not go back only a few years, but all your lives. Habituated from your childhood to your *chérie* as a sister and she loving you as a brother, you have developed an affection that can only end with life itself." Later in their marriage, the cousin/wife addressed her husband in her letters as "my love, my friend, my spouse, my brother."[47]

Another example of the same language, reconfigured in the cultural imaginary, comes from *Frankenstein*, where Dr. Frankenstein's orphaned cousin, raised in his family as a sister, becomes his and his family's object of choice for his wife.[48] The cousin/sister switch was only one part of a new eroticism that placed new emphasis on the close siblings of the opposite sex and on a search for sameness in the object of erotic/spiritual desire.

Obviously "same" and "other" is a very complex problematic for the period. Even as there developed cultural milieus structured around the dynamics of interconnected families—those milieus within which marital choice was shaped and desire given focus—another discourse began to model male and female in terms of otherhood, although both were often understood in correlation with each other or seen as two parts of a necessary unity.[49] Hegel can stand in for many spokesmen of the period. In *Elements of the Philosophy of Right*, in the section on "Ethical Life," which is devoted to the family, he makes a differentiation between male and female that at once echoes and determines a long discourse about sexual characteristics. He distinguishes between two kinds of "spirituality," one oriented toward universality, self-consciousness, and conceptual thought (male) and the other to the concrete, individuality, and feeling (female). The point, however, is that each of these is incomplete without the other.[50] Interestingly, precisely at that point in the nineteenth century when marriage was ever more thought of and practiced in terms of tighter alliances within groups of culturally similar and circles of familiar people, Hegel developed an argument that harks back to marriages among "strangers."

> Since marriage arises out of the *free surrender* by both sexes of their personalities, which are infinitely unique to themselves, it must not be concluded within the *naturally identical* circle of people who are acquainted and familiar with each other in every detail—a circle in which the individuals do not have a distinct personality of their own in relation to one another—but must take place [between people] from separate families and personalities of different origin.[51]

Although this is an argument against incest among blood relations, it is couched in broader terms. He goes on to say: "Familiarity, acquaintance, and the habit of shared activity should not be present before marriage: they should be discovered only within it, and the value of this discovery is all the greater the richer it is and the more components it has."[52]

A particularly good example to illustrate the connection between actual relationships between brothers and sisters and the handling of incest themes in the social imaginary is offered by Clemens Brentano, whose novel *Godwi* (1801) and long poem *Romanzen vom Rosenkranz* (1803–1812) both put brother/sister incest at their center. The history of his relationship with his sister Bettine and the place of incest in his writings is worth considerable attention, but I will only sketch in a few points of a larger argument.[53]

I want to set aside a set of relations to develop a few issues that have to do with Bettine Brentano (von Arnim) and Sophie Mereau, during Brentano's courtship of Mereau. Clemens Brentano saw very little of Bettine as they were growing up, raised in separate households, until he was twenty and she fourteen. He describes her growing erotic attraction in the 1801 novel *Godwi*, which he was writing around that time, expressing pleasure at her maturing breasts.[54] He and Bettine paired off in an intense relationship, frequently carried on in an exchange of letters—part of which she later heavily edited in *Clemens Brentano's Frühlingskranz*.[55] The pairing off of two siblings was typical of many families of the period. For Brentano, Bettine became his ideal, and their relationship, the model of love. From the beginning, and throughout his life, he searched for a woman to act as a mediator between him and God or transcendent reality, constantly moving between images of purity and sensuality. Brentano could only see himself as a self, constituted in an other. Writing in 1802 (6 September) to his friend and the future husband of Bettine, Achim Von Arnim, he said: "My love for her (Bettine) is itself not genuine. I stand shyly next to her because she shows me nothing other than a more beautiful image of my self."[56] A few days later, to a friend (Johanna Kraus, in September 1802), he wrote that "Bettine is my double."[57] Not only had he he been formed by Bettine, but she was in turn formed by him, he maintained. Writing to his fiancée (18 March 1803), he remarked: "This girl, Sophie, is mine, mine alone, and if I am good, I am good in order to be like her [ihr zu gleichen], because of her love, and to earn her sweet reproach that she is everything through me."[58] Earlier in the dedication to the second volume of *Godwi*, he had written to her: "You are my world, and you should create me, stir yourself and open my eyes."[59]

Brentano constantly let the image of his sister and his lover fade into each other. In the same letter, he wrote: "she is beautiful, you are beautiful, oh if only you were beautiful sisters, *belles soeurs* [a pun on sisters-in-law]." To Savigny (another brother-in-law), he wrote (7/8 June 1803) that he would receive Sophie Mereau only from Bettine's hands.[60] Then (mid June 1803), he wrote to his lover that Bettine "is except for God the highest that a human can love, and when I show you to her then you will have gotten everything from me—more than that I have nothing."[61] Several weeks later, he asked her to continue the kind of love he got from his sister (3 June 1803): "oh if only you would really love me, so very intimately, as I hardly can do it myself, as only Bettine has tried."[62] Later (31 August 1803), he wanted Mereau and himself to "unite" with his sister.[63] On the heels of that idea (13/14 September 1803), he imagined what it would be like if Bettine were not his sister and if she were as old as Mereau—which would he choose? Of course he would be passionately in love with Mereau and desire her, but Bettine would win him—although he would not forget Mereau in her. "But since things are otherwise, you are there and are the only one."[64]

Finally, he felt he had to defend himself to his fiancée against charges of incest (7 October 1803):

> the crime that was in me was not against the divine, for I had already rescued the divine in my heart and brought it in safety from myself and my contempt for my destiny ... and that circle of people who constructed incestuous anecdotes out of my poetic fondness for my mother and the deservedly honest love for my sister, can probably regale you with many more of my remarks.[65]

As a final comment on his transition from sister to wife, he wrote to Mereau (17 and 20 January 1804):

> Bettine's connection to me is like the connection of two friends who live somewhere where talking is forbidden. One of them, however, had prayed out loud, told a woman he loved her, comforted a dying person, and called out in the night to someone walking into an abyss. Because of this he had his tongue cut out. That is me. Now the other goes around in all the joys of life, greets the dumb one whenever they meet, but she is fearful and does not talk and the comforting glances become more seldom, and thus everything is ruined, with no injustice or revenge. Oh if the dumb one had his tongue again, he would ask her to love him, but still without hope and would lose his tongue again.[66]

The best way to end any essay is, of course, with Hegel. I might make it clear that my interest in all of these texts is like that of an anthropologist. I see them as symptomatic of a social and cultural situation where like was seeking out like, where ever more active familial life provided cultural sites for the formation of desire, and where schooling in emotion and sentiment connected the problematic of sister and wife together. Just this occurs in the middle of the *Phenomenology*. It is widely known, I think, that the relationship between Hegel and his younger sister was very intense. Just after his marriage at forty, she had a nervous breakdown and was in an asylum for more than a year. Soon after Hegel died, she wrote a letter to his widow about Hegel's childhood and personality development, took a walk, and committed suicide. It seems to me that this is foreshadowed in the discussion of wife and sister in the chapter on the "ethical world." Hegel suggests that the emotional tie for a woman was to marriage itself, but hardly to the particular husband in question—at least in an "ethical" household. Or perhaps feeling is not really the issue, for her relationships "are not based on a reference to this particular husband, this particular child, but to *a* husband, to children *in general*—not to feeling, but to the universal."[67]

The point is that women are fitted for wifehood and motherhood as such, and the particular situation in which they find themselves is of no ethical importance. Above all, a woman as wife cannot know herself, cannot be a particular self in knowing and recognizing and being recognized by the husband (i.e., through an other). Everything is different, however, with respect to the brother, because there is no sexual desire that disturbs the recognition of self:

> The brother, however, is in the eyes of the sister a being whose nature is unperturbed by desire and is ethically like her own; her recognition in him is pure and unmixed with any sexual relation. The indifference characteristic of particular existence and the ethical contingency thence arising are, therefore, not present in this relationship; instead the moment of individual selfhood, recognizing and being recognized, can here assert its right, because it is bound up with the balance and equilibrium resulting from their being of the same blood, and from their being related in a way that involves no mutual desire. The loss of a brother is thus irreparable to the sister, and her duty toward him is the highest.[68]

In many ways, we can clearly see the tensions in the brother/sister, husband/wife dichotomy in Hegel's treatment. Ethical life is rooted in the brother/sister relationship, and it fundamentally eschews desire. But it is precisely desire that the literature of the period between 1740 and 1840 tries to deal with. For Hegel, the indispensable issue is eventually to leave the bosom of the family and attain independence, finding in a new union that which is new and, in a sense, not merely "reproductive," since the object of marriage is to produce children that are independent of their origins. In this understanding of the bourgeois family as the matrix for individuality, free choice, and—essentially—revolutionary activity, Hegel profoundly influenced the historiography of the family, for what he described is what the historians and sociologists found. Yet a closer reading of the texts of the period and an examination of the details of familial alliance shows that families were reorienting themselves toward the creation of networks of similarly situated individuals, reiterating alliances with kin, and finding mates for their members among people from the same neighborhoods, social and cultural milieus, and class position. In the transition period around 1800, when kinship relations were reordered from vertically to horizontally structured forms, siblings offered each other not only the psychological foundations for personality development but also models (and often mediators) for entering into new marriage alliances. Hegel himself was well aware that his sister had a far deeper meaning for him than his wife.

Although I have not been able to say much about the particular forms of selfhood that emerged around 1800, what I have tried to do is to suggest some of the social dynamics and social forms within which people developed a sense of selfhood and schooled themselves in sentiment, moral disposition, and social aesthetics. The exigencies of matching like with like and operating in extensive networks of interconnected families, together with socialization in emotionally laden and sentimentally stylized households, brought about a social pattern of intense sibling interaction and a cultural imaginary of brother/sister incest.

Notes

1. See the discussion in David Warren Sabean and Simon Teuscher, "Kinship in Europe: A New Approach to Long Term Development," in *Kinship in Europe: Approaches to Long-Term Development (1300–1900)*, ed. David Warren Sabean, Simon Teuscher, and Jon Mathieu (Oxford and New York, 2007), 1–32.
2. See the brilliant study by Gérard Delille, *Famille et propriété dans le royaume de Naples (XVe–XIXe siècle)* (Rome and Paris, 1985). There is a long discussion of his findings in David Warren Sabean, *Kinship in Neckarhausen, 1700–1870* (Cambridge, 1998), 399–407.
3. Sabean, *Kinship*, 428–448.
4. Among many other writings on the subject, see Ulrike Prokop, *Die Illusion vom großen Paar*, 2 vols. (Frankfurt am Main, 1991), esp. vol. 1, 52–3, 78ff.
5. Sabean, *Kinship*, 449–508.
6. A good example from among many is offered by Heinz Reif, *Westfälischer Adel 1770–1860: Vom Herrschaftsstand zur regionalen Elite* (Göttingen, 1979), 266–267.
7. Michael Titzmann, "Literarische Strukturen und kulturelles Wissen: Das Beispiel inzestuöser Situationen in der Erzählliteratur der Goethezeit und ihre Funktionen im Denksystem der Epoche," in *Erzählte Kriminalität: Zur Typologie und Funktion von narrativen Darstellungen in Strafrechtspflege, Publizistik und Literatur zwischen 1770 und 1920* (Studien und Texte zur Sozialgeschichte der Literatur, vol. 27), ed. Jörg Schönert, Konstantin Imm, and Joachim Linder (Tübingen, 1991), 229–281.
8. An earlier version of the argument appeared in David Warren Sabean, "Inzestdiskurse vom Barock bis zur Romantik," *L'Homme: Zeitschrift für feministische Geschichtswissenschaft* 13, no. 1 (2002): 7–28.
9. Friedrich Maximilian Klinger, *Geschichte Giafers des Barmeciden: Ein Seitenstück zu Fausts Leben, Thaten und Höllenfahrt*, 2 vols. (St. Petersburg, 1792–1794).
10. Ibid., 9.
11. Ibid., 27–28.
12. Ibid., 92.
13. Ibid., 59–61.
14. When he is taken into the harem and encounters the pleasures of lustful desire, the picture of Fatime with the beauty of innocence presents itself before his eyes, with the memory of the feelings that that flowed into his heart from her last kiss; ibid. Later, thinking he is seeing Fatime, he falls in love with the daughter of the leader of a caravan, who has awakened all the feelings that Fatime had brought about; ibid., 179.
15. Ibid., 92.
16. Ibid., 211.
17. Ibid., 373.

18. Ibid., 365.
19. Ibid., 433.
20. Ibid., 448.
21. Ibid., 450–451.
22. Ibid., 452.
23. C. M. Wieland, *Geschichte des Agathon* [3 vols., Leipzig, 1794], reprinted in *Sämmtliche Werke*, ed. Hamburger Stiftung zur Förderung von Wissenschaft und Kultur, 14 vols. (Hamburg, 1984), vol. 1.
24. Ibid., vol. 1, 37.
25. Ibid., vol. 1, 38.
26. Ibid., vol. 1, 41.
27. Ibid., vol. 1, 58.
28. Ibid., vol. 1, 103.
29. Ibid., vol. 2, 7.
30. Ibid., vol. 2, 24.
31. Ibid., vol. 2, 51.
32. Ibid., vol. 2, 55.
33. Ibid., vol. 2, 56.
34. Ibid., vol. 1, 210–211.
35. Ibid., vol. 1, 237–238.
36. Ibid., vol. 1, 309–310.
37. Ibid., vol. 3, 199.
38. Ibid., vol. 3, 210.
39. Ibid., vol. 3, 237.
40. Ibid., vol. 3, 240.
41. Ibid., vol. 3, 417–418.
42. Ibid., vol. 3, 423.
43. C. M. Wieland, "Die erste Liebe. An Psyche" [1774], in *Sämmtliche Werke*, vol. 9, 165–185.
44. Carl Ludwig Nitsch, *Neuer Versuch über die Ungültigkeit des mosaischen Gesetzes und den Rechtsgrund der Eheverbote in einem Gutachten über die Ehe mit des Bruders Wittwe* (Wittenberg und Zerbst, 1800), 66–74, 92.
45. This is discussed at length in Sabean, *Kinship*, chaps. 21–23.
46. See in this volume Christopher H Johnson, "Siblinghood and the Emotional Dimensions of the New Kinship System, 1750–1850: A French Example."
47. Christopher H. Johnson, "Das 'Geschwister Archipel': Bruder-Schwester-Liebe und Klassenformation im Frankreich des 19. Jahrhunderts," *L'Homme. Zeitschrift für feministische Geschichtswissenschaft* 13 (2002): 50–67, here 63–64.
48. Mary Shelley, *Frankenstein*, ed. J. Paul Hunter (New York, 1966), 19.
49. Karin Hausen, "Die Polarisierung des 'Geschlechtscharaktere': Eine Spiegelung der Dissoziation von Erwerbs- und Familienleben," in *Sozialgeschichte der Familie in der Neuzeit Europas*, ed. Werner Conze (Stuttgart, 1976), 363–393.
50. G. W. F. Hegel, *Elements of the Philosophy of Right*, ed. Allen W. Wood, trans. H. B. Nisbet (Cambridge, 1991), 206.
51. Hegel, *Philosophy of Right*, 207–208.
52. Ibid., 208.
53. There is now a book that chronicles their correspondence: Hartwig Schultz, *"Unsre Lieb aber is außerkohren": Die Geschwister Clemens und Bettine Brentano* (Frankfurt am Main, 2004).

54. Clemens Brentano, *Godwi oder das steinerne Bild der Mutter: Ein verwilderter Roman von Maria*, ed. Werner Bellman, in Brentano, *Sämtlicher Werke und Briefe*, vol. 16 (Stuttgart, 1978), 228.

55. *"Clemens Brentano's Frühlingkranz" und handschriftliche überlieferte Briefe Brentanos an Bettine 1800–03*, in *Sämtliche Werke*, vol. 30 [*Briefe*, book II, ed. Lieselotte Kinskofer] (Stuttgart, 1990).

56. *Sämtliche Werke*, vol. 26 [*Briefe*, book I, ed. Lieselotte Kinshofer] (Stuttgart, 1988), 502.

57. *Briefe* I, 512.

58. *Briefe* III, 62.

59. Cited in Schultz, *Geschwister Brentano*, 28.

60. *Briefe* III, 105.

61. Ibid., 110.

62. Ibid., 123.

63. Ibid., 153.

64. Ibid., 184–185.

65. Ibid., 217.

66. Ibid., 287.

67. G. W. F. Hegel, *The Phenomenology of Mind*, trans. and intro. J. B. Baillie, 2nd ed. (London, 1949), 476.

68. Ibid., 477.

Chapter 10

Sisters, Wives, and the Sublimation of Desire in a Jewish-Protestant Friendship

The Letters of the Historian Johann Gustav Droysen and the Composer Felix Mendelssohn-Bartholdy

Regina Schulte

In the Museum of Prints and Drawings (Kupferstichkabinett) of the Berlin State Museums there is a portrait of the twenty-one-year-old Johann Gustav Droysen. He sits, his folded arms resting on a table, gazing out at the beholder. Before him lies a musical notation in his own hand, and on the lower edge of the picture a Greek text is visible—neither of them legible. This pencil drawing from 1829 is the work of the court painter Wilhelm Hensel.[1] The artist and the date locate the young Droysen within a distinct environment, the Mendelssohn family, and thus within the circles of the educated and artistic elite of the Prussian capital, which in the 1820s gathered at the Mendelssohn home as one of the most important, and with its weekly "Sunday musicales" the most discerning, Berlin salons of that period. Hegel, Heinrich Heine, Bettina von Arnim, Rachel Varnhagen and Karl August Varnhagen von Ense, Alexander von Humboldt, Henriette Herz, Eduard Gans, Ludwig Tieck,

Illustration 10.1. Wilhelm Hensel. Johann Gustav Droysen, 1829. Bleistift-Zeichnung mit einem griechischen Text und einem Noten-Zitat von der Hand des Dargestellten (Kupferstichkabinett, SMPK, Berlin; 9/12)

and E.T.A. Hoffmann were among the guests of the house, along with other famous individuals.[2]

After the initial steps toward emancipation in the 1780s, Berlin's educated circles, with the Mendelssohn family at their center, had witnessed a brief and significant flowering of social and intellectual exchange between Jews and Christians. After this hopeful phase, which was influenced by the spirit of Moses Mendelssohn and its idealization in Lessing's *Nathan the Wise*, anti-Semitism gained ground once again with the victory over Napoleon, the rise of anti-liberal currents, and the beginnings of modern nationalism.[3] It even moved Mendelssohn's son Abraham and his wife Lea to have their children Felix and Fanny baptized as Protestants in 1816 and to convert later themselves. In the process they supplemented their typically Jewish family name—controversially within the family—with an "estate name," thus anchoring themselves to the soil, as it were.[4]

In the 1820s, however, these phenomena remained in the background of elite urban sociability, and gatherings at the Mendelssohn house continued to bring together Christians and Jews in the spirit of intellectual enlightenment and religious tolerance. Among them, apart from the younger Mendelssohns, were also other prominent Jewish converts to Protestantism such as the important Lutheran theologian August Neander; Heinrich Heine; the author of a history of Greek literature G. Bernhardy; the legal scholar Eduard Gans, whose university lectures Droysen and Mendelssohn attended; Eduard Bendemann, one of Droysen's closest friends; and last but not least Gottlieb Friedländer, royal librarian and archivist and Droysen's future brother-in-law.[5] Musical life at the Mendelssohn house was a central medium for the new encounters between Jews and Christians in the 1820s. As Michael Steinberg has noted, the family owed their prominent position to philosophy and commerce, and music now brought the world to them.

In the Berlin of Felix's and Fanny's youth, the Mendelssohn family stood famously at the vanguard of cultural negotiation between Judaism and Lutheranism, and between piety and secularization. In the lives of its patriarchs, this negotiation was conducted in philosophy and commerce. In the lives of its matriarchs, especially Sara Levy, it was conducted in music. Philosophy and commerce brought the family into the world; music invited the world into the household.[6]

The Mendelssohn family home, particularly the town house at Leipziger Straße 3, which they acquired in 1825, was "no common property, no dead pile of stones, but rather a living individual, a member partaking of the family's fortunes ... and to some degree for them and those closest to them also their representative."[7] For contemporaries, it stood for the intellectual space between the public and private spheres, in which this polarity appeared to have been abolished. It was a protective space that the father had created for his children, founded on wealth, a strictly patriarchal model of the family, and the extraordinary education he gave to all of his children. The best teachers, other artists as participants and audience, all of the new musical publications—all of this was delivered to the house, so to speak.[8]

Between the at once prominent and precarious exterior life, represented by the town house and the changes of name and religion, and the interior life of the traditional family with its almost draconian promotion of the children's education as well as its particular emotionality supported equally by family tradition and the style of the age, the children developed a creative emotional culture through the mediums of music, learning, and the new religion. Their teachers too were drawn into this world—at least when their age, education, and temperament so eminently suited them for such a friendship as was the case with Johann Gustav Droysen. His friendship with Felix Mendelssohn—what one might regard as their reciprocal acculturation—allows us to examine more closely the dimensions of an intimacy that appears abstract and questionable in the term "German-Jewish symbiosis."

The portrait sketch by the court and family painter hints at this relationship via both the Greek text and the musical notation. The line of Greek was intended to stand for Droysen, who at the time of this portrait had just completed his dissertation, a translation of Aeschylus,[9] while the musical notes probably did so only indirectly, by way of the writing suggested between the musical notes and the mere fact that Droysen has the musical notation in front of him and perhaps copied it himself. The young Droysen, raised in poor, provincial circumstances in Pomerania, was the son of a Protestant pastor and military chaplain influenced by Halle Pietism. After the early death of the patriarchal and caring father in 1816, the children were raised by their mother, who died in 1828, making orphans of the son, then twenty, and his three sisters. The eldest, 25-year-old Auguste, was married to a pastor; the second, 19-year-old Mathilde, was unmarried and would remain so until her death in 1887; and 13-year-old Ulrike lived under the protection of her sister Mathilde. They had stayed behind in the province when the brother left for the university and Berlin.

On the recommendation of his professor, the ancient historian Philipp August Boekh, young Gustav Droysen had entered the Mendelssohn household in 1827 as a Greek tutor for his almost exact contemporary Felix and his sister.[10] From Fanny's perspective, he was a "philologist with all of the freshness and vivid, active sympathy of his age, knowledge beyond his years, and a pure poetic mind and healthy, amiable temperament."[11] The student-teacher relationship soon turned into a close friendship. But in this moment also began the development of a complex structure that shows that the sisters were an important factor in the formation of the friendship of the young men.

I assume that the musical notes in the portrait of Droysen stand not only for Felix but also for his sister Fanny, who was a composer like her brother. That Droysen appears to be working on them in the drawing suggests the relationship between the Mendelssohns' music and Droysen's writing—he wrote many of the texts that the siblings set to music. According to Eduard Devrient, he was the "candidate for a teaching position who wrote the songs for which Felix and Fanny preferred to compose."[12] The picture thus portrays him as the teacher and "poet" allied with the Mendelssohn siblings that he understood himself to be in a letter of 1829 to his beloved sisters.[13] Finally, the cycle of five poems "To Felix" that Droysen wrote in April–May of that year for Fanny's collection of songs (*Liederkranz*) were dedicated to the brother and friend in faraway London.[14] The sister's yearning-filled music was paired with the poet/friend's melancholy words. An example of these song texts, which are not readily recognizable as poems, is the introductory song "Farewell to Felix," written on the occasion of his first journey to England in 1829:

> I would not disturb your sleep, and yet you depart so soon!
> Would like to steal into your dream, would like to tell you something;
> Are you still asleep? And now I long to hug you and kiss you, brother mine,
> and cannot quite believe that you wish to leave us. Farewell, farewell.[15]

In interpreting the portrait, we also need to keep in mind the time when it was painted. The year 1829 represented a caesura not just in the life of Fanny Mendelssohn: it was, above all, the year of the revival of Bach's St. Matthew Passion by Felix Mendelssohn-Bartholdy with the assistance of the singer Eduard Devrient and—at first reluctantly—of Zelter at the Berlin Singakademie in March and April, and thus of the spectacular resuscitation of an emphatically Protestant piece of music, for which the long, and in those days quite unusual, reception of Bach in the Mendelssohn household had paved the way. In the spring of 1829 Droysen completed the manuscript of his Aeschylus translation and sent it on its way into the public sphere (the translation was published in 1832). Felix embarked on his first major foreign journey to England, and on 6 July Gustav Droysen celebrated his twenty-first birthday at the Mendelssohn home. On 3 October 1829 Fanny Mendelssohn married the court painter Hensel, a Protestant. Finally, after Felix's return, the year ended with the festivities for the elder Mendelssohn-Bartholdys' silver wedding anniversary, complete with recitations, music, and theatrical offerings in which Droysen also participated. In all of these events the lives of Felix Mendelssohn and Gustav Droysen were closely intertwined, and their sisters were also involved through their detailed correspondence.

The Tender Bonds of Masculine Friendship

Thirty letters between Mendelssohn and Droysen as well as others to their sisters and close friends survive as testimony to the friendship between the two men.[16] Mendelssohn wrote the first of these letters to Droysen in November 1829 during his concert tour to England and Scotland.

> When I think that I may be sitting on your sofa a mere three weeks from now, with a very brown slice of bread and butter, and can tell you about the Hebrides, it gladdens my heart ... and I run into the house, rush up the stairs and to that sofa. ... I have said nothing to you in this letter, and the best needs no saying; you already know it as soon as I write my name. And there is nothing to add save Your Felix M.-B.[17]

These sentences begin and end a very long letter in which Felix Mendelssohn-Bartholdy displays his mastery of the epistolary art particularly cultivated in his family. The epistolary culture that developed in the eighteenth century had special significance for Jews. Life in the diaspora, scattered across the world as a minority in frequently hostile surroundings, made it important for Jews to know each other and to create a corresponding network of communication.[18] For the Mendelssohns, writing letters was an art demanding literary skills: "Abraham corrected his children's epistolary style, commenting so relentlessly on details of grammar and content that they sometimes lost all naturalness. Felix knew the very high expectations his parents placed upon his travel letters."[19]

The greater part of Felix's letter to Droysen is thus also a description of the city of London and of his impressions and sentiments, interspersed with at times amusing accounts of high society and individual persons. The expansiveness of this artful travel account creates a contrast, however, with the rather impoverished student Droysen's study, into which he imagines himself, with the sofa that also appears in later letters—"when I congratulated you verbally (on the engagement) and warmed myself at your stove, while you sat on the sofa under Bailly";[20] "I imagined I was sitting beside you on the sofa, pressing your hand."[21] This room with the sofa, over which apparently hung a symbol of the French Revolution and Constitution (a portrait of the man who presided over proceedings in the Tennis Court at Versailles and the Revolutionary mayor of Paris, Jean Sylvain Bailly, who as a Constitutionalist later fell victim to the Terror), contrasts with the expansive Recke Palais with its summerhouse and park at Leipziger Straße 3, where the Mendelssohns had moved in 1825, and which has come down to us in many drawings by Hensel and Felix.[22] The image of Droysen's humble room conveys the atmosphere of conspiratorial familiarity, warmth, and intimacy between young men that is also reflected in Droysen's letters, for example that of 29 November 1829, where he complains to his friend of loneliness.

> Yet I am satisfied with my poverty, or rather, it suffices. What is certain is that I am without company up here, since [Heinrich] Abeken is not enough for me, and [Ludwig] Wiese, who is hungry for love, does not satisfy my needs, and [Adolf Bernhard] Marx, as I have often told you, is immune to the human heart and the gentle rainy gaze of the spring sunshine. I want to love, simply love one person, who would stand here, and to stroke his soft hand and not need to say a word. ... Felix will be here at last in six days.[23]

The friendship between Droysen and Mendelssohn was tightly imbedded in the context of the large, open, and selectively hospitable Mendelssohn family—parents Abraham and Lea, sisters Fanny and Rebekka, and youngest brother Paul. This family was extended by the large number of omnipresent relatives and friends included in their everyday lives, several of whom were always living at the house. Leipziger Straße was a site of musical, intellectual, and literary creativity and communication, which was woven into the very essence of the whole family context, into their home, life rhythms, and annual cycles with all of their rituals, networks of love, piety, kinship and friendship, and also business. A letter that Droysen wrote to his sisters on the occasion of his twenty-first birthday underlines the extent to which he felt integrated into the family, but also how overwhelmed he was by the brilliance of the entertainments laid on for his birthday. This description also shows in exemplary fashion how artfully such events were organized.

> Upon my arrival I found the company already assembled, and was welcomed by all with voluble congratulations. The two sisters had adorned their hair with my favorite flowers, white lilies and cornflowers, as they expressly pointed out, and at my place at table sat a coffee-urn, in a wide covering of napkins embellished with flowers, a present from the mother, who had given me the rest of the coffee service at Christmas, and from the sisters a very tasteful sinumbra lamp. ... The painter Hensel had modeled a dolphin out of the soft mass (anchovy butter); obligingly enough, since I had often enough written poems for his fiancée's and Felix's compositions. After the soup, the three young ladies, in solemn procession, brought me the dolphin, whose eyes were of blue stock leaves, and the spouts of water from his nose were of pale green blades of grass, and which swam on water lilies and cornflowers instead of water, and set it down before me. With a gracious phrase, Mother

put an end to my momentary indecision about what to do: she said that prejudice forbade me to cut the butter, and asked for the dish.[24]

This scene reads like a rite of initiation into the family. Droysen's account, however, also gives us a hint of the great importance—described by Devrient—of the family for Felix, who is inconceivable without this family behind him, into which he also integrated his friend Droysen: "His [Felix's] love for his family still came first in his emotional life. His filial piety for his parents was boundless, and his reverence for his father assumed religious-patriarchal traits. The love he felt for his sisters was of the most affectionate intimacy."[25] According to Marion Kaplan, such profound family ties were common among many nineteenth-century bourgeois Jews.[26] Droysen too, however, came from an emotionally close family, as his letter to his "dear, dear sisters" as well as the memoirs of his father and later of his son attest.[27] The Protestant parsonage of his childhood up to the age of eight bore the imprint of a Pietist-influenced, patriarchal father wholly devoted to his son, whom he taught himself, and "to whom [the boy] looked up with loving admiration," and a mother who "stood by her husband as a loyal companion … and quiet wife," and who tried to support the family after his death by taking in sewing and darning and making rag rugs while assuming sole responsibility for raising the children.[28] For Droysen, now in Berlin, far away from his three sisters in distant Pomerania and still mourning the death of his mother, the Mendelssohn household may well have appeared as a grander substitute family: in the letter to his sisters he also writes of "sisters" when he means Fanny and Rebekka, and "Mother" when he refers to Lea Mendelssohn.

Droysen responded to his acceptance and integration into the Mendelssohn household as the son's tutor and closest friend by actively engaging in its constitutive rituals. This occurred, for example, when he wrote a poem and participated intensively in preparations for the grand celebrations for Abraham and Lea Mendelssohn-Bartholdy's silver wedding anniversary at the end of 1829:

Good morning, Felix! [I have] the following suggestions for the merry performance on December 25th. … To ensure that the suggestion you already heard yesterday is not destroyed or rendered vexatious … by my clumsiness and inopportune earnestness, for although I am sunny and joyful inside, I have little talent for merriment … I will make the choruses of children's music—which could be quite different and perhaps sound in the innermost heart—for you if you wish it.[29]

For a moment, the world appeared to contain all possible gifts at once: friendship, family, and creative artistic collaboration seemingly entered into an intimate symbiosis, which appeared for a short time to be incessantly renewed. Letters were sent and answered on the same day, sometimes several of them, even if the friends were going to see each other later on. "I will tell you ... about it when we see each other this evening."[30] Their communication made use of all forms and levels, letters, poems, sounds, the spring. The occasion might be rewriting a poem that was not quite up to Felix's standards: "But I swear to you, your last two stanzas are impossible to set to music. ... Help me, I am on my knees."[31] The reply turned into an imaginary spring wedding:

> The flowers, intoxicated by spring, are as willful as a young girl ... The dew-fresh rose, in particular, gazes at me with such tremulous melancholy as if she alone made my spring. But I should know better, dearest rose, for poetry says today to music: My dear man ... The children are six songs. 'Tomorrow.'[32]

The brief period of these exuberant encounters in Berlin seems always to have been marked by the premonition of future separation. His father pressed Felix to seek his place in the world and conquer other arenas. When Droysen tried to stop time for a moment, he expressed this awareness of living in a brief transitional phase: "But I am feeling rather low-spirited, as if I were on a nocturnal drive over a wide, deadened snowy field. I beg of you, I would so like to hold and press your warm, soft hand, time is very short now."[33] In spring 1830, the world in Berlin was redolent of parting. Intimate family time in the Mendelssohn house proved brief, and yet so influential and profound that it would shape Droysen's later life with its lasting connections.[34] In a letter of 18 January 1830 to Albert Heydemann he wrote:

> Felix is the warmest, dearest friend. How I love him and his sisters! If only I could prove it by a great sacrifice! It is not enough for me to love them so dearly; I should like to avow it fiercely. Fanny's eye could give me the peace of the sea on a bright, solemn Sunday morning. Rebekka is hardest hit; she will be doubly unfortunate when Felix [goes] to Italy.[35]

Felix—of whom, even as an old man, Droysen said "He was the best we had," speaking of his "obliging tenderness, to produce or even to evoke which is impossible for me"—appeared to be slipping away from him, and Felix's sisters were beyond his reach, and his own sisters far away.[36] It was in this period that he first expressed his desire for a betrothed, which could not, however, be put into practice, so that he must make do with marriage to his own ego, and with the children of his own labor. He does nevertheless unfold his fantastic translation before another friend and correspondent in astonishing images.

At such times you may realize how valuable it is not to be alone; at such times I might even wish for a betrothed, if it were otherwise practicable. But the most loyal, silent and sympathetic betrothed is my own breast, and long has been; the sweet dalliances of the honeymoon are over, and we consider with seriousness and pious diligence how we will set up our life's household and establish the secure hearth of a worthy vocation and the heartfelt, joyful domesticity of a life trusting in God; and we secretly speak and think of our first baptism ... the maternal breast may sicken at the sacred pangs of birth ... and is dressed in white and hugs and kisses the little one who bears not her name, but that of the father, who is the generative spirit.[37]

Sisters and Other Sweethearts

The role of their sisters, who had heretofore shared their brothers' lives, growing up and being educated along with them—Felix and Fanny in music with similar gifts, Felix and Rebekka in their studies of antiquity, while Droysen's letter to his sisters shows that he also took their education as a given—is captured in both Droysen's and Mendelssohn's fantasy about their own lives and their betrothed. Their sisters were also their companions, as were the sisters of their male friends and their sisters' female friends, and the brothers of their female friends. "On Sunday evenings, the larger circle tended to assemble at the Mendelssohn house, which in the summer gathered half in the open garden hall, half in the park-like garden, where a number of blossoming girlfriends of the daughters of the house appeared and gave Felix the opportunity for his first attempts at courtship."[38] When writing to his sisters, Droysen toyed with the idea of Bekkchen Mendelssohn as a possible fiancée: "Wouldn't you say, Mathilde, it is now perfectly clear, you have known about me and Bekkchen for a long time, and this story shows that Mother agrees." But there were also other, "namely younger ladies."[39]

In this Berlin period the sisters were still very much present.[40] For Droysen, who had left them behind in the provinces, they became a reflection of his own awakening and successes.[41] While the brothers set forth to conquer the worlds of science and art, they also developed concepts for their sisters' lives. We will see that these were also the destiny of their future wives, since they tended to be the sisters of friends and moved in the same social and emotional milieu. And at the same time these concepts kept the tenderly loved sisters under their brothers' spell, for these future husbands corresponded to their own self-images.[42] What Droysen remarked in a letter to his sister Mathilde about their sister Ulrike, who was about to marry one of his friends, refers to his model of the ideal sister-wife and the ideal man.

She is all feeling, and it is quite concentrated upon my person; I myself guided and trained her in this, for therein lies the value of the feminine soul, that she loves and only loves, happy when she always knows the point to which she turns her gaze. This unity is all that you have of character, and all you should have. Your relationship is always only to one and for one person, and soon enough that bittersweet hour will come for my dear child when she will, unwillingly and unwittingly, see another and better image in my stead.[43]

"Better", because it is her husband's image, but it is fashioned after her brother's. Droysen, after all, will want to be the better image as a husband.

Felix Mendelssohn appears to have faced greater challenges. He came into more profound and lifelong conflict with the image of his sister Fanny, also a gifted composer, whom he loved dearly. At first it was Fanny who, in the light of her marriage, assured Felix of her continuing love, and "that nothing could ever happen to make me forget you for even the tiniest fraction of a second."[44] In a letter to their mother, however, Felix put his sister in her place once and for all.

And Fanny as I know her has neither the desire nor the vocation to create – she is too much of a proper woman for that, who cares for her house and thinks neither of the public nor of the musical world, nor even of music, except when her first vocation has been fulfilled.[45]

Fanny did think about the public and the musical world, and about music, but after 1830 she brought all of this to the famous Sunday musicales at her house at Leipziger Straße 3, the parental home whose tradition she carried on thereby and that she left at most to travel. Sisters followed their brothers' and husbands' instructions. After his poems for the song cycle, Droysen wrote practically no texts for Fanny. Her fiancé Hensel had reacted with intense jealousy, which finally resulted in Fanny giving up this intimate joint productivity after a "scene" with Droysen in September 1829:

Dear Wilhelm, you expressed with much determination something that pains me greatly. Since you said it with firm intent, however, I can and may say nothing against it, but only base my decision on yours. I shall compose no more songs, at least not by new poets whom I know personally, and certainly not by Droysen. Instrumental music remains, and I can confide to it whatever I wish, it is discreet. ... I now accept ... that art is nothing for women, but only for girls, and at the threshold of my new life I bid farewell to this childhood playmate.[46]

Henceforth, it was Wilhelm Hensel who wrote Fanny's texts. The hus-band provided the "pre-text" for his wife's emotional expressions and "discreet" tones.

Two Kinds of Acculturation: The Mirror Image of Marital Symbioses

At the time when the brothers, scholar and musician alike, believed that they knew their sisters' proper place, they were also choosing their future spouses. These women belonged to a matrix of family, sisters, and the religious and educated bourgeois environment prefigured at Leipziger Straße 3 in Berlin with its multifarious interconnections and symbioses. Johann Gustav Droysen married Marie Mendheim, the sister of the wife of his friend Gottlieb Friedländer, to whom he had dedicated his book about Alexander the Great. Like many of his closest friends, she came from a family of Jewish converts to Protestantism.[47] Marie Mendheim was the granddaughter of the manuscript collector and nu-mismatist Benoni Friedländer, whom Droysen referred to in a letter to Friedrich Gottlieb Welcker as "highly esteemed and famous" and his teacher in numismatics, in whose "rich collection, which is without peer for the Middle Ages," he had worked on numerous occasions.[48] Marie Mendheim's great-grandfather David Friedländer had come to Berlin at the age of twenty-one, married a daughter of Daniel Itzig, and been "welcomed enthusiastically into Mendelssohn's circles as an enlightened, pious Jew" who after Moses Mendelssohn's death in 1786 assumed his mantle as a pioneer in the struggle to modernize and gain civil equality for Prussian Jewry.[49] He died in 1834, the year of Marie Mendheim's fourteenth birthday and her confirmation. During the celebration she fell into a deep swoon and contracted a serious nervous fever. After her recovery she was considered Johann Gustav Droysen's betrothed.[50]

Droysen was a regular visitor to the Friedländer family home—that is, to the house of Marie Mendheim's grandparents, where she and her sister lived after the death of their mother (1826) under the care of her grandmother Rebekka von Halle, who, in the words of her great-grand-son Gustaf Droysen, "in her kindheartedness, found her happiness in caring selflessly for others. [She was] a heart of gold with the greatest delicacy of feeling, a model of every domestic virtue, the very epitome of pure and noble womanly character."[51] She is thus portrayed as the perfect embodiment of the Biedermeier bourgeois female ideal.

Following Felix's departure in 1832, Droysen's visits to the Mendelssohn home became less frequent, but he was now a daily guest at the equally munificent Friedländer house, already familiar to him through his friendship with Gottlieb Friedländer. In a typical brotherly letter to his sisters, the increasingly successful scholar and newly minted fiancé impressively describes his life:

> My dears, you have indeed no idea of the meaning of work and being busy. For a joke I must describe this in detail, just for today. I rise at 6 o'clock, bathe, and must leave at 7:15 for I have a walk of nearly one-half hour to the *Gymnasium*—on the way I visit my betrothed for five minutes. Now 60 to 70 schoolchildren follow from 8 till 12 o'clock. At 12 o'clock I walk 15 minutes to another school where I teach until 1:15. Then I go home and hurriedly change clothes; it is Wednesday; at 2 o'clock sharp I eat at my betrothed's, the way there takes twelve minutes. We are finished at 4 o'clock; I take a walk with my betrothed until five. Then I work, for I lecture tomorrow, and have 56 Latin exercises to mark; it is Wednesday. At 8 o'clock I am back at the Friedländer's, I return home at 11 o'clock, and work for another hour on my lecture for tomorrow. And the same routine begins again the next day.[52]

Clearly, the young Droysen managed to reconcile his strict work ethic with the Friedländer family's internal clock and daily rhythms. Work, visits with his betrothed, "making verses, thinking about love," and meals with the Friedländers were a sequence of seamlessly interwoven daily encounters, each of which he accorded the appropriate amount of time.[53] At any rate, this plan allowed him about six hours daily with his fiancée and her family. On 21 May 1836 he married Marie Mendheim after, as his son later wrote, successfully proposing to her, not just in poems but "in longer conversations in which he acted upon her mind, advising, instructing, and guiding her with a light hand," as he had already done with his younger sister Ulrike.[54] The marriage was celebrated in the garden of another important Jewish friend of Droysen's and Felix Mendelssohn's, the painter Eduard Bendemann, outside the Potsdam Gate on the Schafgraben, now the Landwehrkanal.[55]

That same year, 1836, Felix Mendelssohn became engaged to Cécile Charlotte Sophie Jeanrenaud, the daughter of a deceased pastor of Frankfurt's French Reformed community and the descendant of an old Huguenot family. Since 1835, Mendelssohn had held the position of director of the Gewandhaus in Leipzig, where Droysen sent him the first volume of his Aristophanes translation, which was dedicated to him and Heydemann.[56] Mendelssohn was now famous and much sought-after. In 1835, however, his father Abraham had died, and with him "also the

figure of the 'Great Father' in which many of the traits of Moses Mendelssohn had lived on," to whose memory he had been devoted.[57] In his
suffering, Felix realized that his youth was over, and that the idyll of the
intact family world that had still existed at a distance was no more.[58]
Perhaps he now had to assume the place of these larger-than-life family
men himself; his mother's mentions of looking for a wife would seem to
point to this necessity. In this situation of mourning and loneliness, and
his processing of it in the completion of his oratorio "St. Paul," Mendelssohn met Cécile Jeanrenaud during a sojourn in Frankfurt the following
year and spontaneously fell in love with her. "I am so terribly in love as
never before in my life and I don't know what to do with myself."[59] He
was so taken with the atmosphere in the home of her grandparents—the
important Frankfurt Huguenot patrician family Souchay—where the
Widow Jeanrenaud lived with her children, that he would have liked to
stay in Frankfurt, as he informed his mother,

> with the nice girl I wrote you about the last time, and her amiable family
> ... and Mde. Jeanrenaud, a daughter of the house, with her two delightful
> daughters; they are just the sort of people I like and who do me good, and
> everybody lives together in the house like we do at Leipziger Straße no. 3 ...
> and that did my heart good, and I counted the hours I could spend there.[60]

The homes from which the two men's fiancées came repeat the
structures of the Mendelssohn family clan with its patriarchal traditions,
strict regulation of life and manners, and self-conceptions of Protestant,
Calvinist, and Jewish piety. Love had arrived at a sheltered and, as we
will see, always fragile place. Scholarship and music were the transfor-
mative media of all these overlaps, which required a permanent process
of translation. In Droysen's and Mendelssohn's marriages Christian and
Jewish origins and traditions intersected in an inverse manner. None of
the letters between Droysen and Mendelssohn address this issue. Rather,
they appear to follow a self-conception described as follows by Arnaldo
Momigliano.

> Conversion was taken seriously, but did not mean oblivion of the Jewish an-
> cestry and tradition. Yet surrounding society asked these men and women to
> behave as if they had no Jewish past. ... Silence on Judaism was the official
> line. Droysen seems to have conformed absolutely to this convention in his
> relations with his friends of Jewish origins. ... Even the marriage to Marie
> Mendheim must have happened under this unwritten law.[61]

It was also part of the Mendelssohn family's self-conception to view
themselves as Protestants.[62] This was expressed as well in their marriages,

which were performed out of deep conviction according to Protestant ritual. The "happiness" of these marriages is suggested in the words that the now married Droysen used to congratulate Felix Mendelssohn on his engagement.

> From my brief but rich experience I may avow that we men cannot imagine how much broader and richer and better we can make our lives. It is the fine privilege of such a relationship to promote the closeness and profound intimacy of two personalities, which excludes all selfishness of pleasure and hope and returns us to the most universal human sentiment, and to recast every other relationship and make it appear in a new light. And what virtues, what depths of hope and love we discover there! The scope of life becomes narrower, but the rays of spiritual life become so strongly focused that they suffuse life with truly human and wonderful warmth. My dear Felix, I hope that you will be as happy as I am. May God bless you![63]

It seems that Felix Mendelssohn may have attained just the kind of happiness to which Droysen alludes. Marie and Cécile do not appear very often in the two men's letters, but when they do it is in the guise of quiet, devoted, virtuous, chaste beauties, icons, often mentioned in the context of the children surrounding them, in touching scenes reminiscent of the genre pictures Wilhelm Hensel painted. The women remain rather sketchy—in strong distinction to Fanny Mendelssohn, for example, whose self-expression in her letters as well as her music (which is now receiving more attention) allows an independent portrait to emerge. The family scenes take on emotional power whenever sickness and death invade the familial idyll. How claustrophobic these longed-for domestic scenes could also feel, however, is suggested by Droysen's complaints of loneliness in a letter of 1846 from Kiel to Eduard Heydemann:

> I cannot say that I am missing human hearts. I, at least, cannot live without them, and have never been able to do so; I have the need not to be lonely. Neither a woman's heart nor childish love is enough; there remains a gaping xáoua that demands to be filled.

Collaborating on Protestant Cultural Renaissances and Unprocessed Longings

Finally, let us examine a further layer of the relationship between Droysen and Mendelssohn, which outlasted the departure from Leipziger Straße 3 in Berlin and which seems to be alluded to in the symbols in Wilhelm Hensel's Droysen portrait. I would like to locate it between the words, musical notes, and Greek text, proceeding from the assumption that these elements set up a relationship between Protestantism and Jewish origins.

Michael Steinberg views Mendelssohn's aesthetic in younger years within the dual context of his family life and the Protestant community—promoted within the Mendelssohn family by his early introduction to the North German Bach tradition, which was nurtured "like a cult" in their household.[64] In 1823, Felix received a copy of Bach's St. Matthew Passion as a Christmas present from his grandmother Babette Salomon. The soul mate relationship between the Protestant pastor's son and the "Judenjunge" (Jew-boy), as Felix referred to himself, must also be viewed in this context. Mendelssohn's enthusiasm for Bach, based on the music's spiritual content and emotional expressiveness, was confronted with the young Droysen's worldview and perceptions, deeply rooted in his Protestant background. When he had the opportunity to sing in the choir performing the St. Matthew Passion under the direction of Felix and Devrient in 1829 at the Singakademie in Berlin, he presumably shared the attitude in these circles that Bach's masterpiece was still capable of expressing an important piece of their national and religious self-awareness and that their own cultural perspective found its voice in this music.[65]

Fanny Mendelssohn celebrated the performance of the St. Matthew Passion as a sacred experience.

> The auditorium, which was filled to capacity, had the appearance of a church, the silence, the most solemn reverence reigned among the assembly, and one heard only individual expressions of deeply moved sentiment.[66]

"Never have I seen a holier calm rest upon an assemblage," recalled Devrient in his impressive account of this event.[67] The holy musical community was celebrated, but it was above all Droysen who celebrated the performance of the Leipzig choirmaster's music as an event of Protestant reawakening in his article for the *Berliner Conversationsblatt für Poesie, Literatur und Kritik:*

> Thus we are glad that art, too, and above all art with its all-pervasive power, takes this course with boldness and vigor that the most peaceable effort of truly Protestant knowledge and piety belongs to the age once again and, we hope, shall become the property of our community.[68]

In Kiel, where Droysen had been a professor since 1840, he took up the tradition of the Berlin Singakademie, becoming director of the 150-member student choir, the "Liedertafel," in 1844, and also promoting

Mendelssohn's music in this circle.[69] In a letter to Felix of March 1842, he expressed the view that his friend stood for the revival of Protestantism in music: "It seems that Protestant music, which has lain fallow since J. S. Bach ... is finally being revived."[70]

As if in a repetition of the Berlin St. Matthew Passion of 1829, Droysen was now wholly absorbed by the production of Mendelssohn's St. Paul oratorio in Kiel,

> We are in full swing with your oratorio. We performed the first part a fortnight ago on the piano, and today it is the turn of the second part; in 8 or 10 days the whole will be sung in church: We are proceeding with great diligence. To be sure, our choir is but 50 voices strong; but old Niebuhr's daughter sings your splendid Jerusalem so well. ... The way in which your music is taken up particularly here by the very Protestant and earnest audience is unique. Oh, fortunate ones![71]

For Droysen, Mendelssohn's music did not merely integrate him into the Protestant community of believers; rather, his "St. Paul" became an element of its very foundation. Droysen clearly shared the concept of music that Michael Marissen also finds in Mendelssohn, which aimed in Schleiermacher's sense at a community of feeling and a celebration of reason, and he celebrated Mendelssohn as Bach's heir.[72] "And this is a great achievement for you that you correspond so unambiguously to a certain movement in our time and have stepped to its forefront."[73] In the literature, the St. Paul oratorio, with its themes of religious conversion and redemption, is interpreted as Mendelssohn's way of processing his own experience of baptism, and in Droysen's description the convert becomes the renewer.[74]

The dedicated Protestantism of both Droysen and Mendelssohn and its musical experience in the community of singers, musicians, and listeners was one lasting bond in the biographies and cultural self-images of the two men. The other was their intense mutual interest in the texts of classical Greece, the medium of their first encounter. Droysen had been Mendelssohn's Greek tutor and dedicated the first volume of his epoch-making three-volume Aristophanes translation to him in 1835. Later he also wrote a poem about Nausicaa as the basis for the libretto of a secular oratorio, which was, however, never realized. Droysen incorporated Felix Mendelssohn's music not just into his Protestant-influenced sociability, but also into his attempts to revive classical Greek art. It was not only Droysen's ambition and pride that drove him to write texts for Mendelssohn's music, as he had already done in Berlin; he also saw the music as a means of making the literature of classical Athens accessible to the German public.[75] Just as "the translator of the play [has rendered it accessible] to our understanding," wrote the historian-translator Droysen in a programmatic essay on the production of *Antigone* with Mendelssohn's music in Berlin in 1842, "the music has rendered it accessible to our emotions."[76] The composer had read Sophocles' play with the eyes of the mind,

> With his ear he listened to the sounds of those rhythms, the ringing and echoing of those great events: and his hearing itself was a new and vivid understanding, a translation into our manner of feeling, "out of beauty, the beautiful." For it was in this way that his music seemed to affect us; the sounds with which he speaks to us are alien and yet comprehensible; not ancient music, but the impression of ancient music as it was revealed to him. Indeed, what is more ... the choral singing that followed made us feel utterly at home in this new, ideal world.[77]

Here Droysen brings together the perspective of the Protestant pastor's son with the visions of the historian, also incorporating Mendelssohn and his music. Scholars have demonstrated, however, that various religious currents as well as references to his Jewish origins come together in Mendelssohn's works, including "St. Paul" and the music for *Antigone*. After addressing baptism and conversion in "St. Paul," with its references to his father Abraham, for whom Christianity represented a logical evolution of Judaism, Mendelssohn alludes in *Antigone* to the old law, the Jewish faith and tradition, and thus to his grandfather Moses Mendelssohn.[78] Michael Steinberg has shown that in the context of *Antigone*, the music for which was composed at the king's wish, a close communication is evident between Droysen and Mendelssohn above all in regard to their notions of cultural politics, their relationship to the Prussian state, and their intellectual positioning between Hegel and Nietzsche.[79] Droysen himself did not, however, comment on these new Jewish references in Mendelssohn's music, just as he long regarded Protestantism as a direct successor to Hellenism, with its encounter between Greek and Oriental cultures, and—as Momigliano has pointed out—did not mention the role of Judaism as an important factor in the development of Christianity until 1843.[80]

An additional element may also have played a role in the setting, performance, and discussion of the Antigone theme by Mendelssohn and Droysen: the brother-sister relationship. Hegel, whose lectures both men had attended, had spoken of Antigone's role as her brother's representative and custodian of the old moral law in the family's cult of the dead in her conflict with King Creon and the state.[81] Mendelssohn and Droysen may have (re)dramatized this archaic ethical framework on the level of cultural transformation, and—in contrast to the sibling sociability in Berlin and their simultaneous marriages—this time as a process of textual and musical translation into the modern age. The silence of their sisters and wives is sealed on this level. One might also wonder, however, whether their silence about their sisters was not rather similar to their discussion of religious origins, which was also never explicit. The difference of symbiosis becomes merged in Protestant hegemony.

It seems, however, as if this process was not wholly successful, for it left behind melancholy and encapsulated grief, and the correspondence between Droysen and Mendelssohn after 1840 is shot through with yearning-filled invocations of their shared Berlin "youth," the time of friends, brothers and sisters. In 1842, Mendelssohn wrote:

> You have no idea how terribly attached I am to my entire youth, how it consumes me, and how crushed I am to see on all sides the worn out companions of those years; and how glorious, when among them all one remains my friend as before, and the world is vivid and fresh as before, and suffers and enjoys and works as before, and in a word is the same person he always was, for which constant change is necessary, and not stagnation.[82]

The place of their mutual longing was Berlin, the city by which they had felt betrayed and excluded. After the performance of *Antigone* they never managed to meet there again. Mendelssohn had a touching fantasy, which seems to contain at the same time its impossibility:

> [H]ow dearly I would like to discuss all of this with you in person, for example at Potsdamer Platz, until your wife comes by with her sister and does not greet us, so that we do not notice them.[83]

Droysen's Jewish wife and her sister, who belonged to Mendelssohn's Berlin milieu, are a fundamental component of his fantasy meeting and yet they are simultaneously banished from it, for she does not wish to be seen. What are they not supposed to see? Wife and sister nevertheless belong to the scene as riddles; in this way they can be both present and mythical, leaving brother and husband to their conversation. In 1844, Droysen organized a performance of *Antigone* in Kiel, an attempt to break through the narrowness of provincial life by bringing his friend's music to him, by performing and experiencing it. But all this did not suffice,

> And I sigh to live so far away, where in the end only a distant echo penetrates of what I was once so fortunate to enjoy at close quarters, so vivid and full of joy and hope. I think back with a silent sigh to times past, and the skies above me are gray.[84]

The final years of the correspondence between Droysen and Mendelssohn are marked by deep affection but also by shared grief at the loss of the enthusiasm and ideals of their time together in Berlin. Mendelssohn's violin concerto op. 64 of 1844 has recently been interpreted as his way of working through nostalgia for his lost youth.[85]

For Droysen, the run-up to the Revolution of 1848 was overshadowed by the death, in rapid succession, of the three most important members of his large circle of Protestant friends of Jewish origin. Marie Droysen née Mendheim died in March 1847 at the age of 28, followed in April by Fanny Hensel née Mendelssohn at 41, and on November 4 by Felix Mendelssohn at the age of 38. It is generally accepted that the death of his sister crushed him—at the news of her demise the already exhausted Mendelssohn collapsed with a cry of pain.[86] When he arrived in Berlin months later and entered Fanny's old home, in which she had composed, he suffered another breakdown.[87]

Droysen apparently did not consider his three sisters appropriate caregivers for his four children. In his loneliness and grief, he clung to his chosen family and sent his children to live with their "dearest grandparents" Friedländer in Berlin. Droysen's own path now took him to Frankfurt, but he integrated the male progenitor of this family, Benoni Friedländer, into his path into politics and made the Jewish manuscript collector the archivist of the events about to unfold in the Paulskirche.

> Dear Grandfather, I send you a pair of interesting manuscripts: they are the documentary basis for the "Fundamental Rights of the German People," deliberation upon which begins tomorrow in St. Paul's Church. Most of this, to be sure, is in my hand; but I can't help it that I was involved in the matter. … Your collection may also be lacking a manuscript by Dahlmann; the enclosed is not without interest. … I must close now if I wish to get my packet to the post. My warmest greetings to all. And good luck to Germany too. In faithful love and gratitude, your son, Droysen.[88]

Notes

1. Hans-Günther Klein, ed., *Das verborgene Band: Felix Mendelssohn-Bartholdy und seine Schwester Fanny Hensel. Ausstellung der Musikabteilung der Staatsbibliothek zu Berlin—Preußischer Kulturbesitz zum 150. Todestag der beiden Geschwister, 15 Mai–12 Juli 1997* (Wiesbaden 1997), 131, commentary, 129.

2. See Eduard Devrient, *Meine Erinnerungen an Felix Mendelssohn-Bartholdy und seine Briefe an mich* (Leipzig, 1869), 22ff., 36ff.; Gerhard Schuhmacher, "Felix Mendelssohn Bartholdys Bedeutung aus sozialgeschichtlicher Sicht: Ein Versuch" (first publication 1979), reprinted in G. Schuhmacher, ed., *Felix Mendelssohn-Bartholdy* (Darmstadt, 1982), 138–173, 140.

3. Leon Botstein, "Lieder ohne Worte: Einige Überlegungen über Musik, Theologie und die Rolle der jüdischen Frage in der Musik von Felix Mendelssohn," in *Felix Mendels-*

sohn: Mitwelt und Nachwelt. Bericht zum 1. Leipziger Mendelssohn-Kolloquium, ed. Leon Botstein (Leipzig, 1996), 104–116, here 105–106.

4. See Arnd Richter, *Mendelssohn: Leben, Werke, Dokumente* (Mainz, 1994), 52–53; Hans Christoph Worbs, *Felix Mendelssohn Bartholdy: In Selbstzeugnissen und Bilddokumenten* (Reinbek, 1974), 10–11; in this context see also Abraham's views on the family name change to "Bartholdy" and on baptism: "Whatever the religion, there is but one God, one virtue, one truth, one happiness." Very interesting for the issue of conversion is also Abraham's letter to his daughter Fanny on the occasion of her confirmation, in Sebastian Hensel, *Die Familie Mendelssohn 1729–1847: Nach Briefen und Tagebüchern*, vol. 1 (Berlin, 1898), 112–113; on the wave of baptisms in Berlin from 1770 into the late 1820s, including the Mendelssohn, Friedländer, and Mendheim families, see Steven M. Lowenstein, *The Berlin Jewish Community: Enlightenment, Family, and Crisis, 1770–1830* (New York and Oxford, 1994), 132.

5. These names appear above all from the perspective of their closeness to Droysen in Arnaldo Momigliano, "J. G. Droysen between Greeks and Jews," in *History and Theory* 9, no. 2 (1970): 139–153.

6. Michael P. Steinberg, "Culture, Gender, and Music: A Forum on the Mendelssohn Family," *Musical Quarterly* 77 (1993): 648–650, here 649.

7. Hensel, *Familie*, vol. 1, 167–168.

8. Beatrix Borchard, "'Mein Singen ist ein Rufen nur aus Träumen.' Berlin, Leipziger Straße Nr. 3," in *Fanny Hensel, geb. Mendelssohn Bartholdy: Das Werk*, ed. Martina Helmig (Munich, 1997), 9–21, here 12.

9. See the mention in his letter to his three sisters Auguste, Mathilde, and Ulrike, Berlin, 11 July 1829, in Johann Gustav Droysen, *Briefwechsel*, vol. 1: *1829–1851*, ed. Rudolf Hübner [1929] (Osnabrück, 1967), 3.

10. See also the only major biography of Droysen, written by his son. Gustaf Droysen, *Johann Gustav Droysen*, vol. 1: *Bis zum Beginn der Frankfurter Tätigkeit* (Leipzig and Berlin, 1910), 57.

11. Klein, *Das verborgene Band*, 129.

12. Devrient, *Erinnerungen*, 37.

13. In the letter of 11 July 1829 to his three sisters, Droysen mentions "poetic works, about which you will hear more in perhaps three months." Droysen, *Briefwechsel*, 3.

14. Klein, *Das verborgene Band*, 99. Early on the morning of 10 April 1829, when Felix had left for London, Fanny wrote in her diary, "Droysen brought me the dearest poem to Felix, which put me in the pleasantest mood, since I immediately thought of a melody for it." In a letter of 20 May 1829 to Felix, Fanny wrote: "The chimney sweep woke me at six this morning, otherwise I do not get up so early; the fruit of my self-discipline was a good song, which will please you. The turn of phrase will convince you that it is by Droysen." Quoted from Fanny and Felix Mendelssohn, *"Die Musik will gar nicht rutschen ohne Dich." Briefwechsel 1821 bis 1846*, ed. Eva Weissweiler (Berlin, 1997).

15. Musikabteilung der Staatsbibliothek zu Berlin—Preußischer Kulturbesitz MA Ms. 128, 44.

16. Droysen, *Briefwechsel*; Johann Gustav Droysen and Felix Mendelssohn Bartholdy, *Ein tief gegründet Herz: der Briefwechsel zwischen Felix Mendelssohn Bartholdy mit Johann Gustav Droysen*, ed. Carl Wehmer (Heidelberg, 1959).

17. Felix Mendelssohn-Bartholdy, London, 3 November 1829, in Droysen, *Briefwechsel*, 10ff.

18. Gert Mattenklott, *Über Juden in Deutschland* (Frankfurt am Main, 1992), 13.

19. Eva Weissweiler, "Vorwort," in Eva Weissweiler, ed., *Fanny Mendelssohn: Italienisches Tagebuch* (Hamburg and Zurich, 1993), 27; Hensel, *Familie*, 91ff.

20. Felix Mendlsohn-Bartholdy, Düsseldorf, 15 February 1835, in Droysen, *Briefwechsel*, 72.

21. Felix Mendelssohn-Bartholdy, Leipzig, 5 April 1847, in Droysen, *Briefwechsel*, 351. This was Mendelssohn's last letter to Droysen.

22. See Cécile Lowenthal-Hensel, "Neues zur Leipziger Straße Drei," in *Mendelssohn-Studien: Beiträge zur neueren deutschen Kultur- und Wirtschaftsgeschichte*, ed. Cécile Lowenthal-Hensel and Rudolf Elvers, vol. 7 (Berlin, 1990), 141–151.

23. To Albert Heydemann, Berlin, 18/19 November 1829, in Droysen, *Briefwechsel*, 13ff.

24. Letter to his three sisters, in Droysen, *Briefwechsel*, 4.

25. Devrient, *Erinnerungen*, 71.

26. Marion A. Kaplan, *The Making of the Jewish Middle Class: Women, Family, and Identity in Imperial Germany* (New York, 1991), 83. In this context she also mentions Heinrich Heine, who was a frequent guest at the Mendelssohn house, and who once referred to the family as the Jews' "portable homeland."

27. Letter to his three sisters in Droysen, *Briefwechsel*, 3.

28. Gustaf Droysen, *Droysen*, 25, 30, 31.

29. To Felix Mendelssohn-Bartholdy, December (1829), Droysen, *Briefwechsel*, 17–18.

30. To Felix Mendelssohn-Bartholdy, 26 January 1830, ibid., 21.

31. From Felix Mendelssohn-Bartholdy, 5 January 1830, ibid., 20–21.

32. To Felix Mendelssohn-Bartholdy, 26 January 1830, ibid., 21

33. To Felix Mendelssohn-Bartholdy, 26 January 1830, ibid., 21.

34. To Felix Mendelssohn-Bartholdy, 26 January 1830, ibid., 21.

35. To Albert Heydemann, Berlin, 18 January 1830, ibid., 20.

36. Quoted in Heinrich Eduard Jacob, *Felix Mendelssohn und seine Zeit: Bildnis und Schicksal eines Meisters* (Frankfurt am Main, 1981), 314. To Albert Heydemann, Berlin, 18 January 1830, Droysen, *Briefwechsel*, 19.

37. To Albert Heydemann, Berlin, 18 January 1830, Droysen, *Briefwechsel*, 20.

38. Devrient, *Erinnerungen*, 39.

39. Letter to his three sisters, Droysen, *Briefwechsel*, 5.

40. In 1832, too, Gustav told his sisters of his longing for their presence. "With God's help it will not be long; you girls will be here with me soon, hooray! I intend to tyrannize you, torment and scare you, love you and who knows what; and should you ever clear up my papers, or move a book aside, I will calmly replace it and laugh at your foolish devotion to order! And how neat it will be in your sitting room, flowerpots at the windows, and joy and love always." Quoted in Gustav Droysen, *Droysen*, 70.

41. On Droysen's letter to his three sisters, see also Regina Schulte, "Dokument: ein Historiker an seine Schwestern," *L'Homme. Zeitschrift für Feministische Geschichtswissenschaft* 8, no. 1 (1997): 78–86.

42. On relationships between brothers and sisters in the late eighteenth and early nineteenth century, see Ulrike Prokop, *Die Illusion vom Großen Paar*, 2 vols. (Frankfurt am Main, 1991); on Felix and Fanny Mendelssohn-Bartholdy see also David Sabean, "Fanny and Felix Mendelssohn-Bartholdy and the Question of Incest," *Musical Quarterly* 77 (1993): 709–717.

43. Quoted in Gustaf Droysen, *Droysen*, 72–73.

44. Fanny to Felix, Berlin, 3 October 1829, in Fanny and Felix Mendelssohn, *Briefwechsel*, 101.

45. Quoted in Borchard, "Mein Singen," 16.

46. Fanny Mendelssohn Bartholdy and Wilhelm Hensel, "Briefe aus der Verlobungszeit," ed. Martina Helmig and Annette Maurer, in Helmig, *Fanny Hensel*, 139–163, 155.

47. Lowenstein has carefully worked out the marriage networks among Jewish converts into whose circles Droysen married. "Among the Jewish converts who married other converts were . . . the grandchildren of David Friedländer, some of whom married into the Mendheim family . . . the child of one of David Friedländer's converted grandchildren who married Bendemann and whose son married a Mendelssohn-Bartholdy." *Berlin Jewish Community*, 132.

48. To Friedrich Gottlieb Welcker, Berlin, Hackescher Markt 2, 2 July 1836, Droysen, *Briefwechsel*, 90; on Marie Mendheim's origins see also Gustaf Droysen, *Droysen*, 111–112.

49. Reinhard Rürup, ed., *Jüdische Geschichte in Berlin: Bilder und Dokumente* (Berlin, 1995), 57. "With his brother-in-law Isaac Daniel Itzig, he founded the Jewish Free School in 1778. He supported the translation of liturgical and biblical texts with the aim of holding religious services completely in German, and reconceptualizing Judaism more generally as a confessional community. In 1809 the first Berlin City Council elected him an unsalaried councilor."

50. Gustaf Droysen, *Droysen*, 116.

51. Ibid., 113.

52. To his sister Mathilde, Berlin, 5 November 1835, Droysen, *Briefwechsel*, 81.

53. Ibid., 81.

54. Gustaf Droysen, *Droysen*, 115.

55. Ibid., 116.

56. Eric Werner, *Mendelssohn: Leben und Werk in neuer Sicht* (Zurich, 1980), 299. Wehmer, *Ein tiefgegründet Herz*, 40; cf. the letter of 3 November 1835, with which he sent him "the enclosed little blue book."

57. Werner, *Mendelssohn*, 302.

58. On this see Richter, *Mendelssohn*, 221–222; Werner, *Mendelssohn*, 303, 311.

59. Letter of 24 July 1836 to Rebecka Derichlet, in Hensel, *Familie*, vol. 2, 26.

60. Rudolf Elvers, *Briefe: Felix Mendelssohn-Bartholdy* (Frankfurt am Main, 1984), 194.

61. Momigliano, "J. G. Droysen," 150–51.

62. On Felix's silence about his Jewish origins, see Devrient, *Erinnerungen*, 62.

63. To Felix Mendelssohn-Bartholdy, Berlin, 28 October 1836, Droysen, *Briefwechsel*, 101.

64. Michael Steinberg, "Das Mendelssohn-Bach-Verhältnis als ästhetischer Diskurs der Moderne," in *Felix Mendelssohn: Mitwelt und Nachwelt: Bericht zum 1. Leipziger Mendelssohn, Kolloqium am 8. und 9. Juni 1993*, ed. Leon Botstein and Gewandhaus zu Leipzig (Wiesbaden, 1996), 84–88, here 85–86.

65. John E. Toews, "Memory and Gender in the Remaking of Fanny Mendelssohn's Musical Identity: The Chorale in Das Jahr," *Musical Quarterly* 77 (1993): 727–748, here 736.

66. Quoted in Gustaf Droysen, "Johann Gustav Droysen und Felix Mendelssohn-Bartholdy," *Deutsche Rundschau* 111, no. 3 (1902): 106–126, here 119–120.

67. Devrient, *Erinnerungen*, 63ff. On 62, he cites Felix Mendelssohn's oft-quoted exclamation, "to think that it took an actor and a Jew-boy to revive the greatest Christian music!"

68. Quoted in G. Droysen, "Johann Gustav Droysen und Felix Mendelssohn-Bartholdy," 120.

69. Cf. 31 December 1841, Droysen, *Briefwechsel*, 204–205.

70. To Felix Mendelssohn-Bartholdy, Kiel, 7 March 1842, Droysen, *Briefwechsel*, 211.

71. Ibid., 211.
72. Michael Marissen, "Religious Aims in Mendelssohn's 1829 Berlin-Singakademie Performances of Bach's Matthew Passion," *Musical Quarterly* 77 (1993): 718–726, here 721.
73. To Felix Mendelssohn-Bartholdy, Kiel, 7 March 1842, Droysen, *Briefwechsel*, 211.
74. Botstein, "Lieder," 105. Cf. Droysen's letter of 8 January 1844 to Mendelssohn, in which, after requesting a copy of the *Antigone* score for Kiel, he writes: "I was extremely pleased to hear that you are directly occupied with music for divine service. If anything is desirable for our culture, it is that." Droysen, *Briefwechsel*, 261.
75. Momogliano, "J.G. Droysen," 146.
76. Johann Gustav Droysen, "Die Aufführung der Antigone des Sophokles in Berlin," in his *Kleine Schriften zur Alten Geschichte*, vol. 2 (Leipzig, 1894), 146–152, here 149.
77. Ibid., 148.
78. Botstein, "Lieder," 107. Werner, *Mendelssohn*, 405; for a more detailed account, see Michael P. Steinberg, "The Incidental Politics to Mendelssohn's Antigone," in *Mendelssohn and his World*, ed. R. Larry Todd (Princeton, 1991), 137–157.
79. Steinberg, "The Incidental Politics," 146ff.
80. Momigliano, "J.G. Droysen," 149. "The taboo was deeply ingrained, and I wonder whether it did not affect Droysen as an historian. He had started from the notion that Christianity can be explained with little reference to Judaism. ... Droysen did some work on Jewish texts, but he never brought himself to face the whole problem of the relation between Judaism and Christianity. It was the problem which at a personal level had deeply concerned his best friends, his wife and his relatives—and it was going to affect his children. He must have known that his friends were thinking about it in their silences. He remained silent, too. The *History of Hellenism* was never finished" (p. 151). See also Steinberg, "The Incidental Politics," 146–147.
81. "For this reason, familial piety is expounded in Sophocles' *Antigone*—one of the most sublime presentations of familial piety—as principally the law of the woman, and as the law of a substantiality of subjectivity and feeling. This is the law of the inwardness that has not yet attained full actualization, the law of the old gods, of the subterranean, as an eternal law, of which no one knows when it first appeared. This law is in opposition to the manifest law, the law of the state. This is the highest opposition in ethics and therefore in tragedy; in *Antigone* it is individuated [*individualisiert*], in humanity, into femininity and masculinity." Georg Wilhelm Friedrich Hegel, *Philosophy of Right*, trans. Alan White (Newburyport, MA, 2002), 137. On the family cult of death and the brother-sister relationship, see Hegel's *Phenomenology of Mind*, trans. J. B. Baillie, intro. George Lichtheim (New York, 1967), 475–478.
82. 11 March 1842, Droysen, *Briefwechsel*, 212.
83. 19 January 1844, Droysen, *Briefwechsel*, 263.
84. 5 January 1846, Droysen, *Briefwechsel*, 325.
85. Reinhard Gerlach, "Mendelssohns schöpferische Erinnerung der 'Jugendzeit'. Die Beziehungen zwischen dem Violinkonzert, op. 64 und dem Oktett für Streicher, op. 20," in Schumacher, *Mendelssohn*, 249–62, esp. 261–2.
86. Werner, *Mendelssohn*, 510.
87. Ibid., 514.
88. To his grandparents-in-law, the Friedländers, Frankfurt, 2 July 1848, Droysen, *Briefwechsel*, 339–340.

Chapter 11

Husband, Wife, and Sister

Making and Remaking
the Early Victorian Family

Mary Jean Corbett

With ample selections from contemporary family letters, the sixth chapter of E. M. Forster's *Marianne Thornton: A Domestic Biography* (1956), entitled "Deceased Wife's Sister," tells the story of "a fantastic mishap" that the members of his grandparents' generation "could only regard as tragic."[1] After the death of his first wife, Harriet, in 1840, Henry Thornton decided to take another—Harriet's younger sister, slightly older than Henry himself—and at once, "the situation became very awkward." Having lived with Henry all her life, his sister Marianne "behaved civilly" to Emily Dealtry, who "had continued to frequent the house" after Harriet's demise, helping "to look after her nephew and her nieces," but another Thornton sister "refused to see her anywhere." Spending "vast sums" without success "in trying to get the 1850 bill passed," a bill that would have repealed the 1835 statute invalidating all such future marriages, Henry closed up the family home and took Emily, her mother, and his own daughters abroad to solemnize the marriage in one of the many European states where these unions were legal.[2]

Appalled, the rest of his nine siblings, most of them married, worked to maintain a united front. Upon Henry and Emily's return to England, they prevailed upon the susceptible Marianne to stay away from Battersea Rise: even *"a single visit"* from her, Forster's clerical grandfather insisted at the time, "will be magnified into *countenance* and approval by a leading member of the family: and every artifice be employed to draw others in. ... In the mind of society the family may become mixed with the offenders: and real injury be done without any resultant benefit."[3] By this act of "the Master, the Inheritor, who had betrayed his trust," Forster characterizes the other members of the family as "excluded for ever" from their ancestral home "unless they bent the knee to immorality, which was unthinkable." Marking his own distance from Thornton family values, Forster comments: "To the moralist, so much discomfort will seem appropriate. To the amoralist it will offer yet another example of the cruelty and stupidity of the English law in matters of sex."[4]

Forster knew a good deal at first hand about that "cruelty and stupidity," of course, in all its multifarious forms. So, too, did his contemporary Vanessa Stephen, who fell in love with Jack Hills, her half-sister Stella's widower. That was a legally prohibited match even as late as the 1890s, construed in some quarters as incest and loudly opposed by her half-brother George Duckworth, who had sexually abused both Stephen sisters. Vanessa's sister Virginia no doubt fathomed that irony and expressed a thin slice of it in the voice of Peter Walsh, who calls it "incredible" that Richard Dalloway should ever have pronounced that "no decent man ought to let his wife visit a deceased wife's sister."[5] But reproving the manners and morals of a former age does not quite address the historical circumstances of Forster's biographical subject, the loyal unmarried sister displaced not just by a second wife, but by a woman who could not under English law take her dead sister's place. "Should the law be altered," Marianne Thornton writes, "probably the next [generation] will wonder at our scruples"; Forster confesses that "we do wonder at them," even as he purports to "remember the indignation of Orthodoxy" in 1907, when the prohibition was finally repealed. Marianne, however, makes no reference to law and very little even to religion in characterizing her own attitude. "I have never thought alas as all my family do that it is very wrong," she tells a friend, "only that it is an *impossible* sort of idea—in short it seems not a sin—but a shame." And the shame of it stems from "feelings that I fear nothing can eradicate—for they seem like an instinct planted in ones [*sic*] very nature" (albeit not in her brother's) "that in this generation cannot be worn out." She subsequently gives those feelings a sharper profile in a letter to Henry: "My own brothers- and sisters-in-law have always appeared to me so exactly like real brothers and sisters that any other connection seems an impossibility. I cannot realize a different state of feeling."[6]

Without a grasp on the conditions that produced this "state of feeling," we, too, may continue to interpret the long nineteenth-century debate about marriage with a dead wife's sister (hereafter MDWS) in the way that Forster does, as a species of Victorian foolishness in "matters of sex." In doing so, however, we would miss the ways in which it also illuminates divergent definitions of who belongs to "the family" and what constitutes "incest." Far removed from a time when some relations by marriage, termed "affines," did figure by Anglican marriage law as "exactly like real brothers and sisters," Marianne's shame may be difficult for us to fathom, for she operated under assumptions about the shape and scope of the family that differ from those that underlie the now-naturalized nuclear model. A sibling's marriage would not only create ties between separate families, it would also expand and reshape one's very own family through the incorporation of new members. Regarded in this light, Marianne is herself, as Forster's chapter title attests, a "Deceased Wife's Sister" to the departed Harriet—with neither she nor Emily being legally capable of forming "any other connection" to Henry than the one that already exists: neither sister, that is, can or should become his wife.

In the language she uses to express her feelings, Marianne observes the distinction between "real" siblings and those who are "exactly like" them that both forms a linchpin of the MDWS debate and reveals an ambiguity in the boundaries of "the family."[7] While "exactly like" suggests there is no difference between birth siblings and in-laws, the word "real" assigns priority to the former and dictates the terms in which the latter were and still are represented: no one then or now, that is, ever says, "she's like a sister-in-law to me." Commonsensical as this distinction now appears, even the "real" of Marianne's statement is not entirely stable, though it most often designates those "children of the same family, the same blood, with the same first associations and habits" of whom Jane Austen writes in *Mansfield Park* (1814).[8]

Even if not always raised by the same parents, moreover, "real" siblings must share more than "the same blood." For one thing, as Leonore Davidoff has argued, "the notion of a distinct 'blood relative' … seems to have been fully developed only at about the turn of the twentieth century."[9] And shared blood did not in and of itself form a barrier to marriage: the pervasiveness and legitimacy of cousin marriage in nineteenth-century culture, so endemic as well in nineteenth-century fiction, suggests that a close degree of relatedness between marriage partners was an incentive rather than an impediment, at least among the upper classes.[10] Even in a capacious sense of family, "real" siblings were nonetheless fully recognizable as different in kind from, say, cousins—and not only because one's cousin, unlike one's brother, could become one's spouse, as in *Mansfield Park*. Proximity, association, and habits of language and thought produced not only first families, which may have encompassed birth, adoptive, and fostered siblings, but also second families, of which siblings by marriage formed an integral part, in a far less narrow sense of "family" than our contemporary usage denominates.[11]

That an in-law could become "exactly like" a "real" sister or brother helps especially to demonstrate the broader parameters of "family." As Leila Silvana May perceptively argues in her study of sibling relations, "literal definitions of 'daughter' or 'sister'" constitute only a single dimension of their meaning: "extensions of those terms … produce metaphorical and metonymical parents and siblings," such that (to take an example May does not discuss) Mrs. Hamley of Elizabeth Gaskell's *Wives and Daughters* (1864–1866) can become "like" a mother to Molly Gibson, and her sons "like" Molly's brothers, in the absence of a "real" mother or brothers of Molly's own.[12] Whereas May concludes that the "metaphorization of familial nomenclature" can potentially "prove destructive to the ideal of the family," I follow Elizabeth Rose Gruner's lead in seeing the nineteenth-century family as both "born and made," as evident in Marianne Thornton's sense of relatedness to her siblings-in-law as well as Molly Gibson's family-by-analogy.[13] To privilege the "real" exclusively is to miss that kinship is and has always been a made thing, a human artifact, rather than (as some Victorian anthropologists would argue) a naturally occurring phenomenon based in blood.

In a historical process that unfolded over a long period, we can trace a slow cultural shift, as the protracted span of the MDWS debate itself demonstrates, away from the broader family that marriage had traditionally produced.[14] For a good portion of the nineteenth century, sisterhood or brotherhood was conceived not exclusively as a static relation fixed at and by birth, but also as an achieved and achievable state of relationship to others; not just a legal or biological designation, but also a more-than-metaphorical means of indicating proximity and connection that could both incite and prohibit romantic and sexual attachments between siblings-in-law. The installation of a norm that emphasized the exclusive (and exclusionary) bond of the conjugal, reproductive couple modified the older, larger "ideal of the family," and this transformation generated both extensive resistance and qualified assent.

To illustrate the reshaping of "the family" among the early Victorians, I draw on pamphlets, speeches, and reports about the first phase of the MDWS debate, published primarily in the 1830s and 1840s, that portray the second families formed by first marriages and the desire for second marriages that they sometimes inspired. With very few exceptions, the perspectives expressed in these male-authored, publicly circulated representations support the conclusion that "the MDWS controversy was mainly a battle between men," "an issue that would concern men rather than women as a group."[15] Participants in the public debate largely aimed either to broaden or restrict male prerogative, to permit or prohibit the fantasy that Karen Chase and Michael Levenson have identified as central to both the quarrel and the culture: "that a husband will always have a second choice, a second sister, waiting nearby in domestic reserve."[16]

However, two contemporary novels by women from very different ideological positions—the dissenting Harriet Martineau's *Deerbrook* (1839) and the orthodox Anglican Felicia Skene's *The Inheritance of Evil; Or, the Consequences of Marrying a Deceased Wife's Sister* (1849)—critique that prerogative and chastise that fantasy. Moreover, they also reveal a corresponding female desire, which they likewise work to correct in the interest of solidifying the singular bond of the conjugal pair. Each stages the drama of the husband's illegitimate attraction to his sister-in-law against the backdrop of a wife's fierce attachment to the first-family sister whom she cannot leave behind. The pervasive "jealousy" of the wife operates, I will suggest, as an ambivalent and ambiguous sign that conveys both sisterly desire and sororal solidarity. Reading these novels against the fictions of relatedness contested in the MDWS debate demonstrates something Forster overlooked: that "matters of sex" are also family matters.

I

From almost sister to second wife: an entirely unremarkable movement, to those Victorians who imagined "real" sisters as similar enough to make the substitution of the living for the dead an appropriate and desirable course for a widower to take. However, as Helena Michie observes, "the question of the relation between the sisters" could be posed in "a number of different ways." Those who protested the MDWS ban most frequently cast the living sister as a reminder of the dead one, naturalizing the second choice by emphasizing its inevitability.[17] "The heart, while yearning for a second love," in the words of a pamphlet that tells the widower's conventional story, "shrinks from all contact with that which wears not some impress, or cannot in some measure perpetuate the memory of the first":

> Consider how such a marriage is likely to originate. A man who
> marries the woman he loves, and loves the woman he has married,
> finds himself, after some years of conjugal happiness, a widower.

He may or may not have children—if a father, there is before him
the sight of those who vainly listen for a mother's voice; if childless,
where is the face into which he can look for similitude of her that
is gone?—in either case his bereavement is complete. If, then, in
the hour of his desolation there come to him, with words of comfort
and sympathy, one who in tone and feature—perhaps in heart and
temper too—reminds him of his beloved departed, is it strange,
though it may for a moment sadden him to

> "view the dame
> Resembling her, yet not the same,"

that his heart should yearn towards her? ... To whom but to *her*
could he speak, as he would, of the lost one?—the one dear to,
and lamented by, both—a bond of mutual sympathy and source
of hallowed regret, alone sufficient to impart to such an union
much more of a sacred than a sensual character.[18]

The likeness of the two is the widower's greatest comfort, for the
sister "wears … some impress" of, bears a "similitude" to, the dead wife,
and in that comfort lies the origin of the new "union." The tenor of such
a representation—and there are countless more just like it—leads the
anthropologist Françoise Héritier to conclude that for grieving widowers and their apologists, "two sisters are essentially the same thing …
replacing one sister with another amounts to the same."[19] But the inset
poetic quotation (from Byron's *The Giaour*, of all things) qualifies Héritier's conclusion. "Resembling her, yet *not* the same," the second sister is
not identical to the first, more *aide-mémoire* than exact duplicate. The
point of difference—at a bare minimum, that between the living and
the dead—enables the substitution, most effective when it makes the
least difference. "It would be repugnant to my feeling to displace old associations, and to seek marriage elsewhere," as one anonymous widower
testified before the royal commission convened in 1847 to examine the
issue: "My wife's sister disturbs nothing; she is already in the place of
my wife."[20]

That a second sister might succeed a first wife, a move that casts them
as both actual and "metaphoric replacements" for one another, does
not then mean that they are "essentially the same thing."[21] Rather, each
could occupy the same "place," namely that of "wife," a position that
could never be filled by a man's own first-family sister, rarely mentioned
as a potential surrogate mother for the orphans who typically populate
the standard tableau created by the advocates of repealing the ban. The
latter as a rule subordinate the would-be wife's putative sisterhood to
the widower to testimony that she has been a good sister to his wife.
Indeed, the more a sister devoted herself to the memory of the departed

and shared that unifying bond of grief with her brother-in-law, the more likely that she would be an attentive mother to her nieces and nephews and a fit wife for their father; the widower thus quickly learns just how well (or badly) she would fill that empty "place." Emphasizing that "sacred" rather than "sensual" feeling motivated such marriages, moreover, witnesses before the royal commission represented men as only heeding dead wives' final wishes when they took the momentous step: "it was the dying request of my first wife"; "she should die happy if I could marry her sister"; "my sister ... on her death-bed expressed a wish, that if [her husband] married again, he should marry her sister."[22] The most assiduous wife might take a more active role: as one widower testified, "My former wife expressed a very strong desire that, if I married again, I should marry her sister"; at the same time, "my former wife had also expressed to her sister her desire that if she married she should marry me, if such a marriage was legal; so that, in point of fact, we were both, it might be said, doubly tied up."[23]

Matthew Arnold cleverly pointed up the lack of delicacy such declarations evince in *Friendship's Garland* (1871): "the place of poor Mrs. Bottles will be taken by her sister Hannah, whom you have just seen. Nothing could be more proper; Mrs. Bottles wishes it, Miss Hannah wishes it, this reverend friend of the family [a Baptist minister], who has made a marriage of the same kind, wishes it, everybody wishes it."[24] For the grieving widower of the sentimental scenario, by contrast, honoring a wife's dying declaration, even when it means breaking the law, becomes another means of disavowing everything but the purest intentions and most enduring fidelity to the dead woman on the part of both her sister and their husband. To reinforce "old associations" by forging "a second attachment [that] might seem like the continuance of the first," resembling it, yet not the same, a widower needs a second wife who is like (and presumably liked) her sister.[25]

But to make a wife from a sister-in-law is to deny that sisters-in-law are really a man's own sisters, and this claim was one that advocates of the ban most fiercely contested. A leading figure in the debate who consistently portrayed the effort to legitimate MDWS as an attack on the central principle of holy marriage, the Anglican divine Edward Pusey argued that a married couple, "by their own oneness, incorporates each into the family of the other," because "sexual union" (even outside marriage, some aver) "makes two people 'one flesh.'"[26] Such hard-line opponents of MDWS as Pusey did not subscribe to a firm distinction between "consanguinity, a relation created by 'blood'," and "affinity, a relation created by human law," which "were on precisely the same footing with regard ... to incest" in the ecclesiastical courts even before the passage of Lord Lyndhurst's Act in 1835.[27] And their polemics attempted to persuade others that they did not subscribe to it, either: an essayist in the *London Quarterly Review* proposes, for example, that "in the actual state of public feeling and of the law, a man looks upon the sisters of his wife as upon his own sisters" and a woman regards them as "having such an interest in her husband's affection and attentions as his own sisters by blood. In life they are united as one family."[28]

As Skene's narrator intones, the sister of the dead Elizabeth Maynard Clayton, named Agnes, remains the widower Richard's sister even after Elizabeth's demise: "Death had dissolved the tie between Richard and Elizabeth in one sense only—it had not dissolved the relationship which that tie had produced—Agnes was still sister to her who mouldered in the dust—Richard was still one flesh with her—the fraternity between them remained unbroken as between children of the same parents."[29] "Those, then, who deny that the sister is akin to the husband must deny that the husband and wife are really one"—and when Pusey says "really," he does not mean "exactly like."[30] "If of 'one flesh' with his wife, a man was related by blood to his wife's relations": "If there were any meaning in those words at all," a clergyman tells Richard Clayton, "the sister-in-law be in the sight of heaven counted as the sister in blood."[31] Concretely envisioning sisters as the same substance, opponents of MDWS posited actual identity, rather than exact likeness, between them: a man's sister-in-law is therefore *really* a sister of his own.

The effects of sex and marriage on first and second families were thus very much at issue in this aspect of the debate, and the varied interpretations of "one flesh" in particular illustrated the contested claims about the impact of a man's first marriage on the parameters of the second family that every marriage created. By contrast with the view that would sanction such unions, the high church position asserted that when a man moved from his first family, where he stood as a son to his parents and (typically) a sibling among other siblings, to the one he originated as a husband and a father, the agency of holy marriage created new, real siblings. Against the idea that the husband/father stood alone, accorded the right to take any new wife at his pleasure, Anglican orthodoxy enjoined that his second family reproduce elements of his first by establishing what William Hale Hale called "a real brotherhood and sisterhood" between in-laws.[32] In this light, marriage signified not exclusively as an alliance between individuals, but between families, as in Marianne Thornton's feelings of "real" kinship, or in William Gladstone's claim that by "the conjugal relation you bound families together."[33] A sister of one's wife thus became a sister to oneself: "The husband has not merely the opportunity, but the duty, of paying to his wife's sister those blameless and tender attentions which he pays to his own sister. He can pay them to no other woman except his own sister; he sees his wife's sister as he sees his own."[34]

Underpinning Mrs. Dashwood's remark in *Sense and Sensibility* (1811) that should Elinor marry Edward Ferrars, Marianne and Margaret "will gain a brother, a real, affectionate brother," this line of thought makes siblings-in-law available for intimacy within precisely the same legal and social limits that governed relationships between "children of the same parents."[35] "In whatever degree the marriage law is relaxed," Pusey warned, "in that degree are the domestic affections narrowed": if the nuclear family and the contract model of marriage loosened the ties of kinship by casting affinity as a merely metaphorical relationship, a sister-in-law would lose her privileged status as a sister.[36] And a widowed brother-in-law would lose the benefit of her presence, since relaxing the law must drive her from his house, according to the "rule of society that persons whom the law allows to marry cannot remain under the same roof unmarried."[37] "Change the sister of a wife into a young marriageable stranger" and "the union which is daily seen in families will, where it now exists, be broken": "The relation of brother-in-law and sister-in-law will cease" if not measured by the same standard that applied to "real" brothers and sisters.[38] One side emphasized the similarity between first-family sisters as the very basis for sanctioning second unions; the other cast the analogous relation between first and second families as grounds for prohibiting them.

With so much discord between the competing arguments, it is easy to lose track of where they overlap, but it is certainly the case that on both sides of the debate, "real brotherhood and sisterhood" between in-laws signified an intimate relationship that might generate a desire to marry. James Endell Tylor, a clerical witness to the royal commission who supported the ban, assumed that a man's feelings would naturally and inevitably gravitate toward the sister of the deceased wife, chief among "the memorials" the dead woman leaves behind, a second source of the same "love and devotedness."[39] While some counseled that the very natural attraction to the second sister must be blocked—as the queen's chaplain stated with some asperity, everyone has "desires to approximate, which they will naturally proceed to accomplish, except under powerful restraints"—an anonymous widower spoke for many others in testifying that "the intimate intercourse, which the present state of the law sanctions," itself "has been the cause of the attachment which subsists."[40] A sister-in-law's presence in the household, as a sister to a brother, inspired the feelings the ban aimed to proscribe by allowing for the transfer and extension of "domestic affections" to a not-so-new, not-so-different ob-

ject. Where the two camps differed, then, was on whether an attraction to the second sister was an appropriate outcome of family feeling
or a hideous perversion of it, whether it was most "natural" or all too
"natural." Differently valenced as that term was for each side, their joint
appeal to "nature" demonstrates that neither commanded the full social
assent to the premises each was attempting to legitimate.

Advocates of the ban feared that lifting it would contaminate all sibling bonds by admitting the possibility of adulterous incest into the Victorian home, either before or after the first wife's demise; advocates of
repeal—positing likeness rather than identity between sisters, and affinity rather than consanguinity between brother- and sister-in-law—denied
the charge of incest and disputed the grounds on which it was based. "It
is a curious idea of incest to call it incest to marry an alien in blood when
it is not incest to marry a first cousin," Viscount Gage argued in the
1870s, invoking a frequent reference point for late-century opposition
to the ban; "but are sisters-in-law sisters? This is just what they are not,"
he declared, enumerating legal distinctions of status between siblings
and in-laws regarding the inheritance of property.[41] The acceptability
of cousin marriage, to which no incestuous stigma was attached, might
have provided a model on which MDWS could also be made acceptable to earlier Victorians, for as Gullette writes in her groundbreaking
essay on the subject, "to many people at the time the idea that sex with
such an in-law should be called incest seemed genuinely preposterous."[42]
Undoubtedly it seemed so because to them, as to most of us, "one flesh"
was only a metaphor, siblinghood a relationship conferred only by the
first family, and, increasingly, marriage a potentially dissoluble contract
between individuals rather than a union of families. If, metaphorically
speaking, cousins were far away enough to marry, then wives' sisters
stood at an even further remove from the family of origin (unless, that is,
both wife and sister were already a man's cousins in the first place).

Characterizing the stance of the forces of prohibition, the royal commissioners bluntly stated the rhetorical goal that they had so much
trouble achieving: "the great object ought to be to induce the husband
to regard his wife's sister as his own," an end at which the repeated
references to in-laws as relations "by blood" who are "united as one family" and the characterization of MDWS as "manifest incest" were clearly
aimed.[43] That such rhetoric alone kept the law in place seems unlikely,
but it is just as improbable that belief in "one flesh," and the contests
over the scope of the second family that it generated, had no residual
effect on how relationships between first and second families were conceived. "Preposterous" or not, the characterization of in-law marriage as
incestuous reminds us of the historical variability—and, in Ellen Pollak's

reading of eighteenth-century materials, the cultural contingency—of what constitutes incest.[44] Even as the Victorians progressively adopted a secular view of marriage, some remainder of the older view persisted, and the figure of the wife's sister at the apex of the triangle that forms the second family provided its focal point.

II

Responding to "the only objection" to repealing the law "worth considering"—that it "would destroy the sanction under which the innocent familiarity allowed amongst brothers and sisters-in-law takes place"—one pamphleteer argued that "this familiarity must be attributed to other causes" than the law itself, going on to characterize those causes as something other than innocent familial feeling.[45] He implied that a second sister would continue to appear in the light of a potential marriage partner, even after a first marriage, as a perennial "second choice":

> Up to the period when he makes his selection, the man necessarily regards all the sisters alike: it is absurd to suppose that, the moment he has married one, a complete revulsion in his moral being is to take place, and that he will be enabled to invest her near relations of his own age with the same ideal barrier, the same sin-repelling halo, which nature has cast around his own. If he did, he would never afterwards regard them as objects of sexual passion; for feelings of this kind are the product of habit, and cannot be put off and on with circumstances.[46]

"Men in general," he concluded, "undergo no such change" of perspective: they did not come to see these new sisters as they saw their own and as thus immune to being regarded as "objects of sexual passion."[47] The very charms of "familiarity" derived instead from their having once auditioned for the role of (first) wife, and thus being sexualized to some extent simply by having been made available for male choice—think of Mr. Collins confidently assessing all, but romancing only some of the Bennet sisters in *Pride and Prejudice* (1813). At the level of courtship ideology, women as a group were "not the choosers but the chosen"; and "a pretty, young, unmarried sister," in the view of a male character from Margaret Oliphant's *The Perpetual Curate* (1864), "was perhaps the least objectionable encumbrance a woman could have."[48]

The presumed male prerogative of unfettered selection, however qualified in practice, surely enabled the fantasy of the "second choice" that Chase and Levenson analyze in Dickens's fiction. Its scandalous appeal rested on the double charge of the second sister: both those who accepted and those who discounted the force of "one flesh" invariably constructed her as at once an innocent familiar and a potential object of desire. This double charge involved a double bind. On the one hand, the pamphleteer distinguished a man's attitude to his own sisters from what he might feel for his sisters-in-law, attributing the ban on the former to the quasi-religious feeling ("sin-repelling halo") that "nature" inspired in brothers. On the other, he suggested that there was nothing natural about that "ideal barrier," pointing to the prohibition of sexual feeling as "the product of habit" rather than, say, instinctual taboo. If first-family sisters were not naturally off limits, then second-family sisters were not even habitually so. Having "regard[ed] all the sisters alike," and all as unlike sisters of his own, generic man would see the woman he did not marry as a familiar domestic object that may be wife or sister, containing the latent capacity to occupy either place, or perhaps both.

In *The Inheritance of Evil* as in *Deerbrook*, the woman who becomes the husband's sister is, from the very beginning of their acquaintance, an object of his desire. Narrated from the perspective of the suspicious but observant fiancée, the first meeting of Richard Clayton and Agnes Maynard in *The Inheritance of Evil*—clearly written in the service of Pusey's cause—affords Agnes's sister Elizabeth "an indescribable pang": "Her future husband was standing with his eyes fixed on Agnes, gazing at her with a look of the most warm and unqualified admiration, a look such as had never been bestowed on herself" (Skene 30). After the establishment of their joint household, Agnes fills a spot in Richard's daily life: "Annoyed and often irritated at" his querulous spouse, he would "gladly turn from her to seek the society of Agnes," who forms "so pleasing a contrast to the anxious care-worn wife," "openly preferring the society of" the one who is "virtually his sister" (Skene 36, 66). Here what draws the husband to the sister-in-law is not her sameness to his wife, but her difference: not being Richard's wife but still being close enough, as a virtual sister, to join him unchaperoned during "the long walks and rides which Elizabeth's enfeebled health prevented her from attempting," Agnes innocently but familiarly provides Richard with a source of female companionship that is both sisterly and sexualized (Skene 37).

In the far less orthodox yet equally sensational *Deerbrook*, the husband's passion for the second sister does not arise from her domestication in the second family; it actually precedes it. Having learned that Hester Ibbotson loves him, Edward Hope, a Deerbrook doctor, proposes to the sister he has inadvertently attracted rather than to Margaret, the sister he truly loves. Despite the narrator's emphasis on his moral struggle, Hope finally chooses the course convenient to his desires, knowing that marrying Hester will bring him Margaret, too: "He glanced forward to his desolation when he should lose the society of both sisters—an event likely to happen almost immediately, unless he should so act as to retain them."[49] In both novels, then, the second family incorporates the sister on terms that make the husband's attraction to her an ongoing site of tension and conflict.

From the perspective of these male characters, "two sisters" are thus not "the same thing" at all; and in both cases neither wife nor sister is what she should be to the husband. With each novel asserting the shaping force of male agency, the second family turns out to be something of a nightmare for both husbands, owing in part to the relationship between the sisters, whose first-family circumstances shape their entry into the second. Being orphans unites each pair very tightly: Elizabeth's dying mother had entreated her to "look upon [Agnes] henceforward as a sacred charge" and to promise "that no other tie or affection hereafter springing up in her life should interfere with this her earliest and most binding duty"; on becoming engaged, Elizabeth makes it "the sole condition of her marriage that Agnes should reside with" her and Richard "entirely, and that she should never be separated from her sister so long as [Agnes] remained unmarried" (Skene 11, 28). In *Deerbrook*, Hester and Margaret expect to be all in all to one another, "to be each other's only friend," when they arrive at the rural home of their distant relations after their father's death; and in the prospect of Hester's marriage to Hope, "no one seemed to doubt for a moment that Margaret would live with her sister. There was no other home for her; she and Hester had never been parted; there seemed no reason for their parting now, and every inducement for their remaining together" (Martineau 21, 162). Each new family formed by marriage, then, bears the mark of a woman's first, with the sororal solidarity between orphans requiring the husband to embrace the second sister.

Disaster threatens second-family life, however, not only because of the sisters' solidarity or the husband's fantasy, but also because of his wife's temperament. Even before their marriages, both Elizabeth and Hester are represented as constitutionally jealous, possessed by a possessiveness that borders on mania. While still a child, Elizabeth's "affection for those she loved was of a nature so profound and exacting, that it had engendered that jealousy of disposition which makes such havoc of the soul that harbours it," and the advent of a potential husband focuses her "overwhelming and almost idolatrous love" on him (Skene 8, 34). Explicating Elizabeth's jealous pang at Richard and Agnes' first meeting, the narrator dwells on the "disposition" that gives rise to it: "Her affection for Richard Clayton was so absorbing that her whole heart and mind were bound up in it, and she had not a thought unconnected with him; she felt indeed that it had most utterly superseded all other sentiments and feelings" (Skene 30–31). Looking at Richard looking at Agnes, Elizabeth glimpses the possibility of a second choice in that gaze: coveting her fiancé's attention arouses her jealousy.

Arguably, then, the problem at this point in *The Inheritance* is not so much the presence of the sexualized sister as the inconstancy of the husband and the insecurity of the wife; taken together, the flaws of the conjugal couple make for an imperfect union. The law aims to remedy their weaknesses: Skene insists that the ban on the second sister not only prohibits the husband's desire for a familiar but protects the wife from her own failings. Along these lines, Elizabeth initially rights herself by recalling the doctrine that will safeguard all parties from the near occasion of sin: "In another instant she repelled this unworthy feeling almost with horror, for she remembered how, in a very few days, Richard Clayton would hold for Agnes Maynard the sacred name of brother. They twain were about to be made by a most holy ordinance ONE FLESH, and from that hour her sister must be his sister also, in the sight of God and man" (Skene 31). Had she been formed on a better model, the narrator implies, Elizabeth would not have felt "jealous and suspicious" at all: adapted as it is to human frailty, the law ameliorates the lack of that better, purer self which it is the province of Christian doctrine to inculcate (Skene 30). Knowing enough of religion to believe that Richard and Agnes can only ever be brother and sister to each other and in the eyes of God keeps Elizabeth's "unworthy feeling" in check—at least for a while.

Hester's possessiveness in *Deerbrook* also centers less on the perception of her sister as a rival and more on her desire for undivided affection, but it is her sister, rather than her husband, whose attention she craves. Hester covets Margaret's love as intensely as Elizabeth does Richard's in *The Inheritance*, claiming "there can never be the same friendship between three as between two" and attributing the operation of her "jealous temper" to the intensity of "the strongest affection I have in the world" (Martineau 21, 22). Contrary to May's argument that "one source of the paranoid jealousy with which Hester torments herself" is that she intuits Edward's love for Margaret, Hester does not consistently see Hope as a rival for her sister's affections, nor as someone of whose affections she should be jealous: only once does Hester suspect, before the marriage, "that Margaret had been the more important of the two to him" (Martineau 117).[50]

A more plausible "source" for Hester's seemingly insatiable need emerges in a conversation early in the novel that gives her jealousy a first-family genealogy. Hester and Margaret recall the baby sibling they lost, with Margaret wondering aloud "what difference it would have made between you and me, if we had had a brother." "He would now have been our companion, taking the place of all other friends to us," Hester remarks, then adding that "you and he would have been close friends—always together, and I should have been left alone" (Martineau 21). Fantasizing perpetual exclusion, she subsequently resents the intimacy Margaret forms with a Deerbrook resident, Maria Young: "Hester found that Maria filled a large space in Margaret's mind, and that a new interest had risen up in which she had little share," and turns her resentment against Margaret herself, from saying "a few pettish words" to violently lamenting the alienation of her sister's affections (Martineau 70). Such persistent suspicion provokes even the saintly Margaret to anger: "I have found a friend in Maria; and you poison my comfort in my friendship, and insult my friend. There is not an infant in a neighbour's house but you become jealous of it" (Martineau 288). But struggle as Hester does against her wickedness, Margaret's attention even to her own nephew leads Hester to accuse her sister of having "not a thought to spare for any of us while she has baby in her arms. The little fellow has cut us all out" (Martineau 498). "The empty space that should be filled by the brother," May persuasively claims, "becomes the object of unfulfilled desire": as her own baby replaces the dead baby brother, Hester reproduces in her second family the feelings of exclusion generated in the first.[51]

While Martineau's Hester never learns the truth about her husband's feelings, Skene's Elizabeth undergoes the suffering induced by both her "idolatrous love" and the dying knowledge that her jealousy is not without foundation.[52] Having managed to solace herself with help from the "one flesh" doctrine, Elizabeth comes to believe that, after her death, "Richard would find some unknown stranger, fairer and dearer, to take her place in his love and in his home" (Skene 38). She experiences "the most complete consolation," however, when she lights upon an alternative scenario: "far from her place being filled by a rival," Agnes would stay on, after Elizabeth's demise, "and so long as she continued unmarried, she would prevent the possibility of another wife entering into the house of which she would be the beloved inmate" (Skene 39). Agnes would become chief among the "memorials" to her sister and her enduring love: Elizabeth "repeatedly implored of them both to promise her that Agnes should always remain with her brother-in-law; urging as her reason for wishing it, that to her alone would she commit the care of her little daughter, and the new-born babe if it survived" (Skene 40). The narrative thus casts the dying wife who pleads her sister's suitability as a second mother not as an angelic moral guardian aiming to superintend the happiness of the family circle even from the grave, as proponents of MDWS would have it, but as someone so unprepared to give up worldly affections that "she longed, had it been possible, to have held [Richard] still within the stiff cold arms from which the warmth of life was fled" (Skene 38).

The dénouement follows fast on Elizabeth's overhearing Richard speak "much of the advantage which might result from … procuring for the children of the deceased wife so kind and natural a protectress as their aunt": "There had been an energy and an anxiety in Richard's manner of expressing himself, which proved that, however unconsciously, it was yet for his own sake that he sought so earnestly to prove the truth of his assertions" (Skene 43, 48). The shock precipitates Elizabeth's final illness of both mind and body: "her gaze fell upon Agnes, and her heart revolted with unnatural horror against her dear and only sister," whom she throws against a wall before falling into a fit, delivering her child, and attempting to utter the deathbed words that will prevent the foul incestuous deed (Skene 51). When words do come, the ambiguous sentence they form is "Agnes – not — marry"; as the sister hastens to console Elizabeth with the pledge that "I will never leave this house," "an expression of utter hopelessness settled on [Elizabeth's] features—they had misunderstood her to the last!" (Skene 59).

If the set-up of the second household appears to fulfill the structural requirements of the husband's fantasy, then it also closely corresponds to the shape of the wife's darker imaginings. The truth of the matter notwithstanding—that both Elizabeth and Hester *do* have reason to be jealous of their sisters, who *are* regarded as "objects of sexual passion" by their brothers-in-law—the desire for exclusive possession that motivates both wives, whether understood as excessive love or unmet need, intensifies with the addition of a third party (be it man, woman, or child) who seems to cut them out of the picture. The male character's wish always to have a "second choice" close at hand joins, in very uneasy union, with the female character's fear of being replaced not only by her sister, but also in her sister's affections. The structural likeness of the fear to the wish suggests that they are actually two sides of the same marital coin, two desires that traverse the second family: the wife's negatively coded "jealousy," that is, complements the male fantasy of plenitude.

While a wife's desire to retain her sister for herself even as she also gains a husband of her own does not look particularly scandalous, seeing it *as* desire can help us to recover a dimension of the husband-wife-sister triangle that both nineteenth-century analysts and contemporary critics have largely ignored.[53] In reading only for the wifely rivalry with the sister, we too readily accept the naturalness of the competitive structure between women implied by both sides in the MDWS debate: whereas "nothing may seem more natural to us than female rivalry over men," as Sharon Marcus comments, "nothing seemed more odd to Victorian readers."[54] As much recent queer criticism including Marcus' own work has usefully illuminated, we could consider sororal ties as promoting intimacy, for example, rather than enforcing competition. Eve Kosofsky Sedgwick notes parenthetically in "Jane Austen and the Masturbating Girl" that "there are important generalizations yet to be made about the attachments of sisters, perhaps of any siblings, who live together as adults," and one such enabling generalization may be, as George E. Haggerty argues in relation to Austen's *Sense and Sensibility*, that "the most profoundly emotional and physical relations between women emerge from the family itself."[55] Recognizing the wife's longing to possess sister *and* husband as comparable, indeed structurally parallel, to the husband's wish for "two sisters" enables us to inquire into the conjoined fate of male and female desire in these texts.

III

In an important and exhaustive study entitled *Novel Relations: The Transformation of Kinship in English Literature and Culture, 1748–1818*, Ruth Perry argues that the triangular pattern of husband, wife, and sister that I have traced is best viewed as a "cultural residual of consanguineal kin formations."[56] In the trajectory that she outlines in literary and cultural history from Richardson to Austen, "the biologically given family into which one was born was gradually becoming secondary to the chosen family constructed by marriage."[57] As a result, "it became less and less clear how much one owed to one's family of origin—to siblings and parents and even parents' siblings—and how much to the new family one made for oneself with a stranger."[58] The comprehensive framework Perry develops is especially persuasive in elaborating the ways in which changing economic circumstances shaped and reshaped family formations, with a special emphasis on how women of all classes were massively disadvantaged: by changes in the rules of inheritance that made "women's hereditary rights in property ... secondary to the imperative for accumulation"; by the modernizing practices of land enclosure; and by the diminution of employment opportunities in the transition to wage labor.[59] All of this added up to "a net loss of social power for women."[60] Perry carefully demonstrates that the push and pull toward conjugality as the central form of kinship edged out commitments to the first family, redefining the marriage plot in these terms as "the story of women scrambling to find new homes and to negotiate new families, their rights within the consanguineal family having been undercut by a shift in kinship priorities."[61]

Although her overall thesis stresses the historical shift from first-family consanguinity to second-family conjugality, the main emphasis of Perry's discussion falls on the narrative patterns that derive from the "cultural residual" of consanguineal kinship. She examines a range of plots in which "paternal responsibility for daughters, fraternal responsibilities for sisters, the importance of maternal relatives"—all significantly less dominant in practice by the later eighteenth century because "law and custom increasingly defined women as wives rather than as daughters"—nonetheless constitute the major matter of the domestic fiction of the period.[62] Retaining the sentimental force of an earlier dispensation, eighteenth-century novels relentlessly featured father-daughter reunion in "a nostalgic and compensatory recreation of a time when a father's word protected his daughter"; being "a family obligation from an earlier era, increasingly honored more in the breach than in the observance," "brotherly love came to be a conventional ideal in fiction as it was eroded in life."[63] "In the wish-fulfillment of fiction," Perry argues, "conjugal love creates new affinal sibling bonds that do not compete with earlier ties."[64]

In reading actual early Victorian accounts of comparable circumstances, however, we can see not only the continued persistence of the "cultural residual" that Perry traces, but also the basis it provided for a new resistance, especially on the part of men, to making a second marriage with "a stranger." "It is one of the many advantages of marriage with a sister in law," Henry Thornton wrote to Marianne, "that all things connected with one's former life, instead of raising feelings of jealousy, acquire an increased interest and form a new bond of union" (Forster 208). In undoing the difference that death had made, and even adding a certain luster to what had been lost (and perhaps a necessary one in this case, if we credit the claim that Henry "bore Harriet's decease phlegmatically"), Henry's second marriage continued, indeed renewed the first attachment (Forster 156). Far from being lost, "the new family one made for oneself with a stranger," in Perry's words, was enhanced by a second marriage to another member of that very same "new family." The "jealousy" that a second wife from outside the second family might have felt, in taking the place another had once filled, would not afflict Emily Dealtry. In mourning her sister's loss, she "form[ed] a new bond of union" with the brother-widower, who was thereby spared the search for a new mate, a potentially painful, even alarming undertaking. As one witness to the royal commission put it, "to take a stranger into my house is in itself really a visitation."[65]

Indeed, the threat of the "stranger" to domestic security loomed large in much of the pro-MDWS discourse, especially when the happiness of the children entered the equation: "The aunt, who already stand[s] in a suit of quasi-maternal relation to the children of the first wife, would, *cæteris paribus*, have a better chance than a stranger as a stepmother. … Such marriages have actually turned out happier marriages than in the case of perfect strangers as step-mothers."[66] Another witness similarly preferred the known to the strange, with a special emphasis on his vulnerability to the latter: "With my habits of business, and want of comfort at home, I knew well that I should run great risks in marrying anybody that I might fancy, or that might be thrown in my way," making a fairly explicit reference to the sexual danger a man of some fortune might incur in being thrown onto an open matrimonial market.[67] "My present wife I had known as a child": if this remark had an incestuous overtone, what followed directly after it—"I knew her to be virtuous and good, and I knew that she would make me happy"—reemphasized the importance of knowing the new wife's character, which arose only from sustained familial association.[68]

In the male advocacy for what may be construed as an "endogamous" second union, the "exogamous" imperative that we typically associate with early Victorian marriage among the elite classes—and with the heterosexual courtship plot of nineteenth-century fiction—gave way to a preference for the security of the familiar and the familial. In seeking legal sanction for this "second attachment," arguments based on what men felt, as Chase and Levenson suggest, aimed to legitimate "the desire never to have to leave home" and registered "the longing of these widowed husbands to be allowed to stay within the domestic circle, not to be forced to look outside for a second wife but to find her here, already, the familiar sister."[69] One might say, then, that the increasing cultural emphasis on conjugality—the second family that a man made with a first wife—played a critical part in the formation of a man's desire not to alter that second family any further than death had already done.

For married women, no doubt, the situation differed from that of their male counterparts—but how? Perry's analysis affirms that "it was a mixed blessing for women to exchange whatever power and status they had in their families of origin for the power and status of women in conjugal families," and that in "the movement from father patriarchy to husband patriarchy," daughters who became wives potentially lost sustaining connections to first families.[70] Becoming more isolated in marriage, albeit with the possibility of producing children of their own that might help to repair those losses, women who retained first-family ties to married or unmarried sisters might meet a pressing emotional need. Pitted against the ideological emphasis on conjugal loyalty, however, sisterly solidarity could run a poor second: for example, in an essay on the MDWS debate published more than two decades after the appearance of *Deerbrook*, Martineau recommended to both wives and husbands that they exercise "that prudence which, in the conjugal case, should keep all friendships subordinate to the supreme bond, all companionship secondary to the prime union,—all intercourses immeasurably below the open confidence and tenderness, and understood intimacy of the conjugal friendship."[71] Writing in full consciousness, to be sure, of the implications for wives in particular of the gender-differentiated consequences that might arise from any weakening of "the supreme bond," Martineau clearly subordinated first-family relationships to marital "confidence and tenderness." But her advice might be viewed as strategic rather than normative; it might, that is, have sprung from a recognition that a married woman's only true security would lie with the husband who, for much of the century, controlled her person and her property almost as his own.

Finally, within a cultural framework that vaunted matrimony as woman's destiny, to be the third where there should be only two, to be not a wife but a wife's sister with no living father or brother, as is the case in both *The Inheritance of Evil* and *Deerbrook*, might make marriage both a clear imperative and a prospect that co-residence with a sister and her husband might itself imperil. Reporting some secondhand family intelligence, Marianne Thornton proposed that Henry chose to marry Emily in order to save her honor, so compromised by the scandal their situation aroused that if he did not marry her, no one would: "He feels he has damaged her & owes it to her to make her retribution" (Forster 198).[72] Casting Emily as a fallen woman positioned Henry as her seducer, who might make amends only by making an honest woman of her, even if doing so violated English law. One imagines that from his perspective, it was *not* marrying her that would constitute the real damage, since whatever had already transpired between them had sullied her reputation. To be sure, in his position as scion of a large and influential Clapham Sect family, a father in his own right, an officer of an important local bank, and a leader in the community, his reputation, too, was at stake, even if the stigma he might have incurred would have been broadly social rather than specifically sexual. Henry's act of reparation, then, might have constituted an effort to ward off the ruin of both parties, gender-differentiated though that ruin might be.

So, too, could the differences between Henry's stance and Margaret's perspective have arisen from the gendered asymmetries at the intersection of sexuality and alliance. Discussing cousin marriage and MDWS together as "two contested forms of marriage in eighteenth-century culture [that] illustrate most clearly the cultural shift from consanguineal to conjugal loyalty," Perry suggests that the permissibility of the former and the prohibition on the latter in the eighteenth century depended "on whether or not marriage is understood to sever the consanguineal kin tie and replace it—whether or not marriage creates new families that retroactively suppress and replace the family of origin."[73] She finds that cousin marriage was legitimate because "the sibling tie" between the mothers or fathers of the engaged couple was "dissolved by adulthood and marriage," while affinity marriage with an in-law was not, because a new "sibling tie" was created by the very marriage that also created the affinity.[74]

My research suggests, by contrast, that in nineteenth-century cases of marriage within the family, the distinction that Perry draws between consanguineal and conjugal (or affinal) families was not so clear-cut. It lost force under circumstances in which members of the first family and those who populated the second were made analogous to birth siblings by the "one flesh" doctrine. And it was decidedly blurred, as in my two fictional examples, when married women retained their single sisters as members of the new conjugal household. Both in-law and cousin unions remained "contested forms of marriage" all throughout the nineteenth century, with the terms that governed the debate about them shifting in relation to developments in science and anthropology, which took the meaning of "consanguinity" in particular as a central node of investigation. Finally, the very plot points that, for Perry, exemplify the shift from consanguinity to conjugality—"daughters pressured to marry against their wills, older brothers who gambled away the inheritance of younger children, brothers who lived off the labors and savings of their sisters, mothers who died leaving children ignorant of their paternity" as well as other "elements of disrupted kinship"—so pervade nineteenth-century fiction as to suggest continuous cultural tension between the claims of the first family and the dictates of the second.[75] Such persistent tension over the forms of "the family," ongoing as it is, indicates that "the transformation of kinship," far from ever being completed, is a long, slow, open-ended process, contested and renewed in every succeeding generation—including, of course, our own.[76]

Notes

This chapter was previously published as "Husband, Wife, and Sister: Making and Remaking the Early Victorian Family," which appeared in *Victorian Literature and Culture* 35, no. 1 (2007): 1–19.

1. E. M. Forster, *Marianne Thornton: A Domestic Biography, 1797–1887* (New York, 1956), 189.
2. Forster, 189–192.
3. Forster, 214.
4. Forster, 205, 210.
5. Virginia Woolf, *Mrs Dalloway* [1925] (reprinted New York, 1981), 75. That George's offense was not punishable by English law between 1857 and 1908, while a marriage between Jack and Vanessa would have been illegal, no doubt forms additional and appalling support for Forster's remarks even as it highlights the meanings of "incest" that circulated during this period. For further discussion of this incident and its implications, see Mary Jean Corbett, *Family Likeness: Sex, Marriage, and Incest from Jane Austen to Virginia Woolf* (Ithaca, 2008), 1–4, 177–181.
6 Forster, 190–193.
7. For full discussions of the MDWS debate, see especially Nancy F. Anderson, "The 'Marriage with a Deceased Wife's Sister Bill' Controversy: Incest Anxiety and the Defense of Family Purity in Victorian England," *Journal of British Studies* 21, no. 2 (1982): 67–86; Cynthia Fansler Behrman, "The Annual Blister: A Sidelight on Victorian Social and Parliamentary History," *Victorian Studies* 11 (1968): 483–502; Karen Chase and Michael Levenson, *The Spectacle of Intimacy: A Public Life for the Victorian Family* (Princeton, 2000), 105–20; Elizabeth Rose Gruner, "Born and Made: Sisters, Brothers, and the Deceased Wife's Sister Bill," *Signs* 24 (1999): 423–447; Margaret Morganroth Gullette, "The Puzzling Case of the Deceased Wife's Sister: Nineteenth-Century England Deals with a Second-Chance Plot," *Representations* 31 (1990): 142–166; and Sybil Wolfram, *In-Laws and Outlaws: Kinship and Marriage in England* (London, 1987), 21–51. My work builds on theirs, yet focuses especially on the impact of marriage on the family.
8. Jane Austen, *Mansfield Park*, ed. Claudia L. Johnson (New York, 1998), 161.
9. Leonore Davidoff, "Where the Stranger Begins: The Question of Siblings in Historical Analysis," in *Worlds Between: Historical Perspectives on Gender and Class*, ed. Davidoff (New York, 1995), 208–226, here 208.
10. For a wide-ranging discussion of cousin marriage along these lines, see Adam Kuper, "Incest, Cousin Marriage, and the Origin of the Human Sciences in Nineteenth-Century England," *Past & Present* 174 (February 2002): 158–183. See also Glenda A. Hudson, *Sibling Love and Incest in Jane Austen's Fiction* (reprinted New York, 1999), and Corbett, *Family Likeness*, 30–56, for more on cousin marriage in Austen's fiction.
11. "The first family" is an even more fluid construction than I indicate here, in that in addition to birth, fostered, and adoptive siblings, we should also consider siblings of the half blood, with just one parent in common; the Duckworth brothers and the Stephen sisters, for example, shared just the same mother, which might have made a difference in perceptions or attitudes within the blended household of eight children created by the second marriages of Leslie Stephen and Julia Duckworth. As Jack Wentworth tells his half-brother Frank in Margaret Oliphant's *The Perpetual Curate* (1864), only Gerald "and I are the original brood. You are all a set of interlopers, the rest of you," in being the children of a second wife. Oliphant, *The Perpetual Curate* (Harmondsworth, 1987), 408. Whether half-siblings were related on the father's or the mother's side would certainly make a difference in their status within the family in relation to inheritance practices and related privileges.
12. Leila Silvana May, *Disorderly Sisters: Sibling Relations and Sororal Resistance in Nineteenth-Century British Literature* (Lewisburg, PA, 2001), 29; Elizabeth Gaskell, *Wives and Daughters*, ed. Pam Morris (London, 1996).

13. May, *Disorderly Sisters*, 29; Gruner, "Born and Made."

14. Although they disagree amongst themselves as to the particulars of the family's institutional evolution, the historians of the family who have shaped my thinking on this point include Leonore Davidoff and Catherine Hall, *Family Fortunes: Men and Women of the English Middle Class, 1780–1850* (Chicago, 1987); Edward Shorter, *The Making of the Modern Family* (New York, 1975); Lawrence Stone, *The Family, Sex and Marriage in England, 1500–1800* (New York, 1977); and Randolph Trumbach, *The Rise of the Egalitarian Family* (New York, 1978).

15. Gullette, "Puzzling Case," 146; Behrman, "Annual Blister," 494.

16. Chase and Levenson, *Spectacle of Intimacy*, 106.

17. Helena Michie, *Sororophobia: Differences among Women in Literature and Culture* (New York, 1992), 24. Although her analysis focuses in particular on elements of competition among women, Michie also offers a concise list of the myriad ways in which sisterhood could be configured: "Are sisters reiterations of each other? ... Competitors? Is the deceased sister primarily replaced as wife or mother or as both? Is one sister the most natural or the most unnatural replacement for another? Is marrying your sister's widower the ultimate act of betrayal or the ultimate act of loyalty to her memory? Are sisters too much the same (incest), or comfortingly similar (familial bliss)?" (p. 24).

18. [W. A. Beckett], *The Woman's Question and the Man's Answer; or, Reflections on the Social Consequences of Legalizing Marriage with a Deceased Wife's Sister* (London, 1859), 10–11.

19. Françoise Héritier, *Two Sisters and Their Mother: The Anthropology of Incest*, trans. Jeanine Herman (New York, 1999), 14.

20. *First Report of the Commissioners Appointed to Inquire into the State and Operation of the Law of Marriage as Relating to the Prohibited Degrees of Affinity, and to Marriages Solemnised Abroad or in the British Colonies* (London, 1848; reprinted Shannon, 1969), 66.

21. Michie, *Sororophobia*, 24.

22. *First Report*, 69, 24, 76.

23. Ibid., 67.

24. Matthew Arnold, *"Friendship's Garland,"* in *The Complete Prose Works of Matthew Arnold*, vol. 5., ed. R. H. Super (Ann Arbor, 1965), 315.

25. *First Report*, 88.

26. E. B. Pusey, *Marriage with a Deceased Wife's Sister Prohibited by Holy Scripture, as Understood by the Church for 1500 Years* (Oxford, 1849), 18; Behrman, "Annual Blister," 485–486. Anderson notes that "the contention that sexual intercourse causes an actual physiological change in the marriage partners that makes them blood relations" came under scrutiny later in the century. Anderson, "'Marriage with a Deceased Wife's Sister Bill' Controversy," 75. Even when the specter of shared blood was not invoked as an impediment, however, sex between these in-laws was categorically differentiated from simple adultery because it was construed as incestuous, as sex with a sister "of the same blood" would be; a husband's intercourse with his sister-in-law, for example, "constituted one of the few grounds on which [his wife] could be granted a divorce until 1923." Kuper, "Incest," 165.

27. Gullette, "Puzzling Case," 160; Wolfram, *In-Laws*, 29.

28. "The Marriage Relation," *London Quarterly Review, American Edition* 85 (July and October 1849): 84–98, here 92.

29. Felicia Skene, *The Inheritance of Evil, Or, the Consequence of Marrying a Deceased Wife's Sister* (London, 1849), 96–97; this book is available online in the "Victorian

Women Writers Project directed by Perry Willett at Indiana University. Subsequent references are included in the text.

30. E. B. Pusey, *A Letter on the Proposed Change in the Laws Prohibiting Marriage between Those Near of Kin* (Oxford, 1842), 16–17.

31. Skene, 44. See Anderson, "'Marriage with a Deceased Wife's Sister Bill' Controversy," 74.

32. Quoted in Chase and Levenson, *Spectacle of Intimacy*, 113.

33. *Hansard* 3 (Commons), vol. 106, col. 630, 20 June 1849.

34. "Marriage Relation," 92.

35. Jane Austen, *Sense and Sensibility*, ed. James Kinsley (Oxford, 1990), 14. Widows were also proscribed from marrying their dead husbands' brothers. But as Gullette observes, the only couple that attracted widespread attention was "the man whose desire was to marry his wife's sister, and the woman who reciprocated." Gullette, "Puzzling Case," 154. That there was no comparable MDHB debate suggests, among other things, the persistent presence of what Chase and Levenson call "the usual entrenchments of masculine agency and female passivity." Chase and Levenson, *Spectacle of Intimacy*, 114.

36. *First Report*, 53.

37. Ibid., 53.

38. "Marriage Relation," 92.

39. *First Report*, 112.

40. Ibid., 29, 80.

41. *Hansard* 3 (Lords), vol. 214, col. 1876, 13 March 1873. Wolfram notes that "his wife's sister did not inherit from a man who died intestate, and if a woman were left a legacy by her sister's husband, she paid the death duties customary for unrelated people"; cousins, by contrast, "paid at a reduced rate." Wolfram, *In-Laws*, 34.

42. Gullette, "Puzzling Case," 159. From a financial standpoint, of course, first-cousin marriage would often be not only acceptable but desirable, as an interested mother in Oliphant's *Hester* (1883) points out to both her son and her niece as she aims to encourage their marriage: "She asked her son how he could forget that if Catherine's money went out of the business it would make the most extraordinary difference? and she bade Catherine remember that it would be almost dishonest to enrich another family with money which the Vernons had toiled for." Oliphant, *Hester*, ed. Philip Davis and Brian Nellist (Oxford, 2003), 6.

43. *First Report*, x, 37.

44. See Ellen Pollak, *Incest and the English Novel, 1684–1814* (Baltimore, 2003).

45. [Abraham Hayward], *Summary of Objections to the Doctrine that a Marriage with the Sister of a Deceased Wife is Contrary to Law, Religion, or Morality* (London, 1839), 18, 19.

46. Ibid., 19.

47. Ibid., 19.

48. [Beckett,] *Woman's Question*, 24; Oliphant, *Perpetual Curate*, 386–387.

49. Harriet Martineau, *Deerbrook*, ed. Valerie Sanders (London, 2004), 140; subsequent references are included in the text. Ann Hobart maintains that "though Hope marries a woman he does not love, we are not invited to question his integrity," a conclusion I would challenge on the basis of the passage cited here. Hobart, "Harriet Martineau's Political Economy of Everyday Life," *Victorian Studies* 37 (Winter 1994): 244.

50. May, *Disorderly Sisters*, 101. May relies heavily on René Girard's theory of mediated or mimetic desire to untangle the "thicket of rivalries and jealousies" (p. 91) that constitutes *Deerbrook*, a reliance that occasionally leads her to overemphasize rela-

tively slight textual evidence, as in this example. In making the claim that "true to Girard's schema, Hester desires to *be*—to become—her rival" (p. 92), May imposes a competitive structure on the sisterly relationship. My reading of this passage and others emphasizes instead the way in which the second sister persistently figures the sister/wife's unmet needs and desires as she moves from a first to a second family.

51. May, *Disorderly Sisters*, 28.
52. In an otherwise thoughtful reading of the novel, Gruner asserts that Elizabeth's "jealousy is misplaced," discounting some of the warning notes that Skene strikes earlier in the text. Gruner, "Born and Made," 430.
53. Although the particulars of my analysis differ from hers, May's work yet offers a noteworthy exception to the rule.
54. Sharon Marcus, *Between Women: Friendship, Desire, and Marriage in Victorian England* (Princeton, 2007), 106.
55. Eve Kosofsky Sedgwick, *Tendencies* (Durham, 1993), 118; George E. Haggerty, *Unnatural Affections: Women and Fiction in the Later 18th Century* (Bloomington, 1998), 75.
56. Ruth Perry, *Novel Relations: The Transformation of Kinship in English Literature and Culture, 1748–1818* (Cambridge, 2004), 9.
57. Ibid., 2.
58. Ibid., 24–25.
59. Ibid., 49.
60. Ibid., 34.
61. Ibid., 7.
62. Ibid., 9, 90.
63. Ibid., 90, 144.
64. Ibid., 145.
65. *First Report*, 64.
66. Ibid., 74.
67. Ibid., 82.
68. Ibid., 82.
69. Chase and Levenson, *Spectacle of Intimacy*, 108.
70. Perry, *Novel Relations*, 2, 34.
71. Quoted in Valerie Sanders, *The Brother-Sister Culture in Nineteenth-Century Literature: From Austen to Woolf* (New York, 2002), 78.
72. A slightly earlier incident in Austen's family illuminates this point. When her brother Charles lost his first wife, he installed his surviving three children under the care of his wife's sister Harriet Palmer; according to Austen biographer Park Honan, "when home from the Navy, [Charles] lived with his dead wife's sister respectably at her parents' house; but gossip focused on his behaviour with Harriet." This may well have been the catalyst for their marriage in 1820, at a moment when such marriages did not fall under the legal scrutiny they incurred after 1835. Park Honan, *Jane Austen: Her Life* (New York, 1987), 365.
73. Perry, *Novel Relations*, 119.
74. Ibid., 121.
75. Ibid., 30.
76. Among much else that I could cite, see Judith Butler, *Undoing Gender* (London, 2004), which explores the ground for rethinking the symbolic and social structures of kinship in the new families forged over the last two decades by assisted reproductive technologies and adoptive practices that enable lesbians, gay men, and single people of all genders and sexualities to parent.

Chapter 12

Gender and Age in Nineteenth-Century Britain

The Case Of Anne, William, and Helen Gladstone[1]

Leonore Davidoff

> Sisters are to brothers what
> brothers can never be to sisters
> —Harriet Martineau

> Friendships with women have constituted no small portion
> of my existence. I know the meaning of the words
> "weakness is power; real weakness is real power"
> —William Ewart Gladstone

Introduction

In the voluminous body of writing about the career and personality of William Ewart Gladstone, four times prime minister and one of Britain's most influential, controversial politicians, two elements have constantly puzzled commentators: his habit of nocturnal wanderings in search of high-class prostitutes for redemption, and his uncharacteristically bullying, even hostile, attitude to his younger sister, Helen. Neither of these

issues looms large in the Gladstone corpus, but they make for uneasy assessment of the man.[2] While the relationships of the Gladstone siblings
William, Ann, and Helen together with their brothers Thomas, Robertson, and John will probably never be fully comprehended, their interconnections can be understood as a striking, if somewhat extreme, case
of the role of gender in sibling dynamics, set in a particular economic
social and cultural context.[3]

In the context of the Gladstone story, the aim of this chapter is to
investigate the way only opposite-sex siblings both identify with and
distance themselves from each other, how these relationships can be central in creating a concept of the self, and how family structure, including
birth order and age, influence this process. While these structural elements may be constant to many societies, the psychological and social
features involved are always particular to their historical epoch and social milieu.

Since a keystone of the gender order in modern Western society has
been the equation of masculinity with public life and the relegation of
femininity to a naturalized domestic realm, historical records as well as
attention have been almost all concentrated on the former. Since the
time of his political ascendancy, the life of William Gladstone has been
consistently and minutely documented, while Ann and Helen remain
forgotten shadowy figures. In addition to his own lifelong diary entries,
now in print, there are innumerable biographies and visual representations of William.[4] For Anne and Helen, in addition to a couple of portraits not publicly available, there is only a scattering of private papers.
The best that can be done is to bring together these extremely uneven
bodies of evidence while keeping in mind the inevitable silences.

The construction of masculinity and femininity—of their constraints
and paradoxes and how these played out in the lives of real, embodied,
brothers and sisters—is here set within the context of the British upper
middle class in the first half of the nineteenth century. This was a volatile
period when an empire was being created, new fortunes made, and many
radical innovations such as the railway combined to bring to a climax
the challenge of an expanding bourgeoisie to the established gentry and
aristocracy.[5] The nascent capitalism that had helped to make fortunes
had also flooded towns and cities with working people fueling clamors
for reform. It was in this atmosphere that cultural boundaries were both
broadened and reinforced by placing people in oppositional categories:
civilized and primitive, black and white, British and native, Christian and
heathen, pure and polluting, independent and servile, lady and woman,
gentleman and working man—and embedded in all these, masculine and
feminine. Models of masculinity and femininity were pervasive in fiction

and prescriptive literature, often exemplified through idealized stories of brothers and sisters.

Starting in the mid-eighteenth century, especially among the middling strata, there had been a gradual shift for both men and women from gaining and maintaining a gendered reputation through external *behavior* to an internalized sense of personal and highly differentiated gendered *identity*. Often its first awakening was via experiencing differential treatment meted out to boys and girls within the family.[6] However, as John Tosh has argued, attaining full adult manhood also continued to involve forming a household—preferably through marriage—and protecting and controlling its contents and the people within it.[7] Although the appearance of physical vigor, of resolution and power, was still highly valued for men, where commercial, professional, and political life predominated, intellectual ability and business acumen were at a premium; few had the opportunity or inclination to blatantly prove their manhood in venues such as the hunting field. It was more likely that professional reputation, oratory, and writing skills or a healthy bank balance, ownership of property, and the appearance of his home defined status as a man.

The potential tension between physical and mental measures of manhood was partially resolved through covertly accepting young men's perceived need to sow wild oats including sport, adventurous travel, and attempts at sexual conquest before settling down to the constraints of funding and wielding domestic authority. Nevertheless, conflicts and slippages within the meaning of *manliness* simmered. In this "portmanteau term of overlapping ideologies," adolescents and young men could measure themselves not only against their peers but also in opposition to the feminine development of their sisters.[8] The ideal of manhood flourished in contrast to notions of both childishness and effeminacy, equating these with physical and mental submissive weakness. A woman's youth was ideally passed in innocent domestic activity until the apotheosis of her existence, marriage, materialized at a suitor's instigation. She was then transferred from father, brother, or their substitutes to husband. Customary practices included adoption of a husband's name bolstered by a property law that incorporated a wife into her husband's persona although, in fact, inheritance of both material and cultural capital came from both paternal and maternal sides.

Such strictures had been enhanced by the early nineteenth-century idea that passion, desire, and active initiative were absent from genteel women's makeup or, if present, represented an abhorrent anomaly—the dreaded epithet of "strong woman." Official denial of women's sexual desire fed into the accepted double standard of morality whereby men were expected to stray, women to remain pure. On the other hand, in an effort to disentangle independent man from the snares of personal dependence or being mired in their physicality, women were characterized as "The Sex." Over the period there was an increase in sexualizing the least powerful, exemplified by the content of pornography where women, children, slaves, and "natives" became carriers of sexuality and the uncontrolled body.[9]

For women in this stratum, the idea of all adult women *mothering* children, youths, and other dependents whether or not they were their own offspring evolved into a more individual notion of *motherhood* within marriage and one's own family. Mothers were increasingly seen to bear responsibility for the fate of the family, the stability of their class and nation.[10] Elder sisters were often called upon to act as "apprentice mothers" for younger siblings. By mid-century, femininity itself was becoming synonymous with motherhood, particularly for serious Christians. But such expectations meant that upon marriage, somehow the tender maiden was to be transformed into a competent, managing wife, mother, and household manager while remaining deferential to masculine superior knowledge and experience. Despite the ensuing unrestricted childbearing, her role had to be kept free from the taint of sexual acknowledgement. Under this regime, childless married women and even doubly so unmarried women, while spared such a major transition, were ultimately considered failures, dangerously—or ridiculously—unfeminine despite the fact that many women cared for others' children, especially as aunts or cousins.[11]

These idealized, if confusing, constructions were enhanced by the evangelical religious movement that had swept Britain since the mid eighteenth century. The "Christian tint" that affected many aspects of life called for the submission of self to God and the self-control necessary to carry out His will, along with the constant examination of thoughts and behavior as measured against a rigid moral code.[12] For men brought up in the evangelical tradition, the heightened emotional concentration on one's inward state and self-abnegation to a higher authority ran counter to the demands of active, independent manliness, a tension ratcheted further for men in the full flush of physical and sexual energy. Guilt at not controlling and directing the passions away from sinful desires could wreak havoc for those who took such dictates seriously. For them, the overpowering of what they regarded as baser elements of self became a heroic struggle. This in turn fed into men's perceived need for a pure, genteel lady of their own class to act as moral arbiter—as opposed to the servants or, in some cases, prostitutes whose functions were to soak up polluting elements and sin.[13] In Freud's well known phrase: "where they love they do not desire and where they desire they cannot love."[14]

Submission of self should have come more easily for the serious Christian girl and woman, given its congruity with the feminine ideal. Much depended on the temperament as well as functions available within a woman's domestic milieu. But the denial of desire for autonomy, the lack of opportunities for active intervention in a larger world as well as lack of acknowledgment of erotic feelings could create its own kind of torment.

Such cultural artifacts were just that, mental constructions overlying the messy, conflict-ridden real world of embodied boys and girls, men and women. Recent scholarship has emphasized how often attitudes and behavior deviated from prescriptive portrayals.[15] In a variety of ways people resisted or redefined prescribed roles. Nevertheless, the power of normative expectations should not be lightly dismissed. Those who obviously stood out against the prevailing codes risked not only social ostracism or even financial and material deprivation but also the besmirching of their family and kin when reputation was essential to commercial and professional as well as social survival.

The individual psychic effects on self-confidence could be devastating, especially as ridicule and satire were so often employed to enforce norms of expected gender appearance and behavior. Expectations of gender-appropriate physical appearance and social behavior were part of the training in gentility that would distinguish social position.[16] Body language learned in childhood stressed masculine stance and a striding gait, as opposed to the dainty, gliding steps affected by ladies. Ladies should also not whistle, talk in loud voices, or put themselves forward; they should not eat much rich food, drink, smoke, or ever swear. Gentlemen doffed hats to ladies, stood when they entered a room, carried their parcels, helped them on with their wraps, handed them into vehicles. But among their masculine peers they smoked, drank [in moderation] and could enjoy a risqué story.

Acceptable clothing enhanced gender difference. Upper-class men's dress had shifted radically from the bejeweled and highly colored outfits of the eighteenth century. The early nineteenth-century revolutionary change from breeches and stockings to body hugging trousers accompanied by Byronesque flowing locks, colored fancy waistcoats, and generously flounced cravats gradually gave way to the unadorned, dark-colored, trouser-suited male, his height emphasized by the black stove-pipe hat, his face hidden behind bushy whiskers.

In direct contrast the female figure was outlined in corsets and voluminous petticoated skirts that by mid-century expanded to the cage-supported crinoline. Bright colors and shining fabrics were smothered in ruffles and lace enhanced by beads and earrings, beribboned caps and bonnets. Tight sleeves made lifting arms for many activities difficult while as skirts became ever wider, moving about was not just hampered but at times dangerous, as in maneuvering to get into a carriage. Such restrictions enhanced the need for gestures such as pulling out chairs to allow women to sit down. Thus dress alone necessitated some dependence on servants and male escorts.

Such niceties about men's putative care and protection of women were part of the general training boys had to undergo in preparation for adult status. Active careers usually entailed at least a period away from home, whether as a form of apprenticeship, in education, or for travel. For the wealthiest and ambitious strata of the bourgeoisie it usually implied a period in a prestigious public school with a curriculum based on the classics, where a youth would be able to mix with his more aristocratic fellows. Girls were almost wholly educated and trained at home by mother, elder sisters, or aunts, supplemented by governesses and specialized masters in a diet of social accomplishments, modern languages, and the arts. They would then expect to be "presented" to society, preferably to the court in London but at least locally through a series of balls and assemblies, although this was not an option for serious Christians.

This differentiation continued into young adulthood, when the life course of siblings radically diverged. For brothers a form of engagement with the wider world was needed, for in whatever capacity, "a man must act."[17] Many girls and young women took enthusiastically to domestic concerns as helpmates or even substitutes for a mother. They might also throw themselves into the social round, where their contacts through kin and friends offered considerable influence, or these might be combined with church-related and philanthropic activities. However where opportunities were more limited through family pressures, social isolation, or shyness and lack of social skills, many young women wilted into indeterminate mental as well as physical health. It was assumed that their femininity already placed them at the mercy of their emotions.[18]

In cultural terms brothers and sisters figured as the archetype of the ideal relationship between men and women, but unsullied by erotic attraction. For a provincial clockmaker's daughter, brother and sister represented not only the "winning tenderness of pure love," but also "the respect due to superiority and the sense of weakness on one part and the consciousness of power, affection and support on the other. ... as a protector, a guardian and a friend" the brother will "mark the conduct, the opinions, the principles, the temper and even the little foibles of his sister," especially when it came to choice of marriage partner. Her part was to influence him subtly through her winning, dependent femininity.[19]

In all such modeling, a few selective features were picked out. In representations of the ideal sibling relationship, invariably only one pair, *the* brother and *the* sister, is chosen. And just as in George Eliot's poem "Brother and Sister," the brother is always the elder.[20]

> He was the elder and a little man
> Of forty inches, bound to show no dread,
> And I the girl that puppy-like now ran
> Now lagged behind my brother's larger tread
> I held him wise, and when he talked to me
> Of snakes and birds, and which God loved the best,
> I thought his knowledge marked the boundary
> Where men grew blind, though angels knew the rest
>
> If he said 'Hush!' I tried to hold my breath
> Wherever he said 'Come!' I stepped in faith

How did real brothers and sisters relate to each other in such a milieu? Since even contemporary social-psychological analysis has neglected this topic there is little guidance for the historian.[21] Even when siblings have been acknowledged, modern emphasis on the vertical dimension of parent and child—in Juliet Mitchell's view—"may be a major means whereby the ideologies (including sexism) of the brotherhood are allowed to operate unseen."[22] Mitchell has stressed the antagonistic element in sibling relations, the deep psychic distress caused by displacement in parental attention and affection when a brother or sister is born. Other psychologists have argued against such a bleak view, maintaining that there is also a strong element of common recognition and support among brothers and sisters.[23] But all agree that siblings provide one of the major sites where personality is formed, where the self recognizes *both* similarity and difference in the other—in George Eliot's poem, "a like unlike."

Contradictory tendencies and ambivalent feelings within oneself when observed in a sibling, particularly of the opposite sex, could rouse deep anxiety, even furious antagonism, but also empathy and identification. The strong emphasis on gender difference at this time, while homage was paid to affection and mutual support, may in fact have hidden unacknowledged similarities leading to the kind of *hostile dependence* that marked many brother-sister relationships.[24] The idealized gender models defined "the other in mirror *opposition* to the self," thus precluding the necessity of dealing with such pressures from within the individual.[25] Combined with intense involvement and interdependence between siblings, these feelings could spill over into sexual desire, a covert theme in fiction and one that increasingly appeared in pornography of the period.[26]

Both brothers and sisters played out these psychic processes among and between each other. Whatever the externally sanctioned authority of brothers, their monopoly of resources and opportunities presented problems for overt resistance to their dictates, especially for younger sisters. Some girls and young women strongly identified with and furthered their brothers' lives and careers.[27] Others employed a variety of indirect responses to gain leverage: they might invoke the nature of the sibling tie itself, call on the love they felt for the dominant brother, try to manipulate a special relationship with a parent and/or other family member, or—a favorite device of those with less power in any relationship—delay responding to requests or directions, or simply withdraw into silence.

Modern psychologists work mainly with two-sibling families, but the situation was even more complicated in the nineteenth-century "long family," in which elder siblings could be separated by more than a decade in age from the younger so that they often exercised semi-parental authority.[28] In families of half a dozen or more children there were shifting alliances, shallower or deeper pools of affection. A brother or sister could play one off against another as well as manipulate relationships with parents and other household adults. Dyads and triads developed *within* the group, where psychic projection, identification, and repulsion among a group produced a highly complex dynamic. Aggression and caring, love and hate, desire and disgust, involvement or withdrawal could lie dormant, flare up, or shift among a multitude of players. The intricate web built up in childhood between brothers and sisters became part of an individual's internal and external worlds, their ghostly presence persisting throughout life whether or not they were present in the flesh.

The Gladstone Family

To explore these themes more fully, it is instructive to take one family as a case study.[29] The story of the Gladstone siblings may seem extreme, but for that very reason it is revealing of issues around gender, age, and birth order in their particular milieu.[30] The Gladstone family, part of the aspiring middle strata, was deeply imbued with the language and beliefs of their intensely felt evangelical religion. The children were raised in this atmosphere amid the wealth of commercial Liverpool. Their father, son of a modest Scottish tradesman, was a Liverpool merchant whose fortunes were based on trade in grain, sugar, cotton, and slaves, as well as substantial West Indian properties. Increasing wealth led to his political ambitions, mainly at the local level but eventuating in a baronetcy in old age. His position was socially enhanced by his marriage at age 34 to the 28-year-old Anne Robertson Mackenzie from a prosperous Scots family with gentry connections.[31] The children's milieu was typical of second-generation high bourgeoisie: they took for granted their lifestyle, surrounded by luxury and cared for by servants, yet were never quite sure of their social status.

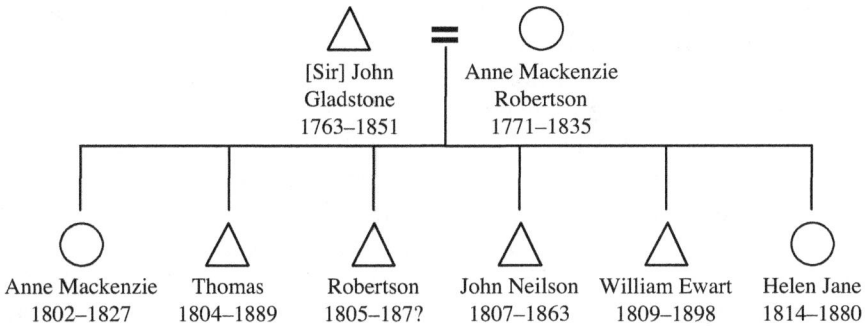

Figure 12.1. The Gladstone Family

In this period of unlimited births there might well have been more children, but their mother had begun childbearing only at age thirty, and after producing six children within the next twelve years her condition was weakened. The family was dominated by John Gladstone, who was fifty-one at the time of his last child's birth. As a virtually self-made man, he made sure that his children felt the full weight of his authority, backed by God's commands (known as "the Juggernaut" by his nieces and nephews).[32] The gentler role of an often ailing mother put guilt high on the list of parental control, allied as it was to a deeply held belief in sin and the necessity of being constantly aware of temptation. Here was a household whose everyday life was steeped in God's immediate presence, and whose denizens yearned for redemption. Self-control and discipline over one's inherently sinful nature defined ultimate virtue. The Gladstone offspring, cushioned as they were by wealth and well advanced within regional if not national economic and social circles, absorbed a paradoxical sense of self at once steeped in feelings of personal unworthiness and possessed of a highly developed self-righteousness. At least consciously, anger and rebellion could not be turned against the all-powerful God and His earthly representative, Father. According to a recent study of William Gladstone, this potent combination could feed "a pooled reservoir of rage," causing issues of anger, restraint, and authority to remain problematic through much of his life.[33]

Elder Sister: Younger Brother

The configuration of the family meant that Anne, as eldest daughter, was close to her mother; the three middle sons formed a masculine group, leaving William somewhat on his own; and Helen played the typical youngest child's role as "pet." Anne, seven years William's senior, had a semi-maternal relationship to her younger brother. Not unusually, she had become William's' godmother at age eight. Anne took her duties seriously with regard to both his intellectual and religious development, devoting to them an attention beyond the capacity of their mother and outside the interests of their father.

Brother and sister shared their deeply felt religious world. For William, Anne was the embodiment of the evangelical view of life. He always remembered her telling him as a small boy that when he arrived in Heaven, St. Peter would ask him to give an account of how he had spent every minute in his life.[34] Despite instilling a lifelong sense of guilt, she was deeply sympathetic to his struggling efforts to live up to the evangelical moral order. Above all, she listened to and soothed his doubts— about his faith, his view of the world, himself and his capacities, and his attraction to a life in the Church as opposed to his father's more worldly ambitions for him.

The boys when young all attended a small school funded and directed by their father, run by an Evangelical clergyman of his choosing. As they grew older, John Gladstone's keen social ambitions led him to send all his sons to Eton, the most aristocratic of public schools, whatever their talents and inclinations. Robertson left early to join the family firm, but Thomas struggled to stay the course. William left his sheltered and puritanical home milieu for the school in his turn, at the age of eleven. Quite aside from the formal teaching, William had to face the rough housing of everyday life in an institution that was still often chaotic and brutal. Physical conditions were harsh, the regime among both boys and masters punitive, even violent, and rivalry was endemic.[35] For example, William described playing a leading part in the Literati Society, where "the atmosphere was both friendly and competitive, with an especial emphasis on prowess of presentation and argument … both a game and a high art."[36]

William felt Anne's values and warm personality as a bulwark against the aggressive, lewd atmosphere of the public school. William took for granted her interest in all his doings, his friends, trials, and accomplishments, as when she wrote about his first debate at age fifteen: "We all congratulate you on the happy commencement of your oratorical career! You may be assured of our best wishes."[37] Anne was educated completely at home. She relayed family news and kept all her brothers up to date on each other's comings and goings. In his letters, William affectionately referred to Anne as "little witch" and the family's "Secretary of State for Foreign Affairs, Home and Colonial Department."[38]

Thomas, as oldest son, was being groomed to inherit the family estate, while Robertson was destined for the family's mercantile firm and John Neilson chose to go to sea. Young William was left to carve out a place for himself. It was Anne who listened, advised, and admonished, for example warning her young brother against being ensnared by the theater. She was instrumental in William's development as he prepared for Confirmation. At that time, he recorded in his diary that he had received a "long and most excellent and pious letter from my beloved sister—unworthy am I of such an one." Sister and brother had long conversations when William was home for the holidays.[39]

Above all it was Anne whose firm belief in her younger brother's destiny and future greatness helped William through difficult decisions about a future public life course. But by the time such career choices became imminent, Anne, who had been ill for several years with what may have been tuberculosis, was dead. In 1827, just after William had begun his first term at Oxford, he was summoned home to attend her deathbed and funeral. Anne remained for William Ewart an icon of all that women could mean, a femininity colored by suffering, especially in illness, bravely borne in an atmosphere of moral purity. Such unworldly grace set demanding standards that William strove to meet throughout his life. A few days after her death, he recorded that he felt apathetic, blaming himself for torpor of mind and habitual selfishness: "how unworthy I had been of the love and attention which the departed saint had honoured me."[40] Into his sixties he was still remembering Anne's birthday in his diary; all the more significant as it fell on Christmas Eve.

Elder Brother: Younger Sister

William's—and to a lesser extent Thomas's and Robertson's—relationship with the baby of the family, Helen Jane, was a complete contrast. Four years younger than William and a dozen years Anne's junior, she was in many ways of a different generation. She had been a bright and spirited, sometimes willful youngster. William, the petted youngest for his first four years, had been displaced by this engaging baby. Yet he was fond of her as an agreeable playmate and enjoyed having someone to look up to him as he had looked up to his elder siblings.

While Anne lived she had taken charge of Helen's life. As the eldest daughter with an invalid mother, from her early days Anne had often been especially responsible for the welfare of her young sister. When Anne was twelve and Helen only a year old, her mother wrote to her that "it is no small comfort to me to know my little pet has one who will pay every kindness and who so well apprehends all her wants."[41] It was Anne who supervised Helen's home-based education, recognizing that her young sister had "no *common share* of talent and apprehension which it has pleased God to gift her with."[42] But as her frailty increased Anne could no longer cope, and Helen, in her mid teens, was left without formal instructors, guidance, or duties. Given these circumstances, Helen's situation is a dramatic illustration of the contrast between William's informal as well as formal educational experience and his stay-at home sister's lack of external demands or competitors against whom to test herself intellectually, physically, or socially.

While William's deep distress and melancholy upon Anne's death is recorded in detail, Helen's loss has to be imagined. Still a young teenager, Helen had inherited, along with Anne's clothes, her position as daughter at home, aid to the timid, invalid mother, and companion and "little housekeeper" to her father. Her sense of desolation was compounded by measuring herself against the much older and universally admired sister, now haloed in death, which only emphasized her sense of inadequacy. "Each day teaches me how weak, how powerless I am and how sweetly bright my sister shone."[43]

At this period in their lives William's relationship to Helen mirrored what Anne's had been to him, but with a superiority born of not only age but also masculine status. William had long had the satisfaction of Helen's childhood worship of her older brother, having been her playmate while home on holiday. When he returned to Eton she missed him sorely, even calling her canary after him.[44] He took his duties as elder brother seriously—for example writing from Eton, when he was thirteen and Helen nine, to criticize her handwriting and question whether she should make better use of her time than spending it writing to him.[45] But during the dark days of Anne's final illness, the two drew even closer. Anticipating her sister's death, Helen wrote to William that "my earliest recollection of you … is as loving you almost more than any other and now cannot avoid looking to you as my principal friend, one day, perhaps my stay."[46]

In the autumn following Anne's death, when Helen was fourteen and William going on nineteen, he proposed a covenant between himself and his young sister that "we have agreed to tell one another's faults, small and great, without fear or favor." But it was William who took by far the major role, pointing out that it was his duty as the elder to make the first move. This took the form of a ten-page letter, steeped in their mutual religious language, in which he especially addressed Helen's dress and her use of time and money, first cautioning her generally: "may you carry through all your dealings with all men the blessed principle of *subordination* and resignation of your own desires, and unqualified disregard of your own conventions; when they come into collision with duty." He ends by recommending again his "old nostrum" of "appropriating specific seasons to specific purposes," in fact particularly difficult for a young teenager without supervision, purpose, work, or study to carry out.[47]

Nevertheless, Helen, overcoming her "natural pride," felt thankful toward this adored elder brother that "I was not left alone and suffered to stray further without being warned." Aside from her Heavenly Father, her darling brother was "her support, comfort and guide, from whom she can never fear anything but kindness."[48] She felt she owed her "friend, my own dear William" a great deal, not only for his advice but also for his example. In turn, as he had with Anne, William confided in Helen his attraction to a religious and scholarly path and a possible clerical career, using the youngster as a sounding board, which aroused the hurt and anger of his elder brothers in not consulting them.

A Brother Grows Up

The roots of William's determination to guide and control Helen's worldly as well as spiritual and moral development are complicated. His political coming of age had coincided with the radical questioning of established order in the agitation over the 1830s reform movement. While still at Oxford he had taken part in raucous election processions and vigorous debate, defending both church and state. He felt that the "subversion of ancient principles of political union" was particularly pernicious, as it freed "ungoverned and uninstructed self-will." From his school days onward, for William order and tradition represented stability, control, and the maintenance of a personal coherence, an issue central to his emotional as well as intellectual equilibrium throughout his life.[49]

In later life, William acknowledged that he saw in Helen many of his own traits of sensuous passion and difficulty of self-control. Given his own adolescent preoccupations, as his sister developed physically as well as emotionally, William may have felt disturbed by her burgeoning sexuality.[50] Something of this is reflected in his opinion that she was becoming too forward in dress and behavior and in the intensity of William's absorption with her state of mind, to the point where his parents became worried and asked Tom to write to William to desist from "religious speculations" with Helen.[51]

It is clear that William found the combination of what he saw in women—misfortune and suffering furthered by attractive appearance—

dangerously enticing. While still at Oxford he had become drawn to rescue work with "fallen women," whom he would accost in the streets.[52] While undoubtedly some of his fascination with the sexual underworld was motivated by a genuine desire to "uplift" these women, it extended to the use of pornography, leading to guilt-ridden anguish over masturbation and feelings of sexual desire.[53] In his middle teens he had purchased a copy of *Aristotle's Masterpiece*, the most widely used guide to sexual matters at the time, and admitted in his diary that while ostensibly looking in bookshops for political volumes he would clandestinely pour over sexually salacious material.[54]

These tussles bedeviled a young man whose sense of manhood was already divided between a spiritual and intellectual personification and his aggressively budding career as politician and statesman. As one commentator put it: "there was a kind of languor and melancholy … of scholarly, poetic temperament" in William Gladstone that did not serve him well in his public life.[55] Yet others sensed in him "repressed aggression, private torments underlying restlessness and guilt." Even in repose, Gladstone hummed with a kind of "restrained violence."[56] These have been seen as opposing aspects of his character—the intellectual as opposed to the practical. But they also represent two shifting facets of masculine identity of the period, witnessed in the almost "effeminate" averted eyes, delicate white hands, and sensuous mouth of an early portrait as contrasted with the massive head and shoulders, thin-lipped authoritarian mouth, and intense gaze of later paintings, as well as the notorious photographs of the erstwhile politician, coatless, attacking trees with his axe on his estate.[57]

To twenty-first–century sensibilities, male attitudes like William Gladstone's toward women seems naïve to a degree. He seems to have taken at face value the belief that women were a different species—pure, noble, and above all without erotic feelings or desires. In his quest for a wife, with the image of Anne always before him, he sought a woman whom God should appoint to be the guardian angel of his soul. In fact, in his wife, Catherine Glynne, he found a woman the opposite of his sisters: a down-to-earth, healthy, and competent partner. Yet long after his marriage he continued his nocturnal pursuit of high-class prostitutes in the streets—even following them to their rooms, to the chagrin of his political friends and delight of his enemies.[58]

A Sister's Youth

William's career through Oxford and beyond to his election as an MP continued to flourish, while Helen's early womanhood was spent at home as companion to her invalid mother and now elderly father. Five years later, the mother had died and Helen had seen her father through critical surgery. Whether or not she found the role of daughter at home congenial, it had given her a function within the household, although the family's intense religiosity would have limited her social contacts. Throughout Helen's twenties, William continued to exhort and instruct her, but with less and less effect. Helen—intelligent, high-spirited, and, despite her patchy education, well read in several languages—had become deeply religious, spending any energies that could be spared from the family furthering Anglican causes, though without the familial backing that her sister Anne had enjoyed. For many young women, the world of Evangelical religion provided not just a sphere for action but also an abiding belief in their direct relationship to a divine power. Submission and obedience to earthly male family members could be bypassed if seen as contradicted by duty to the heavenly Father and His Son.[59] Increasingly this seems to have been the case for Helen Gladstone, although such a judgment is mainly to be inferred by her actions and her silences.

It is difficult to glean a specific picture of Helen's condition from existing sources, covered as they are in Victorian reticence and euphemism. What is clear is that in the Gladstone household the example of the invalid mother and saintly departed Anne left the men convinced that weakness and affliction bravely borne made for the most rarefied and lovely form of womanhood. All the brothers took an intense interest in their young sister, mainly in the form of anxieties about her health. Helen was beginning to replicate her model, Anne, as when their mother commented on her daughter's health: "I must not be too sanguine ... this morning she [Helen] looked so like our departed Angel whose voice and manner she recalled."[60]

In the shadow of Anne, the family's illness-suffering womanhood model must have appeared in a positive light to Helen, for example when her mother proclaimed that although she feared Helen suffered a great deal, "they that suffer and support suffering are far happier than those who do neither."[61] Yet no amount of suffering seems to have been enough to make up for her lost sister. What must it have felt like to hear her mother's reported deathbed statement: "Oh my first—dearest—beloved—precious—she was blessed"?[62] Unlike her sister and mother, Helen did not have tuberculosis. Like her brother William, she appears to have been potentially an active and sensuous young woman with a strongly passionate nature. In the guilt-ridden culture of their home erotic desire had to be repressed, as William had to do, but for a woman, could it even be acknowledged as such?[63]

Helen would have had an orientation similar to William's in seeing self-control, bolstered by faith, as a way of overcoming feelings and desires defined as sinful. But when a woman's whole being was defined by her reproductive cycles, and these were equated with illness, such a woman "by nature" would have a potential for an invalid role.[64] Not surprisingly Helen seems to have suffered from a variety of minor problems, including what William perceived as her "gluttony," which now would be regarded as an eating disorder. As was the case with all ailments at this time, she was treated with laudanum, a concoction of opium steeped in alcohol, a remedy begun in her early teens presumably in connection with menstrual pains.

Undoubtedly Helen's condition was exacerbated by grief over Anne's death and feeling that she could never live up to her sister's standards. But it was also a function of her isolation, mostly endured in Fasque, the Scottish great house built by John Gladstone, where her main companions were her invalid mother and elderly father. Unusually for this type of family, female friends, aunts, and cousins seem to have been absent or kept at bay. Helen's temperament does not seem to have been as well suited to a domestic routine as had Anne's. But as with many upper middle-class young women at this time, her yearning for more intellectually stimulating opportunities was trivialized.[65] From early on, William had put aside Helen's attempts to learn further than her ad hoc situation afforded. When she wanted to study Latin, he wrote to her: "I do not see leaning them [classical languages] at all necessary for women."[66]

Reading between the lines, we can see that Helen's increasing reliance on drugs may have been connected to intense religious guilt punctuated by bouts of frustration and rage, leading to the outbursts that so irritated and frightened William as evidence of loss of self-control mirroring his own culpable shadows. His acknowledged resemblance to Helen elicited some sympathy for what he interpreted as her *moral* weakness. Yet he had little understanding of the fact that while he was able to channel some of his immense restless energy into physical activity and wide political and social action, enlarging his life through friendship and the challenge of maneuvering in the world outside the hothouse family atmosphere, Helen's youth was spent quietly at home with little external stimulation.

A Brother's Career: A Sister At Home

Beginning in his teenage years at Eton, William had begun to make friends with a variety of boys, some from gentry and aristocratic background above his own status. A few made a huge emotional impact, among them the "golden youth" Arthur Hallam, also the object of Tennyson's poem *In Memoriam*. William left Eton with fond memories as he moved on to Oxford. There he was surrounded by a circle of friends from school, which he widened through membership in the nascent Oxford Union and participation in numerous clubs and activities where he rubbed against a range of people, ideas, and values. Most notable was the religious "Oriel College set" that included Newman, Keble, and Pusey, the core of what became the Oxford Movement, keen to revive ritual practice within the established church.

Indeed, William's first two years at Oxford were spent in such a welter of busy occupation that his studies were somewhat neglected. The ensuing scramble to prepare for final examinations was a challenge that taught him a lifelong lesson in applying himself without stint to an external deadline and produced the reward of a double first in classics and mathematics. As was the custom, after his triumph at Oxford William set out on a continental tour with his brother, John Neilson, financed by their father. On his return, through the father of a school and college friend as well as John Gladstone's contacts, he was offered the chance to stand for a seat in Parliament that he duly won, giving a triumphant maiden speech at the age of twenty-four.

The contrast with Helen's experience could not have been greater. Her mother's ill health and shrinking personality made her ever more dependent on her daughter. This, combined with the family's strict evangelical code, meant little entry into social life either in London or when at Fasque. In such a wealthy family with its full complement of servants, her duties would not have been onerous, for her father had always had the effective running of the household. Unlike Anne, she had no troop of younger siblings to care about and direct. No weekly, monthly, or annual external deadlines were imposed to challenge her mind or engage her energy, aside from regular attendance at religious occasions, of which Helen took full advantage. In this period, most types of rigorous physical activity or sport that would have absorbed youthful restiveness and lifted her sprits were out of the question for a young lady. Outdoor activity would be at most sedate strolls in the grounds of the house or gentle "carriage exercise," that is, being driven out for an hour or two, appropriate to her feminine semi-invalid condition.

From the attractive, talented child and early adolescent, Helen intermittently descended into what can only be termed a private hell. She paid a bitter price for the fact that control of her life was totally in the hands of a loving but blinkered father and fond but striving, successful brothers. Given her period and class, only marriage could have radically altered this situation. For William, marriage had been a pressing necessity in terms of his political, sexual, and emotional life (it is speculated that he remained technically a virgin until he married at age thirty).[67] All his courting was of women higher in status, revealing an ambition that was clinched by his eventual marriage, given Catherine Glynne's gentry background and aristocratic social circle. However precipitously he had rushed into action in his three attempts to secure a wife, no such remedy was an option for his sister, for proposals were expected to be instigated by the man and she lacked mother, sisters, or female friends to expedite any potential wooing. Helen probably never knew that for several years she had been courted by the son of a neighboring business associate of her father, whom he had approached for approval as a suitor. The now elderly John Gladstone had dismissed the idea as ridiculous, filing the correspondence as "T.K. Finlay's foolish letters and my answers to them."[68]

It is significant that the periods of Helen's partially recovered health coincided with a need for her to take control of the household, first when the family considered her a rock during her mother's decline and death. Even William had been impressed by her "nerve and fortitude."[69] For the next few years she remained mistress of her father's household and his companion, mainly at Fasque. Of her intellectual, emotional, and sexual development we know nothing except what can be garnered from letters among her mainly male relatives and wholly male physicians.

There is no doubt that somewhere along the way, Helen Gladstone became addicted to opium (and probably alcohol as well). When she had occupation and a stable supply of the drug she seems to have been capable of behaving normally, and her relations with her brothers, including William, were on a more even keel.[70] Even so, their concerns over her medical condition reinforced the default position for Gladstone women. What we know of Helen's life during her twenties and thirties is that it was spent traveling to be "under" the care of one physician or another in search of some vaguely defined health. Rigorous medical regimes such as daily cold showers, warm foot baths, rest, and exercise periods were time consuming and constraining. The laudanum she was being treated with and subsequent attempts at its withdrawal increasingly becoming the principal cause of her physical and mental problems.

Pathways to Adulthood: Sexuality, Marriage, and Religion

In 1838 William was out office, and his two attempted marriage proposals to aristocratic women had been rejected. In a state of some distress he accompanied Helen to the continent, leaving her in a German spa under the care of family friends. Although diary entries show his guilt at leaving her, he went on to join the Glynne party in Italy for nascent wooing of Catherine. Released from the direct presence of father and brothers, Helen, now twenty-four, seems to have recovered. She met and became engaged to a Polish aristocrat, whom she significantly described as "a stouter edition of William." However, the marriage would have removed her entirely from her family's reach.[71] At one level William was pleased for his sister, but he was suspicious of the count's motives and deeply disturbed at the thought of Helen moving to such an alien culture. Remarkably, he was not the first to be told, having learned about the affair only through friends: "a line from her would I think have done everything."[72]

William need not have worried, for the count's family refused to sanction the match. As the potential marriage plans petered out, Helen was forced to return to Fasque. Meanwhile William's third attempt at marriage had culminated in a double wedding in which Catherine's sister Mary married one of William's close friends, the aristocratic George Lyttelton. All the Gladstone brothers were now on the way to successful careers. Thomas, in line for the family estate, was an MP, as was John Neilson, now a rising naval officer, while Robertson, established in the family business, flourished in Liverpool political circles. All were now married, although William and Helen had been censorious about Thomas's Unitarian wife. None of the Gladstone brothers' wives seem to have welcomed what was considered their irksome sister-in-law. Catherine Glynne was exceptionally close to her own sister, Mary. In their wifely and maternal roles (between them they eventually produced twenty-four children), they had little patience with Helen's preoccupations. Catherine also, perhaps, sensing the intense nature of Helen and William's relationship, showed scant compassion for the young woman, considering her tiresomely hysterical.

Back at Fasque, Helen's condition deteriorated, and she was sent once more to try the ministrations of a variety of medical men. Unmarried Aunt Johanna Robertson, her mother's sister who had always been fond of her niece, was assigned to be her companion and relay constant bulletins about Helen's condition. She was now under constant surveillance; every item of her diet and minute of her day was overseen and reported on by doctors and carers. Her attempt at fasting and her preference to slip out for early morning worship as part of her intense religious commitment were negated on medical grounds.

There is no doubt that Helen's condition deeply disturbed William. It is believed that his passionate performance in the parliamentary debate over the Chinese Opium Wars was fueled by personal experience of her addiction. He was also increasingly uneasy about reports of his sister's attendance at "Romish" chapels in London. He warned Helen of the danger, not least to his political career, if these had substance. She did not deny her increasing involvement with Roman Catholicism but refused to discuss the subject with him. Unprepared by the rumors, the family was struck by a bombshell in the spring of 1842. Helen, age twenty-seven, had been received into the Roman Catholic Church, a move William only heard about from his father. William's views and feelings on this subject were deep-seated but complicated. Quite aside from the damage to his political prospects by the taint of popery, this was anathema to his evangelical soul. His beloved sister Anne, like her mother, had been bitterly opposed to Catholic emancipation in the 1830s and considered Catholicism despicable. He had gone deeply into these questions in his just-published book, *The State in Relation to the Church*, and felt hurt that Helen had not consulted him on the subject. And yet William himself was uneasy with the formalistic Anglican Church services and drawn to the ritual and beauty of the Roman Church.

Despite desperate attempts to keep the matter from the public, an announcement in the press headlined Helen's conversion, allowing the world to "read the record of our shame," as William bitterly remarked.[73] William's anger at Helen's move was accentuated by his awareness of many high-profile Anglicans' increasing sympathy for Catholic ritual and dogma, including some of his closest friends from Oxford days. His sister's conversion also coincided with a period of uncertainly in his career, as he had been voted out of Parliament and his financial affairs were going badly. His mood is expressed in a ten-page letter to Helen that indicates his fury, hurt, and feeling of abandonment:

> The recollection that there was a time—although many years back—when we had, or seemed to have, religious union and communication, makes me feel that the event announced yesterday demands from me a few words. I AM STUNNED BY THE MAGNITUDE OF THE JUDGEMENT WHICH IT HAS PLEASED God to send upon you, and upon us: stunned but not surprised, for causes which have been very long in operation. ... That which I have to testify solemnly to you, to you the fruit of my mother's womb, and the beloved associate of my earliest years is this: you have not been an inquirer: you have not endeavoured to inform and discipline yourself respecting the immense issue upon which you have found what you think to be a judgement. ... Have you yet to learn, that it is along the path of obedience and docility, of self denial and self subjugation, that God leads His children into truth?

He goes on to query where she derives the authority to make such a decision: "You have, as it seems by some marvellous Divine ordering, been led to confess that the act you meditate is one of private judgement. But I say it is even less than this. It is one of private will. You have followed instinct and bias." He rhetorically admits that she will ask what right has he to dogmatize. He answers himself that his smattering of inquiry, although narrow, is wide compared to hers (all too true given their unequal circumstances). Although he knows she has acted sincerely, this very fact is the proof of her deep delusion.

> Mark again my words. *This* delusion is not your first. It is the completion of a web, which for many years you have been weaving around you, and which by progressive degrees has enveloped all your faculties and deprived you of true vision. *Not in religion alone.* This last step was not needed to prove, but merely illustrates the fact, that you are living, and have long been living, a life of utter self deception. Not in religion alone—but in all bodily, in all mental habits—in all personal and in all social relations. ... For a very long time you have not known what *study* is; the whole action of your naturally powerful mind has been dissipated and relaxed ... of the subtle and wayward will which has for so long distorted your life and destroyed its liberty, its peace and usefulness—alas! ... is the latest [delusion] born of a whole family of delusions, pervading your life from the highest concerns of your soul down to your very diet and clothing.

He will now open to her the "sealed book" of his opinion of her, which is "that five years have now elapsed since, in discussing matters relating to your health, *I* told my Father that I regarded you as morally beside yourself, and urged upon him that the only way to restore you to yourself ... was to put constraint and coercion upon you."[74]

Frustration at his inability to reach, much less influence Helen, heightened by fears about his own efforts at self-control, lie behind William's almost sadistic outburst in his diary entry for the day following writing the letter: "I write, as one would drag a woman by the hair, to save her from drowning. The best I can hope for is that she should find the words keen and piercing; such ills as these are not curable except by searching pain."[75] Fortunately for Helen, her father, although anxious about her condition and autocratic in his authority, took her conversion seriously. He refused William's demands that Helen should be banished from the family home and allowed her to receive priests in his house on condition that he oversee all her temporal arrangements.[76] Three years later Helen, now aged thirty-one, once again left for Germany but was followed by William, despite the fact that his political career needed nursing and Catherine had very recently given birth to another daughter. There he trailed after his sister, settling in the spa town of Baden.

It was also at this time that his rescue work took a more disturbing turn. As political and financial pressures mounted, a pattern emerged whereby William would first descend into what he regarded as moral weakness, manifested in susceptibility to pornography and enticing responses to his chosen fallen women "cases."[77] Then, after such episodes, he began to scourge himself with a small whip, following the example of his Anglo-Catholic friends. Finding Helen sunk into a desperate state—to the extent that he witnessed her having to be held down—must have inflamed all his own fears about falling into an abyss of unrestrained appetites. Like most educated people, including physicians, he believed that such behavior, even insanity, could be cured by regaining self-discipline under a regime of "moral management."[78] But this solution was hard to practice in the intense individualism of the evangelical tradition inherited from their mother.[79] Whereas Helen had sought support in Roman Catholicism, he found it in the companionship of like-minded ex-Oxonian high church Anglicans, mainly young men moving in high society. To counteract their worldly surroundings, they had come together in concern for good works among the needy in a group self-titled as "The Engagement." They gave William external ratification for his contacts with prostitutes, for he admitted that on his own his conscience was too weak to limit their impact.

It was in this heightened state, when William was with Helen in Germany and keenly aware of her distress, that he drew up what he called the "Baden Rules." This characteristically included meticulous listing of the conditions in which temptations to his "chief besetting sin" might arise. The following list of remedies included prayer, immediate pain, self-examination, and injunctions not to look at images, for example in print shop windows, a prime site for the pornography flooding in with novel forms of reproduction.[80]

Control, Resistance, and Confinement: The Crisis Period

William's heavy-handed concern about his sister is to some extent understandable as Helen's addiction to opium was growing, but the intensity of his punitive hostility still seems out of proportion. William was later joined in his pursuit by their brother Thomas. They had extracted a letter from their father giving authority to fetch her home, and another from her English priest telling her to obey her father's wishes and threatening to cut off her funds.[81] For days she locked her door against the brothers and the doctor, drinking any opiates she could get hold of. If William forced his way in, he might find her paralyzed in both arms and speechless. Her father pleaded with William to treat her with "mildness and consideration" while she was in this extremity. But William was writing to Catherine that nothing "except the expedient we have so often talked of—an engagement to universal obedience" would be of any use and that "the channels of common interest and feeling between a brother and sister are frozen up."[82]

During this period Thomas kept a record of Helen's condition. Clearly she was in a state of breakdown. Once he found her squatted on the ground with nothing on but her night shift, eating on the floor. Pitifully, she had told the doctor that she feared people would think she was going mad. She gave a letter to her German doctor giving him full power to restrain her for her health, even against her own will, but hoping he would not enable force by others (obviously William if not Thomas). The doctor gave her an ultimatum that she see her brothers and return home, or go to Italy with him. At this, Helen effectively dismissed him. Thomas felt that she "will dislike anyone whom she cannot influence and rule over." A note from Helen in January 1846 states lucidly and firmly: "My dear Tom—my answer is given, and to my father directly. I must beg to decline any personal discussion with yourself or with William and I do so from no want of right feeling to either you or him."[83]

By December, doctors were advising against the proposal that Helen be given a limited income from her father and left to her own devices. Rather, she should be "committed to the command of herself entirely to others appointed by her father," for she might get into debt and "a great many misfortunes" if she was allowed to act independently.[84] Pushed to extremes, Helen made a bid to escape. The exact order of events is not clear, but it seems that she tried to go to some of her Catholic friends. Thomas discovered that Helen was trying to sell some jewelry through her maid to finance this plan, and he immediately took steps to dismiss the woman. The bewildered Thomas noted that Helen "says it would be death for her to stay where she is but where will she go ... she is fierce against all of us—told Estelle (the maid) that she would bring her brothers to their knees to her before a month." While the brothers continued to regard this 32-year-old woman as a grown child, chiding her for going out alone or for staying out late, Helen continued to resist through silence and visiting the Catholic friends who had become her alternative world.

By mid January 1846, now firmly back in England, Helen had been confessed by her English priest, who the brothers disgustedly learned was backing her present course. She was also meeting Estelle at the home of a Catholic lawyer. At this point, Helen seems to have had several doctors on her side whom the brothers believed had been completely taken in by her. They also suspected she had sold family valuables. At last

Thomas heard that Helen had finally written to their father—but only "with sheets of grievances." William had also had a note announcing her departure and saying again that she could not endure life in the London family home.[85]

Eventually some compromise was reached and Helen agreed to go back with her father. Gradually her health and peace of mind began to return. At the end of the following year, Helen wrote to William begging for forgiveness for her past conduct, reaffirming her unmixed respect for him in the past and future and wishing anxiously that he know how she valued his love and esteem "from the depths of my heart. ... I feel that I have no other claim upon you, than that of our common blood and of your charity and if these may so far avail I ask you to try and not regret my father's great and unhoped for fondness toward me. ... If my father, who has so much to forgive, can pardon, may I not hope from you?"[86] Despite such approaches, William remained convinced that Helen's whole life commitment via her conversion was not genuine. He told their father that she was not "a convinced Roman Catholic" but that her feelings were "emotional and superficial," and he begged that priests be kept away.

However, matters threatened to go beyond the troubled waters of the Gladstone family when the commissioners in lunacy met to consider a report alleging that Helen Gladstone had been illegally confined on the top floor of the family's London house. By this time Helen had made friends with the Catholic lawyer Henry Bagshawe and his wife, whose son became her godchild and eventual heir. It was Bagshawe who took up Helen's case with the commissioners. The Gladstones vigorously refuted the accusation and the case was dropped, but not before William and Tom had privately met the chairman of the commissioners, Lord Ashley, at the Carleton Club to "arrange matters quietly with him."[87]

Despite the commissioner's withdrawal of the charge, her father's and brothers' methods of control appear draconian. Helen's one constant ally, her maid, had been replaced by Mary, the head housemaid from Fasque, who was detailed to keep a constant watch and report back directly to her father. To this end he instructed William that in the London house "there will be only one approach and that through the dressing room where Mary is to sleep ... that nothing whatsoever or person of any description is to have access to Helen without either your or Tom's or the Doctor's consent ... her food and medicine is all to be directed by him and none else."[88]

In fact, Helen managed to leave for Bath with Catholic friends, only to be returned to Fasque, where a similar regime was instituted. Her father, on whom she was financially completely dependent, reminded her that he had consented to her religious conversion only on condition that she would be advised by his guidance and direction in all temporal concerns. Everything from clothing to the state of her teeth was to be open to inspection and governance by caretakers, father, and brothers. Despite this regime Helen held fast to her religious commitment, but continued as an invalid, struggling, making what seem to have been several suicide attempts. She was now in her mid thirties, yet her life was dominated by the men around her: father, brothers, doctors, priests.

When confinement at home did not seem to produce results she was sent to Leamington Spa under a female minder, Mrs. Elliott, appointed by the well-known physician Dr. Jephson, who was known as a specialist in such cases. A clergyman's wife and friend of the Gladstones, Elizabeth Rawson, was to oversee Helen's welfare. What exactly went on under Dr. Jephson's ministrations is not possible to disentangle from the records, partly because of Victorian reticence about discussing intimate details. Mrs. Elliott had taken Elizabeth Rawson to Helen's rooms to show her some "surgical instruments" used by Jephson, but it is not clear for what purpose. Jephson had reported to her father that aside from the opium addiction, Helen's problems had "another cause" so delicate as to be only discussed privately with her father.

Hints and innuendo make it probable that this was some expression of sexual behavior and that the "instruments" referred to the vaginal speculum.[89] Even Mrs. Elliott complained on Helen's behalf about the absence of any companions or pocket money and insisted that Dr. Jephson displayed no sympathy for his patient. He had called her "wicked, the worst case I have ever seen," in contrast to the tone of his bland letters to her father.[90] Jephson, a "miniature martinet," even forbade access to her maternal Aunt Johannah Robertson: "she shall not see her niece as I am sure it would do much serious permanent mischief."[91]

With no improvement Helen was moved to Edinburgh under a Dr. Miller. Like Jephson, he was annoyed at the behavior of what he regarded as a recalcitrant patient. He reported that he had called on Helen at 1 p.m. "and found that she had left home at 7 a.m. for the nunnery and had not returned. This is so flagrant an infraction of everything like medical subordination" that he would not continue attendance "*without* a distinct understanding on the part of Miss Gladstone that she will be at least somewhat obedient to my advice," suggesting that "measures be taken, as soon as convenient to remove her to Fasque away from temptation to such imprudence."[92]

Eventually Helen was allowed into the care of Aunt Johannah, who had always been fond of her niece. There her most distressing symptoms—the clenched hands and locked jaws (which could be interpreted as symbolic of her lack of action and voice)—were miraculously cured by the intervention of a Catholic cardinal using a relic of a saint and backed by prayers from Catholic supporters. As can be imagined, these events and the publicity surrounding them did not go down well with the Gladstone men. Helen did indeed return to Fasque, and in attending to her father's decline into old age seems to have acquired some purpose in her life congruent with her religious practice that eased her partial recovery from both her symptoms and use of opiates. Her loneliness was alleviated by the appointment of a personal maid, Ann Watkins, who stayed devoted to her for the rest of her life.

Parting of the Ways: Unfinished Business

After their father's death, Helen, now thirty-eight, refused provision given her to stay at Fasque and left for the continent. From then on, the main contact between her and the brothers related to business affairs, as they had control over her finances. She especially resented that she had been given only a life interest in her inheritance, which would go to her brothers after her death.[93] She was convinced that because she had never married she should have received the equivalent to their marriage portions, of which William had persuaded their father to allow her only half. In the struggles over this issue, the brothers were particularly annoyed at Helen's delay in answering queries or signing documents, invoking yet again the silence and evasions that had been one of the few tactics available to her in dealing with them. The fundamental issue at stake was their recognition of her as an adult woman. Her dilemma was that in the ethos of her time and class, this could only be fully claimed if she had married and had children. With dignity she put her case centered on a plea for fairness and autonomy:

> I do not seek to increase my own wealth from any wish to possess or enjoy it; I have wished simply to act on what I was told was justice. I should be perfectly willing to waive all rights that I have been informed are mine at once and forever if it were agreed to place me in something like the position which marriage would place me ... leaving me free to follow what my conscience might dictate, and with regard to the capital at my death, giving me that control over it, which children of mine would, unhesitatingly enjoy.[94]

Helen spent most of the rest of her life in various convents, eventually becoming a lay member of the Order of St. Dominic and adopting nun's clothing. Although never free from her addiction, in this atmosphere she seems to have found some peace and opportunity for rewarding work.[95]

From this base, relations with her family were restored to the point where she visited William's home and came to be familiar with his and Catherine's seven children. Nevertheless, she remained unconvinced of her brothers' affection. William had refused to name one of his daughters after her until their father had chided him that Helen's religion was her own affair. He relented only by saying he would use the name Helen after an elderly aunt who had just died, not his sister.[96]

Tensions between the brothers and Helen were eased after Sir John's death, for like many siblings they had vied over attention and favors from their parent. (In his diary William noted that the only time he had kissed his father was on his deathbed.[97]) William in particular resented his sister's special relationship with their father—which had, in any case, been obligatory given her status as an only, unmarried daughter who was also financially dependent on paternal good will. It had also irked William that his father's authoritative intervention hindered his own elder brother dominance over this younger sister.

Over the years, William continued to carp at Helen in his correspondence. Once again in 1874, on a visit to Germany, determined to bring her back to the fold, he tried to persuade her to give up Roman Catholicism and return with him to his country seat, Harwarden, that he had acquired through Catherine's family. He warned her of the "paralysing effects of inertia," although in fact she led an active life of good works within the convent community. During the visit he even asked for her help in writing a pamphlet *against* the Roman Catholic Church. Although she no longer feared him, this visit worried her until she felt ill, whereas Gladstone, rather spitefully, wrote his wife that the day following the interview Helen was fine and able to walk for miles in the mountains. Catherine, again bemused and possibly somewhat jealous, begged William to leave Helen alone and come home.[98] As late as 1878, when Helen had failed to repay a loan of £20 and to send a promised £50 for a charity, William wrote: "A parcel arrived from you a few days ago. It contains I have no doubt a gift or gifts kindly intended by you for me, or for us." But, he informs her, it would remain unopened: "I can have no other concern with it while matters remain as they are."[99]

These complicated feelings are illustrated in one tragicomic episode in 1848, toward the end of the period of Helen's most severe breakdown in health and struggles with the family. It also coincided with a time when William suffered from both public pressure and emotional/sexual angst. On a visit when Helen was back living with her father at Fasque, William discovered some Protestant texts from the library with pages torn out in the water closet next to Helen's bedroom—why he was in her most private of spaces, accessible only through her bedroom, raises some questions—"under circumstances which admit of no doubt as to the shameful use to which they were put. ... You have no right to perpetrate these indignities against any religion sincerely held." He threatened to tell their father unless she promised never again to tear up the works of Protestant theologians for use as toilet paper.[100] Twice she refused to reply to William's threats, again using silence and defiant covert behavior to express stifled feelings.

Eventually Helen slipped away from the control of her male relatives, especially William, yet at a formidable personal cost. Although her life in the convent appears to have been peaceful, and she was intermittently able to partially give up dependency on opiates, she still retained some emotional involvement with the family in England. In a final attempt to draw his sister back into the fold after her death, William insisted on bringing her body to England to be buried in the family vault according to the rites of the Church of Scotland: "It is my conviction that in loyalty to her we are absolutely bound, when we take her remains to England, to exclude any interposition by a Roman Catholic." His self-delusion on this matter is expressed in almost wistful terms: "Is not all this most extraordinary and a perfect and substantial proof that she lived and died in unity with us ... ?"[101]

Conclusion

As in so many of these struggles between family members, issues over control and recognition fueled by intense emotions lay at the root of Helen's relationships with her brothers, especially William. His angry, punitive attempts to dominate her display a side of his character that historical commentators have found highly troubling. Yet the brother and sister's intense interaction is characteristic of close sibling bonds generally, here molded by their particular historical world and expressed through a deeply religious, highly moralized idiom. In his early twenties, in a letter to Helen, William was disarmingly frank about the characteristics in himself that he later excoriated in her. "The one thing I *dread* is the fierceness of internal excitement, and that from experience as well as anticipation, I *do* dread. May God pour on it his tranquillising influence. It is very painful to feel myself mastered by turbulent emotions which one can condemn but not control."[102]

Catherine Gladstone recognized that for all his formidable controlled energy, sense of purpose, and high-minded morality, William had a darker side. She perceptively described his duality: "impetuous, impatient, irrestrainable, the other all self-control—able to dismiss all but the great central aim. Able to put aside what is weakening or disturbing—self-mastery achieved with great struggle, partly through prayer."[103] Alas, for Helen, circumstances, especially her gender, deprived her of any such "great central aim." While William was able to discuss and argue with friends, colleagues, and rivals, to declare his opinions in public through political oratory and a flood of books and pamphlets on both spiritual and temporal issues, Helen had no voice to express similar struggles or place to exchange views except within the private confines of the Roman church.[104]

For William, as for many Victorian middle- and upper-class men obsessed with a sense of sin, it was a good woman's role in life to be the helpmeet to flawed masculinity in keeping such disturbing urges within the bounds of morality. In his eyes all women were moral but were also weak. Women should use their moral courage to overcome this weakness. His mother and to an even greater extent his sister Anne were the prototype of this vision. These expectations were compounded by age and position in the family: Anne as older guide and protector, Helen as the younger sister, dependent and submissive. Helen, however—independent of spirit but driven to a frenzy by frustration and lack of opportunity for action—failed to comply, keeping her brother at arm's length. Her openly expressed appetites represented the other side of the equation, too close not only to his own weaknesses but also to what he saw in the "fallen women" who so fascinated as well as repelled upright citizens.[105]

The detailed and numerous studies of William Ewart Gladstone's life and character have given scant attention to the sisters' possible influence on his political career.[106] A case study such as this, set in historical context, could give voice to these silences in the record. However, the purpose here has been to focus on the material life chances and psychic development of sisters as well as brothers and on the way gender was played out in the crucible of familial relationships.

Notes

1. This chapter is a revised and extended version of the article "Kinship as a Categorical Concept: A Case Study of Nineteenth-Century Siblings," which appeared in *Journal of Social History* 39 (2005). My thanks to Megan Doolittle, Janet Fink, and Katherine Holden and to the editors of this volume for their helpful comments.
2. There was a court case thirty years after his death concerning his relationship to prostitutes. See Anne Isba, *Gladstone and Women* (London, 2006).

3. The intricate relationship among the Gladstone *brothers* is a related but separate story. See S.G. Checkland, *The Gladstones: A Family Biography 1764–1851* (Cambridge, 1971). This chapter does *not* attempt to deal explicitly with the relationship of William Gladstone's personal life to his political career. For a psychological focus see Travis L. Crosby, *The Two Mr. Gladstones: A Study in Psychology and History* (New Haven, 1997). Unlike women's history, the analysis of connections between men's private and public life in terms of gender construction has only recently begun. For an outstanding example, see Paul White, *Thomas Huxley: Man of Science* (Cambridge, 2003).

4. Ruth Clayton Windscheffel, "Politics, Portraiture and Power: Reassessing the Public Image of William Ewart Gladstone," in *Public Men, Masculinity and Politics in Modern Britain*, ed. Matthew McCormack (Basingstoke, 2007).

5. Jonathan Barry and Christopher Brooks, ed., *The Middling Sort of People: Culture, Society and Politics in England 1550–1800* (London, 1994); Nicholas Rogers, "Introduction to Special Issue on the Middle Classes," *Journal of British Studies* 32 (1995); Margaret Hunt, *The Middling Sort: Commerce, Gender and Family 1680–1780* (Berkeley, 1996); Alan Kidd and David Nicholls, eds., *Gender, Civic Culture and Consumerism: Middle Class Identity in Britain: 1800–1990* (Manchester, 1999); Alan Kidd and David Nicholls, eds., *The Making of the English Middle Class? Studies of Regional and Cultural Diversity Since the Eighteenth Century* (Stroud, 1999); Richard Trainor, "The Middle Class," in *The Cambridge Urban History of Britain*, ed. Martin Daunton (Cambridge, 2000), 673–713.

6. The early romantic sense of self as well as the self lurking behind emerging rational economic man were directed almost wholly to norms of masculinity, what it meant to be a man. See Leonore Davidoff, "Regarding Some 'Old Husband's Tales': Public and Private in Feminist History," in *Worlds Between: Historical Perspectives on Gender and Class* (Cambridge, 1995).

7. What Robert Connell has termed the elements of "hegemonic masculinity." This section is based on the analysis in John Tosh, "The Old Adam and the New Man: Emerging Themes in the History of English Masculinity 1750–1850," in John Tosh, *Manliness and Masculinities in Nineteenth Century Britain* (Harlow, 2005), chapter 3.

8. J. A. Mangan and James Walvin, "Introduction," in *Manliness and Morality: Middle-class Masculinity in Britain and America 1800–1940*, ed. J. A. Mangan and James Walvin (Manchester, 1987), 1–23, here 3.

9. Lisa Z. Sigel, *Governing Pleasures: Pornography and Social Change in England 1815–1914* (New Brunswick, 2002).

10 John Gillis, *A World of Their Own Making: Myth, Ritual and the Quest for Family Values* (New York, 1996); Eileen Yeo, "The Creation of 'Motherhood' and Women's Responses in Britain and France, 1750–1914," *Women's History Review* 8 (1999): 201–218, here 201.

11. Leonore Davidoff, *Thicker than Water: Sisters and Brothers in Nineteenth-Century Britain* (Oxford, 2011).

12. Leonore Davidoff and Catherine Hall, *Family Fortunes: Men and Women of the English Middle Class, 1780–1850* (London, 2002).

13. Leonore Davidoff, "Class and Gender in Victorian England: The Case of Hannah Cullwick and A.J. Munby," in *Worlds Between: Historical Perspectives on Gender and Class* (Cambridge, 1995), 103–150.

14. Sigmund Freud, "On the Universal Tendency to Debasement in the Sphere of Love," in Freud, *On Sexuality* (Harmondsworth, 1977), 251–254.

15. David Yacovonne, "Surpassing the Love of Women: Victorian Manhood and the Language of Fraternal Love," in Laura McCall and David Yacovonne, *A Shared Experience: Women, Men and the History of Gender* (New York, 1998), 195–229; Sharon Marcus, *Between Women: Friendship, Desire and Marriage in Victorian England* (Princeton, 2007).
16. Michael Curtain, *Property and Position: A Study of Victorian Manners* (New York, 1987); Marjorie Morgan, *Manners, Morals and Class in England 1774–1858* (Basingstoke, 1994).
17 Isaac Taylor, *Self Cultivation Recommended* (London, 1817), 24.
18. Elaine Showalter, *The Female Malady: Women, Madness and English Culture: 1830–1980* (London, 1987).
19. Mary Anne Hedge, "On the Reciprocal Duties of Brother and Sister," in Hedge, *My Own Fireside* (Colchester, 1832), 116–118.
20. George Eliot, "Brother and Sister," *The Spanish Gypsy* (Edinburgh, 1901), 579.
21. Prophacy Coles, *The Importance of Sibling Relationships in Psychoanalysis* (London, 2003); Robert Sanders, *Sibling Relationships: Theory and Issues for Practice* (Basingstoke, 2004).
22. Juliet Mitchell, *Siblings: Sex and Violence* (Cambridge, 2003), viii.
23. Coles, *Importance of Sibling Relationships*.
24. Stepher P. Bank and Michael D. Kahn, *The Sibling Bond* (New York, 1982).
25. Jessica Benjamin, *The Bonds of Love: Psychoanalysis, Feminism, and the Problem of Domination* (New York, 1988), 223.
26. Valerie Sanders, *The Brother-Sister Culture in Nineteenth-Century Literature: From Austen to Woolf* (Basingstoke, 2002); J. B. Twitchell, *Forbidden Partners: The Incest Taboo in Modern Culture* (New York, 1987).
27. After the death of her fiancée, Sarah Disraeli threw herself into helping her brother, Benjamin, in his political career as housekeeper and companion until he married. Michael Polowetzky, *Prominent Sisters: Mary Lamb, Dorothy Wordsworth and Sarah Disraeli* (London, 1996).
28. See Davidoff, *Thicker than Water.*
29. There is, meanwhile, a striking resemblance to the relationship of Alice James to her brothers, especially Henry. See Jean Strouse, *Alice James* (London, 1992).
30. While at one time birth order alone was the focus of sibling studies, this is being recognized as only one factor in a complicated picture. See Frank J. Sulloway, *Born to Rebel: Birth Order, Family Dynamics and Creative Lives* (London, 1996); and for a critique B. Powell, L. C. Steedman, and J. Freese, "Rebel Without a Cause: Birth Order and Social Attitudes," *American Sociological Review* 64 (1999): 207–231.
31. John Gladstone was a widower without children at the time of his marriage to Anne Robertson.
32. Checkland, *The Gladstones*, xii.
33. Crosby, *The Two Mr. Gladstones*, pp 15–16.
34. Richard Deacon, *The Private Life of Mr. Gladstone* (London, 1965), 29.
35. John Chandos, *Boys Together: English Public Schools 1800–1864* (Oxford, 1985).
36. H. C. G. Matthew, *Gladstone: 1809–1898* (Oxford, 1997).
37. Letter from Anne M. to William E., 1 November 1825, Flintshire Record Office, Gladstone Collection, No 605.
38. Isba, *Gladstone and Women*, 5.
39. M. R. D. Foot, ed., *The Gladstone Diaries* (Oxford, 1968), vol. 1, 53. This type of moral oversight of boys at school or in apprenticeships by a home-based elder sister was by no means unusual. See, for example, Judith Flanders, *The Circle of Sisters:*

   Alice Kipling, Georgiana Burne-Jones, Agnes Poynter, and Louisa Baldwin (London, 2001), 51.

40. Foot, *The Gladstone Diaries*, 228.
41. Isba, *Gladstone and Women*, 4.
42. Letter from Anne M. to William E., 30 March 1824, Gladstone Coll. No 605.
43. Checkland, *The Gladstones*, 230.
44. Ibid., 165.
45. Isba, *Gladstone and Women*, 51.
46. Letter from Helen Jane to William E., 2 February 1829, Gladstone Coll. No 629.
47. Letter William E. to Helen J., 10 November 1829, Gladstone Coll. No 751.
48. Letter Helen J. to William E., 18 November 1829, Gladstone Coll. No 629.
49. Crosby, *The Two Mr. Gladstones*, 20.
50. Isba, *Gladstone and Women*, 10.
51. Shannon, *Gladstone*, 25.
52. Matthew, *Gladstone*, 91–93.
53. These were rooted not only in religiously inspired notions of sin but also in fear that impotence would result. Michael Mason, *The Making of Victorian Sexuality* (Oxford, 1994).
54. See Davidoff, "Class and Gender in Victorian England."
55. Windscheffel, "Politics, Portraiture and Power," 97.
56. Crosby, *The Two Mr. Gladstones*, 2–3.
57. Windscheffel, "Politics, Portraiture and Power."
58. This mixture of sexual attraction and inability to view women as full-bodied human beings reached a peak in his relationship with the ex-courtesan Laura Thistlethwayte, with whom he was involved late in life. She titillated him by slowly releasing installments of her "autobiography," detailing the many personal slights and adventures she had supposedly overcome.
59. See Midori Yamaguchi, "The Religious Rebellion of a Clergyman's Daughter," *Women's History Review* 16 (2007): 641–660.
60. Isba, *Gladstone and Women*, 11.
61. Ibid., 11.
62. Ibid., 26.
63. Upper middle-class girls appeared to have had more freedom than their continental counterparts, resulting in some innocent flirting but giving little sexual knowledge. Mason, *The Making of Victorian Sexuality*. Desire in women in this period has only recently been seriously studied. Marcus, *Between Women*.
64. Barbara Harrison, "Women and Health," in *Women's History: 1850–1945*, ed. June Purvis (London, 1995). It may be significant that in his youth Tom had a series of illnesses from which he subsequently recovered, "toughened" by a rather miserable spell at Eton.
65. For example, when William Sewell found his younger sister Elisabeth reading Butler's highly influential religious text, *Analogy*, he told her she was not capable of understanding serious theological works, and she never again admitted to having read the book. Eleanor Sewell, ed., *The Autobiography of Elizabeth M. Sewell* (London, 1908).
66. Isba, *Gladstone and Women*, 52
67. M.R.D. Foot and H. C. D. Matthew, *The Gladstone Diaries*, vol, 3 (Oxford, 1974), liv.
68. Ibid., 69.
69. Checkland, *The Gladstones*, 287.

70. This type of addiction need not necessarily lead to incapacity and deterioration if the supply of the drug is stable and other life situations are favorable. Information kindly supplied by Marion Bernstein, St. Thomas's Hospital, London.
71. Checkland, *The Gladstones*, 290.
72. Foot, *The Gladstone Diaries*, 6 December 1838, vol. 2.
73. Clipping from Birmingham paper, Gladstone Coll. No 630.
74. Letter of William E. to Helen J., 30 May 1842, Gladstone Coll. No. 751. The impetus to lock away seemingly wayward young women did not, unfortunately, end in the nineteenth century. See Diana Gittins, *Madness in Its Place: Narratives of Severalls Hospital 1913–1997* (London, 1998).
75. Foot and Matthew, *The Gladstone Diaries*, vol. 3, 202.
76. Philip Magnus, *Gladstone: A Biography* (London, 1954), 82.
77. William was beset by a similar period, "lacerated and I may say barely conscious morally," of pursuing prostitutes and looking at pornography in the early 1850s, when he was cut off from two of his closest friends and advisors, James Hope and Henry Manning, who had converted to Roman Catholicism. Richard Aldous, *The Lion and the Unicorn: Gladstone Versus Disraeli* (London, 2006), 55.
78. Showalter, *Female Malady*.
79. William had never experienced the conversion experience expected of evangelicals. H. C. G. Matthew, "Gladstone, Evangelicalism and 'The Engagement,'" in *Revival and Religion Since 1700: Essays in Honor of J.C. Walsh*, ed. Jane Garnett and H. C. G. Matthew (London, 1993).
80. Crosby, *The Two Mr. Gladstones*, 56; also see Sigel, *Governing Pleasures*.
81. Magnus, *Gladstone: A Biography*, 71.
82. Ibid., 74–75.
83. Papers of Sir Thomas Gladstone, 1844–46, Gladstone Coll. No. 1304.
84. The brothers could have feared Helen falling into the hands of fortune hunters.
85. Papers of Sir Thomas Gladstone, 13, 16, 18 and 19 January.
86. Letter of Helen to William, 12 May 1846, Gladstone Coll. No 630.
87. Magnus, *Gladstone: A Biography*, 81–82. Gladstone's diary entries record several meetings with Ashley in the days preceding the hearing. For the practice of controlling women through incarceration in lunatic asylums, see Showalter, *Female Malady*.
88. Isba, *Gladstone and Women*, 60.
89. This interpretation depends heavily on Isba, *Gladstone and Women*, 105; uncontrolled sexuality in women seemed almost a defining symptom. Medical intervention in such cases included putting leeches on the labia and cervix: Showalter, *Female Malady*, 74.
90. Isba, *Gladstone and Women*, 62.
91. Checkland, *The Gladstones*, 170; letter from Dr. Jephson, 2 November 1847, Gladstone Collection No 360.
92. Letter from Dr. Miller, 8 November 1848, Gladstone Coll. No. 360.
93. She received £65,000 compared to Tom's £277,000. Checkland, *Gladstones*, 375.
94. Letter Helen Jane to William, 24 July 1853, Gladstone Coll. No. 629.
95. See Barbara Walsh, *Roman Catholic Nuns in England and Wales 1800–1937* (Dublin, 2002).
96. Magnus, *Gladstone: A Biography*, 60.
97. H. C. G. Matthew, *Gladstone: 1809–1874* (Oxford, 1988), 101.
98. Magnus, *Gladstone: A Biography*, 234.
99. Matthew, *Gladstone: 1809–1898*, 329.

100. Letter from William to Helen Jane, 24 November 1848, quoted in Magnus, *Gladstone: A Biography*, 84.
101. Magnus, *Gladstone: A Biography*, 268.
102. Deacon, *Private Life of Mr. Gladstone*, 179.
103. John Morley, *The Life of Gladstone* (London, 1927), 44.
104. The only time Helen's name appeared in public was on a ship built for the family firm. Checkland, *Gladstones*, 287.
105. William's ambivalence around admiration for suffering womanhood is expressed in his view of Queen Victoria, frustrated as he was by her unavailability when needed: "For fanciful ideas of a woman about her own health encouraged by a feeble minded doctor, become realities [with the effect of] producing in a considerable degree the incapacity but for them would not exist." Isba, *Gladstone and Women*, 183.
106. Although it is evident that his view of women was related to his hostile stance on women's suffrage.

Notes on Contributors

Mary Jean Corbett is the John W. Steube Professor of English and an affiliate of the Women's Studies Program at Miami University in Oxford, Ohio. She is the author of *Representing Femininity: Middle-Class Subjectivity in Victorian and Edwardian Women's Autobiographies* (Oxford University Press, 1992); *Allegories of Union in Irish and English Writing, 1790–1870: History, Politics, and the Family from Edgeworth to Arnold* (Cambridge University Press, 2000); and *Family Likeness: Sex, Marriage, and Incest from Jane Austen to Virginia Woolf* (Cornell University Press, 2008).

Leonore Davidoff is research professor in the Department of Sociology, University of Essex, United Kingdom. She was the founding editor of the international journal *Gender & History* in 1987 and was associated with its publication for over two decades. She has held visiting professorships and fellowships in Australia, North America, and Scandinavia. Her research has focused on gender, the family, kinship, and domestic service in nineteenth-century Britain at the conceptual as well as empirical level. She is currently working on a major project on kinship with special reference to siblings, to be published by Oxford University Press. Her previous work has been translated into German, Spanish, French, Japanese, and Turkish. In addition to many articles in the field her previous publications include: (with Catherine Hall) *Family Fortunes: Men and Women of the English Middle Class 1780–1850* (1987; new edition 2002); *Worlds Between: Historical Perspectives on Gender and Class* (1995); (with Megan Doolittle, Janet Fink, and Katherine Holden), *Blood, Contract and Intimacy, 1830–1960* (1999).

Gérard Delille has been a professor at the European University Institute in Italy. Currently he is Directeur de recherche at the Centre National de la Recherche Scientifique (CNRS) and Directeur d'études at the Ecole des Hautes Etudes en Sciences Sociales (EHESS) in Paris. He teaches in Paris and Rome. As a specialist on early modern Italy, he has conducted research on family systems (*Famille et propriété dans le Royaume de Naples, XVe–XIXe siècle* [Rome and Paris, 1985]) and on the relationships between kinship, alliance, and political coalitions (*Le maire et le prieur: Pouvoir central et pouvoir local en Méditerranée Occidentale, XVe–XVIIIe siècle* [Rome and Paris, 2003]). He is engaged in an extensive study on the mechanisms of alliance construction in Western Europe from the Middle Ages to the modern period, from which he has already published certain results ("Echanges matrimoniaux entre lignées alternées et système européen de l'alliance: une première approche," in *En substances: Mélanges pour F. Héritier* [Paris, 2000]).

Bernard Derouet was a member of the Centre National de la Recherche Scientifique (CNRS) and the Centre de Recherches Historiques at the Ecole des Hautes Etudes en Sciences Sociales (EHESS) in Paris. He was especially interested in issues of family, kinship, marriage, inheritance practices, and social reproduction in general in France and Europe (sixteenth to nineteenth centuries). His publications include "Territoire et parenté: Pour une mise en perspective de la communauté rurale et des formes de reproduction familiale," *Annales: Histoire, Sciences Sociales* 50 (1995); "Nuptiality and Family Reproduction in Male Inheritance Systems: Reflections on the Example of Franche-Comté (17th–18th Centuries)," *The History of the Family: An International Quarterly* 1 (1996); "Les pratiques familiales, le droit et la construction des différences (15e–19e siècles)," *Annales: Histoire, Sciences Sociales* 52 (1997); "Parenté et marché foncier à l'époque moderne: une reinterpretation," *Annales: Histoire, Sciences Sociales* 56 (2001); "La terre, la personne et le contrat: exploitation et associations familiales en Bourbonnais (XVIIe–XVIIIe siècles)," *Revue d'Histoire Moderne et Contemporaine* 50 (2003); and "Political Power, Inheritance, and Kinship Relations: The Unique Features of Southern France (Sixteenth–Eighteenth Centuries)," in David Warren Sabean, Simon Teuscher, and Jon Mathieu, eds., *Kinship in Europe: Approaches to Long-Term Development (1300–1900)* (New York and Oxford: Berghahn Books, 2007).

Michaela Hohkamp is a professor at the Free University Berlin. A graduate of the University of Göttingen, where she studied under Rudolf Vierhaus, she has been a research assistant at the Max Planck Institut for history in Göttingen and a fellow at the European University Institute in Florence (Italy). Her main interests in research concern rural society as well as European court society, aristocratic power and kinship, issues of gender and power in early modern Europe, and the history of early modern historiography. Her writings include "Sisters, Aunts, and Cousins: Familial Architectures and the Political Field in Early Modern Europe," in David Warren Sabean, Simon Teuscher, and Jon Mathieu, eds., *Kinship in Europe: Approaches to Long-Term Developments (1300–1900)*, (New York and Oxford, 2007); "Eine Tante für alle Fälle: Tanten-Nichten-Beziehungen und ihre politische Bedeutung für die reichsfürstliche Gesellschaft der Frühen Neuzeit (16. bis 18. Jahrhundert)," in Margareth Lanzinger and Edith Saurer, eds., *Politiken der Verwandtschaft* (Vienna, 2007); "Grausamkeit blutet – Gerechtigkeit zwackt: Überlegungen zu Grenzziehungen zwischen legitimer und nicht-legitimer Gewalt," in Barbara Krug-Richter and Magnus Eriksson, eds., *Streitkultur(en): Studien zu Gewalt, Konflikt und Kommunikation in der ländlichen Gesellschaft (16. bis 19. Jh.)* (Cologne, 2003); and *Herrschaft in der Herrschaft: Die vorderösterreichische Obervogtei Triberg von 1737 bis 1780* (Göttingen, 1998). Currently she is engaged in a study on transmission of kinship and power in European noble society (sixteenth to eighteenth centuries).

Christopher H. Johnson is professor emeritus of history and a member of the Academy of Scholars at Wayne State University. He has held fellowships from the Leverhulme and the Guggenheim Foundations as well as the Social Science Research Council and the National Endowment for the Humanities. He is currently engaged in research on the history of kinship and the family. He has published "Die Geschwister Archipel: Bruder-Schwester Liebe und Klassenformation im Frankreich des 19. Jahrhunderts," *L'Homme. Zeitschrift für feministische Geschichtswissenschaft* 13, no. 1 (2002) and "Kinship, Civil Society, and Power in Nineteenth-Century Vannes," in Sabean, Teuscher, and Mathieu, eds., *Kinship in Europe: Approaches to Long-Term Development (1300–1900)* (New York and Oxford, 2007). His book manuscript on kinship and bourgeois class formation in Vannes is nearing completion. Johnson is also at work on a study of family conflict and women's rights in eighteenth-century Paris. His earlier publications include *Utopian Communism in France: Cabet and the Icarians, 1839–1851* (Ithaca, 1974) (nominated for a National Book Award in 1975); *Maurice Sugar: Law, Labor, and the Left in Detroit, 1912–1950* (Wayne State, 1989), and *The Life and Death of Industrial Languedoc, 1700–1920: The Politics of De-Industrialization* (Oxford, 1995).

Benjamin Marschke is associate professor of history at Humboldt State University in Arcata, California. He holds a PhD in history from UCLA (2003), where he studied under David Warren Sabean and Geoffrey Symcox. Marschke has held fellowships from the DAAD, the Fritz Thyssen Stiftung, and the Max Planck Institut für Geschichte. His publications include *Absolutely Pietist: Patronage, Factionalism, and State-Building in the Early Eighteenth-Century Prussian Army Chaplaincy* (Tübingen, 2005). He is currently working on a close study of the court and monarchical self-representation of King Frederick William I of Prussia (1713–1740), from which he has already published tentative results with "'Von dem am Königl. Preußischen Hofe abgeschafften Ceremoniel': Monarchical Representation and Court Ceremony in Frederick William I's Prussia," in Randolph C. Head and Daniel Christensen, eds., *Orthodoxies and Diversity in Early Modern Germany* (Boston, 2007).

Ruth Perry is the Ann Fetter Friedlaender Professor of Humanities at the Massachusetts Institute of Technology, past president of the American Society for Eighteenth-Century Studies, and founding director of the MIT Women Studies program. She has published widely on eighteenth-century literary history and cultural change. Her most recent book on the family is *Novel Relations: The Transformation of Kinship in English Literature and Culture 1748–1818* (Cambridge, 2004). Her newer interests include balladry, orality, and traditional culture. She guest-edited a double issue of *The Eighteenth Century: Theory and Interpretation* on *Ballads and Songs in the Eighteenth Century* in 2008, with musical examples, including a version of the article included here. To hear the ballad analyzed in this volume sung, visit http://ecti.english.illinois.edu/RecentIssues/47/balladsissuev47i2-3.htm. Dr. Perry is currently working on a biography of Anna Gordon Brown, an eighteenth-century Scotswoman whose magnificent repertoire of ballads, learned as a child, was the first to be collected from a living person.

Sophie Ruppel, PhD, graduated from the Albert Ludwigs University of Freiburg (Germany). She is currently a lecturer at the University of Basel (Switzerland). She has been a member of a research project of the Schweizer Nationalfonds on early modern letter writing and did research as a senior research associate at Oxford University. Her main fields of interest are historical anthropology, gender history, the history of science, and the history of communication in early modern Europe. Currently she is working on her habilitation thesis, dealing with man and nature in early modern Europe with a focus on the changing debates on plants. Her publications include *Verbündete Rivalen: Geschwisterbeziehungen im*

Hochadel des 17. Jahrhunderts (Cologne, Weimar, and Vienna, 2006). And she edited (together with Aline Steinbrecher, University of Zurich) a volume on man and nature in early modern Europe: *Die Natur ist überall bey uns. Mensch und Natur in der Frühen Neuzeit* (Zurich, 2009).

David Warren Sabean is Henry J. Bruman Professor of German History at the University of California at Los Angeles. A graduate of the University of Wisconsin, where he studied under George Mosse, Sabean has taught at the University of East Anglia, University of Pittsburgh, and Cornell, and he has been a fellow at the Max Planck Institute for History in Göttingen, the Maison des Science de l'Homme, the Wissenschaftskolleg zu Berlin, the American Academy in Berlin, and the National Humanities Center. He is a fellow of the American Academy of Arts and Sciences. His publications include *Power in the Blood: Popular Culture and Village Discourse in Early Modern Germany* (Cambridge, 1984); *Property, Production, and Family in Neckarhausen, 1700–1870* (Cambridge, 1990); and *Kinship in Neckarhausen, 1700–1870* (Cambridge, 1998). He is co-editor with Simon Teuscher and Jon Mathieu of *Kinship in Europe: Approaches to Long-Term Development (1300–1900)* (New York and Oxford: Berghahn Books, 2007). Currently he is engaged in an extensive study on the history of incest and other fields of European cultural history.

Regina Schulte is professor of modern and contemporary history/gender history at the Ruhr-University of Bochum. In 1992 she held the Luigi Einaudi Chair in European and International Studies at Cornell University. From 1998 to 2003 she taught European history and women's and gender studies at the European University Institute, Florence. She has published, among others, *Sperrbezirke, Tugenhaftigkeit und Prostitution in der bürgerlichen Welt* (Frankfurt, 1984); *The Village in Court: Arson, Infanticide, and Poaching in the Court Records of Upper Bavaria, 1848–1910*, English translation (Cambridge, 1994); *Die verkehrte Welt des Krieges: Studien zu Geschlecht, Religion und Tod* (Frankfurt a. M. and New York, 1998); ed., *The Body of the Queen: Gender and Rule in the Courtly World 1500–2000* (New York and Oxford, 2006). She is co-editor of *L'Homme. Europäische Zeitschrift für Feministische Geschichtswissenschaft*, (Böhlau, Cologne, and Vienna) and of *Historische Anthropologie. Kultur – Gesellschaft – Alltag* (Böhlau, Cologne, and Vienna).

Karl-Heinz Spieß is professor of Allgemeine Geschichte des Mittelalters und Historische Hilfswissenschaften at the Ernst-Moritz-Arndt-Universität Greifswald in Germany. He is a member of the Konstanzer Arbeitskreis für Mittelalterliche Geschichte, and he is an advisor for the Deutsche Forschungsgemeinschaft. Selected books include *Lehnsrecht, Lehnspolitik und Lehnsverwaltung der Pfalzgrafen bei Rhein im Spätmittelalter* (Wiesbaden, 1978); *Familie und Verwandtschaft im deutschen Hochadel des Spätmittelalters (13. bis Anfang des 16. Jahrhunderts)* (Stuttgart, 1993); *Prozesse der Normbildung und Normveränderung im mittelalterlichen Europa* (Stuttgart, 2000); *Das Lehnswesen in Deutschland im hohen und späten Mittelalter* (Idstein, 2002, 2nd ed.: Stuttgart, 2009); *Principes. Dynastien und Höfe im späten Mittelalter* (Stuttgart, 2002); *Medien der Kommunikation im Mittelalter* (Stuttgart, 2003); *Die Familie in der Gesellschaft des Mittelalters* (Ostfildern, 2009); and *Fürsten und Höfe im Mittelalter* (Darmstadt, 2008).

Bibliography

Accampo, Elinor. *Industrialization, Family Life, and Class Relations: Saint-Chamond, 1815–1924*. Berkeley: 1989.

Adams, Christine. *A Taste for Comfort and Status: A Bourgeois Family in Eighteenth-Century France*. University Park, PA: 2000.

Adelung, Johann Christoph, ed. "Geschwister." In *Grammatisch-kritisches Wörterbuch der Hochdeutschen Mundart, mit beständiger Vergleichung der übrigen Mundarten, besonders der Oberdeutschen*. Vol. 3 of 5. Leipzig: 1793–1818.

Aldous, Richard. *The Lion and the Unicorn: Gladstone Versus Disraeli*. London: 2006.

Altman, Janet Gurkin. "The Letter Book as a Literary Institution, 1539–1789: Toward a Cultural History of Published Correspondences in France." In *Yale French Studies* 71 (1986): 17–62.

Anderson, Michael. *Family Structure in Nineteenth-Century Lancashire*. Cambridge: 1971.

Anderson, Nancy F. "The 'Marriage with a Deceased Wife's Sister Bill' Controversy: Incest Anxiety and the Defense of Family Purity in Victorian England." In *Journal of British Studies* 21:2 (1982): 67–86.

Ariès, Philippe. *Centuries of Childhood*. Translated by Robert Baldick. New York: 1962.

Arnim, Bettina von and Clemens Brentano. *"Clemens Brentano's Frühlingskranz" und handschriftliche überlieferte Briefe Brentanos an Bettine 1800–03*, edited by Lieselotte Kinskofer. In Brentano *Sämtliche Werke und Briefe*, Vol. 30. Stuttgart: 1990.

Arnold, Matthew. *"Culture and Anarchy" with "Friendship's Garland" and Some Literary Essays: The Complete Prose Works of Matthew Arnold*. Vol. 5, edited by R. H. Super. Ann Arbor: 1965.

Atkinson, David. *The English Traditional Ballad*. Burlington, VT: 2002.

Austen, Jane. *Mansfield Park*. Edited by Claudia L. Johnson. New York: 1998.

Austen, Jane. *Sense and Sensibility*. Edited by James Kinsley. Oxford: 1990.

Bank, Stephen P. and Michael D. Kahn. *The Sibling Bond*. New York: 1982.

Barbéris, Pierre. *A la recherche d'une écriture: Chateaubriand*. Paris: 1974.

Bardet, Jean-Pierre. *Rouen aux XVIIe et XVIIIe siècle: Les mutations d'un espace social*. Vol. 1. Paris: 1981.

Barker-Benfield, G. J. *The Culture of Sensibility: Sex and Society in Eighteenth-Century Britain*. Chicago: 1992.

Barmeyer, Heide, ed. *Die preußische Rangerhöhung und Königskrönung 1701 in deutscher und europäischer Sicht.* Frankfurt a. M.: 2002.

Barry, Jonathan and Christopher Brooks, eds. *The Middling Sort of People: Culture, Society and Politics in England 1550–1800.* London: 1994.

Barthes, Roland. *Mythologies,* trans. Annette Lavers. New York: 1972.

Barthes, Roland. *Sade, Fourier, Loyola.* Paris: 1971.

Barthes, Roland. *Sur Racine.* Paris: 1983.

Bastl, Beatrix. *Tugend, Liebe, Ehre: Die adelige Frau in der Frühen Neuzeit.* Vienna: 2000.

Baum, Wilhelm. *Die Habsburger in den Vorlanden 1386–1486: Krise und Höhepunkt der habsburgischen Machtstellung in Schwaben am Ausgang des Mittelalters.* Vienna: 1993.

Baumgart, Peter. "Ein neuer König in Europa: Interne Planung, diplomatische Vorbereitung und internationale Anerkennung der Standeserhöhung des brandenburgischen Kurfürsten." In Windt, *Preußen 1701,* pp. 166–176. Berlin: 2001.

Baumgart, Peter. "Kronprinzenopposition: Friedrich und Friedrich Wilhelm I." In *Friedrich der Große in seiner Zeit (Neue Forschungen zur Brandenburgisch-Preussischen Geschichte 8),* edited by Oswald Hauser, pp. 1–16. Cologne and Vienna: 1987.

Beau de Loménie, Emmanuel. *Les responsabilités des dynasties bourgeoises.* 5 vols. Paris: 1977.

Beckett, W. A. *The Woman's Question and the Man's Answer; or, Reflections on the Social Consequences of Legalizing Marriage with a Deceased Wife's Sister.* London: 1859.

Beebee, Thomas O. *Epistolary Fiction in Europe, 1500–1850.* Cambridge: 1999.

Behringer, Wolfgang. *Thurn und Taxis: Die Geschichte der Post und ihrer Unternehmen.* Munich and Zurich: 1990.

Behrman, Cynthia Fansler. "The Annual Blister: A Sidelight on Victorian Social and Parliamentary History." In *Victorian Studies* 11 (1968): 483–502.

Beik, William. *Absolutism and Society in Seventeenth-Century France: State and Provincial Aristocracy in Languedoc.* Cambridge: 1985.

Benjamin, Jessica. *The Bonds of Love: Psychoanalysis, Feminism, and the Problem of Domination.* New York: 1988.

Bergeron, Louis. *Banquiers, négociants et manufacturiers à Paris pendant le Directoire et l'Empire.* The Hague: 1978.

Bettenhäuser, Erwin, ed. *Familienbriefe der Landgräfin Amalie von Hessen-Kassel und ihrer Kinder.* Marburg: 1994.

Beuys, Barbara. *Der Große Kurfürst: Der Mann, der Preußen schuf. Biographie.* Reinbek bei Hamburg: 1979.

Bodemann, Eduard, ed. *Aus den Briefen der Herzogin Elisabeth Charlotte von Orléans an die Kurfürstin Sophie von Hannover – Ein Beitrag zur Kulturgeschichte des 17. und 18. Jahrhunderts.* 2 vols. Hanover: 1891.

Bodin, Jean. *Les six livres de la République.* 1576. Reprinted, Paris: 1986.

Boehm, Laetitia. "Konservativismus und Modernität in der Regentenerziehung an deutschen Höfen im 15. und 16. Jahrhundert." In *Humanismus im Bildungswesen des 15. und 16. Jahrhunderts,* edited by Wolfgang Reinhard, pp. 61–93. Weinheim: 1984.

Borchard, Beatrix. "'Mein Singen ist ein Rufen nur aus Träumen.' Berlin, Leipziger Straße Nr. 3." In *Fanny Hensel, geb. Mendelssohn Bartholdy: Das Werk,* edited by Martina Helmig, pp. 9–21. Munich: 1997.

Botstein, Leon. "Lieder ohne Worte: Einige Überlegungen über Musik, Theologie und die Rolle der jüdischen Frage in der Musik von Felix Mendelssohn." In *Felix Mendelssohn: Mitwelt und Nachwelt. Bericht zum 1. Leipziger Mendelssohn-Kolloquium,* edited by Leon Botstein, pp. 104–116. Leipzig: 1996.

Bourdieu, Pierre. *Outline of a Theory of Practice.* Cambridge: 1977.

Brentano, Clemens. *Briefe*, edited by Lieselotte Kinshofer. In Brentano, *Sämtlicher Werke und Briefe*. Vol. 26 and vol. 30. Stuttgart: 1988 and 1990.

Brentano, Clemens. *Godwi oder das steinerne Bild der Mutter: Ein verwilderter Roman von Maria*, edited by Werner Bellman. In Brentano, *Sämtlicher Werke und Briefe*. Vol. 16. Stuttgart: 1978.

Brewster, P. G. "The Incest Theme in Folksong." In *FF Communication* 80: 212 (1972): 3–36.

Breyvogel, Bernd. "Die Rolle Henriettes von Mömpelgard in der württembergischen Geschichte und Geschichtsschreibung." In *Württemberg und Mömpelgard: 600 Jahre Begegnung*, edited by Sönke Lorenz et al., pp. 47–76. Leinfelden-Echterdingen: 1999.

Breyvogel, Bernd. "Anna von Württemberg." In *Das Haus Württemberg: Ein biographisches Lexikon*, edited by Sönke Lorenz, pp. 79–80. Stuttgart: 1997.

Broglie, Gabriel de. *Madame de Genlis*. Paris: 2001.

Brown, Mary Ellen. *William Motherwell's Cultural Politics*. Lexington, KY: 2001.

Buchan, Peter. *Ancient Ballads and Songs of North of Scotland*. 2 vols. Edinburgh: 1828.

Burguière, André. "'Cher cousin': les usages matrimoniaux de la parenté proche dans la France du 18e siècle." In *Annales HSS* 55:6 (1997): 1339–1360.

Butler, Judith. *Undoing Gender*. London: 2004.

Caemmerer, Hermann von (ed.). *Die Testamente der Kurfürsten von Brandenburg und der beiden ersten Könige von Preußen*. Munich: 1915.

Cameron, Rondo. *France and the Economic Development of Europe, 1800–1914*. Princeton: 1961.

Caty, Roland and Elaine Richard. *Armateurs marseillais au XIXe siècle*. Marseille: 1986.

Chaline, Jean-Pierre. *Les Bourgeois de Rouen: une élite urbaine au XIXe siècle*. Paris: 1982.

Chartier, Roger. *The Cultural Origins of the French Revolution*. Durham, NC: 1989.

Chartier, Roger, Alain Boureau and Cécile Dauphin, eds. *Correspondence: Models of Letter-Writing from the Middle Ages to the Nineteenth Century*. Translated by Christopher Woodhall. Princeton: 1997.

Chandos, John. *Boys Together: English Public Schools 1800–1864*. Oxford, 1985.

Chase, Karen and Michael Levenson. *The Spectacle of Intimacy: A Public Life for the Victorian Family*. Princeton: 2000.

Chassagne, Serge. *Le coton et ses patrons: France, 1760–1840*. Paris: 1991.

Chateaubriand, René. *Atala/René*. Translated and introduced by Irving Putter. Berkeley and Los Angeles: 1980.

Châtelain, Abel. *Les migrations temporaires en France de 1800 à 1914*. 2 vols. Lille: 1977.

Checkland, S.G. *The Gladstones: A Family Biography 1764–1851*. Cambridge: 1971.

Child, Francis James. *The English and Scottish Popular Ballads*. 5 vols. 1882–1898. Reprinted, Northfield, MN: 2001–2010.

Circirelli, Victor G. "Sibling Relationships in Cross-Cultural Perspective." In *Journal of Marriage and the Family* 56 (1994): 7–20.

Clark, Christopher. *Iron Kingdom: The Rise and Downfall of Prussia, 1600–1947*. Cambridge, MA: 2006.

Claverie, Elisabeth and Pierre Lamaison. *L'impossible mariage: Violence et parenté en Gévaudan XVIIe, XVIIIe, et XIXe siècles*. Paris: 1982.

Cocceji, Samuel de. *Jus controversum civile: ubi illustriores juris controversiae breviter et succincte deciduntur, difficiliores materiae explicantur, objectiones solide solvuntur, et legum dissensus nova saepe ratione, ubi hactenus satisfactum non videntur, conciliantur*. Frankfurt and Leipzig: 1713–1718.

Coleman, D. C. *Courtaulds: An Economic and Social History*. Vol. 1, *The Nineteenth Century*. Oxford: 1969.

Coles, Prophacy. *The Importance of Sibling Relationships in Psychoanalysis.* London: 2003.
Cook, Elizabeth Heckendorn. *Epistolary Bodies: Gender and Genre in the Eighteenth-Century Republic of Letters.* Stanford: 1996.
Corbett, Mary Jean. *Family Likeness: Sex, Marriage, and Incest from Jane Austen to Virginia Woolf.* Ithaca: 2008.
Couchman, Jane and Ann Crabb, eds. *Women's Letters Across Europe, 1400–1700: Form and Persuasion.* Aldershot: 2005.
Crawford, Katherine. *European Sexualities: 1400–1800.* Cambridge: 2007.
Crosby, Travis L. *The Two Mr. Gladstones: A Study in Psychology and History.* New Haven: 1997.
Curtain, Michael. *Property and Position: A Study of Victorian Manners.* New York: 1987.
Darnton, Robert. *The Forbidden Bestsellers of Pre-Revolutionary France.* New York: 1995.
Daumas, Maurice. *La tendresse amoureuse: XVIe–XIXe siècles.* Paris: 1997.
Daumas, Maurice. *Le syndrome des Grieux: La relation père/fils au XVIIIe siècle.* Paris: 1990.
Dauphin, Cécile, Pierrette Lebrun-Pézerat and Danielle Poubron. *La correspondance: les usages de la lettre au XIXe siècle.* Paris: 1991.
Davidoff, Leonore. "Class and Gender in Victorian England: The Case of Hannah Cullwick and A.J. Munby." In Davidoff, *Worlds Between: Historical Perspectives on Gender and Class,* pp. 103–150. Cambridge: 1995.
Davidoff, Leonore. "Regarding Some 'Old Husband's Tales': Public and Private in Feminist History." In Davidoff, *Worlds Between: Historical Perspectives on Gender and Class,* pp. 227–250. Cambridge: 1995.
Davidoff, Leonore. *Thicker than Water: Sisters and Brothers in Nineteenth-Century Britain.* Oxford: forthcoming.
Davidoff, Leonore. "Where the Stranger Begins: The Question of Siblings in Historical Analysis." In Davidoff, *Worlds Between: Historical Perspectives on Gender and Class,* pp. 208–226. Cambridge: 1995.
Davidoff, Leonore and Catherine Hall. *Family Fortunes: Men and Women of the English Middle Class, 1780–1850.* Chicago: 1987, reprinted London: 2002.
Deacon, Richard. *The Private Life of Mr. Gladstone.* London: 1965.
Delille, Gérard. "Échanges matrimoniaux entre lignées alternées et système européen de l'alliance: une première apporoche." In *En substances: Textes pour Françoise Héritier,* edited by Jean-Luc Jamard, Emmanuel Terray and Margarita Xanthakou, pp. 219–252. Paris: 2000.
Delille, Gérard. *Famille et proprieté dans le royaume de Naples (XVe–XIXe siècle).* Rome and Paris: 1985.
Delille, Gérard. "Kinship, Marriage, and Politics." In Sabean, Teuscher and Mathieu, *Kinship in Europe,* pp. 163–183. Oxford and New York: 2007.
Delille, Gérard. *Le maire et le prieur: Pouvoir central et pouvoir local en Méditerranée occidentale (XVe–XVIIIe siècle).* Paris and Rome: 2003.
Demandt, Karl E. "Die Grafschaft Katzenelnbogen und ihre Bedeutung für die Landgrafschaft Hessen." In *Rheinische Vierteljahresblätter* 29 (1964): 73–105.
Demandt, Karl E. "Die letzten Katzenelnbogener Grafen und der Kampf um ihr Erbe." In *Nassauische Annalen* 66 (1955): 93–132.
Demandt, Karl E. *Regesten der Grafen von Katzenelnbogen 1060–1486,* 4 vols. Wiesbaden: 1953-1957.
Derouet, Bernard. "Cycle de vie, marché du travail et transferts fonciers: Chayanov et la paysannerie française d'Ancien Régime." In *Migrations, cycle de vie familial et marché*

du travail (Cahier des Annales de démographie historique, Nr. 3), edited by D. Barjot and O. Faron, pp. 305–317. Paris: 2002.

Derouet, Bernard. "La terre, la personne et le contrat: exploitation et associations familiales en Bourbonnais (xvii–xviiie siècles)." In *Revue d'histoire moderne et contemporaine* 50:2 (2003): 27–51.

Derouet, Bernard. "La transmission égalitaire du patrimoine dans la France rurale (xvie–xixe siècles): Nouvelles perspectives de recherché." In *Historia de la Familia*. 3 vols. Vol. 3, *Familia, Casa y Trabajo*, edited by F. Chacón Jiménez, pp. 73–92. Murcia: 1997.

Derouet, Bernard. "Le partage des frères: Héritage masculin et reproduction sociale en Franche-Comté aux 18e et 19e siècles." In *Annales ESC* 48:2 (1993): 453–474.

Derouet, Bernard. "Les pratiques familiales, le droit et la construction des différences (15e–19e siècles)." In *Annales HSS* 52:2 (1997): 369–391.

Derouet, Bernard. "Nuptiality and Family Reproduction in Male-Inheritance Systems: Reflections on the Example of Franche-Comté." In *The History of the Family: An International Quarterly* 1:2 (1996): 139–158.

Derouet, Bernard. "Parenté et marché foncier à l'époque moderne: une reinterpretation." In *Annales HSS* 56 no. 2 (2001): 337–368.

Derouet, Bernard. "Political Power, Inheritance, and Kinship Relations: The Unique Features of Southern France (Sixteenth–Eighteenth Centuries)." In Sabean, Teuscher and Mathieu, *Kinship in Europe*, pp. 105–124. Oxford and New York: 2007.

Derouet, Bernard. "Pratiques de l'alliance en milieu de communautés familiales (Bourbonnais, 1600–1750)." In *Le choix du conjoint*, edited by G. Brunet, A. Fauve-Chamoux and M. Oris, pp. 227–251. Lyon: 1998.

Derouet, Bernard. "Pratiques successorales et rapport à la terre: Les sociétés paysannes d'ancien régime." In *Annales ESC* 44 no. 1 (1989): 173–206.

Derouet, Bernard. "Territoire et parenté: Pour une mise en perspective de la communauté rurale et des formes de reproduction familiale." In *Annales HSS* 50:3 (1995): 645–686.

Derouet, Bernard and Joseph Goy. "Transmettre la terre: Les inflexions d'une problématique de la difference." In *Mélanges de l'école française de Rome, Italie et Méditerranée (MEFRIM)* 110 (1998): 117–151.

Desan, Suzanne. *The Family on Trial in Revolutionary France*. Berkeley: 2004.

Devrient, Eduard. *Meine Erinnerungen an Felix Mendelssohn-Bartholdy und seine Briefe an mich*. Leipzig: 1869.

Dorgerloh, Annette. "'Mon autre moi-même': Zum Verhältnis der Brüder Heinrich und Friedrich." In Generaldirektion der Stiftung, *Prinz Heinrich von Preußen*, pp. 49–51. Munich: 2002.

Dorsen, Henrich (ed.). *Genealogia oder Stammregister der durchläuchtigen hoch- und wohlgeborenen Fürsten, Grafen und Herren des uhralten hochlöblichen Hauses Nassau samt etlichen konterfeitlichen Epitaphien*. Saarbrücken: 1983.

Dorst, Klaus and Stefan Schimmel. "'Sibi et urbi': Die Berliner Residenz des Prinzen Heinrich." In Generaldirektion der Stiftung, *Prinz Heinrich von Preußen: Ein Europäer in Rheinsberg*, pp. 265–272. Munich: 2002.

Droysen, Gustaf. *Johann Gustav Droysen*. Vol. 1, *Bis zum Beginn der Frankfurter Tätigkeit*. Leipzig and Berlin: 1910.

Droysen, Gustaf. "Johann Gustav Droysen und Felix Mendelssohn-Bartholdy." In *Deutsche Rundschau* 111:3 (1902): 106–126.

Droysen, Johann Gustav. *Briefwechsel, 1829–1851*. Vol. 1, edited by Rudolf Hübner. 1929. Reprinted, Osnabrück: 1967.

Droyson, Johann Gustav. *Friedrich I., König in Preußen.* Berlin and New York: 2001.
Droysen, Johann Gustav. *Kleine Schriften zur Alten Geschichte.* Vol. 2. Leipzig: 1894.
Droysen, Johann Gustav and Felix Mendelssohn Bartholdy. *Ein tief gegründet Herz: der Briefwechsel zwischen Felix Mendelssohn Bartholdy mit Johann Gustav Droysen,* edited by Carl Wehmer. Heidelberg: 1959.
Duby, Georges. *Le chevalier, la femme et le prêtre.* Paris: 1981.
Duchhardt, Heinz. "Die preußischen Nicht-Krönungen nach 1701." In *Dreihundert Jahre Preußische Königskrönung: Eine Tagungsdokumentation,* edited by Johannes Kunisch, pp. 257–263. Berlin: 2002.
Duchhardt, Heinz. "'Petite Majesté' oder unterschätzter Architekt? Ein Barockfürst in seiner Zeit." In Windt, *Preußen 1701,* pp. 47–56. Berlin: 2001.
Duhamelle, Christophe. "Die Krönung von 1701 und ihre Wahrnehmung in Frankreich." In Windt, *Preußen 1701,* pp. 240–246. Berlin: 2001.
Duhamelle, Christophe. *L'héritage collectif: La noblesse d'Eglise rhénane, 17. et 18. siècles.* Paris: 1998.
Dupâquier, Jacques, ed. *Histoire de la population française.* 4 vols. Paris: 1988.
Eliot, George. "Brother and Sister." In Eliot, *The Spanish Gypsy,* p. 159. Edinburgh: 1901.
Elvers, Rudolf. *Briefe: Felix Mendelssohn-Bartholdy.* Frankfurt a. M: 1984.
Ergang, Robert. *The Potsdam Führer: Frederick William I, Father of Prussian Militarism.* New York: 1941.
Farge, Arlette. *La vie fragile: Violence, pouvoirs et solidarités à Paris au XVIIIe siècle.* Paris: 1986.
Farr, James R. *Hands of Honor: Artisans and Their World in Dijon, 1550–1650.* Ithaca and London: 1988.
Ferguson. Niall. *The World's Banker: The History of the House of Rothschild.* London, 1998.
Fichtner, Paula Sutter. *Protestantism and Primogeniture in Early Modern Germany.* New Haven: 1989.
First Report of the Commissioners Appointed to Inquire into the State and Operation of the Law of Marriage as Relating to the Prohibited Degrees of Affinity, and to Marriages Solemnised Abroad or in the British Colonies. London: 1848. Reprinted, Shannon: 1969.
Flanders, Judith. *The Circle of Sisters: Alice Kipling, Georgiana Burne-Jones, Agnes Poynter, and Louisa Baldwin.* London: 2001.
Flandrin, Jean-Louis. *Families in Former Times: Kinship, Household, and Sexuality.* Translated by Richard Southern. Cambridge: 1979.
Flint, Christopher. *Family Fictions: Narrative and Domestic Relations in Britain, 1688–1798.* Stanford: 1998.
Foot, M. R. D. ed. *The Gladstone Diaries,* vols. 1–2. Oxford, 1968.
Foot, M.R.D. and H. C. D. Matthew. *The Gladstone Diaries,* vol. 3. Oxford: 1974.
Forster, E. M. *Marianne Thornton: A Domestic Biography, 1797–1887.* New York: 1956.
Förster, Friedrich Christoph. *Friedrich Wilhelm I., König von Preußen.* 3 vols. Potsdam: 1834–1835.
Foucault, Michel. *The History of Sexuality: An Introduction.* Translated by Robert Hurley. New York: 1990.
Fouquet, Gerhard. "Kaiser, Kurpfalz, Stift: Die Speyerer Bischofswahl von 1513 und die Affäre Ziegler." In *Mitteilungen des Historischen Vereins der Pfalz* 83 (1985): 193–271.
Fouquet, Gerhard. *Das Speyerer Domkapitel im späten Mittelalter (ca. 1350–1540). Adlige Freundschaft, fürstliche Patronage und päpstliche Klientel, vol. 1.* Mainz: 1987.
Frederick II, King of Prussia. *Briefwechsel Friedrichs des Grossen mit Grumbkow und Maupertius, 1731–1759,* edited by Reinhold Koser. 1898. Reprinted, Osnabrück: 1966.

Freud, Sigmund. "On the Universal Tendency to Debasement in the Sphere of Love." In Freud, *On Sexuality*, pp. 251–254. Harmondsworth: 1977.

Frey, Linda and Marsha Frey. *Frederick I: The Man and His Times*. Boulder: 1984.

Friedman, Albert B. *The Ballad Revival*. Chicago: 1961.

Fuchs, Thomas. "Dynastische Politik, symbolische Repräsentation und Standeserhöhung: Die preußische Königskrönung 1701." In *Von Kurfürstentum zum "Königreich der Landstriche." Brandenburg-Preußen im Zeitalter von Absolutismus und Aufklärung*, edited by Günther Lottes, pp. 15–35. Berlin: 2004.

Garden, Maurice. *Lyon et les Lyonnais au XVIIIe siècle*. Paris: 1970.

Garrioch, David. *Neighbourhood and Community in Paris, 1740–1790*. Cambridge: 1986.

Gaskell, Elizabeth. *Wives and Daughters*, edited by Pam Morris. London: 1996.

Geiseler, Udo. "'Daß ich nicht allein sein Vater, sondern auch sein König und Herr sey.' Die Beziehungen der Markgrafen von Brandenburg-Schwedt zu den Hohenzollernkönigen im 18. Jahrhundert." In *Pracht und Herrlichkeit: Adlig-fürstliche Lebensstile im 17. und 18. Jahrhundert*, edited by Peter-Michael Hahn and Hellmut Lorenz, pp. 45–93. Potsdam: 1998.

Generaldirektion der Stiftung Preußische Schlößer und Gärten, ed. *Prinz Heinrich von Preußen: Ein Europäer in Rheinsberg*. Munich: 2002.

Genlis, Stéphanie de. *Alphonse et Dalinde*. In *Contes choisis des veillées du château*, pp. 124–300. London: 1828.

Genlis, Stéphanie de. *Les petits émigrés*. 2 vols. Paris: 1798.

Gille, Bertrand. *Histoire de la maison Rothschild*. 2 vols. Geneva: 1965, 1967.

Gillis, John. *A World of Their Own Making: Myth, Ritual and the Quest for Family Values*. New York: 1996.

Ginzburg, Carlo. "Ein Plädoyer für den Kasus." In *Fallstudien: Theorie – Geschichte – Methode*, edited by Johannes Süßmann et al., pp. 29–48. Berlin: 2007.

Gittins, Diana. *Madness in Its Place: Narratives of Severalls Hospital 1913–1997*. London: 1998.

Given-Wilson, Chris and Alice Curteis. *The Royal Bastards of Medieval England*. London et al.: 1984.

Gloger, Bruno. *Friedrich Wilhelm, Kurfürst von Brandenburg: Biografie*. Berlin: 1985.

Godineau, Dominique. *The Women of Paris and Their French Revolution*. Translated by Katherine Streip. Berkeley and Los Angeles: 1998.

Goldring-Zukow, Patricia, ed. *Sibling Interaction Across Cultures: Theoretical and Methodological Issues*. New York: 1989.

Goldsmith, Elizabeth C. *Exclusive Conversations: The Art of Interaction in Seventeenth-Century France*. Philadelphia: 1988.

Goldstein, Jan. *The Post-Revolutionary Self: Politics and Psyche in France, 1750–1850*. Cambridge, MA: 2005.

Goodale, Jane C. "Siblings as Spouses: The Reproduction and Replacement of Kaulong Society." In *Siblingship in Oceania: Studies in the Meaning of Kin Relations*, edited by Mac Marshall, pp. 275–306. Lanham, MD: 1983.

Goody, Jack. *Production and Reproduction: A Comparative Study of the Domestic Domain*. Cambridge: 1976.

Goody, Jack, ed. *Succession to High Office*. Cambridge: 1966.

Gouesse, Jean-Marie. "Mariages de proches parents (XVIe–XXe siècle): Esquisse d'une conjoncture." In *Le modèle familial européen: Normes, déviances, contrôle du pouvoir*, edited by Gérard Delille and Franco Rizzi, pp. 31–61. Rome: 1986.

Graf, Klaus. "Graf Heinrich von Württemberg († 1519)—Aspekte eines ungewöhnlichen Fürstenlebens." In *Württemberg und Mömpelgard. 600 Jahre Begegnung*, edited by Sönke Lorenz and Peter Rückert, pp. 107–120. Leinfelden-Echterdingen: 1999.

Großmann, Julius. "Jugendgeschichte Friedrichs I.: Ersten Königs in Preußen." In *Hohenzollern-Jahrbuch* 4 (1900): 19–59.

Gruner, Elizabeth Rose. "Born and Made: Sisters, Brothers, and the Deceased Wife's Sister Bill." In *Signs* 24 (1999): 423–447.

Gullette, Margaret Morganroth. "The Puzzling Case of the Deceased Wife's Sister: Nineteenth-Century England Deals with a Second-Chance Plot." In *Representations* 31 (1990): 142–166.

Gullickson, Gay. *The Spinners and Weavers of Auffay: Rural Industry and the Sexual Division of Labor in a French Village, 1750–1850*. Cambridge: 1986.

Gutwirth, Madelyn. "The Engulfed Beloved: Representations of Dead and Dying Women in the Art and Literature of the Revolutionary Era," in Sara E. Melzer and Leslie W. Rabine, eds., *Rebel Daughters: Women and the French Revolution*. Oxford, 1992: 198–227.

Häberlein, Mark. *Brüder, Freunde und Betrüger: Soziale Beziehungen, Normen und Konflikte in der Augsburger Kaufmannschaft um die Mitte des 16. Jahrhundert*. Berlin: 1998.

Haggerty, George E. *Unnatural Affections: Women and Fiction in the Later 18th Century*. Bloomington IN: 1998.

Hahn, Peter-Michael. "Pracht und Selbstinszenierung: Die Hofhaltung Friedrich Wilhelms I. von Preußen." In *Der Soldatenkönig: Friedrich Wilhelm I. in seiner Zeit*, edited by Friedrich Beck and Julius H. Schoeps, pp. 69–98. Potsdam: 2003.

Hahn, Peter-Michael. "Prinz Heinrich von Preußen: Ein königlicher Prinz ohne Herrschaft." In Generaldirektion der Stiftung, *Prinz Heinrich von Preußen: Ein Europäer in Rheinsberg*, pp. 15–19. Munich: 2002.

Hallmann, Hans. "Die letztwillige Verfügung im Hause Brandenburg 1415–1740." In *Forschungen zur brandenburgischen und preussischen Geschichte* 37 (1925): 1–30.

Hammerstein, Notker. "'Großer fürtrefflicher Leute Kinder'. Fürstenerziehung zwischen Humanismus und Reformation." In *Renaissance—Reformation. Gegensätze und Gemeinsamkeiten*, edited by August Buck, pp. 265–285. Wiesbaden: 1984.

Hanagan, Michael. *The Logic of Solidarity: Artisans and Industrial Workers in Three French Towns*. Champaign: 1980.

Hanawalt, Barbara. *The Ties that Bound: Peasant Families in Medieval England*. Oxford: 1986.

Hartmann, Stefan. "Der Thronwechsel als Krise und Entwicklungschance am Beispiel des Kurfürstentums Brandenburg." In *Aus der Arbeit des Geheimen Staatsarchivs Preußischer Kulturbesitz*, edited by Jürgen Kloosterhuis, pp. 3–15. Berlin: 1996.

Hauck, Karl, ed. *Die Briefe der Kinder des Winterkönigs*. Heidelberg: 1908.

Hausen, Karin. "Die Polarisierung des 'Geschlechtscharaktere': Eine Spiegelung der Dissoziation von Erwerbs- und Familienleben." In *Sozialgeschichte der Familie in der Neuzeit Europas*, edited by Werner Conze, pp. 363–393. Stuttgart: 1976.

Hayman, Ronald. *Marquis de Sade: Genius of Passion*. New York: 2003.

Hayward, Abraham. *Summary of Objections to the Doctrine that a Marriage with the Sister of a Deceased Wife is Contrary to Law, Religion, or Morality*. London: 1839.

Hedge, Mary Anne. "On the Reciprocal Duties of Brother and Sister." In Hedge, *My Own Fireside*, pp. 116–118. Colchester: 1832.

Hegel, Georg Wilhelm Friedrich. *Elements of the Philosophy of Right*, edited by Allen W. Wood, translated by H. B. Nisbet. Cambridge: 1991.

Hegel, Georg Wilhelm Friedrich. *The Philosophy of Right*. Translated by Alan White. Newburyport, MA: 2002.

Hegel, Georg Wilhelm Friedrich. *The Phenomenology of Mind*, translated and introduced by J. B. Baillie. 2nd ed. (London: 1949; introduced by George Lichtheim, New York: 1967).

Heinig, Paul-Joachim. "Fürstenkonkubinat um 1500 zwischen Usus und Devianz." In *"…wir wollen der Liebe Raum geben". Konkubinate geistlicher und weltlicher Fürsten um 1500*, edited by Andreas Tacke, pp. 11–37. Göttingen: 2006.

Heinig, Paul-Joachim. "'Omnia vincit Amor'—Das fürstliche Konkubinat im 15./16. Jahrhundert." In *Principes. Dynastien und Höfe im späten Mittelalter*, edited by Cordula Nolte, Karl-Heinz Spieß, and Ralf-Gunnar Werlich, pp. 277–314. Stuttgart: 2002.

Hensel, Sebastian. *Die Familie Mendelssohn 1729–1847: Nach Briefen und Tagebüchern* Vol. 1. Berlin: 1898.

Héritier, Françoise. *L'exercise de la parenté*. Paris: 1981.

Héritier, Françoise. *Two Sisters and Their Mother: The Anthropology of Incest*. Translated by Jeanine Herman. New York: 1999.

Hesse-Fink, Evelyne. *Etudes sur le thème de l'inceste dans la littérature française*. Bern: 1972.

Heuer, Jennifer Ngaire. *The Family and the Nation in Revolutionary France, 1789–1830*. Ithaca: 2005.

Highfill, Philip H., Kalman A. Burnim and Edward A. Langhans. *A Biographical Dictionary of Actors, Actresses, Musicians, Dancers, Managers & Other Stage Personnel in London, 1660–1800*. Vol. 10. Carbondale, IL: 1973.

Hinrichs, Carl. *Friedrich Wilhelm I., König in Preußen: Eine Biographie, Jugend und Aufstieg*, 2nd ed. Hamburg: 1941.

Hinrichs, Carl. "Der Konflict zwischen Friedrich Wilhelm I. und Kronprinz Friedrich." Reprinted in *Preussen als historisches Problem: Gesammelte Abhandlungen*, edited by Gerhard Oestreich, pp. 185–202. Berlin: 1964.

Hobart, Ann. "Harriet Martineau's Political Economy of Everyday Life." In *Victorian Studies* 37 (Winter 1994): 223–251.

Hohkamp, Michaela. "Eine Tante für alle Fälle: Tanten-Nichten-Beziehungen und ihre politische Bedeutung für die reichsfürstliche Gesellschaft der Frühen Neuzeit (16. bis 18. Jahrhundert)." In *Politiken der Verwandtschaft*, edited by Margareth Lanzinger and Edith Saurer, pp. 149–171. Vienna: 2007.

Hohkamp, Michaela. *Herrschaft in der Herrschaft: Die vorderösterreichische Obervogtei Triberg von 1737 bis 1780*. Göttingen: 1998.

Hohkamp, Michaela. "Sisters, Aunts and Cousins: Familial Architectures and the Political Field in Early Modern Europe." In Sabean, Teuscher and Mathieu, *Kinship in Europe*, pp. 128–145. Oxford and New York: 2007.

Holbach, Rudolf. *Stiftsgeistlichkeit im Spannungsfeld von Kirche und Welt. Studien zur Geschichte des Trierer Domkapitels und Domklerus im Spätmittelalter, vol. 1*. Trier: 1982.

Hollmann, Michael. *Das Mainzer Domkapitel im späten Mittelalter (1306–1476)*. Mainz: 1990.

Honan, Park. *Jane Austen: Her Life*. New York: 1987.

Houbre, Gabrielle. *Le discipline de l'amour: L'éducation sentimentale des filles et des garçons à l'age du romanticisme*. Paris: 1997.

Hudson, Glenda A. *Sibling Love and Incest in Jane Austen's Fiction*. London: 1992. Reprinted, New York: 1999.

Hunt, Lynn. *The Family Romance of the French Revolution*. Berkeley: 1992.

Hunt, Margaret. *The Middling Sort: Commerce, Gender and Family 1680–1780*. Berkeley: 1996.

Hunter, Richard and C. Rimington. "Porphyria in the Royal Houses of Stuart, Hanover, and Prussia: A Follow-Up Study of George III's Illness." In *Porphyria – A Royal Malady: Articles Published in or Commissioned by the British Medical Journal*. London: 1968.

Hüttl, Ludwig. *Friedrich Wilhelm von Brandenburg, der Große Kurfürst, 1620–1688: Eine politische Biographie*. Munich: 1981.

Isba, Anne. *Gladstone and Women*. London: 2006.

Jacob, Heinrich Eduard. *Felix Mendelssohn und seine Zeit: Bildnis und Schicksal eines Meisters*. Frankfurt a. M.: 1981.

Johnson, Christopher H. "Die Geschwister Archipel: Bruder-Schwester-Liebe und Klassenformation in Frankreich des 19. Jahrhunderts." In *Die Liebe der Geschwister*, edited by Karin Hausen and Regina Schulte, *L'Homme: Zeitschrift für Feministische Geschichtswissenschaft* 13, (2002): 50–67. Reprinted as "The Sibling Archipelago: Brother-Sister Love and Class Formation in Nineteenth-Century France." In *Remapping the Humanities*, edited by Mary Garrett, Heidi Gottlieb and Sandra Van Burkleo, pp. 94–111. Detroit: 2007.

Johnson, Christopher H. "Into the World: Kinship and Nation-Building in France, 1750–1885." In *Trans-regional and Transnational Families in Europe and Beyond: Experiences since the Middle Ages*, edited by Christopher H. Johnson, David Warren Sabean, Simon Teuscher, and Francesca Trivellato. New York: forthcoming.

Johnson, Christopher H. *The Life and Death of Industrial Languedoc, 1700–1920: The Politics of De-industrialization*. Oxford: 1995.

Kale, Stephen. *French Salons: High Society and Political Sociability from the Old Regime to the Revolution of 1848*. Baltimore: 2004.

Kania, Hans. *Der Große Kurfürst*. Leipzig and Berlin: 1930.

Kaplan, Marion A. *The Making of the Jewish Middle Class: Women, Family, and Identity in Imperial Germany*. New York: 1991.

Kasten, Brigitte. *Königssöhne und Königsherrschaft. Untersuchungen zur Teilhabe am Reich in der Merowinger- und Karolingerzeit*. Hannover: 1997.

Kathe, Heinz. *Der "Soldatenkönig": Friedrich Wilhelm I, 1688–1740, König in Preußen – Eine Biographie*. Cologne: 1981.

Kidd, Alan and David Nicholls, eds. *Gender, Civic Culture and Consumerism: Middle Class Identity in Britain: 1800–1990*. Manchester: 1999.

Kidd, Alan and David Nicholls, eds. *The Making of the English Middle Class? Studies of Regional and Cultural Diversity Since the Eighteenth Century*. Stroud: 1999.

Kirchner, Ernst Daniel Martin. *Die Churfürstinnen und Königinnen auf dem Throne der Hohenzollern: im Zusammenhange mit ihren Familien- und Zeit- Verhältnissen: aus den Quellen*. 3 vols. Berlin: 1866–1870.

Klein, Hans-Günther, ed. *Das verborgene Band: Felix Mendelssohn-Bartholdy und seine Schwester Fanny Hensel. Ausstellung der Musikabteilung der Staatsbibliothek zu Berlin – Preußischer Kulturbesitz zum 150. Todestag der beiden Geschwister, 15 Mai – 12 Juli 1997*. Wiesbaden: 1997.

Kleinjung, Christine. "Geistliche Töchter—abgeschoben oder unterstützt? Überlegungen zum Verhältnis hochadeliger Nonnen zu ihren Familien im 13. und 14. Jahrhundert." In *Fürstin und Fürst. Familienbeziehungen und Handlungsmöglichkeiten von hochadeligen Frauen im Mittelalter*, edited by Jörg Rogge, pp. 21–44. Ostfildern: 2004.

Klinger, Friedrich Maximilian. *Geschichte Giafers des Barmeciden: Ein Seitenstück zu Fausts Leben, Thaten und Höllenfahrt*. 2 vols. St. Petersburg: 1792–1794.

Koch, Elisabeth. "Die Frau im Recht der Frühen Neuzeit: Juristische Lehren und Begründungen." In *Frauen in der Geschichte des Rechts: Von der Frühen Neuzeit bis zur Gegenwart*, edited by Ute Gerhard, pp. 73–93. Munich: 1997.

Koch, Herbert. "Herzog Wilhelms von Sachsen erste Hochzeit vom 20. Juni 1446. Nach den Akten dargestellt." In *Zeitschrift des Vereins für Thüringische Geschichte und Altertumskunde* 30 (1915): 293–326.

Köcher, Adolf. *Geschichte von Hannover und Braunschweig von 1648 bis 1714*, vol 1. Leipzig: 1884.

Köcher, Adolf, ed. *Memoiren der Herzogin Sophie nachmals Kurfürstin von Hannover: Publikationen aus den Königl. Preuss. Staatsarchiven*, vol. 4. Leipzig: 1879.

Kocka, Jürgen. "Familie, Unternehnmer und Kapitalismus: An Beispielen aus der frühen deutschen Industrialisierung." In *Zeitschrift für Unternehmergeschichte* 24 (1979): 99–135.

Krimm, Konrad. "Markgraf Christoph I. und die badische Teilung. Zur Deutung der Karlsruher Votivtafel von Hans Baldung Grien." In *Zeitschrift für die Geschichte des Oberrheins* 138 (1990): 199–215.

Krockow, Christian Graf von. *Die preußischen Brüder: Prinz Heinrich und Friedrich der Große. Ein Doppelportrait*. Stuttgart: 1996.

Kronenberg, Kurt. *Die Äbtissinnen des Reichsstiftes Gandersheim*. Bad Gandersheim: 1981.

Kunisch, Johannes. "Friedrich der Große und die preußische Königskrönung von 1701." In *Dreihundert Jahre Preußische Königskrönung: Eine Tagungsdokumentation*, edited by Johannes Kunisch, pp. 265–284. Berlin: 2002.

Kuper, Adam. "Incest, Cousin Marriage, and the Origin of the Human Sciences in Nineteenth-Century England." In *Past & Present* 174 (2002): 158–183.

Lambert-Dansette, Jean. *Quelques familles du patronat textile de Lille-Armentières (1789–1914)*. Lille: 1954.

Landes, David. *Dynasties: Fortunes and Misfortunes of the World's Great Family Businesses*. New York: 2006.

Lanza, Janine. *From Wives to Widows in Early Modern Paris: Gender, Economy, and Law*. Aldershot and Burlington, VT: 2007.

Lanzinger, Margareth. "Mitgift." In *Enzyklopädie der Neuzeit*. Vol. 8, pp. 606. Stuttgart: 2008.

Lavater-Sloman, Mary. *Der vergessene Prinz: August Wilhelm, Prinz von Preussen, Bruder Friedrichs des Grossen*. Zurich: 1973.

Le Fahler, Michelle. *Recherche de documents maçonniques au XVIIIe–XIXe siècles: Mémoire de Maîtrise*. Rennes: 1976.

Le Roy Ladurie, Emmanuel. "Système de la coutume: Structures familiales et coutumes d'héritage en France au XVIe siècle." In *Annales ESC* 27 (1972): 825–846.

Lebrun, François. *La vie conjugale sous l'Ancien Régime*. Paris: 1985.

LeFanu, William F., ed. *Betsy Sheridan's Journal*. New Brunswick: 1960.

Lehning, James. *The Peasants of Marlhes: Economic Development and Family Organization in Nineteenth-Century France*. Chapel Hill: 1980.

Lemberg, Margaret. *Eine Königin ohne Reich: Das Leben der Winterkönigin Elisabeth Stuart und ihre Briefe nach Hessen*. Marburg: 1996.

Lévi-Strauss, Claude. *Les structures élémentaires de la parenté*. Paris: 1949; 2nd ed., 1968.

Levy, Darlene Gray, Harriet Branson Applewhite and Mary Durham Johnson, eds. *Women in Revolutionary Paris, 1789–1795: Selected Documents*. Urbana and Chicago: 1980.

Lévy, Marie-Françoise, ed. *L'enfant, famille et la Révolution Française*. Paris: 1990.

Lilienthal, Andrea. *Die Fürstin und die Macht: Welfische Herzoginnen im 16. Jahrhundert: Elisabeth, Sidonia, Sophia*. Hanover: 2007.

Lipp, Carola. "Verwandtschaft: ein negiertes Element in der politischen Kultur des 19. Jahrhunderts." In *HZ* 283 (2006): 31–77.

Lison Tolosana, Carmelo. *Antropologia cultural de Galicia*. Madrid: 1971.

Liu, Tessie. *The Weaver's Knot: The Contradictions of Class Struggle in Western France, 1750–1914*. Ithaca and London: 1994.

Loudon, Irvine. *Death in Childbirth: An International Study of Maternal Care and Maternal Mortality, 1800–1950*. Oxford: 1992.

Lowenstein, Steven M. *The Berlin Jewish Community: Enlightenment, Family, and Crisis, 1770–1830*. New York and Oxford: 1994.

Lowenthal-Hensel, Cécile. "Neues zur Leipziger Straße Drei." In *Mendelssohn-Studien: Beiträge zur neueren deutschen Kultur- und Wirtschaftsgeschichte*, edited by Cécile Lowenthal-Hensel and Rudolf Elvers. Vol. 7, pp. 141–151. Berlin: 1990.

Lüdke, Dietmar et al. (ed.). *Spätmittelalter am Oberrhein. Große Landesausstellung Baden-Württemberg 29. September 2001–3. Februar 2002, vol. 1: Maler und Werkstätten 1450–1525*. Stuttgart: 2001.

Luh, Jürgen. "Der Prinz und die Politik." In Generaldirektion der Stiftung, *Prinz Heinrich von Preußen*, pp. 123–125. Munich: 2002.

Luh, Jürgen. "Frondeur, Feldherr, Diplomat: Das Bild des Prinzen Heinrich in Wissenschaft und Öffentlichkeit des späten 19. und 20. Jahrhunderts." In Generaldirektion der Stiftung, *Prinz Heinrich von Preußen*, pp. 543–546. Munich: 2002.

MacAlpine, Ida, Richard Hunter, and C. Rimington, "Porphyria in the Royal Houses of Stuart, Hanover, and Prussia: A Follow-up Study of George III's Illness." *British Medical Journal* 5583 (6 January 1968): 7–18.

MacCannell, Juliet Flower. *The Regime of the Brother: After the Patriarchy*. London: 1991.

Machilek, Franz. "Markgraf Friedrich von Brandenburg-Ansbach, Dompropst zu Würzburg (1497-1536)." In *Fränkische Lebensbilder* 11 (1984): 101–139.

Mangan, J. A. and James Walvin. "Introduction." In *Manliness and Morality: Middle-class Masculinity in Britain and America 1800–1940*, ed. J. A. Mangan and James Walvin, pp. 1-23. Manchester: 1987.

Marcus, Sharon. *Between Women: Friendship, Desire, and Marriage in Victorian England*. Princeton: 2007.

Marissen, Michael. "Religious Aims in Mendelssohn's 1829 Berlin-Singakademie Performances of Bach's Matthew Passion." In *Musical Quarterly* 77 (1993): 718–726.

"The Marriage Relation." In *London Quarterly Review, American Edition* 85 (July and October 1849): 84–98.

Marschke, Benjamin. "'Von dem am Königl. Preußischen Hofe abgeschafften *Ceremoniel*': Monarchical Representation and Court Ceremony in Frederick William I's Prussia." In *Orthodoxies and Diversity in Early Modern Germany*, edited by Randolph C. Head and Daniel Christensen, pp. 227–252. Boston: 2007.

Marshall, Mac, ed. *Siblingship in Oceania: Studies in the Meaning of Kin Relations*. Lanham, MD: 1981.

Martineau, Harriet. *Deerbrook*, edited by Valerie Sanders. London: 2004.

Martin-Fugier, Anne. *La vie élégante ou la formation du Tout-Paris, 1815–1848*. Paris: 1990.

Mathieu, Jon. "Verwandtschaft als historischer Faktor: Schweizer Fallstudien und Trends, 1500–1900." In *Historische Anthropologie* 10:2 (2002): 225–244.

Mattenklott, Gert. *Über Juden in Deutschland*. Frankfurt a. M.: 1992.

Matthew, H. C. G. *Gladstone: 1809–1898*. Oxford:1997.

Matthew, H. C. G. "Gladstone, Evangelicalism and 'The Engagement'." In *Revival and Religion Since 1700: Essays in Honor of J.C. Walsh*, ed. Jane Garnett and H. C. G. Matthew. London: 1993.

Mauss, Marcel. "A Category of the Human Mind: The Notion of Person; The Notion of Self." In *Journal of the Royal Anthropological Institute* 68 (1938). Reprinted and discussed in *The Category of the Person: Anthropology, Philosophy, History*, edited by Michael Carrithers, Steven Collins and Steven Lukes, pp. 1–25. Cambridge: 1985.

May, Leila Silvana. *Disorderly Sisters: Sibling Relations and Sororal Resistance in Nineteenth-Century British Literature*. Lewisburg, PA: 2001.

Maynes, Mary Jo. "Women and Kinship in the Propertyless Classes in Western Europe in the Nineteenth Century." In *Gender, Kinship, Power: A Comparative and Interdisciplinary History*, edited by Mary Jo Maynes, Ann Waltner, Brigette Soland and Ulrike Strasser, pp. 261–274. New York: 1996.

McKay, Derek. *The Great Elector*. Harlow: 2001.

Medick, Hans and David Warren Sabean. "Emotionen und materielle Interessen in Familie und Verwandtschaft: Überlegungen zu neuen Wegen und Bereichen einer historischen und sozialanthropologischen Familienforschung." In *Emotionen und materielle Interessen: Sozialanthropologische und historische Beiträge zur Familienforschung*, edited by Hans Medick and David Warren Sabean, pp. 27–54. Göttingen: 1984.

Medick, Hans and David Warren Sabean, eds. *Interest and Emotion: Essays on the Study of Family and Kinship*. Cambridge: 1984.

Mendelssohn-Bartholdy, Fanny and Wilhelm Hensel. "Briefe aus der Verlobungszeit," edited by Martina Helmig and Annette Maurer. In *Fanny Hensel, geb. Mendelssohn Bartholdy: Das Werk*, edited by Martina Helmig, pp. 139–163. Munich: 1997.

Mendelssohn, Fanny and Felix Mendelssohn. *"Die Musik will gar nicht rutschen ohne Dich." Briefwechsel 1821 bis 1846*, edited by Eva Weissweiler. Berlin: 1997.

Mengel, Ingeborg. "Politisch-dynastische Beziehungen zwischen Albrecht von Preussen und Elisabeth von Braunschweig-Lüneburg in den Jahren 1546–1555." In *Jahrbuch der Albertus-Universität zu Königsberg/Preussen* 5 (1954): 225–241, reprinted in Ingeborg Klettke-Mengel, *Fürsten und Fürstenbriefe*, pp. 11–23. Köln: 1986.

Merkel, Johannes. "Die Irrungen zwischen Herzog Erich II. und seiner Gemahlin Sidonie (1545–1575)." In *Zeitschrift des Historischen Vereins für Niedersachsen* (1899): 11–101.

Merten, Detlef. *Der Katte-Prozeß: Vortrag gehalten vor der Berliner Juristischen Gesellschaft am 14. Febrary 1979*. Schriftenreihe der juristische Gesellschaft e.V., vol. 62. Berlin and New York: 1980.

Mertens, Dieter. "Württemberg." In *Handbuch der baden-württembergischen Geschichte*. Vol. 2, edited by Meinrad Schaab et al., pp. 1–99. Stuttgart: 1995.

Michie, Helena. *Sororophobia: Differences among Women in Literature and Culture*. New York: 1992.

Minden, Michael. *The German Bildungsroman: Incest and Inheritance*. Cambridge: 1997.

Mitchell, Juliet. *Siblings: Sex and Violence*. Cambridge: 2003.

Moch, Leslie Page. "Bretons in Paris: Regional Ties and Urban Networks in an Age of Urbanization." In *Quaderni storici* 86:106 (2001): 177–199.

Momigliano, Arnaldo. "J. G. Droysen between Greeks and Jews." In *History and Theory* 9:2 (1970): 139–153.

Mommertz, Monika. "'Imaginative Gewalt' – praxe(n)ologische Überlegungen zu einer vernachlässigten Gewaltform." In *Gewalt in der Frühen Neuzeit. Beiträge zur 5. Tagung der Arbeitsgemeinschaft Frühe Neuzeit im VHD*, edited by Michaela Hohkamp and Claudia Ulbrich, pp. 343–357. Berlin: 2005.

Morgan, Marjorie. *Manners, Morals and Class in England 1774–1858*. Basingstoke: 1994.

Mundt, Bernhard. *Prinz Heinrich von Preussen 1726–1802: Die Entwicklung zur politischen und militärischen Führungspersönlichkeit (1726–1763)*. Hamburg: 2002.

Neumann, Hans-Joachim. *Friedrich I.: Der erste König der Preußen*. Berlin: 2001.

Neumann, Hans-Joachim. *Friedrich Wilhelm der Große Kurfürst: Der Sieger von Fehrbellin, mit 63 Abbildungen*. Berlin: 1995.

Neumann, Hans-Joachim. *Friedrich Wilhelm I.: Leben und Leiden des Soldatenkönigs*. Berlin: 1993.

Nitsch, Carl Ludwig. *Neuer Versuch über die Ungültigkeit des mosaischen Gesetzes und den Rechtsgrund der Eheverbote in einem Gutachten über die Ehe mit des Bruders Wittwe*. Wittenberg and Zerbst: 1800.

Nolte, Cordula. *Familie, Hof und Herrschaft. Das verwandtschaftliche Beziehungs- und Kommunikationsnetz der Reichsfürsten am Beispiel der Markgrafen von Brandenburg-Ansbach (1440–1530)*. Ostfildern: 2005.

Nuland, Sherwin B. *The Doctors' Plague: Germs, Childbed Fever, and the Strange Story of Ignác Semmelweis*. New York: 2003.

Oestreich, Gerhard. *Friedrich Wilhelm: Der Große Kurfürst*. Göttingen: 1971.

Offen, Karen. *European Feminisms, 1700–1950: A Political History*. Stanford: 2000.

Olden-Jørgensen, Sebastian. "Ceremonial Interaction across the Baltic around 1700: The 'Coronations' of Charles XII (1697), Frederick IV (1700) and Frederick III/I (1701)." In *Scandinavian Journal of History* 28:3/4 (December 2004): 243–251.

Oliphant, Margaret. *Hester*, edited by Philip Davis and Brian Nellist. Oxford: 2003.

Oliphant, Margaret. *The Perpetual Curate*. Harmondsworth: 1987.

Oncken, Wilhelm. "Sir Charles Hotham und Friedrich Wilhelm I. im Jahre 1730: Urkundliche Ausschlüsse aus den Archiven zu London und Wien." In *Forschungen zur Brandenburgisch und Preußischen Geschichte* 7 (1894): 377–407.

Ong, Walter. *Orality and Literacy*. London: 1988.

Opgenoorth, Ernst. *Friedrich Wilhelm: Der Große Kurfürst von Brandenburg. Eine politische Biographie*, 2 vols. Göttingen: 1971, 1978.

Oppeln-Bronikowski, Friedrich von. *Der Alte Dessauer: Fürst Leopold von Anhalt-Dessau. Eine Studie seines Lebens und Wirkens (Bilder aus dem deutschen Leben)*. Potsdam: 1936. Reprinted, Stuttgart: 1941.

Oppeln-Bronikowski, Friedrich von. *Der Baumeister des preussischen Staates: Leben und Wirken des Soldatenkönigs Friedrich Wilhelms I*. Jena: 1934.

Ozment, Steven. *When Fathers Ruled: Family Life in Reformation Europe*. Cambridge, MA: 1985.

Pacheco, Anita, ed. *A Companion to Early Modern Women's Writing*. Oxford: 2002.

Pantenius, Wilhelm Moritz. *Der Prinz von Preussen: August Wilhelm als Politiker*. Historische Studien 108. 1913. Reprinted, Vaduz: 1965.

Papataxiarchis, Eythimuos and Socrates D. Petmezas. "The Devolution of Property and Kinship Practices in Late- and Post-Ottoman Ethnic Greek Societies: Some Demo-economic Factors of Nineteenth and Twentieth Century Transformations." In *Mélanges de l'Ecole française de Rome* (1998): 217–241.

Pardaihle-Galabrun, Annik. *The Birth of Intimacy: Privacy and Domestic Life in Early Modern Paris*. Translated by Jocelyn Phelps. Cambridge: 1991.

Pateman, Carol. *The Sexual Contract*. Stanford: 1988.

Paulig, F. R. *Friedrich I., König in Preußen: Ein Beitrag zur Geschichte seines Lebens, seines Hofes und seiner Zeit*. Frankfurt an der Oder: 1887.

Perrier, Sylvie. "The Blended Family in Old-Regime France: A Dynamic Family Form." In *History of the Family* 3:4 (1998): 459–471.

Perry, Ruth. *Novel Relations: The Transformation of Kinship in English Literature and Culture 1748–1818*. Cambridge: 2004.

Perry, Ruth. "The Finest Ballads: Women's Oral Traditions in Eighteenth-Century Scotland." In *Eighteenth-Century Life* 32:2 (2008): 81–97.

Pierach, Claus A. and Erich Jennewein. "Friedrich Wilhelm I. und Porphyrie." In *Sudhoffs Archiv* 83:1 (1999): 50–66.

Pollak, Ellen. *Incest and the English Novel, 1684–1814*. Baltimore: 2003.

Pollock, Linda A. "Parent-Child Relations." In *The History of the European Family*, edited by David I. Kertzer and Marzio Barbagli. Vol. 1, *Family Life in Early Modern Times 1500–1789*, pp. 191–220. New Haven: 2001.

Pollock, Linda A. "Younger Sons in Tudor and Stuart England." In *History Today* 39 (1989): 23–29.

Polowetzky, Michael. *Prominent Sisters: Mary Lamb, Dorothy Wordsworth and Sarah Disraeli*. London: 1996.

Pomata, Giana. "Blood Ties and Semen Ties: Consanguinity and Agnation in Roman Law." In *Gender, Kinship, Power: A Comparative and Interdisciplinary History*, edited by Mary Jo Maynes, Ann Waltner, Brigette Soland and Ulrike Strasser, pp. 43–64. New York: 1996.

Posse, Otto. *Die Hausgesetze der Wettiner bis zum Jahre 1486: Festgabe der Redaktion des Codex Diplomaticus Saxoniae Regiae zum 800-jährigen Regierungsjubiläum des Hauses Wettin mit 109 Tafeln in Lichtdruck*. Leipzig: 1889.

Powell, B., L. C. Steedman, and J. Freese, "Rebel Without a Cause: Birth Order and Social Attitudes," *American Sociological Review* 64 (1999): 207–231.

Prokop, Ulrike. *Die Illusion vom Großen Paar*. 2 vols. Frankfurt a. M.: 1991.

Puppel, Pauline. *Die Regentin: Vormundschaftliche Herrschaft in Hessen 1500–1700*. Frankfurt a. M.: 2004.

Pusey, E. B. *A Letter on the Proposed Change in the Laws Prohibiting Marriage between Those Near of Kin*. Oxford: 1842.

Pusey, E. B. *Marriage with a Deceased Wife's Sister Prohibited by Holy Scripture, as Understood by the Church for 1500 Years*. Oxford: 1849.

Racine, Jean. *Phèdre*. Edited and with a preface by Raymond Picard. Paris: 2000.

Raff, Gerhard. *Hie gut Wirtemberg allwege: Das Haus Württemberg von Graf Ulrich dem Stifter bis Herzog Ludwig*. Stuttgart: 1988.

Rand, Richard, ed. *Intimate Encounters: Love and Domesticity in Eighteenth-Century France*. Princeton: 1997.

Rank, Otto. *The Incest Theme in Literature and Legend*. Translated by Gregory Richter. Baltimore: 1992.

Ranke, Leopold von. *Preußische Geschichte, 1415–1871*, edited by Hans-Joachim Shoeps. Mühltal: 1981.

Ranke, Leopold von. "Zur Kritik Preußischer Memoiren." In *Abhandlungen und Versuche, Erste Sammlung. Leopold von Ranke's Sämmtliche Werke*. Vol. 24, pp. 41–70. Leipzig: 1872.

Ravis-Giordani, Georges and Martine Segalen. *Les cadets*. Paris: 1994.

Rehtmeier. Philipp. *Braunschweig-Lüneburgische Chronica Oder Historische Beschreibung der Durchlauchtigsten Herzogen zu Braunschweig und Lüneburg…zum Erstenmal in dreyen Theilen ans Licht gestellet von Philippo Julio Rehtmeier*. Braunschweig: 1722

Reif, Heinz. *Westfälischer Adel 1770–1860: Vom Herrschaftsstand zur regionalen Elite*. Göttingen: 1979.

Reinle, Christine. "'Id tempus solum'. Der Lebensentwurf Herzog Johanns von Mosbach-Neumarkt (†1486) im Spannungsfeld von dynastischem Denken, kirchlicher Karriere und gelehrten Interessen." In *Der Pfälzer Löwe in Bayern. Zur Geschichte der*

Oberpfalz in der kurpfälzischen Epoche, edited by Hans-Jürgen Becker, pp. 157–199. Regensburg: 1997.

Richter, Arnd. *Mendelssohn: Leben, Werke, Dokumente.* Mainz: 1994.

Riggert, Ida-Christine. *Die Lüneburger Frauenklöster.* Hannover: 1996.

Ritter, Gerhard. *Frederick the Great: A Historical Profile.* Translated by Peter Paret. Berkeley: 1968.

Roberts, Marilyn. "The Memoirs of Wilhelmina of Bayreuth: A Story of Her Own." In *Eighteenth-Century Women: Studies in Their Lives, Work, and Culture,* edited by Linda Troost, pp. 129–164. New York: 2001.

Roche, Daniel. *The People of Paris: An Essay in Popular Culture in the Eighteenth Century.* Translated by Marie Evans in association with Gwynne Lewis. Berkeley: 1987.

Roche, Daniel. "Work, Fellowship, and Some Economic Realities of Eighteenth-Century France." In *Work in France: Representations, Meaning, Organization, and Practice,* edited by Steven Laurence Kaplan and Cynthia J. Koepp, pp. 54–73. Ithaca and London: 1986.

Röckelein, Hedwig. "De feudo femineo: Über das Weiberlehen." In *Herrschaftspraxis und soziale Ordnungen im Mittelalter und in der frühen Neuzeit: Ernst Schubert zum Gedenken,* edited by Peter Aufgebauer et al., pp. 267–284. Hanover: 2006.

Rogers, Nicholas. "Introduction to Special Issue on the Middle Classes." *Journal of British Studies* 32, 1995.

Rogge, Jörg. "Gefängnis, Flucht und Liebeszauber: Ursachen und Verlaufsformen von Geschlechterkonflikten im hohen Adel des deutschen Reiches im späten Mittelalter." In *Zeitschrift für historische Forschung* 28 (2001): 487–511.

Rogge, Jörg. *Herrschaftsweitergabe, Konfliktregelung und Familienorganisation im fürstlichen Hochadel. Das Beispiel der Wettiner von der Mitte des 13. bis zum Beginn des 16. Jahrhunderts.* Stuttgart: 2002.

Rohrschneider, Michael. "'… vndt keine favoritten ahn Euerem hoffe haltet': Zur Stellung Ottos von Schwerin im Regierungsystem des Großen Kurfürsten." In *Der Zweite Mann im Staat: Oberste Amtsträger und Favoriten im Umkreis der Reichsfürsten in der Frühen Neuzeit,* edited by Michael Kaiser and Andreas Pecar, pp. 253–269. Berlin: 2003.

Rome, Yannick. *La Franc-maçonnerie à Vannes, Auray, Belle-Ile, Ploërmel au XVIIIe et XIXe siècle.* Vannes: n.d. [1985?].

Ronsin, François. *Le contrat sentimental: Débats sur le mariage, l'amour, le divorce, de l'Ancien Régime à la Restauration.* Paris: 1990.

Rosenband, Leonard. *Papermaking in Eighteenth-Century France: Management, Labor, and the Revolution at the Montgolfier Mill, 1761–1805.* Baltimore: 2000.

Rostaing, Leon. *La famille de Montgolfier: ses alliances, ses descendants.* Lyon: 1933.

Ruppel, Sophie. *Verbündete Rivalen: Geschwisterbeziehungen im Hochadel des 17. Jahrhunderts.* Cologne: 2006.

Rürup, Reinhard, ed. *Jüdische Geschichte in Berlin: Bilder und Dokumente.* Berlin: 1995.

Sabean, David Warren. "Fanny und Felix Mendelssohn-Bartholdy and the Question of Incest." In *Musical Quarterly* 77 (1993): 709–717.

Sabean, David Warren. "From Clan to Kindred: Kinship and the Circulation of Property in Pre-modern and Modern Europe." In *Heredity Produced: At the Crossroads of Biology, Politics, and Culture, 1500–1870,* edited by Staffan Müller-Wille and Hans-Jörg Rheinberger, pp. 37–60. Cambridge, MA: 2007.

Sabean, David Warren. "German International Families in the Nineteenth Century: The Siemens Family as a Thought Experiment." In *Trans-regional and Transnational Families: Experiences in Europe and Beyond since the Middle Ages,* edited by Christopher

H. Johnson, David Warren Sabean, Simon Teuscher and Francesca Trivellato. Oxford and New York: forthcoming.

Sabean, David Warren. "Inzestdiskurse vom Barock bis zur Romantik." In *L'Homme: Zeitschrift für feministische Geschichtswissenschaft* 13:1 (2002): 7–28.

Sabean, David Warren. "Kinship and Prohibited Marriages in Baroque Germany: Divergent Strategies among Jewish and Christian Populations." In *Leo Baeck Institute Yearbook* 47 (2002): 91–103.

Sabean, David Warren. *Kinship in Neckarhausen, 1700–1800.* Cambridge: 1998.

Sabean, David Warren. *Property, Production and Family in Neckarhausen, 1700–1870.* Cambridge: 1990.

Sabean, David Warren and Simon Teuscher. "Kinship in Europe: A New Approach to Long Term Development." In Sabean, Teuscher and Mathieu, *Kinship in Europe*, pp. 1–32. Oxford and New York: 2007.

Sabean, David Warren, Simon Teuscher and Jon Mathieu, eds. *Kinship in Europe: Approaches to Long-Term Development (1300–1900).* Oxford and New York: 2007.

Sablonier, Roger. "Die Aragonesische Königsfamilie um 1300." In *Emotionen und materielle Interessen. Sozialanthropologische und historische Beiträge zur Familienforschung,* edited by Hans Medick and David Warren Sabean, pp. 282–317. Göttingen: 1984.

Sanders, Robert. *Sibling Relationships: Theory and Issues for Practice.* Basingstoke: 2004.

Sanders, Valerie. *The Brother-Sister Culture in Nineteenth-Century Literature: From Austen to Woolf.* New York: 2002.

Sarasin, Philipp. *La ville des bourgeois: Élites et société urbaine à Bâle dans la deuxième moitié du XIXe siècle.* Paris: 1998.

Scharmann, Rudolf G. "'Ich habe mir die Ketten der Ehe anlegen lassen, um meine Freiheit zu gewinnen.' Prinz Heinrich und Wilhelmine von Hessen-Kassel." In Generaldirektion der Stiftung, *Prinz Heinrich von Preußen*, pp. 65–68. Munich: 2002.

Schlotheuber, Eva. "Familienpolitik und geistliche Aufgaben." In *Familie und Gesellschaft im Mittelalter,* edited by Karl-Heinz Spieß. Ostfildern: 2007.

Schlotheuber, Eva. *Klostereintritt und Bildung. Die Lebenswelt der Nonnen im späten Mittelalter.* Tübingen: 2004.

Schlumbohm, Jürgen. *Lebensläufe, Familien, Höfe: Die Bauern und Heuerleute des Osnabrückischen Kirchspiels Belm in proto-industrieller Zeit, 1650–1860.* Göttingen: 1994.

Schmidt, Werner. *Friedrich I.: Kurfürst von Brandenburg, König in Preußen.* Munich: 1996.

Schorske, Carl. *Fin de Siècle Vienna: Politics and Culture.* New York, 1980.

Schraut, Sylvia. *Das Haus Schönborn: eine Familienbiographie (1640–1840).* Paderborn: 2005.

Schuhmacher, Gerhard. "Felix Mendelssohn Bartholdys Bedeutung aus sozialgeschichtlicher Sicht: Ein Versuch." 1979. Reprinted in *Felix Mendelssohn-Bartholdy,* edited by G. Schuhmacher, pp. 138–173. Darmstadt: 1982.

Schulte, Regina. "Dokument: ein Historiker an seine Schwestern." In *L'Homme. Zeitschrift für Feministische Geschichtswissenschaft* 8:1 (1997): 78–86.

Schultz, Hartwig. *"Unsre Lieb aber is außerkohren": Die Geschwister Clemens und Bettine Brentano.* Frankfurt a. M.: 2004.

Schwennicke, Detlev. *Europäische Stammtafeln, neue Folge.* Vol. 1.1–1.3. Frankfurt a. M.: 1998.

Schwennicke, Detlev. *Europäische Stammtafeln, Neue Folge, vol. I.2: Přemysliden, Askanier, Herzoge von Lothringen, die Häuser Hessen, Württemberg und Zähringen.* Frankfurt am Main: 1999.

Schwennicke, Detlev. *Europäische Stammtafeln, neue Folge.* Vol. 17, *Hessen und das Stammes-herzogtum Sachsen.* Frankfurt a. M.: 1998.

Scott, Joan Wallach. *Gender and the Politics of History.* New York: 1988.

Scott, Joan Wallach. *Only Paradoxes to Offer: French Feminists and the Rights of Man.* Cambridge, MA: 1996.

Sedgwick, Eve Kosofsky. *Tendencies.* Durham, NC: 1993.

Sedgwick, Romney. "Introduction." In *Letters from George III to Lord Bute, 1756–1766,* edited by Romney Sedgwick, pp. vii–lxviii. London: 1939.

Segalen, Martine. *Fifteen Generations of Bretons: Kinship and Society in Lower Brittany, 1720–1920.* Translated by J. A. Underwood. Cambridge and Paris: 1991.

Segalen, Martine. "Mariage et parentèle dans le pays bigouden sud: un exemple de renchaînement d'alliances." In *Les complexités de l'alliance.* Vol. 2, *Les systèmes complexes d'alliance matrimoniale,* edited and introduced by Françoise Héritier-Augé and Elisabeth Copet-Rougier, pp. 177–205. Paris: 1991.

Segalen, Martine. "'Avoir sa part': Sibling Relations in Partible Inheritance Brittany." In Medick and Sabean, *Interest and Emotion,* pp. 129–144. Cambridge: 1984.

Segalen, Martine. "'Sein Teil haben': Geschwisterbeziehungen in einem egalitären Vererbungssystem." In *Emotionen und materielle Interessen: Sozialanthropologische und historische Beiträge zur Familienforschung,* edited by Hans Medick and David Warren Sabean, pp. 181–198. Göttingen: 1984.

Severidt, Ebba. *Familie, Verwandtschaft und Karriere bei den Gonzaga: Struktur und Funktion von Familie und Verwandtschaft bei den Gonzaga und ihren deutschen Verwandten (1444–1519).* Leinfelden-Echterdingen: 2002.

Shelley, Mary. *Frankenstein,* edited by J. Paul Hunter. New York: 1966.

Shire, Helena Mennie, ed. *Poems from Panmure House.* Cambridge: 1960.

Shorter, Edward. *The Making of the Modern Family.* New York: 1975.

Showalter, Elaine. *The Female Malady: Women, Madness and English Culture: 1830–1980.* London: 1987.

Siegel, Jerrold. *The Idea of the Self: Thought and Experience in Western Europe since the Seventeenth Century.* Cambridge: 2005.

Sigel, Lisa Z. *Governing Pleasures: Pornography and Social Change in England 1815–1914.* New Brunswick: 2002.

Simon, Gerhard. "Der Prozeß gegen den Thronfolger in Rußland (1718) und in Preußen (1730): Caravic Aleksej and Kronprinz Friedrich. Ein Vergleich." In *Jahrbücher für Geschichte Osteuropas* 36:2 (1998): 218–247.

Simpson, Claude M. *The British Broadside Ballad and Its Music.* New Brunswick: 1966.

Skene, Felicia. *The Inheritance of Evil, Or, the Consequence of Marrying a Deceased Wife's Sister.* London: 1849.

Smith, Bonnie G. *Ladies of the Leisure Class: The Bourgeoises of Northern France in the Nineteenth Century.* Princeton: 1984.

Smith, Jay. *Nobility Re-imagined: The Patriotic Nation in Eighteenth-Century France.* Ithaca and London: 2005.

Spalatin, Georg [Georgii Spalatini Historici Saxonici]. *Vitae aliquot electorum et ducum saxoniae inde A. Fridrico I. usque ad JO. Fridericum ...,* in: *Scriptores rerum Germanicarum, praecipue Saxonicarum, in quibus scripta et monumenta illustria. Pleraque hactenus inedita, tum ad historiam germaniae generatim, tum speciatim saxoniae svp. misniae, thuringiae et varisciae spectantia....* Leipzig: 1728.

Spangler, Jonathan. "Those in Between: Princely Families on the Margins of the Great Powers." In *Trans-regional and Transnational Families: Experiences in Europe and Beyond since the Middle Ages,* edited by Christopher H. Johnson, David Warren Sabean, Simon Teuscher and Francesca Trivellato. Oxford and New York: forthcoming.

Spieß, Karl-Heinz. *Familie und Verwandtschaft im deutschen Hochadel des Spätmittelalters: 13. bis Anfang des 16. Jahrhunderts.* Stuttgart: 1993.

Spieß, Karl-Heinz. "Lordship, Kinship and Inheritance in the Middle Ages and Early Modern Period." In Sabean, Teuscher and Mathieu, *Kinship in Europe*, pp. 57–75. Oxford and New York: 2007.

Spieß, Karl-Heinz. "Reisen deutscher Fürsten und Grafen im Spätmittelalter." In *Grand Tour. Adeliges Reisen und europäische Kultur vom 14. bis zum 18. Jahrhundert*, edited by Rainer Babel and Werner Paravicini, pp. 33–51. Ostfildern 2005.

Spieß, Karl-Heinz. "Witwenversorgung im Hochadel. Rechtlicher Rahmen und praktische Gestaltung im Spätmittelalter und zu Beginn der Frühen Neuzeit." In *Witwenschaft in der Frühen Neuzeit. Fürstliche und adlige Witwen zwischen Fremd- und Selbstbestimmung*, edited by Martina Schattkowsky, pp. 87–114. Leipzig: 2003.

Spitzer, Alan. *The Generation of 1820.* Princeton: 1987.

Spring, Eileen. *Law, Land, and Family: Aristocratic Inheritance in England 1300–1800.* Chapel Hill: 1993.

Stearns, Peter. *Paths to Authority: The Middle Class and the Industrial Labor Force in France, 1820–1848.* Urbana: 1972.

Steinberg, Michael P. "Culture, Gender, and Music: A Forum on the Mendelssohn Family." In *Musical Quarterly* 77 (1993): 648–650.

Steinberg, Michael P. "Das Mendelssohn-Bach-Verhältnis als ästhetischer Diskurs der Moderne," in *Felix Mendelssohn – Mitwelt und Nachwelt: Bericht zum 1. Leipziger Mendelssohn – Kolloqium am 8. und 9. Juni 1993*, edited by Leon Botstein and Gewandhaus zu Leipzig, pp. 84–88. Wiesbaden: 1996.

Steinberg, Michael P. "The Incidental Politics to Mendelssohn's Antigone." In *Mendelssohn and his World*, edited by R. Larry Todd, pp. 137–157. Princeton: 1991.

Steinhausen, Georg (ed.). *Deutsche Privatbriefe des Mittelalters, vol. 1: Fürsten und Magnaten, Edle und Ritter.* Berlin: 1899.

Stollberg-Rilinger, Barbara. "Höfische Öffentlichkeit: Zur zeremoniellen Selbstdarstellung des brandenburgischen Hofes vor dem europäischen Publikum." In *Forschungen zur Brandenburgischen und Preußischen Geschichte, Neue Folge* 7:2 (1997): 145–176.

Stone, Lawrence. *The Family, Sex and Marriage in England, 1500–1800.* New York: 1977.

Strouse, Jean. *Alice James.* London: 1992.

Sulloway, Frank J. *Born to Rebel: Birth Order, Family Dynamics and Creative Lives.* London: 1996.

Sutter, Jean. "Fréquence de l'endogamie et ses facteurs au XIXe siècle." In *Population* 23 (1968): 303–324.

Sutter, Jean and Léon Tabah. "Fréquence des mariages consanguins en France." In *Population* 3–4 (1948): 607–630.

Tadmor, Naomi. *Family and Friends in Eighteenth-Century England.* Cambridge: 2001.

Tassin, Guy. *Mariages, ménages au XVIIIe siècle: Alliances et parentés à Haveluy.* Paris: 2001.

Taylor, Charles. *Sources of the Self: The Making of Modern Identity.* Cambridge, MA: 1989.

Taylor, Isaac. *Self Cultivation Recommended.* London: 1817.

Teuscher, Simon. *Bekannte, Klienten, Verwandte: Soziabilität und Politik in der Stadt Bern um 1500.* Vienna and Cologne: 1998.

Teuscher, Simon. "Property Regimes and Migration of Patrician Families in Western Europe around 1500." In *Trans-regional and Transnational Families: Experiences in Europe and Beyond since the Middle Ages*, edited by Christopher H. Johnson, David Warren Sabean, Simon Teuscher and Francesca Trivellato. Oxford and New York: forthcoming.

Tilly, Charles, ed. *Historical Studies of Changing Fertility.* Princeton: 1978.

Titzmann, Michael. "Literarische Strukturen und kulturelles Wissen: Das Beispiel inzestuöser Situationen in der Erzählliteratur der Goethezeit und ihre Funktionen im
Denksystem der Epoche." In *Erzählte Kriminalität: Zur Typologie und Funktion von
narrativen Darstellungen in Strafrechtspflege, Publizistik und Literatur zwischen 1770
und 1920*, edited by Jörg Schönert, Konstantin Imm and Joachim Linder, pp. 229–
281. Tübingen: 1991.

Toews, John E. "Memory and Gender in the Remaking of Fanny Mendelssohn's Musical
Identity: The Chorale in *Das Jahr.*" In *Musical Quarterly* 77 (1993): 727–748.

Trainor, Richard. "The Middle Class." In *The Cambridge Urban History of Britain*, ed. Martin Daunton, pp. 673–713. Cambridge: 2000.

Tosh, John. "The Old Adam and the New Man: Emerging Themes in the History of
English Masculinity 1750–1850." In John Tosh, *Manliness and Masculinities in Nineteenth Century Britain*, chapter 3. Harlow: 2005.

Trumbach, Randolph. *The Rise of the Egalitarian Family.* New York: 1978.

Twitchell, James. *Forbidden Partners: The Incest Taboo in Modern Culture.* New York:
1987.

Ulrich, Laurel Thatcher. *A Midwife's Tale.* New York: 1990.

United Kingdom, *Hansard Parliamentary Debates*, 3rd and 4th series.

Valynseele, Joseph and Henri-Claude Mars. *Le sang des Rothschilds: familles alliés.* Paris,
2004.

Van de Walle, Etienne. "Alone in Europe: The French Fertility Decline until 1850." In
Historical Studies of Changing Fertility, edited by Charles Tilly. Princeton: 1978.

Vedder, Ulrike. "Continuity and Death: Literature and the Law of Succession in the Nineteenth Century." In *Heredity Produced: At the Crossroads of Biology, Politics, and Culture, 1500–1870*, edited by Staffan Müller-Wille and Hans-Jörg Rheinberger, pp.
85–102. Cambridge, MA: 2007.

Venohr, Wolfgang. *Der Soldatenkönig: Revolutionär auf dem Thron.* Frankfurt a. M.: 1988.
Reprinted, *Friedrich Wilhelm I.: Preußens Soldatenkönig.* Munich: 2001.

Vernier, Bernard. *La genèse sociale des sentiments: Aînés et cadets dans l'île grecque de Karpathos.* Paris: 1991.

Vincent-Buffault, Anne. *Histoire des larmes: XVIIIe–XIXe siècle.* Paris: 1986.

Vincent-Buffault, Anne. *L'exercice de l'amité: Pour une histoire des pratiques amicales aux
XVIIIe et XIXe siècles.* Paris: 1995.

Volz, Gustav Berthold. "Die Politik Friedrichs des Großen vor und nach seiner Thronbesteigung." In *Historische Zeitschrift* 151 (1935): 486–527.

Waller, Margaret. "Being René, Buying Atala: Alienated Subjects and Decorative Objects
in Postrevolutionary France." In *Rebel Daughters: Women and the French Revolution*,
edited by Sara E. Melzer and Leslie W. Rabine, pp. 157–177. Oxford: 1992.

Walpole, Horace. *The Correspondence of Horace Walpole.* Vol. 20. Compiled by Edwin M.
Martz with Ruth K. McClure and William T. LaMay. New Haven: 1983.

Walter, Jürgen. *Wilhelmine von Bayreuth: Die Lieblingsschwester Friedrichs der Grossen.*
Munich: 1981.

Walton, Whitney. *Eve's Proud Descendants: Four Women Writers and Republican Politics in
Nineteenth-Century France.* Stanford: 2000.

Weber, Eugen. *Peasants into Frenchmen.* Stanford: 1977.

Wehinger, Brunhilde. "Denkwürdigkeiten des Hauses Brandenburg: Friedrich der Große
als Autor der Geschichte seiner Dynastie." In *Von Kurfürstentum zum "Königreich
der Landstriche": Brandenburg-Preußen im Zeitalter von Absolutismus und Aufklärung*,
edited by Günther Lottes, pp. 137–174. Berlin: 2004.

Weinfurter, Stefan. "Die Einheit Bayerns. Zur Primogeniturordnung des Herzogs Albrecht IV. von 1506." In *Festgabe Heinz Hürten zum 60. Geburtstag*, edited by Harald Dickerhof, pp. 225–242. Frankfurt am Main: 1998.

Weissweiler, Eva, ed. *Fanny Mendelssohn: Italienisches Tagebuch*. Hamburg and Zurich: 1993.

Weller, Karl. *Geschichte des Hauses Hohenlohe, vol. 2*. Stuttgart: 1908.

Werner, Eric. *Mendelssohn: Leben und Werk in neuer Sicht*. Zurich: 1980.

White, Paul. *Thomas Huxley: Man of Science*. Cambridge: 2003.

Wichmann, Manfred. "Die Rezeption der Krönungsfeiern 1701 in der Zeitgenössischen Presse." In Windt, *Preußen 1701*, pp. 237–239. Berlin: 2001.

Widder, Ellen. "Karriere im Windschatten. Zur Biographie Erzbischof Ruprechts von Köln (1427–1478)." In *Vestigia Monasteriensia. Westfalen—Rheinland—Niederlande*, edited by Peter Johanek, Mark Mersiowsky, and Ellen Widder, pp. 29–72. Bielefeld: 1995.

Widder, Ellen. "Konkubinen und Bastarde. Günstlinge oder Außenseiter an Höfen des Spätmittelalters." In *Der Fall des Günstlings. Hofparteien in Europa vom 13. bis zum 17. Jahrhundert*, edited by Jan Hirschbiegel and Werner Paravicini, pp. 417–480. Ostfildern: 2004.

Wieland, C. M. "Die erste Liebe: An Psyche" [1774]. In C. M. Wieland, *Sämmtliche Werke*. Vol. 9, edited by Hamburger Stiftung zur Förderung von Wissenschaft und Kultur (14 vols.), pp. 165–185. Hamburg: 1984.

Wieland, C. M. *Geschichte des Agathon*. 3 vols. Leipzig: 1794. Reprinted in C. M. Wieland, *Sämmtliche Werke*. Vol. 1, edited by Hamburger Stiftung zur Förderung von Wissenschaft und Kultur. 14 vols. Hamburg: 1984.

Windscheffel, Ruth Clayton. "Politics, Portraiture and Power: Reassessing the Public Image of William Ewart Gladstone," in *Public Men, Masculinity and Politics in Modern Britain*, ed. Matthew McCormack. Basingstoke: 2007.

Windt, Franziska. *Preußen 1701: Eine Europäische Geschichte*. Vol. 2. Berlin: 2001.

Wintzingerode, Heinrich Jobst Graf von. "Preussens Erste Prinzen von Geblüt: Die Markgrafen von Brandenburg-Schwedt." PhD dissertation, Freie Universität Berlin, 2009.

Wolfram, Sybil. *In-Laws and Outlaws: Kinship and Marriage in England*. London: 1987.

Woolf, Virginia. *Mrs Dalloway*. San Diego: 1981.

Worbs, Hans Christoph. *Felix Mendelssohn Bartholdy: In Selbstzeugnissen und Bilddokumenten*. Reinbek: 1974.

Wright, Constance. *A Royal Affinity: The Story of Frederick the Great and His Sister, Wilhelmina of Bayreuth*. New York: 1965.

Yacovonne, David. "Surpassing the Love of Women: Victorian Manhood and the Language of Fraternal Love." In Laura McCall and David Yacovonne, *A Shared Experience: Women, Men and the History of Gender*, pp. 195–219. New York: 1998.

Yamaguchi, Midori. "The Religious Rebellion of a Clergyman's Daughter." *Women's History Review* 16 (2007): 641–660.

Yeo, Eileen. "The Creation of 'Motherhood' and Women's Responses in Britain and France, 1750–1914." *Women's History Review* 8 (1999): 201–218.

Yver, Jean. *Essai de géographie coutumière: Egalité entre héritiers et exclusion des enfants dotés*. Paris: 1966.

Zanetti, Dante E. *La Demografia del patriziato milanese nei secoli XVII, XVIII, XIX. Con una appendice genealogica di franco Arese Lucini*. Pavia: 1972.

Zedler, Johann Heinrich, ed. "Frater." In *Zedler's Universal-Lexicon*. Vol. 9. Leipzig: 1735. Reprinted, Nachdruck Graz: 1961.

Zedler, Johann Heinrich, ed. "Nachfolge oder Erbfolge deren Seiten-Freunde." In *Zedler's Universal-Lexicon*. Vol. 23. Leipzig: 1740. Reprinted, Nachdruck Graz: 1961.

Zedler, Johann Heinrich, ed. "Schwester." In *Zedler's Universal-Lexicon*. Vol. 36. Leipzig: 1743. Reprinted, Nachdruck Graz: 1961.

Ziebura, Eva. "'Das göttliche Trio': Die Prinzen Heinrich, August Wilhelm und Ferdinand von Preußen." In Generaldirektion der Stiftung, *Prinz Heinrich von Preußen*, pp. 55–58. Munich: 2002.

Ziebura, Eva. "Prinz Heinrich und seine Schwestern." In Generaldirektion der Stiftung, *Prinz Heinrich von Preußen*, pp. 58–62. Munich: 2002.

Zimmerman, Francis. *Enquête sur la parenté*. Paris: 1993.

Zonabend, Françoise. "Le très proche et le pas trop loin: Réflections sur l'organisation du champ matrimonial des sociétés à structures de parenté complexes." In *Ethnologie française* 11 (1981): 311–317.

Zunkel, Friedrich. *Der Rheinisch-Westfälische Unternehmer, 1834–1879*. Cologne: 1962.

Index